Media Argumentation

Dialectic, Persuasion, and Rhe

Media argumentation is a powerful force in our lives. From political speeches to television commercials to war propaganda, it can effectively mobilize political action, influence the public, and market products. This book presents a new and systematic way of thinking about the influence of mass media in our lives, showing the intersection of media sources with argumentation theory, informal logic, computational theory, and theories of persuasion. Using a variety of case studies that represent arguments that typically occur in the mass media, Douglas Walton demonstrates how tools recently developed in argumentation theory can be usefully applied to the identification, analysis, and evaluation of media arguments. He draws on the most recent developments in artificial intelligence, including dialogical theories of argument, which he developed, as well as speech act theory. Walton provides a structural analysis not only of individual types of argument commonly employed in the mass media, but also of pragmatic frameworks (models of goal-directed conversation) in which such arguments are used. Each chapter presents solutions to problems central to understanding, analyzing, and criticizing media argumentation.

Douglas Walton is professor of philosophy at the University of Winnipeg. An internationally known scholar and author of more than thirty books in the areas of argumentation, logic, and artificial intelligence, he has received major research grants from the Social Sciences and Humanities Research Council of Canada and the Isaak Walton Killiam Memorial Foundation. Dr. Walton also received the ISSA Prize from the International Society for the Study of Argumentation for his contributions to research on fallacies, argumentation, and informal logic.

Media Argumentation

Dialectic, Persuasion, and Rhetoric

DOUGLAS WALTON

University of Winnipeg

CAMBRIDGE UNIVERSITY PRESS
Cambridge, New York, Melbourne, Madrid, Cape Town, Singapore, São Paulo, Delhi

Cambridge University Press
32 Avenue of the Americas, New York, NY 10013-2473, USA

www.cambridge.org
Information on this title: www.cambridge.org/9780521876902

First published 2007

Printed in the United States of America

A catalog record for this publication is available from the British Library.

Library of Congress Cataloging in Publication Data

Walton, Douglas N.
Media argumentation : dialectic, persuasion, and rhetoric / Douglas Walton.
   p. cm.
Includes bibliographical references and index.
ISBN 978-0-521-87690-2 (hardback) – ISBN 978-0-521-70030-6 (pbk.)
1. Reasoning.   2. Fallacies (Logic)   3. Mass media.   I. Title.
BC177.W3245   2007
168–dc22   2006101030

ISBN   978-0-521-87690-2 hardback
ISBN   978-0-521-70030-6 paperback

For Karen, with love

Contents

Color plate section follows page 34.

Acknowledgments

Some of the material in this book is based on material in journal articles previously published by the author. The previously published materials have been modified to fit as revised material in parts of chapters.

Chapter 3 is based on "What Is Propaganda and Exactly What Is Wrong with It?" *Public Affairs Quarterly* 11 (1997): 383–413. The work in chapter 3 was supported by a Fellowship from the Netherlands Institute for Advanced Study in the Humanities and Social Sciences (NIAS) and a Research Grant from the Social Sciences and Humanities Research Council of Canada during the academic year of 1990–1991. Thanks are due to Erik Krabbe for discussions and to the members of the NIAS Research Group on "Fallacies as Violations of Rules of Argumentative Discourse," Frans van Eemeren, Rob Grootendorst, Sally Jackson, Scott Jacobs, Agnes van Rees, Agnes Verbiest, Charles Willard, and John Woods.

Material from two previously published papers is included in chapter 5: "Use of *Ad Hominem* Argument in Political Discourse: The Battalino Case from the Impeachment Trial of President Clinton," *Argumentation and Advocacy* 36 (2000): 179–195, and "Case Study of the Use of Circumstantial *Ad Hominem* in Political Argumentation," *Philosophy and Rhetoric* 33 (2000): 101–115. The former paper was written while I was on study leave in Perth, Australia, and Eugene, Oregon, in 1997. I would like to thank the Department of Philosophy of the University of Western Australia for providing facilities for research, and the Oregon Humanities Center (University of Oregon) for supporting my research on this paper. I would also like to acknowledge some comments made by Henry W. Johnstone, Jr. The latter paper arose out of the graduate seminar on argumentation I gave as a visiting professor at Northwestern

University in the Department of Communication Studies in 1999 and a public lecture given at Northwestern in April 1999. My visit was also supported by a Fulbright Senior Research Fellowship. Among the many individuals who contributed to the paper by raising questions and making comments, I would especially like to thank Mike Leff, Jean Goodwin, Steve Wildman, David Zarefsky, Robert McKown, Lynn Clarke, Adrienne Brovero, Michael Geiser, Horoko Okuda, Susan Sattell, and Michael Pfau. For support of the research in this paper, I would like to thank the Canada-U.S. Fulbright Foundation, the Department of Communication Studies of Northwestern University, and the Social Sciences and Humanities Research Council of Canada. During a later phase of the work in 2004, discussions with Mark Aakhus and David Zarefsky turned out to be extremely helpful.

Chapter 6 is partly based on "Evaluating Appeals to Popular Opinion," *Inquiry: Critical Thinking Across the Disciplines* 20 (2000): 33–45. The material in the paper has been considerably revised, and much new material has been added.

Chapter 8 is based on "Persuasive Definitions and Public Policy Arguments," *Argumentation and Advocacy: The Journal of the American Forensic Association* 37 (2001): 117–132. Much of the paper has been revised, and considerable new material has been added.

I gained some valuable insights into argumentation and computing at the Symposium on Argument and Computation at Bonskeid House in Perthshire, Scotland, in June and July 2000. I would especially like to thank Tim Norman and Chris Reed for organizing the conference. I would also like to thank the following conference participants for lectures and discussions that have influenced my thinking on models of argumentation and deliberation: Trevor Bench-Capon, Daniela Carbogim, Jim Crosswhite, Aspassia Daskalopulu, John Fox, Jim Freeman, Janne Maaike Gerlofs, Michael Gilbert, Rod Girle, Floriana Grasso, Leo Groarke, Corin Gurr, David Hitchcock, Hanns Hohmann, Erik Krabbe, Peter McBurney, Henry Prakken, Theodore Scaltsas, Simone Stumpf, and Bart Verheij. In the second term of 2001, during my time as visiting professor in the Department of Communication at the University of Arizona, I began to appreciate how the study of some phenomena central in rhetorical persuasion could benefit from new tools developed in computing and argumentation. For helpful discussions during this period, I would like to thank Joe Bonito, Michael Dues, Hans Hansen, Scott Jacobs, Sally Jackson, Raymie McKerrow, Robin Nabi, Chris Segrin, Kyle Tusing, David Williams, and Ron Wright. Support during this period was provided by a half-year study leave granted by the University of Winnipeg and a research grant from the Social Sciences and Humanities Research Council of Canada.

Finally I would like to thank Tom Gordon, Henry Prakken, Chris Reed, and Bart Verheij for many discussions over the period of 2002–2006 that helped to sharpen my grasp of new developments in artificial intelligence that are turning out to be essential to recent advances in argumentation technology. I would like to thank Christian Kock for allowing me to preview his paper for the 2006 ISSA Conference. And I would like to acknowledge the support for my continuing research through my Research Grant on Dialogue Systems for Legal Argumentation given by the Social Sciences and Humanities Research Council of Canada in 2005. For help during this latter period leading up the publication of the book, I would like to thank David Godden and Fabrizio Macagno. Rita Campbell prepared the index, and Ruth Lowe helped with proofreading.

Introduction

What initially led me to start work on this project was the observation that the examples of fallacies and questionable argument tactics studied in textbooks of informal logic often featured examples of advertisements and political arguments of the kind that have to do with elections or with public policies. Many of them are media arguments from sources such as political speeches, commercial ads, or Internet blogs. Such arguments are especially interesting when it is evident that they were used – for example, in ads – as rhetorically effective techniques to persuade a mass audience. Formerly (and often still), such arguments tended to be classified in logic as fallacious. But more and more they are now seen as fallible (but slippery) heuristics useful to reach a tentative conclusion under conditions of uncertainty, but subject to critical questioning. The theory put forward in this book strikes a judicious balance between analyzing them as fallible but basically reasonable arguments in some cases, and criticizing them as fallacious arguments used as tactics to unfairly get the best of an opponent or deceive a mass audience in other cases.

More specifically, the kinds of arguments considered throughout the book are ones often used in various communication media, including written texts, television, and the Internet, to attempt to persuade an audience to do something or accept something as true. A broad variety of such arguments are analyzed, but they prominently include political arguments and appeals, especially as used in electoral campaigns, encompassing persuasion attempts in which politicians, corporations, or advocacy groups put forward arguments using mass media and the Internet. They also include staged public debates in legislatures and parliaments and arguments found in commercial ads, in news reports or editorials in newspapers and magazines, and in written transcripts of television broadcasts and other media programs. They include any specimens of argumentation that have appeared in the various mass media and can be taken to try to influence a mass audience in some way. The aim of such an argument is typically to get action or to change public opinion on an issue, although other goals can be involved as well. The problem is to unlock the mystery of how persuasion works in such arguments using a dialogue model.

Despite a large body of experimental work in the social sciences that has studied the persuasive effectiveness of messages, for example, we still have very little precise understanding of exactly what persuasion is and how it works in mass media. As O'Keefe (2001, p. 575) put it, "Persuasion has been one of the great continuing mysteries of rhetoric and related disciplines." This book dissipates some of the mystery by building on recent work in argumentation theory and multi-agent systems in artificial intelligence (AI). These fields have developed new tools that have been applied to argumentation, leading to the development of new argumentation technologies, but one of the problems has been to extend them to argumentation of a kind that has traditionally been studied in rhetoric and speech communication.

The contemporary field of argumentation derives from three different disciplinary roots: logic, dialectic, and rhetoric. Logic is the science of reasoning. Dialectic is the study of two parties reasoning together with each other by argument and objection. Rhetoric is the use of argument to persuade.[1] Each has been somewhat suspicious of the claims advanced by the others, reflecting a tension going back to the ancient origins of all three fields. Rhetoric especially has been suspect, seen by philosophers as a sham and a deception, trading on the biases of audiences and not advancing claims that demand to be taken seriously. Philosophy has long been at war with rhetoric, since the time of Plato. Plato said that rhetoric is used by Sophists, is based only on appearances, and is used to persuade audiences by arguments that are fallacious. According to Plato, the Sophist has no regard for the truth of the matter, and can make the worse argument look better, or the better argument look worse, by tricky arguments. Philosophy, in contrast, on the Platonic theory, can take us to the fixed and unchanging truth of a matter being discussed by means of a method he called dialectic. Rhetoric produces only belief, which is

---

[1] These are superficial initial definitions for the beginner, subject to considerable refinement as the book proceeds. They are controversial and very much at issue.

constantly changing, while philosophy yields knowledge. The word "dialectic" (in this special sense) derives from the ancient Greek term for conversation, *dialectikos*, evoking the Platonic dialogues. Both Plato and Aristotle saw dialectic as a highly important method of rational discussion.[2] Plato couldn't really make up his mind what dialectic was, but by showing his paradigm exponent of it, Socrates, practicing it in his dialogues, gave examples of it at work. Later, Aristotle tried to redress Plato's antagonistic view of the relationship between rhetoric and dialectic by inventing formal logic, trying to reconcile rhetoric with a field he called dialectic. He defined dialectic as a way of criticizing popularly accepted opinions by finding contradictions and logical weaknesses in them and by considering arguments on both sides of a contested issue. But dialectic died out after some attempts to revive it in the Middle Ages.[3] The outcome, which has persisted for over two millennia, is that philosophy and rhetoric are still at war.

Recent developments demand a new look into this conflict. Because of the need to devise systems for electronic communication on the Internet, computing is moving more and more to a model of argumentation as a dialogue between rational agents. Current technologies of artificial intelligence are now widely based on the possibility of communications among entities that can act, reason, ask questions, and exchange information. For example, you might have an agent that filters out your E-mail messages, deletes some, and marks others with a high priority. Or you might have an agent that searches around the Net, collects certain kinds of information, and then processes it in a format you can use for some purpose. To collect this information, the agent will have to ask questions of other agents. Goal-directed communication between agents, or among groups of agents engaged in projects that require teamwork, is more and more important for many applications in electronic commerce and information retrieval. These developments provide an argumentation technology that offers new insight into mass media argumentation through an interlocking of dialectic and rhetoric.

In this book it is argued that rhetorical and dialectical argumentation need to be fitted together as complementary fields integrating two main tasks, the invention of arguments and their critical evaluation. The main

---

[2] But the term, in its Greek meaning, is likely to be unfamiliar to the majority of present-day readers, who are most likely to associate it with (quite different) Marxist-Hegelian notions.

[3] In modern times, Marxist-Hegelian theorists took over the term, signaling its death.

rhetorical task is to devise new arguments that can be used to persuade an audience to come to accept a viewpoint it has doubts about, based on what are taken to be its commitments and values. The main dialectical task is to judge which arguments are stronger and which are weaker (or even fallacious) by appealing to structures based on forms of argument and procedural rules that specify conditions for appropriate uses of an argument. It is argued in this book that even though these two goals are inherently different in theory, in practice they are closely connected. The reason is that audiences generally tend to be persuaded by arguments that are fallible (defeasible, to use the current term), and can sometimes be highly deceptive and even fallacious, but if used rightly, are inherently reasonable. Such defeasible arguments are very common, for example, in politics, where situations are highly complex, and a decision has to be made under conditions of uncertainty and lack of knowledge. In showing us how to use and judge such arguments, rhetoric and dialectic can combine to be a powerful force in the new argumentation technology that is emerging, especially in a democracy.

Whereas rhetorical and dialectical arguments are usually seen as very different, this book shows how they are both built on the same underlying structures of argumentation. Both are built on argumentation schemes, or stereotypical forms of argument. Both are built on the cognitive structure of the speech act of rational persuasion, requiring a dialogue format in which a message sender (called the "proponent" in this book) uses an argument to try to overcome the doubt expressed by another agent (called the "respondent") she is communicating with. To do this successfully, the proponent has to understand "where the respondent is coming from." She has to make some estimate of what premises he accepts or can be persuaded to accept as the dialogue proceeds.

The book shows that the tool of simulative reasoning is the means needed for this purpose, in both dialectic and rhetoric. It explains what arguers do in rhetorical situations: they imagine a dialogue to establish the initial position of the audience, and they then work within that framework to persuade the audience through dialectically secured claims. This works just like a dialogue except that the audience can't respond to the arguer's questions, so he or she must anticipate and account for what the audience would say. However, modifying the notion of dialogue so that it can accommodate simulative reasoning of this sort requires a complex and careful process of adaptation. The treatment of arguments based on definitions or on a variety of other different kinds of evidence – studied in the middle chapters of the book – identifies some of the ways in which this is done. The book shows how simulative reasoning can be captured in a dialogue model of argumentation that integrates reasoning used in dialectical and rhetorical argumentation, explaining how each component is needed to understand what is really going on in mass media argumentation.

The dialogue model has recently been adopted in multi-agent computing, and one can see why, because automated agents are used in communication on the Internet for purposes such as electronic commerce. The way argumentation is presented on the Internet fits the dialogue format in a way that is evident to all of us as users. The dissemination of news and information is becoming less centralized, and with this fragmentation we are continually returning to a "conversational" model of communication and information exchange. For example, it is not just that news networks such as CNN report the results of daily, Internet-based, opinion polls from their viewers. They now include blogs as a regular segment of their newscasts in recognition that an increasing portion of the population is seeking their information from this type of source. Yet the medium of a blog is inherently interactive. It is a kind of "online diary," usually of a single individual, which allows comments and feedback from the readers of the blog. Just as readers can immediately engage with the material on the blog as they read it, the author of the blog, through her continued updates, is able to respond to her interlocutors as individuals. The central task undertaken in this book is to apply this conversational model to media argumentation by integrating rhetorical and dialectical factors in the model.

Media argumentation is a powerful force in our lives. From political speeches to TV commercials to war propaganda, it can appeal to emotions that mobilize political action, influence public opinion, market products, and even enable a dictator to stay in power. If we could study this kind of argumentation using precise models of a kind that are clear enough to build into implemented computing systems, we might be in a much better position to deal with it in an intelligent and balanced way. But there are certain central mechanisms of media argumentation that are still not well enough understood. This book presents a new theory that displays its key structural components and shows how they fit together. The evidence in the case studies and analyses lead to the formulation of a new system to model the structure of rhetorical argumentation, which I call the Persuasion System. This system, along with the other tools and structural components deployed and refined through the case studies, reveal that media arguments have precisely definable characteristics of their own that make them a distinctive use of argumentation with a dialectical structure and rhetorical trajectory fitted together in a dialogue framework. By seeing how they work in typical and in problematic cases of mass media persuasion, fresh light is thrown on important and influential techniques of argumentation in the communication media. Each chapter presents solutions to problems central to understanding, analyzing, and criticizing media argumentation.

1

Logic, Dialectic, and Rhetoric

The three fields of logic, rhetoric, and dialectic are all about arguments, as Aristotle showed, but each takes a different viewpoint on them.[1] Logic is the science of reasoning that studies formal inferential links between sets of propositions designated as premises and conclusion of an argument. Dialectic, usually taken to be a branch of logic, analyzes arguments given in a text of discourse, including fallacious arguments, evaluating them as weak or strong by examining criticisms of them (Kapp 1942; Walton 1998b; Finocchiaro 2005, ch. 13). Rhetoric studies persuasive arguments based on the beliefs, commitments, or values of the target audience to be persuaded (Kennedy 1963; Tindale 1999, 2004; Jacobs 2000). However, the long history of the relationship between logic and rhetoric has been an antagonistic one, characterized by strife and sniping on both sides, beginning with Plato's attack on the Sophists on the basis that they took fees to teach argumentation skills.[2] This attack on rhetoric is visible in many places in Plato's dialogues (Krabbe 2000, p. 206).[3] Aristotle took a balanced view of what he saw as a close relationship between rhetoric and dialectic, but an opposition between the two subjects remained (Hohmann 2000, p. 223). Aristotle thought of dialectic

---

[1] The first sentence of the *Rhetoric* (1354a1) is: "Rhetoric is the counterpart of dialectic." Aristotle saw both arts as about persuasion (*Rhetoric*, 1354a13–1354a14). See Kennedy 1991, 1994).

[2] The ancient history of dialectic as a branch of logic is well described by Kapp (1942), while that of rhetoric as a subject designed for persuasion is equally well described by Kennedy (1963).

[3] In the *Georgias* (463a–463d), Socrates denounced rhetoric as nothing more than "flattery" (*kolakeia*).

as "a rather pure and theoretically sound method aimed at a cooperative search for cognitive truth" (Hohmann 2000, p. 223),[4] and hence by
comparison, rhetoric still had negative implications that are still present.

The aim of rhetorical argumentation seems to make it subjective,
because it needs to persuade by picking premises that represent the values of the specific audience (Johnstone 1981; Tindale 2004), values that
can vary from one group to another. To do this successfully, the proponent has to understand "where the audience is coming from." Using a
fictional example from *Star Trek*, featuring Klingons, Ferengi, and Vulcans, this chapter shows how dialectic also needs to base arguments on
premises that represent the values of the specific audience or respondent to whom the argument is addressed. Another goal of this chapter
is to introduce the reader to some new tools of argumentation theory,
such as argument diagramming and argumentation schemes, forms of
argument representing stereotypical types of reasoning used in everyday
conversational interactions. Thus this chapter will show how dialectical
argumentation, especially as it is being refashioned by recent developments of argumentation technology in AI, has become a much better
developed branch of logic, which has moved more into a rapproche-
ment with rhetoric. This chapter will take the first steps toward achieving
the ultimate goal of displaying the key structural components of rhetorical argumentation, and will show how they fit together with logical and
dialectical approaches to argumentation. What used to be called dialectic, and is coming to be so called again, has often been called informal
logic in recent years. Informal logic has a special viewpoint, setting it
apart from the much better developed field of formal logic.

1. The Viewpoint of Informal Logic

When it comes to studying arguments, there are two points of view, or ways
of analyzing and evaluating an argument, that need to be distinguished.
First, you can study the argument empirically to try to judge what effect
it had, or will be likely to have, on an audience. This viewpoint would
seem to be one that would fit the kind of approach and methods of the
social sciences. The other point of view is logical. You can classify the \

---

[4] Aristotle portrayed rhetoric as "a seriously tainted and practically compromised knack
serving a competitive quest for persuasive success" by contrasting it with the purely intellectual subject of dialectic (Hohmann 2000, p. 223), which studies reasoning supporting
or criticizing an argument.

argument as being of a particular type. By means of such a classification, you show the given argument to be an instance of some abstract form of argument. Then you can analyze it by finding missing assumptions it is based on. Then you can determine whether the argument is correct or incorrect (valid or invalid, reasonable or fallacious). In other words, you can evaluate it according to the normative standards of correctness that this type of argument is supposed to meet. It has been thought, since the end of the nineteenth century, that these two tasks were entirely independent from each other and that they should be carefully separated and never mixed in together. But recently, the feeling has been that this separation is not as clean as was once thought (Johnson 2000).

The following thumbnail sketch of the history of logic will amplify this point. Aristotle's syllogistic, along with the Stoic logic of propositions, developed into the science of deductive logic, which, in the twentieth century, became mathematical logic. On the other hand, Aristotle's practical logic – which comprised the study of "sophistical refutations" or fallacies, which comes under the heading of "dialectical reasoning," in which two parties reason with each other – fell into obscurity and neglect. Something approximating a resurrection of it was attempted in the nineteenth century, most notably, when idealist philosophers wrote about so-called laws of thought. With the ascendancy of formal (mathematical) logic, however, the whole idealist vision of laws of thought was repudiated, and called psychologism – a pejorative term, as then used in logic. A sharp separation was made between how people actually think (psychologically) and how they ought to think (logically) if they are to be rational.

Now to return from this thumbnail sketch, it can be seen why in logic there is thought to be a sharp separation between the empirical and normative viewpoints. Recent developments, however, have started to indicate that this separation is not as clean or sharp as it was thought to be. One recent development is the return to the quest, originating in Aristotle's older logic of the *Topics* and *On Sophistical Refutations*, of studying informal fallacies. It has been found that to study the fallacies with any hope of success, attention must be paid to realistic cases in which arguments are used for various conversational purposes in different contexts. Such an approach requires getting beyond simplistic one-liner examples of fallacies and looking at individual cases in some detail on their merits. Needless to say, such a pragmatic case-oriented approach to realistic argumentation introduces something of an empirical component. While the abstract form of the argument (the so-called argumentation scheme) is still very important, one also has to look seriously at how an argument has been used for some conversational purpose (supposedly, from what can be judged from the given text of discourse). The pragmatic study of arguments used in a given case is no longer purely formal and abstract. It has become contextual. Much depends on how you interpret a given text of discourse as expressing an argument or some other speech act. This pragmatic approach seems to make the traditional separation of abstract form and contextual content much more difficult to maintain.

This pragmatic approach to taking actual cases seriously is characteristic of the schools of thought now called informal logic and argumentation theory. The general theoretical approach can be described briefly as follows. The goals are the identification, analysis, and evaluation of argumentation. The field of argumentation is centrally concerned with arguments, but must also take account of related things, such as explanations and the asking of questions, that are not themselves arguments but nevertheless occur in an important way in sequences of argumentation. The ultimate goal is to evaluate arguments – that is, to judge in a given instance of its use how strong or weak an argument is and to judge whether the premises support the conclusions as good reasons for accepting them (Johnson 2000; Finochiarro 2005; Vorobej 2006).

The typical kind of case dealt with is one in which an argument of some sort has supposedly been put forward in a text of discourse in a given case. In this typical kind of case, the proponent is not around to defend her argument. The argument is expressed in some fairly short text of discourse presented in the logic classroom. The source of the text is known. It may be a magazine or newspaper article, a book, a transcript of a political speech, a transcript of a legal case, or any sort of text of discourse that appears to contain an interesting argument of some sort. The critics, usually a professor and a group of students, then undertake the task of identifying, analyzing, and evaluating the argument. Usually, an argument is selected because it fits the format of one of the famous informal fallacies. However, such arguments can be quite reasonable in many instances and are by no means necessarily fallacious. The game is to try to judge, in a given case, how the given argument, as far as it can be analyzed and pinned down, should be evaluated – is it fallacious, or just weak in certain respects and not so badly off that it should be called fallacious? Or is it reasonable – that is, should it be judged to be basically correct from a structural point of view, even though it may have parts that are missing or that are not very well backed up, as far as can be judged from what is known from the given text of discourse and its presumed context? In many cases, there simply isn't enough context given to support a definitive evaluation. Even in such cases, however, what is called a conditional evaluation can be very informative and even enlightening.

The viewpoint of informal logic is typically from a backward perspective. That is, you are typically confronted with a "dead specimen" – an argument that has already been put forward and is now embedded in some text of discourse that is being examined. The argument, presumably, is already over, and you are looking it at retrospectively. For example, the case you are studying may be from a political debate in a parliament or legislative assembly. The debate has already been concluded, perhaps long ago. So you are looking at it with all the benefit of 20/20 hindsight.

This normative viewpoint characteristic of modern argumentation theory and informal logic has ancient roots. It goes back to the ancient but much neglected and misunderstood field called "dialectic" by the Greeks. To begin to grasp the nature of the interdisciplinary tensions between logic and rhetoric, it is necessary to go back to the roots of both subjects.

2. The Old Dialectic of the Greeks

In the ancient world, dialectic was an art of questioning and replying in which two speech partners took turns. The questioner begins by asking a question that requires the respondent to make a choice on an issue. Once the respondent has chosen a position, the questioner can pursue the discussion further by drawing inferences based on the respondent's answers (Kapp 1942, p. 12). The exact purpose of dialectic is not known. But the best-known examples of it are the dialogues written by Plato in which Socrates plays the role of questioner. Plato called dialectic "the art concerning discussions" (Robinson 1953, p. 69). As we see Socrates using dialectic in the Platonic dialogues, it appears to be a critical art. Socrates uses a series of questions to probe into a respondent's position on some issue or problem, and he tends to finds weaknesses and contradictions in the position. In the early dialogues, dialectic seems like a critical art that has a negative aspect. But Plato had a very high opinion of dialectic as a method of finding the truth of a matter. His view of what dialectic is changed in his writings, but the term was always used to describe "the ideal method, whatever that might be" (Robinson 1953, p. 70). The best we can say is that in Plato's view, dialectic was a method of question and answer, of the kind used by Socrates in the dialogues to cast philosophical light on a question by examining in a critical way answers that seem plausible to some.

Aristotle defined "dialectic" in a more practical and more exact way. Like Plato, he saw it as a way of critically examining opinions that seem plausible. But he tied plausibility to the notion of the *endoxon*, or generally accepted opinion. In *On Sophistical Refutations* (165b10), Aristotle defined dialectical arguments as "those which, starting from generally accepted opinions [*endoxa*], reason to establish a contradiction." This definition makes dialectic similar to the way Plato saw it, but it is more precise, because it is tied to the notion of a generally accepted opinion. According to the *Topics* (100a25), generally accepted opinions are "those which commend themselves to all or to the majority or to the wise – that is, to all of the wise or to the majority or to the most famous and distinguished of them." For Aristotle, then, dialectic was the use of reasoning to draw logical consequences, and especially contradictions, from premises that are generally accepted opinions. Aside from its uses in philosophy, dialectic of the kind defined by Aristotle could be used to teach skills of arguing and debate. It could have everyday uses in casual conversations, and Aristotle also claimed that it is useful for critically questioning and discussing scientific axioms (*Topics*, 101b4). It is clear that for Plato and Aristotle, and for the Greek philosophers generally, dialectic was an important method. It was their attempt to reply to the criticism that argumentation skills could be used in sophistry to deceptively make the weaker argument appear stronger.

Aristotle saw dialectic and rhetoric as closely connected. The first sentence of the *Rhetoric* (1354a1) is: "Rhetoric is the counterpart of dialectic." He saw both arts as having to do with persuasion. Regarding rhetoric, he wrote, "The modes of persuasion are the only true constituents of the art: everything else is merely accessory" (*Rhetoric*, 1354a13–1354a14). He criticized the writers of the manuals on rhetoric for saying nothing about enthymemes, for they are "the substance of rhetorical persuasion." What did he mean by "enthymeme"? The conventional opinion throughout the history of logic since Aristotle has been that an enthymeme is an argument with an implicit premise that needs to be made explicit so that the argument becomes deductively valid. The traditional example, with the implicit premise in parentheses, is the argument "All men are mortal (Socrates is a man), therefore Socrates is mortal." In the *Prior Analytics* (70a10) Aristotle wrote: "An enthymeme is an incomplete argument [*syllogismos*] from plausibility or sign." This passage has long been taken as evidence for the conventional opinion that an

Aristotelian enthymeme is an argument with a missing premise. The word "incomplete" (*ateles*) shifts attention away from Aristotle's primary concern with arguments from plausibility and sign (Hitchcock 1995). However, a minority of Aristotle scholars, notably including Burnyeat, have felt that the traditional view of the enthymeme as an incomplete syllogism is an error. Burnyeat (1994, p. 6) argued on the basis of textual evidence that the key word "incomplete" (*ateles*) may have been inserted in the eleventh century. The sentence without the term *ateles* is repeated three times in the Rhetoric: "An ethymeme is *syllogismos* from plausibility or sign" (Tindale 1999, p. 10). Burnyeat argued that Aristotle meant by "enthymeme" an argument from plausibility that does not have to be incomplete. What Aristotle really referred to, according to his view, is a kind of argument that rests on a premise that is only true "for the most part." In terms of modern argumentation theory, it would be called a defeasible argument of the kind represented by an argumentation scheme. As a warrant, instead of a universal generalization of the syllogistic type, it would have a defeasible generalization that is subject to exceptions. Tindale (1999, p. 11) characterizes them as forms of probable argument that can "take on a number of different strategies or lines of argument." He identified these types of argument with the Aristotelian topics. Topics represent defeasible forms of argumentation or strategies of argumentation, such as argument from consequences.

As Tindale (1999, p. 12) has explained, the enthymeme was seen by Aristotle as connected to a special kind of audience that is interested in non-scientific arguments that are less rationally compelling than scientific arguments tend to be. Thus the enthymeme is the vehicle for mass media rhetorical arguments in which the audience is active and autonomous. If Burnyeat's view is right, both Aristotelian rhetoric and Aristotelian dialectic need to be viewed in a new light. Both subjects need to be rethought and seen as based on what Aristotle called their "true constituents," namely, enthymemes or argumentation schemes representing plausible arguments. Be that as it may, the history of the two subjects is that they grew apart. Rhetoric survived, but not in the form Aristotle would have liked, and dialectic faded into obscurity.

Dialectic failed to survive in the mainstream as a significant skill or method after the fall of the ancient civilizations of Greece and Rome. Especially after the Enlightenment, science came to represent the only reliable model of rational argument and evidence. In the new model of scientific reasoning, theorems were to be rigorously deduced from self-evident axioms by deductive logic. The idea of dialectical critical argumentation commanding rational assent outside science, or questioning scientific knowledge, had no important place in modern thinking after the rise of science. But Kant and Hegel attempted to find a place for it. Kant saw it as a negative art that inevitably leads to contradictions because it tries to resolve problems that are beyond the reach of empirical data and human understanding. According to Kant, we can know the world of appearances only as structured by our own understanding of it. We cannot know the world of "things in themselves," even though we have a strong urge to think we can. For Kant, dialectic represents the limits of human understanding. Basing his philosophy on the empiricism of David Hume, Kant saw empirical science and mathematics (represented by Euclidean geometry) as representing the kind of knowledge that is possible for humans. Although we naturally try to go beyond these limits of our understanding to abstract metaphysics, Kant argued that this quest is futile. And it was dialectic, or his version of it, that was used by Kant as the tool to show that we cannot go beyond these limits. In this respect, Kant was a modern thinker who took scientific knowledge as the model of rationality and saw dialectic only as a lesser art. Dialectic, on Kant's view of it, could be used only in a negative or critical way to show the futility of trying to go beyond the limits of mathematical reasoning and scientific observation.

Hegel, unimpressed by Kant's warning, saw dialectic as the way of going beyond mere appearances and investigating "things in themselves." Karl Marx built his philosophy of communism on Hegelian foundations. Hegel and Marx did not see dialectic as a purely verbal art of conversation, in the Greek way. They saw dialectic as studying contradictions between events in the real world. For example, Marx wrote about the contradictions in capitalism. In modern language, the term "dialectic" has come to be equated with Hegelian-Marxist notions. Thus it has been discredited as a serious scientific or philosophical notion. One takes some risks now by even using the term. But given the heritage of the term as representing such an important and central notion in Greek philosophy, it is better not to give up on it. Thus the new dialectic needs to be seen as having Greek roots. What is needed is a Greek revival.

By linking dialectic to the *endoxon*, Aristotle had done something highly significant. Dialectic was no longer confined to abstract philosophical discussions on arcane and technical philosophical problems. It now became linked to public opinion and widely held views that could be on any subject. The premises of a dialectical argument were taken by Aristotle to be the received views held to be plausible by both the public and the experts at any given time. Note that such views can change over time and can be different in different cultures or countries. Dialectic, on this view of it, is flexible. Of course, on the modern view of rational argumentation, this flexibility is precisely the defect that makes dialectic unfit to command rational assent. For in the modern view, as emphasized by Descartes, knowledge can come only from true and self-evident axioms that are fixed as true and never change. This static view of rationality was also that so highly promoted by Plato. In contrast, on the Aristotelian view of dialectical argument, it is based on premises that are not fixed and that change over time. Thus it is easy to see why dialectic has not been highly valued for so long and has been seen as an ancient notion of no use to represent a kind of argument or evidence of serious worth to command rational assent. At the same time, it is becoming increasingly apparent, as we overcome our modernistic preconceptions, that something like dialectic of the Aristotelian sort can be extremely useful as a method. Of course, where it can be most useful is in the evaluation of argumentation, especially the kinds of arguments used in law and public affairs. Indeed, the notion of democracy, as well as our Anglo-American system of law, would seem to rest on our capability of understanding and judging arguments on matters of public opinion.

3. The Opposition between Rhetoric and Dialectic

The Sophists were itinerant teachers who taught rhetorical techniques of argumentation, especially of the kind that could be used in the courts or in political speeches. Greek philosophy was strongly influenced by the Sophists, and it was through them that both rhetoric and dialectic emerged as significant philosophical subjects, taking the shape they did. However, as philosophy grew, it came to be seen as an abstract and general subject motivated by finding the truth of a matter. Philosophy took on a critical and skeptical tone; rhetoric, as developed by Sophists, had always been seen as a practical subject. The aim of rhetoric was that of persuasion or advocacy. This aim often requires examining both sides of an argument, but the aim, in the end, is to advocate the one side. Philosophy came to regard itself as a discipline that needed to consider both sides of an argument, looking at strengths and weaknesses in arguments on both sides in a balanced way. Given this perceived divergence of aim, it was natural that an opposition grew between rhetoric and dialectic.

The criticism of rhetoric, and even suspicion and hostility toward it, is perhaps most pronounced and sharply formulated in the philosophy of Plato. Plato often compared dialectic and rhetoric and consistently portrayed rhetoric as inferior and even untrustworthy. His method of attack was to use the bias *ad hominem* argument against the Sophists. Plato argued from the premise that the Sophists took fees for their lectures, whereas Socrates talked to anyone without charging any fee. He argued that because the Sophists were motivated by financial gain, it can be concluded that they have no regard for the truth of a matter. In other words, Plato charged the Sophists with being biased. He used this argument against them to discredit rhetoric as a discipline, or at least to compare rhetoric unfavorably with dialectic. This attack on rhetoric emerged in many places in the Platonic dialogues. Krabbe (2000, p. 206) has cited a few of the leading passages. For example, in the *Georgias* (463a–463d), Socrates denounced rhetoric as nothing more than "flattery" (*kolakeia*). Plato used the word "semblance" (*eidolon*) in describing the role of rhetoric in politics, and for Plato appearances are misleading and are not a good guide to the truth.

After Plato portrayed rhetoric as inferior to dialectic and emphasized its capability for deception, the *ad hominem* argument he used against it seemed to stick. For over two thousand years, the term "rhetoric" has taken on negative connotations. Although Aristotle took a more balanced view of the two subjects, and saw rhetoric in a more positive light than Plato, an opposition was still evident in his treatment of them. Hohmann wrote that Aristotle thought of dialectic as "a rather pure and theoretically sound method aimed at a cooperative search for cognitive truth" (2000, p. 223). By contrast to such a pure method, rhetoric is seen as compromised and even as untrustworthy. As Hohmann phrased it, rhetoric is portrayed as "a seriously tainted and practically compromised knack serving a competitive quest for persuasive success."

Even in Aristotle, then, because of the contrast with dialectic, rhetoric still comes across as a subject with negative implications. While in the present day, it is not hard to find suspicion and mistrust about rhetoric, there is not much respect for philosophy as a subject, either. By the close of the twentieth century, philosophy had become a highly abstract subject for the most part, seen by the public as removed from reality and useless. By the second half of the nineteenth century, neither rhetoric nor logic were subjects held in high esteem in public opinion. As Whatley wrote (*Elements of Rhetoric*, 1863, preface, p. 1): "The subject [rhetoric] stands perhaps but a few degrees above Logic in popular estimation; the one being generally regarded by the vulgar as the Art of bewildering the learned by frivolous subtleties; the other, that of deluding the multitude by specious falsehood." At the beginning of the twentieth century, mathematical logic soared to new heights in both philosophy and mathematics. But the promise of formal symbolic logic to provide a dialectical method for the evaluation of philosophical or practical argumentation was never fulfilled. The parts of logic relating to argumentation in natural language, like the subject of informal fallacies, remained undeveloped.

Even now, the rift between dialectic and rhetoric remains, and it seems very hard to break down the barriers between the traditional disciplines of logic and rhetoric. It is perhaps for this very reason that neither field seems to be capable of growing and fulfilling its potential for usefulness as a scientific discipline. This problem is more than a mere matter of historical accident. There are fundamental differences between the two fields in what they do and how they do it. Even if we consider dialectic, which could also be called informal logic or applied logic, there is one very great difference between it and rhetoric. In dialectical argumentation, two participants take turns. First, the proponent makes a move and then the respondent makes a move responding to that prior move. Dialectic always takes as its framework of argumentation a connected sequence of moves in which the parties take turns. Rhetoric does not appear to fit this model. In traditional rhetorical argumentation, a speaker is seen as making a presentation to an audience, typically a mass audience. They listen to and/or watch the performance. The speaker is active. He is an arguer who makes claims and supports them with arguments. But the audience is relatively passive with respect to advancing argumentation. The audience may respond through eye contact, by shouting "hurrah" or "boo," or by responding to a public opinion poll after the speech. But they don't seem to be active respondents of the kind that one would expect in dialectical argumentation. Many examples of mass media argumentation, while they appear to fit the rhetorical format obviously enough, do not seem to fit the dialectical format at all, or at best only indirectly. This contrast of structure is perhaps the deepest and most impressive difference between rhetoric and dialectic.

Leff (2000, p. 247) recognized this difference and expressed it concisely by writing that dialectic proceeds by question and answer, whereas rhetoric proceeds through uninterrupted discourse. He also cited three other differences between rhetoric and dialectic, which he called "differences of degree": (1) Dialectic deals with abstract issues, whereas rhetoric deals with specific issues. (2) Dialectic deals with propositions and inferences, whereas rhetoric deals with how propositions relate to social norms and circumstances. (3) Dialectic uses technical language, while rhetoric accommodates and embellishes ordinary language. Leff argued (p. 247) that despite their very different orientation and emphasis, the differences between rhetoric and dialectic are not as sharp or irreconcilable as tradition has long held. Dialectic, if it is to be a practical subject that is useful to analyze and evaluate actual arguments in given texts of discourse in natural language, does have an empirical aspect. If applied to cases of fallacies of the kind that deceive or trip up arguers, dialectic will have an empirical and even psychological or sociological aspect. If it is applied to real cases, it can scarcely be denied that it has some sort of empirical component. Thus the contrast between rhetoric as having an empirical method and dialectic as having a normative method may not be as sharp or absolute as it is often taken to be.

Another difference between rhetoric and dialectic is that their methods appear to contrast. Rhetoric aims at directing argumentation to a specific target audience, and the role of a normative or cognitive component may not necessarily support this aim, depending on how the rational the audience is (Perelman and Olbrechts-Tyteca 1969). According to a conventional view, rhetoric has to do with the effectiveness of argumentation to persuade or influence a target audience (Tindale 2004). The presumption of this view is that this influence is one of changing the beliefs or behavior of the audience. Such a change, it might seem to follow, is purely a matter of the psychology of the audience. For example, in the case of a commercial ad used in the mass media, the persuasive impact of the ad can be judged, it may be assumed, by the subsequent increase or decrease in sales, measured in numbers of transactions or in dollars. In the case of a political message, the persuasive impact can be measured in public opinion polls or in votes. On this view, rhetoric is a branch of psychology, and the element of persuasion can be measured by empirical indicators. So conceived, it seems that rhetoric has nothing to do with the dialectical structure of the argument used to make the persuasive appeal. It seems to have nothing to do with whether the argument is structurally correct by some standard, such as that of deductive logic. The reason presumably is that an argument could be structurally correct, but an audience could fail to find it quite persuasive. Or on the other hand, it could fail to be structurally correct as an argument, but an audience could find it quite persuasive anyway. Thus, for example, in public relations, advertising, or mass marketing, the concern seems to be exclusively with the effectiveness of the argument. The concept of persuasion effectiveness is seen as purely instrumental and psychological, so that rationality has no part in it.

Those working in the fields of rhetorical persuasion often operate on the assumption that effectiveness is the exclusive technical aim of their craft. The corollary of this assumption is that matters of the rationality of the arguments they use, or their structure as correct arguments, are of no concern or utility. But more recently, there has appeared a certain ambivalence about this view, as observed by Schiappa (1995) and Jacobs (2000). Schiappa commented that despite the occasional impulses of rhetorical theorists to take the rationality of argumentation into account, how they actually treat argumentation in practice often seems to reduce to the issue of effectiveness. Jacobs (2000, p. 273) made the similar comment that while rhetorical analysts don't explicitly accept the criterion of effectiveness as their exclusive aim in theory, they "tend to accept it in practice." Its methodology is to measure how successful argumentation is to persuade an audience or secure compliance to an action or policy. This goal appears to be psychological in nature, and therefore rhetorical argumentation, it would appear, needs to be evaluated empirically by the methods of the social sciences. The usual method is to run a poll to judge how successful argumentation was in a given case. In cases of argumentation techniques used in mass media ads, collection of numerical data measures empirically how many more units of a product were sold. The methods of dialectic are visibly different, and do not appear to fit with social science methodology. The question to be determined is whether a given move in argumentation serves to contribute to some type of dialogue of which it is a part. This contrast also seems fairly deep and dramatic. Dialectic is a normative subject, whereas rhetoric is conventionally seen as an empirical subject that fits in fairly well with the usual social science model for collecting data by empirical observation and testing. However, Leff (2000, p. 245) has argued convincingly that the issue should not be seen as one of "a contrast between a normative art of dialectic and a merely empirical art of rhetoric." He noted (p. 244) that Aristotle defined rhetoric not in terms of persuasive effect but as a faculty for observing in a given case the available means of persuasion. Following this viewpoint, the sharp division between dialectic as purely normative and rhetoric as purely empirical is not sustainable.

4. Topics and Fallacies

The term "topics," from the Greek word for "having to do with commonplaces," refers to classical and medieval sets of generally accepted arguments that can be used in a speech or composition (Bloomer 2001,

p. 779). Topics have long been recognized as rhetorical devices representing common forms of argument that can be used for inventions of arguments in a speech. However, they have never proved to be very useful for this purpose, despite the attempts to make them so, especially by Aristotle and Cicero (Bloomer 2001, p. 781). The topics appear to be very similar to what are now called argumentation schemes. However, it is uncertain what the function of the topics is supposed to be. Because they didn't prove to be useful for assisting argument invention, later writers, especially in medieval logic, tried to recast them in a dialectical role as devices that might be used to judge the worth of arguments already given. Perhaps the topics were not stated clearly enough or perhaps they were not fitted well enough into any general system of argument invention to be useful for rhetorical argumentation.

Any system of argument invention will have to be built on several basic components, so that arguments needed to prove a claim or to persuade can be constructed out of them. Basically, there will have to be a target proposition that is supposed to be proved or refuted, a given base of premises, and a tool for constructing chains of arguments that move forward from the premises toward proving this target proposition. Such systems have been attempted, but not in a formalized way, from ancient times onward. In modern times, formal systems have been constructed, called theorem-proving machines. However, these systems work only for deductive logic, and systems designed to use defeasible argumentation schemes have not yet been attempted. But it is the defeasible schemes that would prove most useful for inventing arguments in everyday reasoning, for example, in forensic debating and in legal argumentation.

One important function especially applicable to rhetorical argumentation is that of argument construction, providing means for the invention of new arguments. According to Kienpointner (1997), such topic-based systems of argument invention in antiquity, medieval, and early modern times had the following three characteristics.

1. The aim of the system is to search for arguments that could be used to support or attack some claim that is open to dispute (p. 225).
2. The search process looks not for all conceivable arguments but for ones that the audience either accepts or can be gotten to accept the premises, as well as the form of argument leading to the disputed claim from these premises.
3. The system can have stronger or weaker standards on what counts as a form of argument by means of which a conclusion can be shown to follow from a set of premises.

An invention device of this sort could be used to cast around among a set of facts, or a set of premises accepted by an audience, and find arguments (argumentations schemes, or forms of argument) that could be used to prove some claim to the audience that it does not presently accept.

On the other hand, the topics were sometimes represented by the medievals as having a logical or dialectical function, in contrast to their invention function. Fallacies are forms of argument that represent weak inferences, or even deceptive argumentation tactics used to unfairly get the best of a speech partner. Fallacies are not just arguments that are logically incorrect. They are logically incorrect arguments that appear to be correct. Fallacies tend to be either erroneous arguments of kinds that look persuasive, or deceptive arguments that appear to be rationally persuasive. In the latter case, they are sophistical tactics that can be used to try to get the best of a speech partner unfairly, because they look reasonable to that partner. Thus the concept of fallacy does have a rhetorical element, meaning that fallacies are kinds of arguments that generally appear to be reasonable as attempts to persuade a speech partner or a target audience. In fallacies of mass media argumentation, the fallacious argument is one that appears reasonable and is persuasive to a mass audience.

Jacobs (2000, p. 273) observed that fallacies are argumentative moves that seem good when they are not. He also commented that just because an argument seems reasonable or seems unreasonable, it does not follow that "it is what it seems" (p. 273). Of course, if an argument looks reasonable to a mass audience, they might be persuaded by it more easily than by an argument that looks fallacious or unconvincing to them. Or would they? The P. T. Barnum approach is to assume that the audience is emotional rather than logical, and can be persuaded even by the most fallacious argument. Barnum said that you can never go broke underestimating the intelligence of an audience. Le Bon is noted for a similar skepticism. He felt that crowds are moved by emotion, not reason, and that it is pointless to try to use reason to persuade them. There is something in these admonitions, for appeals to emotion really are the key to persuasion of a mass audience. But the Barnum/Le Bon approach restricts the role of logic (if we can include dialectic and informal logic) too narrowly. The reason is that even appeals to emotion have argumentation schemes, and thus they have a "logic" or argumentation structure. Even an audience that responds to an emotional appeal to fear or pity, or a vicious personal attack, needs to be persuaded by orchestrating that appeal through forms of argumentation the audience can follow and respond to. They need to draw the conclusions suggested by the speaker, following the inferences set up by the speaker in his argumentation. It is for this reason that dialectic is connected to rhetoric so that the one subject is useful and even necessary for the other. Dialectic is about fallacies, and explains how arguments that seem correct can be flawed underneath because the argumentation is defective or used for a communicative purpose in some deceptive way.

Rhetoric, when viewed through the framework laid out by Aristotle, is based on topics or argumentation schemes, and thus has a methodology with fundamental normative components. The importance of these argumentation schemes can be appreciated if one looks at Aristotle's *Rhetoric* in a new light. Aristotle began the *Rhetoric* by drawing a distinction between deliberative and forensic oratory. But from the very beginning (*Rhetoric* 1355a11), he emphasized that the method of constructing argumentation in either type of oratory is concerned with proof. This seems a peculiar word to use. It even seems inappropriate, because to us the term suggests a conclusive type of type of proof that you might find, for example, in Euclidean geometry. So what does he mean by the term in this context? He went on to explain that proof is "a sort of demonstration," suggesting that the Euclidean type of proof from axioms to theorems is exactly what he has in mind. But then in the next sentence he wrote, "We are most strongly convinced when we suppose anything to have been demonstrated." What did he mean by these remarks? To the modern reader, they just seem wrong. They seem to say that argumentation in rhetoric should be based on the same kind of deductive form of argument called "proof" that is characteristic of argumentation in science. This claim just seems wrong to us, because we think that argumentation in rhetoric is generally inconclusive and is based only on persuasion. Later, in fact (*Rhetoric* 1355b2), Aristotle defined rhetoric as "the faculty of discovering the possible means of persuasion in reference to any subject whatever." This definition appears to be at odds with the hypothesis that rhetoric is all about scientific proof or "demonstration." So how can we resolve this puzzle? The answer seems to lie in how Aristotle uses the term "enthymeme." Evidently, he thinks of an enthymeme as a kind of argument that is syllogistic in its form. It may not be the same as a logical (deductively valid) syllogism. But for Aristotle, it appears to be syllogism-like. He wrote (1355a11) that "the enthymeme is a kind of syllogism."

These remarks seem very puzzling because it is unclear what rhetoric has to do, at its core, with logical syllogisms of the kind we are so familiar with in deductive logic. But Aristotle's remarks start to make a good deal of sense as expressing a plausible hypothesis about rhetoric once we adopt Burnyeat's view. This view is that the enthymeme represents a presumptive form of argument that is like a syllogism but is based on a generalization that is held to be true "only for the most part." Supporting this interpretation is the passage at 1355a12 where Aristotle wrote that in forensic rhetoric, it is not easy to persuade an audience by even the most accurate scientific knowledge, and therefore, "our proofs and arguments must rest on generally accepted principles." On this view, an enthymeme, in the Aristotelian sense, is a presumptive argumentation scheme based on a warrant that is claimed to hold generally, but is subject to exceptions. Given this interpretation, Aristotle's view of the relationship between rhetoric and dialectic becomes much clearer and easier to appreciate. For example, when he wrote (*Rhetoric* 1355a11) that rhetorical skills are much more powerful when the speaker can detect bad arguments, we can easily appreciate how rhetoric and dialectic are connected, and how both are based on argumentation schemes and both relate to persuasion. He defines rhetoric (*Rhetoric* 1355a14) as "the faculty of discovering the possible means of persuasion in reference to any subject whenever." So defined it might initially seem that rhetoric has very little to do with dialectic. But a key term is "persuasion." How is an audience influenced by a means of persuasion? The answer is that it is persuaded by means of arguments that are (at least typically) not syllogisms, but kinds of arguments they are familiar with in everyday thinking and discourse. Once this connection is made, it is not hard to appreciate the plausibility of the assumption that an audience will be more effectively persuaded by arguments that they think are reasonable.

5. Persuasion, Social Influence, and Democracy

Now that these various dialectical tools have been explained, they can be applied to various problems, phenomena, and cases of mass media argumentation. But of course, many of the readers of this book will still not be convinced that these tools really can be applied in a useful way to mass media arguments in the realities of the marketplace and public discourse. What should really matter, according to the conventional viewpoint, are arguments that have social influence in the marketplace of a free economy and in the marketplace of social decision making in a democratic political system. The conventional view is that such matters should be studied by the empirical methods of the social sciences. To set the direction for the investigations in the rest of the book, and try to put such readers in a receptive frame of mind, two points are made in the final section of this chapter. The first relates to some recent findings on persuasion in social psychology. The second has to do with the wider implications of rhetoric and dialectic in relation to argumentation in the public sphere, especially in law and democratic politics.

Robert B. Cialdini, a social psychologist, has studied techniques of persuasion empirically. In his popular book (Cialdini 1993), he recognized seven techniques that he saw as basic to social influence.

Contrast is a technique concerning the sequence in which a persuasive message is presented. For example (Cialdini 1993, pp. 25–26), a salesperson in a clothing store, in order to sell an expensive sweater, may show the customer an even more expensive sweater first. Then by comparison, the cost of the sweater presented second may not seem so exorbitant.

Reciprocity is a technique by which a proponent makes a respondent more likely to consider or accept his argument by making the respondent obliged to the proponent in advance of the argument. For example, in an experiment by Regan (1971), raffle sales were increased when participants were given a free soft drink before being asked to buy a raffle ticket.

Consistency is the technique of using an arguer's previous commitments, or getting him to commit to propositions that will support the conclusion you want to persuade him to accept. Cialdini (1993, pp. 76–77) gave the example of how the Chinese interrogators during the Korean war began the process of indoctrinating American prisoners of war by asking each prisoner to prepare a list of problems in the United States. This seemed harmless at first, but later it turned out to be a powerful device to assist persuasion.

Social proof presents evidence of what other people think as a reason for accepting a proposition or going along with a recommended course of action. A case cited by Cialdini was the mass suicide in Jonestown, Guyana, in which 910 people voluntarily drank poison in an orderly way. Conformity seemed to play a large role in the technique the charismatic leader, Rev. Jim Jones, used to persuade the group to carry out this extraordinary action.

Liking is the positive attitude that the person or group persuaded has toward the persuader. The example given by Cialdini (1993, pp. 163–166) is the hostess who invites all her friends to a Tupperware party. They like the hostess, and this attitude makes the persuasive task of the hostess that much easier.

Authority is the use of an expert opinion or accepted authority as a technique of persuasion. Cialdini (1993, pp. 212–213) uses the example of a physician who tells a patient that he should take a particular medication.

Scarcity is the technique of telling a respondent that the item he is thinking of buying is in short supply, possibly because there is competition for it. Cialdini (1993, p. 197) used the example of a salesperson who told a customer that the machine the customer is looking at has just been bought by another person, but there might be one left.

Cialdini classified these seven techniques as cognitive short cuts, meaning that they go straight to a conclusion when there is no time to engage in a more lengthy analytical process of thinking. They are thinking techniques we all use in situations where hard evidence is insufficient to resolve a problem or make a decision by more thoughtful cognitive processing, but where a quick decision can be made on the basis of a guess or presumption. Thus when used by an arguer at the opportune moment in a deliberation, they can be powerful techniques of persuasion.

In the following chapters, these seven techniques will be encountered with some regularity. Some of them are associated with argumentation schemes and also with traditional fallacies. For example, the technique of authority is obviously related to the argumentation scheme for appeal to expert opinion. Social proof is very closely related to the appeal to popular opinion, a form of argument studied in chapter 2. Others of the techniques are not forms of argument, but argumentation strategies of various kinds. Contrast is an argumentation strategy that is not closely associated with any particular form of argument, but can be devised in advance by a persuader as a framework into which to fit a sequence of argumentation. It is related to the argumentation strategy called dissociation by Perelman and Olbrechts-Tyteca (1969) as explained in chapter 8. Consistency falls into both categories. It is associated with a form of argumentation called argument from commitment in chapter 3, section 3. Using this argumentation scheme, the proponent argues from the commitments of the respondent. But commitment-based argumentation is central to all the types of dialogue in the new dialectic, and is a strategy used in all the various argumentation schemes.

At any rate, awareness of the seven powerful persuasion techniques shown to be so important in social influence by Cialdini is extremely useful for linking dialectic to empirical work on how people respond to persuasion. We now proceed to the second point, as the closing consideration of this chapter, thus pointing the way to the studies undertaken in the next chapters. Many of the case studies of argumentation treated in these chapters concern arguments that can't just be viewed from a simple rhetorical or dialectical framework of a persuading arguer and a single respondent who is the target of the argument message. Many of the arguments involve policies that are public in nature and may even be cast in law as rules binding at the national level. Of course, if we look back to the Greek origins of dialectic and rhetoric once again, these subjects originally rose out of the need to contend with legal and political argumentation in the democratic form of government of the Greek city-states. As Wenzel (1990, p. 14) emphasized, Aristotle, Cicero, Isocrates, and other ancient rhetorical theorists linked rhetoric to politics and law. Wenzel (p. 13) argued that in fact rhetoric, dialectic, and logic all originated in ancient Greece "to meet certain practical needs of people who were learning how to manage democratic government." It is, of course, fairly obvious how rhetoric applies to politics in democratic government. What is less obvious is how dialectic might apply to the public sphere. Wenzel (p. 14) showed very clearly how it does when he wrote: "Democratic government requires the exercise of human judgment to choose among alternatives and that judgment requires skilled advocates to articulate the various options in public deliberation." At the same time, this remark hints at the interdependence of rhetoric and dialectic. Dialectic has to examine and weigh all the relevant arguments on both sides of an issue to be decided. But it requires a skilled advocate, a rhetorician, to articulate the arguments in a persuasive way.

6. Argumentation Schemes

It wasn't until the recent exploration of new methods of argumentation theory and the study of fallacies that prospects for either dialectic or rhetoric began to improve. One especially important tool is the classification and analysis of so-called argumentation schemes, or common forms of argumentation. Argumentation schemes are premise-conclusion inference structures that represent common types of arguments used in everyday discourse, as well as in special contexts, such as those of legal or scientific argumentation. They include deductive and inductive forms of argument, but also forms of argument that fall into a third category, called defeasible, presumptive, or abductive. The study of schemes gradually began to be developed, motivated partly by rhetoric, but also by the need in logic to deal with informal fallacies and other problems of informal logic. This work originated mainly in philosophy departments and in speech communication departments, but after a while it became interdisciplinary, including researchers from fields such as linguistics and computing. Joint projects developed; for example, the recent Perthshire Conference on Argument and Computing had working groups combining expertise in the fields of law, computing, communication, and philosophy.

The new rhetoric of Perelman and Olbrechts-Tyteca (1969) began to study various common forms of argument used not only in rhetorical and philosophical argumentation but in law, science, and many other contexts of discourse as well. Of course, many such forms of argument are listed and treated quite extensively by Aristotle in his *Topics*. A table drawing up comparisons among the list of twenty-eight topics found in Arsitotle's *Rhetoric* and the thirteen argumentation schemes in *The New Rhetoric* (1969) of Perelman and Olbrechts-Tyteca has been constructed by Warnick (2000). Throughout the long history of the study of so-called topics (*topoi*), or common forms of argument, their role in dialectic and rhetoric has been controversial. Were they aids to memory in debate, were they rhetorical devices for arguing in a speech, or were they logical forms of argument of some undetermined sort? They are often referred to as "places" where you can find an argument. In rhetoric, they have often been seen as useful for invention – that is, to help a speaker think up a new argument to support advocacy of a claim.

As one looks over the comparative table of argumentation schemes from Pereleman and Olbrechts-Tyteca and topics from Aristotle's *Rhetoric* listed in Warnick (2000, pp. 120–128), one finds some common and familiar forms of argument represented. Other forms appear obscure and are hard to relate to common argumentation. A familiar one is argument from example, a weak form of argument that is sometimes hard to distinguish from explanation. Argument from analogy is another familiar one found in both sources. The table shows that there are forms of argument common to both the ancient and modern accounts. But it also points up the difficulties with Aristotelian topics and the argumentation schemes of Perelman and Olbrechts-Tyteca. The forms of argument are not worked out clearly by formalizing them and using case studies or realistic examples to show how the form applies to a common variety of cases. To advance the subject a bit further, we have to turn to the more systematic accounts of schemes given in Kienpointner (1992) and Walton (1996). The best introduction to this work is to give the example of argument from expert opinion, developed at length in Walton (1997a).

Presumptive argumentation schemes are modeled with the help of two components. One is a representation of the form of the argument. The other is a set of critical questions matching that form of argument. The appeal to expert opinion, also called argument from expert opinion, is an example of a common presumptive form of argument. For example, in court, a ballistics expert may be called in as a witness to testify about a bullet found at a crime scene. The first component of the argumentation scheme for argument from expert opinion is the following form of argument (Walton 1997a, p. 210).

Form of Argument from Expert Opinion

Major Premise: Source E is an expert in subject domain S containing proposition A.

Minor Premise: E asserts that proposition A (in domain S) is true (false).

Conclusion: A may plausibly be taken to be true (false).

Argument from expert opinion is typically a presumptive form of argument, meaning that it carries tentative probative weight in a dialogue. But presumptive arguments of this kind are defeasible, meaning that they are subject to defeat at some next point in the dialogue. As the logic textbooks tell us, appeal to expert opinion can even be fallacious in some cases. The problem is that there is a natural tendency to defer to an expert, and it is easy to give in to this tendency uncritically, without making the effort to ask critical questions. Thus the second component of the argumentation scheme for appeal to expert opinion is the following list of six basic critical questions (Walton 1997a, p. 223).

Critical Questions for the Argument from Expert Opinion

1. *Expertise Question*: How credible is E as an expert source?
2. *Field Question*: Is E an expert in the field that A is in?
3. *Opinion Question*: What did E assert that implies A?
4. *Trustworthiness Question*: Is E personally reliable as a source?
5. *Consistency Question*: Is A consistent with what other experts assert?
6. *Backup Evidence Question*: Is A's assertion based on evidence?

The evaluation of argumentation based on appeal to expert opinion takes the form of a dialogue. If a proponent puts forward an argument that has the form of the argumentation scheme above, and the premises are based on good evidence, then the argument carries probative weight. This means that the respondent in the dialogue is obliged to provisionally accept the conclusion of the argument. But the respondent also has the option of asking appropriate critical questions. If he asks such a critical question, the proponent has the burden of proof, meaning that he must either answer the question or the argument is defeated. That is, the proponent must answer the critical question adequately or he must give up the appeal to expert opinion as an argument carrying presumptive weight in the dialogue.

The technique of evaluating arguments defeasible through the use of a set of special critical questions matching each argumentation schemes is due to Arthur Hastings (1963). Hastings, in his innovative Ph.D. thesis at Northwestern University, set out a list of many common schemes with a set of critical questions accompanying each scheme. An argument fitting a scheme is defeated if an appropriate critical question is asked but not answered. As the field of argumentation studies developed, this approach became widely adopted, for example, by Kienpointner (1992) and Grennan (1997). Now argumentation schemes are being used in artificial intelligence, logic programs, natural language text generation, argumentation systems for legal reasoning, and multi-agent technology used on the Internet.[5] The most useful and widely used tool so far developed in argumentation theory is the set of argumentation schemes, especially those representing defeasible argumentation. A defeasible argument is one in which the conclusion can be accepted tentatively in relation to the evidence known at a given point of the investigation in a case, but may need to be retracted as new evidence comes in.

A defeasible argument is typically not very strong by itself, but still may be strong enough to provide evidence to warrant rational acceptance of its conclusion on a balance of considerations as an investigation moves forward. The investigation can then move ahead, even under conditions of uncertainty and lack of knowledge, using the conclusion tentatively accepted. The recognition of defeasible argumentation has led to a paradigm shift in logic, artificial intelligence (AI), and cognitive science concerning forms of argument, such as argument from expert opinion, traditionally categorized as fallacious in logic textbooks. Among the defeasible argumentation schemes that have been studied are argument from sign, argument from example, argument from commitment, argument from position to know, argument from expert opinion, *ad hominem* argument, argument from analogy, argument from precedent, argument from gradualism, and several types of slippery slope argument.

---

[5] Recent conferences and workshops dedicated to the theory of argumentation in artificial intelligence include the International Conference on Computational Models of Argument (COMMA 2006), the Computational Models of Natural Argument (CMNA) workshop series, and the Argumentation in Multi-Agent Systems (ArgMAS 04, 05, 06) workshop series. In 2007, there has been a call for papers on a special issue of the IEEE journal *Intelligent Systems* on the topic of argumentation technology.

Among others that might be mentioned are argument from popular opinion, argument from verbal classification, practical reasoning, argument from sunk costs, argument from ignorance, argument from cause to effect, argument from correlation to cause, argument from positive or negative consequences, argument from threat, and fear appeal argument. Such arguments are now admitted to be reasonable in many instances, even if they are tricky and not always reliable because they are defeasible and hence inherently subject to failure. Argument from expert opinion, for example, had traditionally been treated in logic textbooks under the category of the fallacy of appeal to authority. And we can get into a lot of trouble, for example, concerning "junk science," with such arguments. However, currently it is admitted that we could not get by without such arguments, for example, in the courts, where testimony by scientific experts and much of the evidence, including ballistics and DNA evidence, is based on appeal to expert opinion. Hence the importance of defeasible argumentation schemes has become readily apparent in the recent body of work on informal fallacies, leading to the new idea that such "fallacies" should no longer be treated as fallacies. We will see in this book that one of the most central argumentation schemes underlying many arguments associated with the traditional informal fallacies is the scheme for practical reasoning.

7. Basic Practical Reasoning

An important point made recently by Kock (2003, 2006) is that contemporary theories of argumentation have tended to define rhetorical argumentation with reference to the arguer's goal of effective persuasion. For example, Johnson (2000) has made a contribution to argumentation theory by emphasizing the dialectical aspect of rhetoric in which he sees rhetorical argumentation as underpinned by an informal logic that has the aim of rational persuasion as its goal. Van Eemeren and Houtlosser (1999b, 2000, 2001, 2002) advocate a view in which rhetoric is seen as a persuasive effort at winning a discussion by resolving a difference of opinion in one's favor. Although acknowledging the importance of both these views, Kock (2006) has also criticized them because they overlook the view of Aristotle that rhetoric is rooted in deliberation, a form of decision making that comes to a conclusion about which action to take given choices among alternative courses of action. The problem pointed out by Kock is that although these contemporary theories of argumentation have taken steps toward reconciling rhetoric and dialectic, they haven't gone far enough. By emphasizing the view that argumentation is exclusively about giving reasons to accept a proposition is true or false, they have tended to overlook deliberative rhetoric. The purpose of a deliberative discussion is not to prove that a designated proposition is true or false but to select a prudent course of action by looking at the reasons for and against this action compared with the alternative actions available in a given situation. To follow up on Kock's insight and pave the way for our analysis of deliberation as contrasted with persuasion dialogue in chapter 2, we now turn to the argumentation scheme most characteristic of deliberative reasoning.

The form of reasoning used in appeals to fear and pity is the so-called Aristotelian practical syllogism, or what is more often called practical reasoning (Perelman and Olbrechts-Tyteca 1969; Walton 1990). To use a simple example for illustration, consider the following inference.

My goal is to be in London before 4:30.
The 2:30 train from here arrives in London at 4:15.
So, I shall catch the 2:30 train.

There might be all kinds of complications. It might be cheaper or faster to fly to London. Still, one can appreciate how this kind of reasoning works in its simplest form. Aristotelian practical reasoning has now been much studied, both in philosophy and in computer science (particularly in AI), and its properties as a structure of logical inference are now becoming better known and formalized. Practical reasoning is carried out by an agent (or group of agents), an entity that has goals (intentions) and can carry out actions. Practical reasoning is made up of a chain of practical inferences. A practical inference has two premises. One states that an agent has a certain goal, meaning something that she thinks ought to be realized if possible. The other premise cites some form of action as a means, or part of a means, of carrying out the goal. Goals are often stated at a high level of abstraction. For example, an agent's goal could be to maximize her health. The question then is one of which specific means would contribute to this general goal. Practical inference meshes such abstract goals with the specifics of an agent's given situation. So, for example, some action that would contribute to my health might actually be harmful to your health. Here, there is a conflict of goals at an abstract level. However, in some cases, goals are highly specific. For example, my goal might be to arrive at a specific destination at a specific time. Practical reasoning is the form of argumentation underlying deliberative rhetoric. In section 9 below, a more complex example that brings out the rhetorical dimension will be offered.

Practical reasoning is a chaining together of practical inferences of the following form, where the first-person pronoun represents an agent (Walton 1990). An *agent* is an entity capable of carrying out actions, of seeing the consequences of these actions, and of modifying its subsequent actions on the basis of what it has seen (Wooldridge and Jennings 1995). The structure of practical reasoning as an argumentation scheme is built on the assumption that there can be a theory of action representing the logical form of imperative reasoning that concludes in a directive for an agent to carry out an action. According to one theory, an action may be analyzed as the bringing about of an event or state of affairs, represented as a proposition made true or false by what an agent does (Horty and Belnap 1995). As shown in an overview of this type of formal action system (Segerberg 1984), actions fit into sequences called routines (sometimes called scripts in AI) that represent standard ways of doing things. A good example described by Segerberg is a recipe for a culinary dish that lists a series of actions as steps that need to be carried out in a certain order in order to realize a goal, such as baking a chocolate cake, for example. On this model, outcomes of actions are represented as propositions A, B, C, . . . , so that carrying out an action can be described as bringing about a stated proposition by making it true.

Agents are seen as having the capability to bring about entities called states of affairs (Walton 1990). States of affairs can obtain or not obtain in a given case. They can be thought of as propositions that can be made true or false by an agent. Using the primitive notions of agent and state of affairs, the structure of the practical inference can be represented as follows. The letters A, B, C, . . . , stand for states of affairs, or propositions brought about (made true) by agents.

Instrumental Practical Reasoning
Bringing about A is my goal.

Bringing about B is a necessary (or in some cases sufficient) condition for bringing about A.

Therefore I should bring about B.

The first premise could be called the goal premise, and the second premise the conditional premise, because it expresses a conditional relationship of a practical sort. Bringing about one state is said to be necessary or sufficient for bringing about another. The conclusion expresses a so-called prudential, or practical, ought-statement.

In multi-agent practical reasoning, a group of agents communicate with each other in order to collectively carry out some shared goals, or at least to deliberate on how to proceed in a situation that requires some sort of group action. The "should" in the conclusion is a practical "ought" that expresses a kind of prudential imperative that binds these agents. It means that if the agents are to be practically rational, they should become committed to bringing about B, once they know that bringing about B is necessary (or sufficient) for bringing about A, and they are committed to bringing about A. In multi-agent reasoning (Wooldridge and Jennings 1995), one agent puts forward an argument in the form of a practical inference, and another is designated as the respondent of the argument. A typical context of use of such argumentation would be in planning, where the two agents are jointly trying to bring about some shared goal. Another context of use might be that of advice-giving dialogue, where the one agent is asking the other (an expert) how to carry out some task requiring technical expertise.

Practical reasoning is defeasible, meaning that it leads to a conclusion that is only provisionally acceptable, subject to the asking of appropriate critical questions. The key critical questions are the following.

(Q1) Are there alternative courses of action apart from B?
(Q2) Is B the best (or most acceptable) among the alternatives?
(Q3) Should goals other than A be considered?
(Q4) Is it really possible to bring about B, in the situation?
(Q5) What bad consequences of bringing about B should be taken into account?

The practical inference, as used in the argumentation in a given case, should be evaluated positively to the extent that it stands up to this kind of critical questioning. As noted above, practical reasoning is defeasible in nature. It holds tentatively, subject to rebuttal by critical questions. If the critical questions are asked but not answered adequately, the practical inference fails. The asking of any one, or any group of such critical questions, can lead to argumentation of kinds we are highly familiar with. For example, if it appears that carrying out the action considered may have bad consequences – that is, consequences that go against the goals of the agent – a critic may argue that the action should not be carried out because it is likely to have these bad consequences. This form of argument is called argumentation from negative consequences. In another common type of case, an agent may have a conflict of goals. If it carries out an action to realize its goal $G1$, that same action may go against its goal $G2$. Such conflicts often take the form of a dilemma, in which there is a choice between two incompatible actions.

So far, we have taken into account only the simpler kind of practical reasoning that is purely instrumental, in that it does not take values into account. Values are sometimes in the background in practical reasoning, and do not need to be considered. In such cases the basic instrumental scheme can be used to analyze and evaluate practical reasoning. In other cases, for example, those typical in political deliberation in electronic democracy, values often need to be taken into account. In these cases, for example, in ethical dilemmas, the more complex scheme for value-based practical reasoning needs to be applied. Note that in Q5, the term "bad" is used to denote negative value, and in Q2, the term "best" is used to denote a comparative rating of values.

8. Value-Based Practical Reasoning

Atkinson, Bench-Capon, and McBurney (2004, p. 88) have studied examples from the development of AI tools to assist electronic democracy that involve a more complex kind of practical reasoning based on values. Their example can be adjoined to the simple train example of practical reasoning stated above.

> Friendship requires that I see John before he leaves London.
> The 2:30 train arrives in London at 4:15.
> So, I shall catch the 2:30 train.

Atkinson et al. (p. 88) showed how the action in the conclusion in this case is justified by citing an underlying general social value, friendship. On their account, there are three components of such value-based practical reasoning: the action, the goal, and the reason why the goal is desired, namely, an underlying value. They describe values as social interests that support goals by explaining why goals are desirable.

Thus there are two notions of practical reasoning, a simpler instrumental one and a deeper one that takes values into account. In political deliberations, such as those assisted by electronic democracy tools, an arguer may be trying to persuade an audience to see a course of action as practically reasonable for the group to adopt, based on their presumed values. In such an instance it is important to take values into account, even if they are implicit premises as opposed to clearly articulated goals. In addition to the instrumental basic scheme for practical reasoning, a new value-based scheme is also formulated below. The difference between this new scheme and the instrumental one above is that an additional premise, below, has been inserted to account for values.

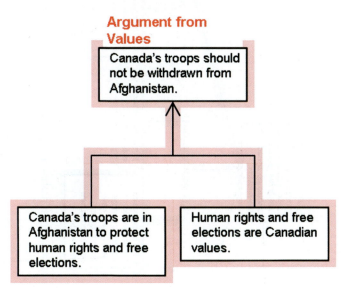

PLATE 1 Araucaria diagram of example of political value-based argumentation.

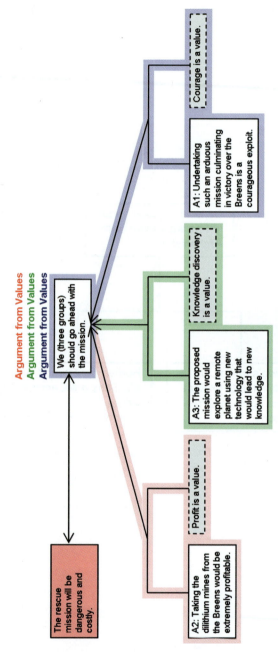

PLATE 2 Araucaria diagram representing Captain Picard's argument.

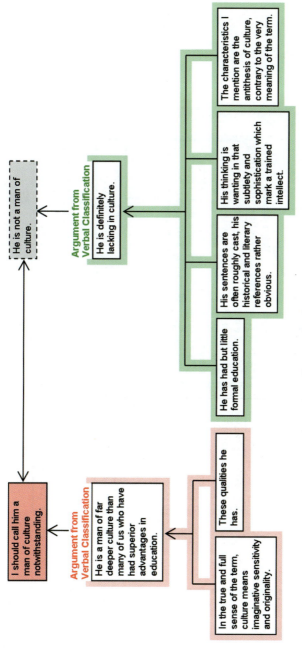

PLATE 3 Argument diagram for Stevenson's culture example.

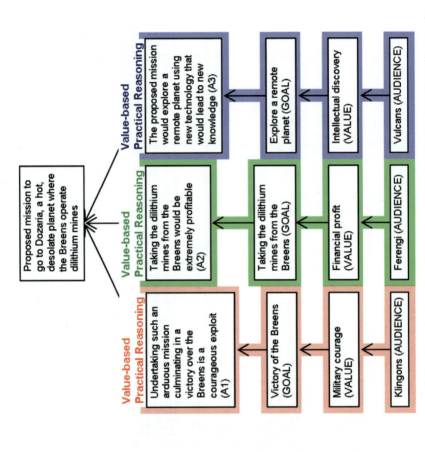

PLATE 4 Value-based structure of argument invention in Captain Picard's speech.

Scheme for Value-Based Practical Reasoning
I have a goal *G*.
G is supported by my set of values, *V*.
Bringing about *A* is necessary (or sufficient) for me to bring about *G*.
Therefore, I should (practically ought to) bring about *A*.

Both the instrumental scheme and the value-based one should be regarded as representing defeasible forms of reasoning that can be rebutted by asking any one of a set of critical questions in a dialogue, such as: Which alternative actions to my bringing about *A* that would also bring about *G* should be considered? In the case of value-based practical reasoning, the following critical question is appropriate: How well is *G* supported by (or at least consistent with) my values *V*? Another is this one: Among bringing about *A* and these alternative actions, which is arguably the best of the whole set, in light of my values *V*?

In a speech reported in a newspaper article (Ivison 2006), the front runner in a liberal party leadership debate defended his support for extending the Canadian mission in Afghanistan using argument from positive values. He was quoted below as saying that the mission was based on Canadian values.

He said there is fear that if the international effort fails, Afghanistan will fall back into the hands of extremist Taliban forces, and argued Canada's troops are there to protect human rights and free elections, which he said are "Canadian values."

In this part of the speech, as reported above, two arguments are put forward. The first one is based on the alleged fear that if the international effort fails, Afghanistan will fall back into the hands of extremist Taliban forces. It is presumed as an implicit premise that the outcome of falling back into the hands of extremist Taliban forces would be a bad thing. The evaluation of this outcome as negative is partly based on the use of the negative term "extremist." Hence this argument, although mainly an argument from negative consequences, is also partly based on argument from values and argument from verbal classification. For present purposes, however, the second argument is more interesting as an example for analysis. The speaker argued that Canada's troops are there to protect human rights and free elections, and he claimed these to be Canadian values. The audience of his speech was composed, we may presume, of Canadians who might or might not support his side in the party leadership debate. We can assume that protecting human rights and free elections would be taken as positive values by this audience of Canadians. And we can assume that the speech was aimed at this audience. Hence the argumentation in his speech can properly be fitted into the argumentation scheme for argument from positive values.

Based on this analysis, the argumentation in the politician's speech can be represented diagrammatically as in Plate 1. The figure was constructed using Araucaria, a freeware system for automating argument diagramming. In an Araucaria diagram, each premise or conclusion (proposition) in an argument appears in a text box, while the inference between a set of premises and a conclusion is drawn as an arrow (Reed and Rowe 2002). Araucaria can also be used to display the argumentation scheme linking a set of premises to a conclusion (Reed and Walton 2003). As shown in Plate 1, the two premises are in a linked configuration supporting the conclusion. The argumentation scheme for argument from values is displayed on the linked inference.

The argumentation scheme for argument from values has the following structure.

Argument from Values

Variant: Argument from Positive Value

Premise 1:   Value *V* is *positive* as judged by agent *A* (judgment value).

Premise 2:   The fact that value *V* is *positive* affects the interpretation and therefore the evaluation of goal *G* of agent *A* (if value *V* is *good*, it supports commitment to goal *G*).

Conclusion: *V* is a reason for retaining commitment to goal *G*.

Variant 2: Argument from Negative Value

Premise 1:   Value *V* is *negative* as judged by agent *A* (judgment value).

Premise 2:   The fact that value *V* is *negative* affects the interpretation and therefore the evaluation of goal *G* of agent *A* (if value *V* is *bad*, it goes against commitment to goal *G*).

Conclusion: *V* is a reason for retracting commitment to goal *G*.

Given this argumentation scheme, a set of premises can be identified as supporting a conclusion in virtue of the scheme linking them to the conclusion.

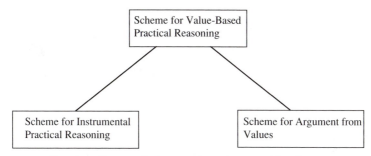

FIGURE 1.1 Ontology for practical reasoning schemes with values.

In value-based practical reasoning, argument from values is grafted onto basic practical reasoning, forming the composite argumentation scheme called value-based practical reasoning. To have a classification system for this family of argumentation schemes, we propose the ontology represented in Figure 1.1. This type of diagram is called an ontology in computer science, because it classifies key concepts in a systematic way so that operations concerning them can be automated in the semantic web. An ontology can be seen as a way of partially defining a term by classifying it in relation to other key terms in a subject or field.

Practical reasoning typically takes place in the context of a deliberation in which two parties are trying to decide on a best course of action for one or both of them in a situation of uncertainty. Public debates on complex social issues, such as the question of gun control legislation, take place in a context of deliberation in which the goal is to come to a decision on a prudent course of action. But the issue and its ramifications are so complex, with so many variables, that there can be no mechanical procedure, as in mathematical decision theory, for example, that is of much use in coming to a rational decision on what to do. Many factors are involved, and not all of them are purely factual. Deliberation is often based on goals and values, and the rhetorical speaker who wants to influence public deliberation must ground persuasive argumentation on what are taken to be the goals and values of the groups who are taking part in the deliberation and who will decide the outcome.

9. The Star Trek Example

A small story can be used to illustrate how values can vary in different groups or cultures, and how the different values from each group can support the same goal. In the television show *Star Trek: The Next Generation*, there were three types of beings from different planets, and each had values that were very different from those of the other group. The Klingons were warlike and have values of courage and honor. For them, dying in battle, especially when outnumbered by a worthy enemy, is very valuable. For them, being in any way perceived as cowardly, or avoiding confrontation or battle, would be the worst thing, implying great dishonor. The Ferengi were commercially minded. They constantly think about making deals that are in their best economic interest. Their values were the accumulation of property, goods and money. They constantly negotiate on everything, scheming and swindling people into bad deals. For them, dying in battle would be impractical, unless it were merely a risk to take that would somehow be financially profitable. The Vulcans were very intellectual, noted for knowing a lot about science and computers and for making decisions based on reason and logic. They valued science and intellectual pursuits.

Now let's consider the reasons each group might have for the goal of attempting to reach new planets by space exploration. The Klingons would see it as inviting possibilities of conquest and exploits in battle. Their value is courage. The Ferengi would see it as a way of exploiting resources that might be found on these other planets that could be sold or otherwise used to make profits. The Vulcans would see it as a way of finding new knowledge not only about distant planets, but also through the development of technology by building new spaceships and better computers. Their value is discovery. In this case, each group has the same goal – that of attempting to reach new planets by space exploration – but the values each has that support that goal are quite different.

The episode of *Star Trek* set out below is based on a real episode, but details have been changed, and the plot has been simplified. On Dozaria, a hot, desolate planet, the Breens operate dilithium mines. A Cardassian prison transport has crash-landed on Dozaria after being attacked by Breen warships. The survivors, Bajorans and Cardassians, are forced to labor in the mines, and Starfleet Command is to mount a rescue mission. Now let's suppose that Captain Jean-Luc Picard is giving a speech to the three groups who are expected to take part in the rescue mission, the Klingons, the Ferengi, and the Vulcans. Such a mission would mean a long, dangerous trip to Dozaria, and all three groups might be opposed to such a hazardous undertaking. Picard is assigned the job of trying to persuade the three groups to go ahead with the mission, and gives the following speech:

I admit that the rescue mission will be dangerous and costly. Still, I think that we should go ahead with it as a group undertaking, for three reasons. First, undertaking such an arduous mission culminating in victory over the Breens is a courageous exploit. Second, taking the dilithium mines from the Breens would be extremely profitable. Third, the proposed mission would explore a remote planet using new technology that would lead to new knowledge.

Essentially, Picard presented three arguments in favor of undertaking the mission.

> A1: Undertaking such an arduous mission culminating in victory over the Breens is a courageous exploit.
>
> A2: Taking the dilithium mines from the Breens would be extremely profitable.
>
> A3: The proposed mission would explore a remote planet using new technology that would lead to new knowledge.

Even judging from what we have been told in the condensed presentation of Picard's speech given above, it has many interesting aspects that could be commented on from the point of view of argumentation. It was the outcome of a deliberation process. It depends on practical reasoning, or so-called means-end reasoning, concerning a decision of whether a proposal for action should be undertaken. But most interesting, from our point of view, is the aspect of persuasion. Captain Picard's goal was to persuade his audience to undertake a dangerous mission; of the arguments he used, each of them was directed to a specific value that he thought each of the groups in the audience would have. This type of argumentation is clearly connected somehow with practical reasoning. The goal-directed reasoning combining means and ends is based not only on the practicality and possibility of undertaking the proposed action, but also on the values of the groups that are to take part in carrying out the action.

Here we have looked at the argument in a rhetorical light, by showing how Picard's speech was specifically targeted to the values of the groups he needed to persuade to undertake the mission that Starfleet Command had assigned. Once Picard made the speech, and put his argumentation forward to the three groups, there is another way it can be studied. It can be studied from a dialectical perspective by analyzing the arguments as premises and conclusions, aiming at evaluating how strong each component argument is, and how each of them fits together as supporting an ultimate conclusion.

Picard explicitly put forward three arguments, A1, A2, and A3. More precisely, each of these arguments can be seen as a claim or premise that supports his conclusion that undertaking the mission by the three groups would be a good idea. In addition to these three explicit premises, Picard also appealed to the values of each of the groups in his audience. In the argument diagram in Plate 2, each of these values is represented as an implicit premise of one of the three subarguments leading to the ultimate conclusion. Each of these subarguments is a linked argument, meaning that each of the premises is required in order to provide an argument that strongly supports the conclusion. In other words, the two premises function together to support the conclusion, rather than being independent lines of argument for that conclusion.

Picard's argument is based on an argumentation scheme called argument from values. This form of argument uses values to support goals. It is a presumption of the use of this argumentation scheme that the participants in an argument have certain values that can be identified. It is assumed that these values can play a role as premises in arguments in which a proponent puts forward rational arguments that are supposed to be based on the commitments and accepted premises of the respondents to whom the argument is addressed. It was based on three explicit arguments that appealed to implicit values of the audience that can be viewed as additional assumptions. Araucaria can be used to insert implicit premises (or conclusions) in a given argument, by using the argumentation scheme to link a given set of premises with an added premise that was not given but is needed as part of the linked argument supporting the conclusion. The combination of these tools represents a method for analyzing arguments of the kind called enthymemes, where premises or conclusions are implicit (Walton and Reed 2005). It can be seen with the aid of Plate 2 not only what the explicit and implicit premises of Picard's argument are, but how they are all connected together in a structure that can be displayed in an argument diagram. Plate 2 represents each of the three implicit premises in a darkened box with a border made up of dashes. Within each of the boxes representing these implicit premises, the owner of the premise is indicated. For example, in the box representing the premise that profit is a value, the owner of that premise is indicated as the Ferengi. Also, in each case, the argumentation scheme that fits the structure of the linked argument is indicated. For example, in the argument on the right, composed of the two premises A1 and the statement that courage is a value, the structure of the linked inference leading from these two premises to the conclusion that the three groups should go ahead with the mission is labeled as argument from values. This labeling indicates that the argumentation scheme for argument values is applied to these two premises to support the conclusion that the three groups should go ahead with the mission. To sum up, then, we see that the argumentation as a whole is built up from three linked arguments, each of which is an instance of argument from values.

One other part of the argument also needs commentary. The proposition on the left in the darkened box joined by a double arrow to the conclusion of the previous argument represents what is called a refutation. A refutation consists of a proposition that is opposed to a previous claim. Such a refutation functions as a counter-argument or rebuttal that attacks a prior argument. Thus the argument diagram in Plate 2 represents the argumentation content of Captain Picard's speech, showing not only all the positive arguments he used to support the conclusion he advocates, but also the arguments against that conclusion that he mentioned.

10. **The Aims of Dialectical and Rhetorical Argumentation**

The problem is that dialectical and rhetorical argumentation, while they share many of the same argumentation schemes (topics), appear to be different methods that have different aims and that use these schemes for different purposes. Take the example of a commercial ad for a product. Let's say it is an ad to sell jeans, and the target audience is teenagers. Let's say the ad uses an appeal to popular opinion, arguing that this brand is very popular and is widely seen as the best by teenagers. What is the argumentation in this ad? Evidently, it contains an argument with premises and a conclusion. But what is the purpose of the ad as a speech act that is presumably goal-directed and aimed with specific purpose at an audience? Popular opinion is basically in agreement with expert opinion in the field of rhetoric that the speech act is essentially one of persuasion and in this case that the purpose of the ad is to persuade the target audience to buy the jeans. Or perhaps it might be thought that the purpose of the ad is to persuade the audience that the jeans are desirable or that buying them would be a good idea. On the surface, this hypothesis seems reasonable. The aim of the ad is persuasion, and so the speech act is one of persuasion of some sort. There are two parties involved in the speech act. One is the writer of the ad, the group who thought it up, or the company that sponsored it. We can see this group as one entity, a single agent who constructed the ad as its message. The other key party is the target audience. Of course, this entity is not a single person, or even a clearly designated group of persons. Various people will see the ad and be influenced by it. But the second party to the communicative act is really a construct. It is the presumed target audience. And so, if we can see the ad as containing a communicated message with a sender and receiver, the argumentation in it can be viewed as a dialogue. The one participant in the dialogue is the sender of the ad to the mass media. The other is the mass audience to whom the ad was sent. The type of message communicated, as indicated above, would be widely taken to be classifiable as one of persuasion, attempted persuasion, or an influence attempt.

But there is a problem with the hypothesis that the purpose of this message is one of persuasion. The problem is that interests are involved, in the form of money. In some cases, the ad will say nothing explicit about money. It may say very little. It may just picture the jeans and say that teenagers find them so "cool" that inventory is running out, or something of that sort. In other cases, the ad may tell you where the jeans are being sold, or even tell you they are on sale and give a price. In the second kind of case, an offer is being made. The ad is a form of so-called commercial speech. The store can even be held to selling the jeans at the offered price, because the ad offered to do that. The ad is seen as "making a deal," or an offer as part of a transaction. In this kind of case, interests are clearly involved. The ad comes under the category of interest-based bargaining as well as the category of persuasion. Even if nothing explicit is said about prices or where you can buy the jeans, clearly commercial interests are involved. The company who paid for the ad and the firm who designed it are not just trying to persuade the audience about some property of the jeans. They are trying to sell the jeans. They are trying to get the audience to buy them. So even in this case, financial interests are involved. The purpose of the ad is not purely one of abstract persuasion. It is one of trying to get action, and action that has a measurable financial outcome. The hypothesis that the purpose of the ad as a speech act is simply that of persuasion is not quite right, or adequate to the reality of the ad. It may be partly a goal of persuasion, but the ad is also about promoting the proponent's interests.

A comparable analysis can be made of political argumentation of the kind commonly found in the media. For example, consider a political ad used in Senator Smith's election campaign. Once again, on the surface, the purpose of the ad as a piece of mass media discourse seems to be one of persuasion. An argument used in the ad, for example, may cite Senator Smith's past record of good deeds. Presumably, then, the argument has premises and a conclusion. The conclusion is a proposition to the effect that voting for Senator Smith is a good thing to do, or would be the right action to take. Even though the conclusion is best expressed as an action that is being recommended or advocated, still the speech act seems to be one of persuasion essentially. But once again, as in the ad case, interests are involved. In some cases, the ad may even appeal directly to these interests, by promising tax breaks to corporations, for example, or by making concessions to union interests. It may even appeal to certain groups that favor policies of a certain sort identified in it. We all know that politics is not pure persuasion dialogue in the same way an abstract philosophical discussion might be. People in identifiable interest groups vote for elected officials who they think will be most likely to support the interests of the group – or what the group thinks or says are its interests. The interests of one group may conflict with the interests of another group, in a way that has definite financial implications. So we know that it is naïve to think of argumentation in a political mass media message as having a purpose of pure persuasion.

To make the point in a more concrete way, consider the type of persuasion dialogue that goes on in a forensic debate. Let's say the issue being debated is that of euthanasia, and the question is whether a physician should be allowed to stop treatment that will prolong life (such as removing a ventilator) if the patient voluntarily requests it. In a forensic debate, each side has a thesis, and during the debate each side brings forward its best arguments to support that thesis. At the end, a judge, or perhaps an audience, makes a ruling on which side won the debate. The debate is not a case of what might be called rational persuasion. For the opinion of the judge or audience on which side won does not necessarily coincide with the reality of which side had the stronger argumentation. Judges and audiences can, after all, be deceived by fallacious arguments that look strong when they are not. But even so, the purpose of argumentation in a debate can rightly be seen, on both sides, as one of persuasion. On the other hand, of course, interests may be involved. There may be a monetary prize for winning the debate. A debater on one side may be a health care professional who might see his interest compromised by certain kinds of rulings on policies of stopping treatment in the hospitals. Interests can never be absolutely excluded in real cases of argumentation. But the primary purpose of the argumentation used by the debating team on one side or the other is not really to bargain, to win financial gain, or to promote the interests of some specific group to whom one of the debaters may belong. The purpose of the argumentation is just to win the debate. And given the structure of the forensic debate as a format for argumentation, this aim is accomplished by bringing forward the strongest and most persuasive arguments to support the designated thesis of your side.

In a forensic debate, then, it is appropriate to see the purpose of an argument as a speech act of persuasion, even if that analysis is subject to some qualifications. The purpose is not one of interest-based bargaining, as it would be in a negotiation type of dialogue. Now contrast the forensic debate type of case with those of the commercial ad and the election campaign ad in politics. Here, too, persuasion is a central aim, but it is mixed with interest-based bargaining in a different way. Here the central purpose of the ad is to sell. If the ad appeals to the interest of the audience in an implicit or even in an explicit way, the argument could be perceived as not inappropriate. In the debate, however, suppose an arguer for the one team appeals to the interests of the opposing team by indicating they will gain financially if they make some concessions in their arguments. This kind of move is not appropriate. The users of this kind of argument have gone outside the boundaries of the kind of argumentation that is appropriate for the debate.

Of course, observations about any real examples of argumentation will never be sufficient to resolve normative questions about whether certain kinds of argumentation are appropriate or not for certain types of communication frameworks. To answer such questions, it is necessary to make hypotheses about the aims of rhetorical and dialectical argumentation, and the methods used to achieve those aims, or help users to achieve them, by studying how arguments can be used and evaluated in different communicative frameworks. In argumentation theory and informal logic, the framework that defines such an idealized structure of goal-directed communication is called a normative model of dialogue. Specific types of normative models of dialogue are introduced in chapter 2. Abstract normative models are not meant to be instantiated in every respect in any real example of argumentative discourse. But by bringing in consideration of normative models, we can study how common and familiar examples of argumentation are treated differently in dialectic and rhetoric. We can ask what the purpose of the argument is supposed to be, or what it should ideally be taken to be. Of course, in reality, the designers or users of argumentation like that used in an ad may have all sorts of purposes, and the ads themselves can vary tremendously in the kinds of strategies they appear to employ. But to understand how these strategies work, and to understand how the arguments in the ads work, it will be argued in subsequent chapters that applying normative models to them can help, beginning with a normative model of the speech act of persuasion.

2

The Speech Act of Persuasion

The subject of this chapter is the meaning of the term "persuasion" as a speech act in argumentation theory. Terms like "persuading" and "persuasion" are pervasive and central in recent work in argumentation, along with closely related terms like "convince" and "convincing." It is often said that the purpose of an argument, for example, is to persuade or convince someone to accept something as true.[1] Wenzel (1990, p. 13) stated that "the purpose of rhetoric is persuasion." The problem is to define exactly what is meant by the term "persuasion." For as Wenzel pointed out (p. 13), simply stating that the purpose of rhetoric is persuasion "evokes all the negative connotations associated with both rhetoric and persuasion." Both are then linked with deception and sophistical trickery. That line of thought was, of course, Plato's view of both rhetoric and the Sophists, as shown in chapter 1. In this chapter it will be shown that persuasion is a legitimate function of argumentation. What does this remark mean? It seems to imply that persuasion is a distinctive type of communicative act in dialogue, a speech act of some sort.[2] From the previous chapters, many clues can be gathered about what persuasion is, within a multi-agent framework. Obviously, it involves some sort of change of opinion or acceptance of a belief, from an initial state to a new state

---

[1] Van Eemeren and Grootendorst (1984, 1992) seem to prefer "convince," while Walton and Krabbe (1995) tend to use the term "persuade."

[2] A speech act is a verbal utterance of the kind that can change events in the world in the same way as a physical action. The classic illustration is the minister's speech act of saying, in the wedding ceremony, "I now pronounce you husband and wife." Requesting and informing are common types of speech acts.

that is the outcome of the act of persuasion. The transition from the one state to the other takes place within an agent, and is brought about by a second agent. The two agents, it is presumed, are engaged in a conversational interaction. Thus the speech act of persuasion is based on a conversational or dialogue structure, and can best be understood within such a structure. One party persuades another party normally through some sort of verbal communication with the other. These clues are put together here to work toward clarifying the notion of persuasion. This chapter will also show, however, that even if the speech act of persuasion can be formally defined, identifying its occurrence in specific cases, and its role in different dialogues, is non-trivial. It will even be shown that it is controversial to determine whether persuasion is the same thing as argument or is something different. Thus the analysis of persuasion as a speech act takes the form of an investigation.

In this investigation into dialectical theory, the hypothesis is put forward that there is a distinctive and clearly definable speech act of persuasion that can be identified as central to persuasion dialogue. A distinction is drawn between a persuasion attempt and a successful act of persuasion in a dialogue. It is argued that while the speech act of persuasion can be present in other types of dialogue, such as deliberation and negotiation, it is not central to them in the same way. In particular, the act of persuasion is contrasted with the act of putting forward inducements as a form of argumentation that appeals to an arguer's interests. Both these speech acts are also compared with the speech act of making a threat. The analysis on these points centers around the observation that threats and inducements are a normal part of negotiation dialogue in many cases (Donohue 1981), whereas they tend to be regarded as inappropriate or irrelevant in persuasion dialogue. Indeed, it is hypothesized that interest-based inducement attempts are central to negotiation dialogue in the same way that persuasion attempts are central to persuasion dialogue.

1. The Belief-Desire-Intention Approach and the Commitment Approach

According to O'Keefe (2001, p. 575), quantitative research on persuasion has centrally consisted of experimental work in the social sciences studying the effects of persuasion under controlled conditions. But many other fields are interested in persuasion and have studied it. Thus the study of persuasion is not restricted to a single discipline, nor does it have a conceptual framework within any single discipline. O'Keefe's remarks surveying persuasion research are worth quoting.

> Persuasion research is not unified within any single discipline or conceptual framework. Research has been conducted in a number of academic fields, with few efforts after integration or connection. Nearly all the social sciences (including psychology, communication, sociology, political science, and anthropology) and related applied endeavors in which social-scientific questions and methods appear (such as advertising, marketing, and public health) contain relevant research. (p. 575)

Of course, persuasion has always been regarded as central to rhetoric as a discipline, as reflected in Aristotle's view of rhetoric and the long tradition stemming from it. But somehow no attempt to analyze the cognitive structure of persuasion in a precise or logical way has ever been undertaken, or ever been successful at any rate. Persuasion has always seemed too psychological for logic, and the social sciences have concentrated on the experimental and empirical aspects of it. Perhaps they did not want to venture into the study of abstract normative and logical structures or were not familiar with new tools being developed in argumentation theory and AI. Thus, as O'Keefe indicated, although persuasion is important to many disciplines, research on it has not been unified within a single discipline or conceptual framework.

In empirical psychology, persuasion is defined in a stimulus-response framework. An act of persuasion is characterized as a stimulus that changes, shapes, or reinforces a response (Simons, Morreale, and Gronbeck, 2001, p. 29). The response is a change in the beliefs, values, and attitudes of the subject of the act of persuasion. Such changes take the form of "response shaping," "response reinforcing," and "response changing" (p. 30). This approach defines the act of persuasion in terms of an input that can be empirically observed and an output that represents some change in the behavior of the individual or mass audience that has received this input. But this purely empirical approach to persuasion by itself can take us only so far in studying how interpersonal argumentation works as a device of persuasion. For interpersonal argumentation depends on a cognitive component. Persuasive messages, for example, in political campaign rhetoric or in advertising, often strongly depend on the capability of the respondent to recognize and interpret actions and statements as being forms of rational argument connecting sequences of reasoning. This lesson will be shown time and time again in the following chapters. These patterns of rational thinking, familiar to both the message sender and the message receiver, enable the sender to leave out certain parts of the message that he knows the receiver will fill in. The cognitive structures shared by both parties enable the receiver to decode implicatures in the form of indirectly implied suggestions. The capability to persuade by this means is based on the presumption that both speaker and hearer know that they are taking part in a collaborative conversation of a kind that both recognize. So to understand persuasion of the kind important for rhetoric in an adequate way, an act of persuasion needs to be seen as more than just empirically a stimulus and an observed response. It needs to be seen as having a cognitive and dialectical component that allows one party to communicate with the other by understanding the implications of certain forms of argument and certain kinds of moves that are appropriate and relevant in a collaborative conversation.

Immediately, however, there is an objection that calls for clarification. Dialectic imports rationality into the subject of persuasion. A dialogue, in the sense of the term used in argumentation and computational dialectics, is a collaborative goal-directed conversation between two (in the minimal case) parties who contribute to the conversation by following certain rules. For example, at a minimum, in order to have a dialogue in this sense, the two parties must take turns making "moves" or "speech acts." Each move must be responsive to the previous move, according to conversational rules or maxims. Many in the social sciences will say that they want no part of such rules, or even of rationality in any form. They see persuasion as purely psychological. Persuasion is simply change of belief, according to this view, and belief is psychological, meaning that it is measured by stimulus and response, or by other empirical parameters.

To respond to this sort of objection, we must revert to the distinction drawn in chapter 1 between two approaches to cognitive science, artificial intelligence, and argumentation. One is called the belief-desire-intention (BDI) approach. The other is called the commitment, or commitment-based, approach. The BDI approach has been the dominant model of thinking in cognitive science and in the social sciences generally. It has been the main model in the development of multi-agent systems in distributed computing, and continues to be advocated in recent research (Wooldridge 2000). It has also been the dominant model in analytical philosophy. For the past fifty years or so, the leading work in analytical philosophy of mind has been built around the central notions of belief, intention, and desire, and it still is (Bratman 1987). It is only recently, in argumentation theory, and especially with the advent of Hamblin's work on fallacies, that the commitment-based approach has even been articulated as a distinctive viewpoint or analytical tool. The dialogue structures proposed as models of rational argumentation by Hamblin (1970, 1971, 1987), van Emeren and Grootendorst (1992), and Walton and Krabbe (1995) are all based on a central notion of an arguer's commitment. Leading recent work in AI has now shifted to a commitment-based model of communication in multi-agent systems (Singh 1991, 1997).

As applied to the simplest kind of case in which there are two parties in a dialogue, a proponent and a respondent, argumentation can be defined as commitment-based in the following sense. The proponent has a claim to be proved, and he must use the respondent's commitments as premises in an argument having his own (the proponent's) claim as the conclusion. Similarly, the respondent, to prove his opposed claim, must use only the proponent's commitments as premises. The principle of commitment-based argumentation represents a normative ideal that is present in all my previous writings on argumentation. It derives from the notion of commitment first set out by Hamblin (1970, 1971) as the core of the method of formal dialogue theory used to analyze fallacies. An equivalent term for commitment is acceptance. Commitment in this sense, deriving from Hamblin's use of the term, refers to what an arguer has gone on record as accepting, as far as one can tell from the moves he has already made in a dialogue. An arguer is committed to a proposition, in this special sense, when he has gone on public record as having asserted it. But outright assertion is not the only way someone can become committed to a proposition or make his commitment to it evident. A participant in a dialogue can become committed to a proposition by putting forward any kind of speech act. The commitment rules for that type of dialogue determine what kind of move implies what kind of commitment. For example, asking a question of a certain sort can imply, in a certain sort of dialogue, that the questioner is committed to a presupposition of the question. Or when the respondent gives a certain sort of reply or answer to the question, that reply can imply that he is committed to a certain proposition. In short, commitment is determined by given speech acts or moves in a dialogue, in line with the type of dialogue and the rules governing the moves in that type of dialogue. Commitment also has some other key characteristics. It can be retracted. But it can't be retracted freely in all cases. Sometimes there is a cost or penalty attached to retraction. How freely commitments can be retracted depends on the type of dialogue. In persuasion dialogue, commitments need to be retractable without severe penalties.

We must now come to the distinction between commitment and belief. Belief is an internal psychological notion. Beliefs and desires are private "mental states." In contrast, commitments are public. Hamblin (1970, p. 257) compared commitments to sentences written on a blackboard. They are there and visible, or at least they can be traced. They are in a dialogue somewhere in a database. At the beginning point of any dialogue, there is a set of commitments called a commitment store. As the dialogue proceeds through the various moves, propositions are added to this set or deleted from it. In a dialogue, when a commitment is incurred or retracted, the act is external and public. Belief is different. It is a matter of private mental states. Bob Smith's beliefs are private to him. Nobody else may know what they are. He may not even know himself. Beliefs are obviously very important in psychology. But from a viewpoint of critical argumentation, or informal logic and the study of fallacies, it may not be necessary to know what an arguer's actual beliefs are. What matters is how he argued and what positions he took. The reason for utilizing the notion of commitment in argumentation theory is that the goal is the evaluation of an argument in a given text of discourse. It is not necessary to probe into an arguer's real beliefs to evaluate his argument. But although commitment is different from belief, there is no doubt some sort of indirect relationship between the two. As Hamblin put it (1970, p. 257), commitment can act as a kind of *persona* of belief.

Of course, some would object to the whole basis of the distinction between commitment and belief, as outlined above. They would say that it's all a matter of semantics. What does it matter whether you call it commitment or belief? This objection is accurate and reasonable, up to a point. Yet it is useful and even necessary to make some distinction of this sort, no matter what terms we use for the two concepts. The basic difference is that commitment, by its nature, has a rationality component built in. It is all about rationality, even though it represents a kind of rationality tied into the instrumental use of argumentation in dialogue. Belief, on the other hand, could be rational belief. But it is basically an empirical and internal psychological matter. I, and all of us, do believe certain propositions; there are others we don't believe. I don't believe that Santa Claus really exists, for example. But there are people, especially small children, who do seem to believe that he exists. Later they reach an age where that belief changes, and they begin to be doubters. Commitments are different. They are just propositions inferred from the speech acts you have put forward in a dialogue. You may believe them, or you may not. But if challenged, you must defend them or retract them.

If these remarks are right, there is a real opposition between the commitment-based approach to rationality and the BDI approach. It seems reasonable that both approaches could have places of importance in the study of rational thinking and argumentation in communication and computing. But one approach might be more difficult to implement than the other, and one may be more applicable to various cases and problems of interest as a theoretical model of how rational thinking works. Our central concern in this book is with argumentation, and with mass media argumentation in particular. It is my opinion that the BDI approach has its place, but it has turned out to be more complex and cumbersome as a tool than many initially anticipated. Trying to give BDI sets of conditions that define the most basic and apparently simplest kinds of speech acts has turned into a messy business, resulting in an abstruse metaphysics of speech acts that just hasn't been very helpful in devising clear and useful protocols and standards for computer communication. On the other hand, the commitment-based approach, according to its advocates, is much easier to work with and is proving more useful in computing. Which approach will win out is impossible to say at the moment. I have been an advocate of the commitment approach for many years in the field of argumentation studies, and also think it will turn out to be the most useful approach for the study of communication in computer models like multi-agent systems. Whatever the outcome of the debate, the commitment approach is easier to grasp and to apply to cases of argumentation.

Various types of dialogue have now been recognized in the literature, as indicated in Table 2.1 below (p. 60). The commitment-based approach, according to the analysis of argumentation presented in Walton and Krabbe (1995) and Walton (1998b), is applicable to all of them. What is common to all argumentation in dialogue is that there are two participants (in the minimal case), and the arguments of the one should always (ideally) be based on the commitments of the other. Such a commitment-based argument structure is modeled in Figure 2.1.

The sort of structure represented by Figure 2.1 is typical of all argumentation in the various types of dialogue. But it is implemented in different ways in the different types of dialogue. For example, in persuasion dialogue, one party attempts to persuade a second party to come to accept a claim by using a set of premises that are commitments of the second party. In negotiation dialogue, the commitment-based pattern represented by Figure 2.1 is still characteristic, but how it is implemented in that type of dialogue is different. In negotiation dialogue, the one party makes an

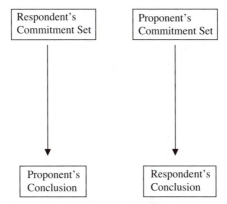

FIGURE 2.1 Commitment-based argumentation in a dialogue.

offer and then tries to get the second party to accept that offer by arguing that accepting the offer is in the interests of the second party. In this
model, commitment is not to the truth or falsity of a proposition but to
interests, usually in the form of goods or services.

2. Basic Components of Persuasion

The fundamental structure of the persuasion dialogue can be stated very
simply. The central notion is that there are two participants, and one is
trying to persuade the other to accept a designated proposition as true.
Let us say that the party who is trying to persuade is the proponent. The
proponent is trying to persuade the respondent to accept a designated
proposition as true. This is the central idea of persuasion dialogue. But
what does "persuasion" mean in this context? To define the notion of persuasion appropriate for persuasion dialogue, we must view persuasion as
a kind of speech act that gets its meaning within dialogue theory. Singh
has defined and analyzed many speech acts central to communication
and computing. An example of the speech act of asserting is the utterance "The door is shut" (Singh 1999, p. 52). An example of the speech
act of committing is the utterance "I will shut the door." Other speech
acts defined by Singh include permitting, prohibiting, and commanding
(directing). But Singh did not even mention the possibility of defining
a speech act of persuading, nor does persuasion seem to be included in
other lists of speech acts of the kind now common in the literature and
technology of computer communications systems. To define it, we must

express it in terms of other notions that are also fundamental to dialogue theory.

To grasp the root notion of persuasion, we must appeal to two other notions, the notion of commitment and the notion of an argument that is structurally correct, according to some standard. Each participant in a dialogue has a set of propositions called his commitment set. These are the propositions he is already committed to, at any given point in the dialogue. And there must some notion in a dialogue of a structurally correct argument. For example, an argument is deductively valid where if the premises are true, then necessarily the conclusion is true. Notions of an inductively strong argument and a presumptively plausible argument need to be added as well. But to keep matters simple for purposes of exposition, let us assume that deductive validity is the standard that matters in the dialogue we are considering. Given a grasp of these prior notions, we can now explain what is meant by "persuasion."

Persuasion: The First Definition

The proponent persuades the respondent to accept a designated proposition A as true if and only if the proponent puts forward a deductively valid argument, the premises of the argument are all propositions that are commitments of the respondent, and the conclusion of the argument is the proposition A.

This definition represents the basic idea of persuasion as the aim of the kind of argumentation used in a critical discussion. So defined, persuasion has three elements. The first element is that the argument put forward by the proponent is deductively valid or is otherwise structurally correct. This indicates that the inference in the argument is such that the conclusion follows from the premises. It means that if a rational respondent accepts all the premises, then he must also accept the conclusion. Such an argument rationally forces acceptance downward from the premises to the conclusion. This forcing is sometimes called the probative function of an argument, meaning that the argument can be used to prove something to somebody. The second element is the commitment of the respondent to the premises of the argument. In persuasion, commitment is transferred from the premises to the conclusion of an argument. The third notion is that of the special proposition that is designated as the conclusion of the argument. This proposition is the aiming point of the persuasion. It is what the proponent must aim at, and must successfully arrive at in his argument, in order to accomplish the speech act of persuasion. The first definition defines what might be called a successful act of persuasion. It is also possible to have what is sometimes called a persuasion attempt.[3] A persuasion attempt could be defined as an attempt to carry out the successful speech act putatively defined by the conditions stated in the first definition above. There are various ways an arguer might attempt to persuade another arguer to accept something or to do something without being successful or without completing all the requirements of the first definition. So we might say that the first definition defines persuasion, but only in a limited sense. It is possible that there might be cases in which there is only unsuccessful or incomplete persuasion, although the attempt might still be called an act of the persuasion type. Thus the first definition needs to be extended to capture the meaning of "persuasion" in such cases. But even so, by defining successful persuasion as the aiming point of the speech act of persuasion, the first definition is useful.

An example might help to relate this definition to everyday argumentation. Suppose that Bob and Helen are having a critical discussion on tipping. Bob is for tipping. He thinks it is a good social practice. Helen is against tipping. She thinks it is a bad social practice. Both present various arguments to support their views. For example, Bob argues that tipping supports free enterprise. Helen argues that tipping supports inequality. Each uses arguments to try to rationally persuade the other to change her or his opinion about tipping. In such a dialogue, we have all the elements of persuasion dialogue. Bob accepts a proposition that is his ultimate thesis in the dialogue. It is the proposition that tipping is a good social practice. Helen has as her ultimate thesis the proposition that tipping is a bad social practice. Assuming that "good practice" is the opposite of "bad practice," we can say that the one thesis is the opposite (negation) of the other. The one proposition is true if and only if the other proposition is not true. The conflict of opinions in the dialogue represents what is often called "strong opposition." Presumably, each party in the dialogue is trying to persuade the other to abandon his or her old thesis and come to accept the opposed thesis. The means used for this purpose are arguments. These arguments can be of various sorts, but they

---

[3] The notion of an attempt is fundamental to the agent-based formalization of communication developed by Wooldridge (2000). He gave a definition of it (p. 134) in terms of the BDI approach as an intention that is not satisfied by an agent's action. But the notion of an attempt can also be defined in a commitment-based approach, as an action that falls short of achieving a goal. A commitment-based analysis of speech acts can be found in Singh (1999).

can supposedly be evaluated by some sort of structural standard. In the example, then, each party has an ultimate conclusion to be proved by means of argumentation. And each party tries to prove that conclusion and thereby successfully persuade the other. Here we have the basic idea of persuasion, which is encapsulated in the first definition above.

It is now time to introduce the first objection to the first definition.

First Objection

> It isn't really persuasion if the respondent is already committed to the proposition A. For the speech act to be one of persuasion, the respondent must not accept the proposition A prior to the act of persuasion. After the act of persuasion by the proponent, the respondent then comes to accept A, due to the argument presented by the proponent.

This objection makes sense intuitively. Persuasion involves a changing of one's mind. Before the act of persuasion the respondent must be committed to one proposition. But after the act of persuasion he must become committed to a different proposition. But a problem arises here. How different must the one proposition be from the other?

There is a nice way of solving this problem. The way is to add a further requirement to the first definition. That requirement is that the proposition A must be the ultimate conclusion that the proponent is trying to prove in the dialogue. Because such a dialogue is based on a conflict of opinions, the respondent will be opposed to it. Thus the very act of getting him to come to accept it will imply that he is changing his mind. The opposition in the dialogue itself will always mean that the respondent is opposed to A. So if he does come to accept A at any point in the dialogue, then that is a change from his initial opinion. That might seem to solve the problem, and rescue the first definition of persuasion. But there is another objection waiting in the wings.

3. Chaining of Argumentation

The first definition is helpful as a first step because it expresses very simply the fundamental notion of persuasion in dialogue theory. But it is simplistic in one vitally important respect. It does not take the chaining of arguments into account. In persuasion dialogue, the speech act of persuasion is typically not a one-step process. Instead, it starts out with one small step of argument, and then proceeds through a series of connected steps forming a chain of argumentation. The typical case can be represented by the example of the Socratic *elenchus* in the earlier dialogues of Plato (Robinson 1962). At the start Socrates gains some relatively small and apparently harmless concessions from his respondent. But then, as the chain of argumentation gets longer, even though the respondent is still making only small concessions, the direction of the argumentation ultimately moves toward a conclusion that is quite serious and dangerous for the respondent's view. This step-by-step process is fundamental to the notion of persuasion in dialogue. It is familiar in the Socratic dialogues.

The reason that the chaining notion is so important to persuasion dialogue is that a respondent will naturally tend to resist any argument that seems to go directly against or refute his ultimate thesis. Once he sees that the conclusion is contrary to his ultimate conclusion and that the argument is valid, he will see the obvious. He will then take the route of denying the premises, or of retracting his commitment to them. This issue of retraction is central to persuasion dialogue. A participant must be fairly free to retract commitments, at least in the normal kind of persuasion dialogue that is typical of everyday argumentation. He can't be entirely free, but he must be free to retract if he is presented with an argument that calls for changing his previous view of a matter. For this reason, it is not possible to rationally persuade a respondent in one step. He must be drawn along by small steps, so that retraction at any step is not so easy.

For example, suppose that Helen presents the following argument to Bob.

Example of a One-Step Argument
   First premise: Any practice that supports inequality is a bad social practice.
   Second premise: Tipping is a practice that supports inequality.
   Conclusion: Tipping is a bad social practice.

Suppose that Bob accepts each premise individually, as a proposition he is committed to. Suppose that Bob accepts that the argument is deductively valid. Then Bob must accept the conclusion. He has no choice. Once he has accepted the conclusion, the persuasion dialogue is over. Bob has lost. He has converted to Helen's view on the tipping issue. Of course, in any realistic persuasion dialogue, Bob would not be likely to accept defeat so easily. He might take issue with one of the premises. Or he might argue that one premise or the other is not absolutely true as a universal generalization, but is subject to exceptions and counter-vailing considerations. He might argue that yes, something that supports inequality tends to be bad, but something that tries to enforce equality in a rigid way could be even worse. He might concede that tipping does support inequality to some extent, but that this bad consequence of it is outweighed by good consequences of it. And so forth. Bob, the exponent of tipping, is going to find all kinds of ways of either denying one premise or the other, or denying that the inference is valid. That is the way of persuasion dialogue. That is what makes it interesting and revealing.

This idea of a chain of argumentation is familiar not only in Socratic dialogues. It is also a familiar tool in artificial intelligence. The techniques called "forward chaining" and "backward chaining" are commonly used in AI when formulating how reasoning is carried out from a set of premises in a database. To see how the essential structure works in a simple case, consider a *modus ponens* inference.

$(I1)$ If A then B
$$\frac{A}{B}$$

This inference can be chained forward by using its conclusion as a premise in a next step.

$(I2)$ If B then C
$$\frac{B}{C}$$

The two single-step inferences, once chained together, form a longer sequence of argumentation. The second step could then be chained to a third inference. The conclusion of the second inference then becomes a premise in the third inference. This type of sequence can be expanded indefinitely. In a lengthy sequence of persuasion dialogue, as in a Socratic dialogue, for example, it is common to find quite lengthy chains of argumentation of this sort.

Having introduced the basic notion of persuasion and having added the notion of chaining of argumentation, we arrive at a structure with four components. In an analysis of relevance in dialogue (Walton 1998b, p. 43), these four components have already been identified as characteristic of argumentation in persuasion dialogue.

(R1) The respondent accepts the premises as commitments.

(R2) Each inference in the chain of argumentation is structurally correct.

(R3) The chain of argumentation must have the proponent's thesis as its (ultimate) conclusion.

(R4) Arguments meeting R1, R2, and R3 are the only means that count as fulfilling the proponent's goal in the dialogue.

These four requirements seem to form a core around which the rules of the critical discussion are built. They represent the idea of how logical reasoning is used for some purpose in a critical discussion. The aim of the critical discussion can be seen as one of rational persuasion of one party by the argumentation of the other. Hence the four requirements can be taken (by hypothesis) to form the fundamental characteristics of persuasion as a speech act. Several other assumptions are implicit in this new definition of persuasion. One assumption is that two parties, called the proponent and the respondent, are engaged in a dialogue. Another is that the proponent has an ultimate conclusion (thesis) to be proved in the dialogue. Putting these assumptions together with the four requirements above leads to the formulation of a second definition of the speech act of persuasion.

Persuasion: The Second Definition

The proponent persuades the respondent to accept a designated proposition A as true if and only if the proponent puts forward a chain of argumentation meeting the following requirements. First, each step, or single inference in the chain, is a deductively valid argument. Second, the premises of the argument are all propositions that are already commitments of the respondent in the dialogue. Third, the ultimate conclusion of the chain of argumentation, at the final step of inference, is the proposition A.

Another background assumption is that the respondent is (at least initially) opposed to A in the dialogue. Either he holds an ultimate conclusion that is the opposite of A or he has taken a position of doubting that A is true. Thus, if the proponent gets him to come to accept A by the process of argument indicated in the four requirements above, we can say that the proponent has persuaded the respondent to accept A. Accordingly, the requirements R1 through R4 make up a second definition of the speech act of persuasion. The second definition provides a set of criteria that are both necessary and sufficient for the speech act of persuasion. For as R_4 makes clear, R_1, R_2, and R_3 are taken to be the only means that count as persuasion in a dialogue. This definition takes chaining into account. Thus, it overcomes the objection to the first definition of persuasion. Even so, there is another objection waiting in the wings.

4. Types of Dialogue

Evaluating an argument using argumentation schemes presupposes a context of dialogue in which the argument has been put forward. For example, the argument from expert opinion might be used in a persuasion dialogue, in which the one party is trying to persuade the other party to accept some claim as true. But as the appeal to expert opinion is deployed, the argument may shift to an information-seeking type of dialogue. For example, in court, the expert might be brought forward to provide testimony based on having studied the facts and on being an expert in a scientific discipline. Thus, the other important tool for the study of argumentation is the classification of the types of dialogue. So far, six basic types of dialogue have been recognized that are centrally important to analyzing common arguments. Table 2.1, based on the types of dialogue recognized in Walton (1998b, p. 31), represents the standard classification of the basic types of dialogue. It is also very similar to the

TABLE 2.1. *Types of Dialogue*

Type of Dialogue	Initial Situation	Participant's Goal	Goal of Dialogue
Persuasion	Conflict of opinions	Persuade other party	Resolve or clarify issue
Inquiry	Need to have proof	Find and verify evidence	Prove (disprove) hypothesis
Negotiation	Conflict of interests	Get what you most want	Reasonable settlement that both can live with
Information-seeking	Need information	Acquire or give information	Exchange information
Deliberation	Dilemma or practical choice	Coordinate goals and actions	Decide best available course of action
Eristic	Personal conflict	Verbally hit out at opponent	Reveal deeper basis of conflict

typology presented in Walton and Krabbe (1995, p. 66), except that various hybrid types of dialogue are also recognized in that typology.

One type of persuasion dialogue that has been clearly recognized and defined is called the critical discussion by van Eemeren and Grootendorst (1984, 1992). The goal of a critical discussion is to resolve the initial conflict of opinions. At an earlier, opening stage of the dialogue, the participants have agreed to engage in argumentation in order to try to resolve the conflict. At a later argumentation stage, they put forward their arguments. There are ten rules for conducting the critical discussion during this argumentation stage (van Eemeren and Grootendorst 1987, pp. 184–293). These ten rules can be summarized as follows. (1) Parties must not prevent each other from advancing arguments. (2) An arguer must defend her argument if asked to do so. (3) An attack on an arguer's position must relate to that position (and not some other position). (4) A claim can only be defended by giving relevant arguments for it. (5) An arguer can be held to his implicit premises. (6) and (7) An argument must be regarded as conclusively defended if its conclusion has been inferred by a structurally correct form of inference from premises that have been accepted by both parties at the outset of the discussion. (8) Arguments must be valid or be capable of being made valid by the addition of implicit premises. (9) If a proponent fails to defend his argument successfully, he must withdraw it. (10) Formulations must not be unduly vague or ambiguous.

Rule 3 states that an attack on a point of view must be directed to the point of view really advocated by the protagonist. In the theory of van Eemeren and Grootendorst, fallacies are violations of the rules of a critical discussion. For example, violations of Rule 3 cited are "imputing a fictitious standpoint to someone" and "distorting someone's standpoint" (p. 286). These violations correspond to the *straw man fallacy*, the fallacy of setting up a distorted version of an opponent's thesis (standpoint), and then demolishing this distorted version, thereby claiming to have refuted the opponent's argument. An example would be the person who argues against an environmentalist position by setting up an extreme or exaggerated version of that position – for example, "You are trying to make the world a pristine wilderness. That is not practical!" – and who then proceeds to demolish that extreme position by using arguments against it.

The critical discussion is a subtype of a more general type of dialogue called persuasion dialogue. The critical discussion can be seen as a species of persuasion dialogue because each party is trying to persuade the other to come to accept the thesis of the first party. The inquiry is a type of dialogue in which an investigating group tries to prove some designated proposition, to disprove it, or to show that it cannot be either proved or disproved. To achieve this goal, the group collects data or "the facts" that can be verified, and the group also tries to assess what is not known. Negotiation is a type of dialogue in which there are some goods or resources that are in short supply, and the two parties try to reach some agreement on how to share them. Each side makes offers and concessions.

Information-seeking is a type of dialogue in which one party tries to communicate information to another party. The importance of information-seeking as a type of dialogue does not appear to have been noticed very much, if at all, in the history of either rhetoric or dialectic. But intelligent deliberation clearly depends on the ability of a decision maker to take in relevant information on a current situation. A type of mass media format that fits the normative model of information-seeking dialogue is that of the presentation of the news in the media.

Eristic dialogue is a quarrelsome type of dialogue in which the two parties "hit out" at each other and try to attack each other verbally. The goal of each participant is to articulate some grudge or grievance against the other. Plato and Aristotle equated eristic dialogue with sophistry. Thus, a clear distinction can be drawn between persuasion dialogue and eristic dialogue. From a dialectical point of view, persuasion can be described as a process of rational argumentation in which one agent uses premises that a second agent is committed to, or can be gotten to commit to, through a sequence of argumentation chained together in a dialogue, with the aim of getting the second agent to come to accept an ultimate conclusion that he doubts. In all the types of dialogue in Table 2.1, there is an ultimate issue, a problem to be solved or a conflict to be resolved, and argumentation using rational persuasion seems to be the main tool for the job.

Actually, no mention is specifically made of persuasion in the account of the four elements presented in section 3 above. In all these types of dialogue, the respondent has to overcome an opposed view initially held by the respondent. If so, the definition of persuasion given above could be too wide. The structure comprised of the four elements R_1 through R_4 could be characteristic of argumentation in other types of dialogue, such as negotiation or deliberation, as well as persuasion dialogue. So here we have a puzzle. It has been shown above how R_1 through R_4 are quite characteristic of how an argument is used to persuade in a persuasion dialogue. The four components above do seem to intuitively represent the speech act of persuasion. Does this mean that persuasion is involved in these other types of dialogue as well? Or is the second definition above unique to persuasion dialogue, and can what is going on in these other types of dialogue be shown to be something different from persuasion? To solve this puzzle, it is necessary to examine the characteristics of these other types of dialogue, referring again to Table 2.1.

If we look at what happens in all the types of dialogue represented in Table 2.1, we see that the initial situation is always some disagreement between the proponent and respondent. There is some unsettled issue or difference of opinion, and each side tries to get the other side to change his or her opinion so that the issue becomes settled. In the inquiry, there is some open factual proposition that needs to be proved or disproved by collecting all the available evidence. If the proposition can neither be proved nor disproved, then that could be an outcome of the inquiry as well. In the inquiry, the participants are not literally trying to persuade each other. At least it does not appear that way. "Persuasion" is not a strong enough word. Instead, they are trying to collectively prove something by establishing it with evidence that cannot later be challenged. They are looking for a kind of conclusive proof, whereas persuasion is generally less than conclusive when it comes to settling an issue beyond reasonable doubt by an exhaustive search that collects all the relevant evidence.

In both the information-seeking and the eristic types of dialogue, it also appears plausible, even on a superficial analysis, to say that persuasion is not the central kind of move made in the dialogue. In an information-seeking dialogue, one party asks the other a question that is a request for some information. The other then answers that question by trying to supply the information, if possible, or indicating where it can be obtained. Persuasion may be involved in how the information is later used, but the speech of persuasion is not central to the exchange of information that is the principal function of information-seeking dialogue. In eristic dialogue, each party attacks the other, often using personal attack argumentation. The ultimate purpose is to bring hidden grievances that are not normally articulated to the surface for discussion. In a quarrel, one party will sometimes put on a show of trying to rationally persuade the other party. And one will sometimes accuse the other of falling below a level of argumentation appropriate for rational persuasion dialogue. But these moves are deceptive. The purpose of making any move in an eristic dialogue is not to persuade the other party by using a chain of reasoning with premises that are commitments of the other party. The move may look like this on the surface, but under that appearance, it is simply meant to be an attack on the other party, meant to accuse the other party of being a bad person or of having done something wrong. Each move is really a "hitting out" at the other party. Thus, it is fairly easy to rule out the information-seeking dialogue and the eristic dialogue as having the speech act of persuasion as a type of move that is central to the dialogue.

This leaves us with the deliberation and negotiation types of dialogue. It seems initially much more plausible that the speech act of persuasion could be a central kind of move in these types of dialogue. In deliberation an agent, or group of agents, examines the arguments for and against a particular action being considered. Of course, one agent will often try to persuade another that this course of action is a good idea, or a bad idea. So it seems that persuasion, or something very much like it, is quite common in deliberation dialogue. In negotiation dialogue, one party is trying to persuade the other to accept some sort of offer or proposal that the first party has made. So here, too, the speech act of persuasion seems to have a central place as a move in the argumentation. The job that confronts this investigation then is to examine the role of persuasion in these two types of dialogue more closely. We begin with deliberation dialogue. Having reached some conclusions about it, we then move on to consider negotiation dialogue.

5. Deliberation

Deliberation as a type of dialogue has been recognized as important in both rhetoric and dialectic. The deliberative genre in rhetorical studies is described by Hart and Dillard (2001, p. 209) as a kind of ideal model or "act of faith" that proposals can be decided on in the best way when persons have a discussion with four characteristics. First, the persons are "gathered together with their peers." Second, they are "discussing important matters of the day." Third, the atmosphere is "nonautocratic." Fourth, public policy can be changed by the discussion. But Hart and Dillard admit that this framework is an "idealized model" that can easily lose its way, in a real instance, and not "prove worthy." In postmodern times, the advent of mass media political rhetoric has cast doubt on the ancient Greek notion that deliberation is a form of rational discussion that people can engage in with their peers in a city-state. Even so, in the theory of democracy that came to us from the Greeks, deliberation is an ideal we can still strive for. Hart and Dillard have expressed this ideal concisely: "Deliberative reason is . . . a special kind of reason, the kind of sense people make when thinking aloud together."

The paradigm case of deliberation is the kind of case where a person is trying to decide what to do. For example, suppose I am trying to decide whether to take radiation therapy or chemotherapy in a medical treatment. Deliberation arises out of the need to take action. An agent finds himself in a certain situation, and he needs to make a decision on Wednesday. There are two kinds of problems typically encountered by an agent in a deliberation. One is to find out what the relevant facts of the given situation are. The other is for the agent to try to determine what his goals are (and possibly also the goals of other affected agents). In the medical treatment case, the agent presumably needs to find a lot of relevant medical facts. This is normally done by getting input in the form of expert advice from physicians. But then the agent has to decide what his own goals are, or what he takes them to be. Some goals are obvious. For example, presumably in this case one of the agent's main goals is to preserve his life. The goals always need to be evaluated in relation to a possible trade-off against other things that may be consequences of bringing about the goals in the given situation. For example, chemotherapy may extend his life, but the side-effects may be severe, and therefore he may want to take into account factors concerning the quality of the life so extended.

Deliberation is a type of dialogue in which an agent or group of agents is confronted with having to make a decision about which course of action to take in a given situation. All of the agents involved have goals, and given their knowledge about the situation as they see it, they try to cooperate among themselves and with others to carry out these goals as well as they can. Hitchcock, McBurney, and Parsons (2001) have devised a formal model of deliberation dialogue as a framework of argumentation. According to this model, a deliberation dialogue arises from a need to take action, and begins by posing a "governing question" that expresses a problem to be solved. At the opening stage, the governing question is posed, and then during the argumentation stage there are "propose" moves where possible action options appropriate to the governing question are put forward by both parties. These proposals can then be revised, considered, rejected, recommended, or confirmed at subsequent moves. Finally, there is a closing stage at which agreement is reached on which course of action of those proposed is the best one to take. Both parties have commitment sets, and the argumentation stage proceeds by both parties putting forward arguments of various kinds. Rules define what kinds of moves are permitted, and how each move affects the given commitment of either participant at any point in a dialogue. In their model (p. 7), a deliberation dialogue goes through the following seven stages.

1. Opening of the deliberation dialogue, and the raising of a governing question about what is to be done.

2. Discussion of: (a) the governing question, (b) desirable goals, (c) any constraints on the possible actions that may be considered, (d) perspectives by which proposals may be evaluated, and (e) any premises (facts) relevant to this evaluation.

3. Suggesting of possible action options appropriate to the governing question.

4. Commenting on proposals from various perspectives.

5. Revising of (a) the governing question, (b) goals, (c) constraints, (d) perspectives, and/or (e) action options in the light of the comments presented, and the undertaking of any information gathering or fact checking required for resolution. (Note that other types of dialogues, such as information-seeking or persuasion, may be embedded in the deliberation dialogue at this stage.)

6. Recommending an option for action, and acceptance or non-acceptance of this recommendation by each participant.

7. Confirming acceptance of a recommended option by each participant. We have assumed that all participants must confirm their acceptance of a recommended option for normal termination.

6. **Closing of the Deliberation Dialogue**

These stages do not necessarily occur in the order above, in actual cases. Some of the stages represent kinds of moves that are repeated. But the outline of the stages gives the reader an idea of how a deliberations dialogue proceeds. Of course, there are rules governing each type of move in the sequence. Using a formal model of deliberation dialogue can help us to evaluate, in any given case, whether an argument is relevant or not as a move made when two parties are deliberating with each other.

In this model, two agents engage in argumentation by making proposals and counter-proposals that are meant to represent actions that can solve a problem. A deliberation dialogue arises out of a need to take action to solve a problem, expressed in the form of a governing question, such as, "How should we respond to the prospect of global warming?" Both participants in the dialogue are agents who have goals and who are presumed to have the capability of practical reasoning. First, there is an opening stage, then a stage where information is shared, then a stage for making proposals and counter-proposals, then a stage for confirming accepted proposals, and finally a closing stage. The third stage is the one where something most closely approximating a speech act of persuasion would take place. A key move at this stage is the speech act for making a proposal. In one kind of move, a participant can *propose* a proposition. In another kind of move, a participant can *prefer* one action option over another. In a third kind of move, one participant can ask another to *justify* a proposal. It would seem that justifying a proposal might be close to a speech act of persuasion. How Hitchcock et al. handle sequences of dialogue surrounding such a justification request is very interesting. Suppose, for example, that the respondent has requested that the proponent justify a proposition *A* that the proponent has previously put forward as a proposal in the deliberation dialogue. According to the rule governing such a move, the proponent must reply by either retracting *A* or shifting into an embedded persuasion dialogue in which the proponent seeks to persuade the respondent to accept *A*.

How would this model work as applied to the medical treatment case outlined above? It would mean that when the patient examines the arguments for or against chemotherapy, he shifts to a persuasion dialogue. When this dialogue comes to a conclusion, or closing stage, he then uses the outcome as input into the deliberation dialogue that then continues. Thus the persuasion dialogue is embedded in the deliberation dialogue. In the persuasion dialogue phase, the patient lists all the pros and cons of the proposed course of action. This dialogue can then be transported into the deliberations. In another shift, all the pros and cons of radiation therapy could be considered. Then both options could be weighed more thoughtfully in the ensuing deliberations.

Although this single-agent type of case is the most obvious kind of example of deliberation, it is helpful to also consider a multi-agent case. For example, let's consider a case of deliberation where two parties are trying to arrive at a common course of action, even though they disagree on what is the best thing to do. An example cited in Walton (1998b, p. 169) is the debate in the Rhode Island Assembly on whether or not to bring in no-fault insurance.

Case 1: The No-Fault Insurance Example

One side wanted to bring in a new system of no-fault insurance similar to one that had recently been adopted by other states. The problem perceived by the citizens of Rhode Island was that insurance rates were too high, and paying the premiums had become burdensome. The goal of both sides then was presumably to deal with this problem by, if possible, lowering insurance rates in some way. One side had made a proposal to do this, and the other side opposed it. Of course, in all such cases there are other goals in the background that would come into consideration. The opposed side, for example, argued that the no-fault system would unfairly make good drivers pay for bad drivers. The opposed side also argued that the proposed no-fault system would fail to lower insurance premiums.

In this case, then, we have a deliberation dialogue in which there were two groups engaged in debate with each other. The argumentation appears to be similar to the notion of persuasion in the speech act definitions above. We need to ask whether the arguments used in this dialogue meet the requirements of the second definition of persuasion. Were the two groups trying to persuade each other to accept a particular designated proposition using arguments based on the commitments of the other side? It may seem so. But it is possible to argue that the argumentation in such a case does not fit the second definition of persuasion. The reason is that both sides are arguing from common commitments. They are arguing that the proposals for action put forward by the other side will not fulfill the goals they both agree on. For example, both sides began the discussion by agreeing on common goals. Both wanted lower insurance rates. The argument of the one side was that the new system of no-fault insurance would in fact succeed in producing lower insurance rates. The other side denied this claim. They might give reasons to support their contentions. For example, the first side might cite what was happening in other states. The other side might then come forward and argue that the no-fault system in other states has failed to lower premiums there. So what is happening here is different from persuasion dialogue. It is not that the one side is trying to use the commitments of the other side as premises to get the other side to agree to a different view. It seems more like both sides have common goals and the one side is trying to argue that the proposal of the other side would not in fact be successful in leading to these goals.

The formal model of negotiation dialogue given by Hitchcock et al. (2001) shows how deliberation dialogue is structurally different from persuasion dialogue in the kinds of moves that are appropriate and in how these moves are used at different stages. In deliberation, persuasion, of the kind represented in the two definitions above, is not the central goal, nor is it the function of the arguments used at the various moves. In this model of deliberation as a type of dialogue, the two sides have common goals, or at least they have some commonality of goals. It is this common element that steers them through the various proposals and counter-proposals toward agreement on the best course of action to resolve the problem posed by the governing question. So while persuasion may be involved at various points, it is not the central theme or mechanism that drives the deliberation dialogue forward toward its goal. To see more clearly why this is so, however, persuasion must be contrasted with other kinds of argument moves.

7. Acts of Persuasion, Inducement, and Making a Threat

Simons et al. (2001, p. 7) put forward the following definition of persuasion. Persuasion is "human communication designed to influence the autonomous judgments and actions of others." According to this definition, persuasion is a form of attempt by one party to alter the way another party thinks, feels, or acts. This definition does make persuasion take the form of a dialogue between two parties. But one of the most interesting aspects of the way Simons et al. defined persuasion is the way they distinguished it from other forms of influence, such as coercion and inducement. They offered the toy truck example to illustrate the difference between persuasion and these other two forms of speech act. The outline of the truck example presented below has been paraphrased from Simons et al. (2001, p. 7), but the six arguments (A1–A6) are quoted verbatim.

Case 2: The Truck Example
A boy called Reynaldo has been sitting on a toy truck. A girl called Janie wants to play with the truck. To get the toy truck, according to the example, Janie has three options. Each of these options is characterized by certain sorts of typical argument moves, as indicated below. Persuasion is characterized by the following two arguments.

> (A1) Aren't you tired of being on the truck?
> (A2) That doll over there is fun. Why don't you play with it?

The speech act called inducement is typified by the following two arguments.

> (A3) If you let me play on that truck, I'll play with you.
> (A4) I'll stop annoying you if you let me play with that truck.

The speech act of coercion is characterized by the following two arguments.

> (A5) If you stay on that truck, I'll stop being your friend.
> (A6) Get off that truck or I'll tell Mrs. S.

The role of Janie is described as persuader insofar as "she identifies the benefits or harms from the adoption or nonadoption of the proposal but does not claim to be the agent of those consequences" (p. 8). By contrast, in the speech acts of inducement and coercion, she is the agent. The difference between inducement and coercion is that inducement offers positive consequences, whereas coercion threatens negative consequences.

Let us examine the various arguments A1 to A6. A1 takes the form of a question. But by examining the indirect speech act structure under the question, it is possible to reconstruct it as an argument. Janie is suggesting to Reynaldo that he may be tired of playing with the truck. And if it were true that he was tired of playing with the truck, that would be a reason for him to get off the truck and play with something else. So Janie's argument could be described as a persuasion attempt. She is trying to persuade Reynaldo to get off the truck by giving him a reason to do so that might be acceptable to him. Let's say that Reynaldo has been sitting on the truck for while. It is known that kids tend to get bored with activities that are prolonged. Thus Reynaldo might well be moved by this argument. Notice also that A1 is an example of a speech act of persuasion used to try to get the respondent to take action. A2 can also be described as an argument and as a persuasion attempt. Janie is giving Reynaldo a reason to move off the truck in order to play with something else. Here she is giving him a more positive reason by suggesting that playing with the doll would be fun. A3 and A4 can be contrasted with A1 and A2. The latter pair of arguments are not really persuasion attempts, although they may initially seem to fall under this category. They are more like the kind of *quid pro quo* moves typical of arguments used in negotiation dialogue. They have the form "If you give me this, I'll give you that." Loosely speaking, they may be called attempts to persuade the respondent to take a certain action. But really they are not attempts to persuade in the sense captured by the first or second definitions above. They are not attempts to prove to the respondent that a designated proposition is true or that the act it describes is a good thing for the respondent to carry out, based on the respondent's prior commitments. Instead, they are proposing a trade-off so that the respondent can get something he presumably wants – some goods, commodities, or outcomes that he might like to have and would enjoy. In other words, with A3 and A4, we are entering into the area of the arguments of the kind centrally used in negotiation dialogue. Can they be classified as speech acts of persuasion? Simons et al. seem to be right in not so classifying them and in contrasting them with persuasion.

Finally, we come to A5 and A6. These examples are classified by Simons et al. under the heading of coercion. Coercion has been recognized as being antithetical to the aims of persuasion. As noted above, the first rule of critical discussion formulated by van Eemeren and Grootendorst is to the effect that parties must not prevent each other from putting forward arguments. One of the defining hallmarks of persuasion is freedom. The respondent of a genuine act of persuasion must freely decide to accept the conclusion that the other party is trying to persuade him to accept. Borderline cases, like "brainwashing," can be denied the status of genuine persuasion. They are not intended to be captured by the first and second definitions above. Examples A5 and A6 correspond to a type of speech act that is both very familiar and important in the world of argumentation. It is the speech act of making a threat. This, of course, is the very kind of move meant to be banned by the first rule of a critical discussion, and it corresponds to a known fallacy, the *argumentum ad baculum*. Thus the question is posed of how the speech act of making a threat should be defined. For if it could be clearly defined, the contrast with the speech act of persuasion might be made evident.

The speech act of making a threat has been defined in Walton (2000, pp. 113–114). It is presupposed that there are two parties engaging in a dialogue. In line with the definitions of persuasion given above, let us designate these two parties as the proponent and the respondent. It is also presupposed that there is some designated event or outcome that is perceived as bad by the respondent. This event represents something that the respondent would prefer to avoid if possible. The definition of a threat involves three conditions. The preparatory condition states that the respondent has reason to believe that the proponent can bring about the event and that without the intervention of the proponent, the event will not occur. The sincerity condition states that both parties think that the event is not in the respondent's interest. The sincerity condition assumes that the respondent would like to avoid this event's occurring if possible. By the same condition, it is also presupposed that the respondent would take steps to avoid the offensive event coming about if he thought these steps were necessary to avoid the event coming about. The essential condition requires that the proponent is making a commitment to bring about the event unless the respondent carries out the action designated by the proponent. The third (essential) condition is part of the notion of a credible threat. A credible threat is one that the respondent thinks that the proponent really can bring about, and one that the respondent thinks that the proponent seriously intends to bring about if the respondent fails to comply. This third condition, the necessary condition, is very important because it marks the distinction between a warning and a threat. The condition characteristic of a threat, as opposed to a warning, is that the proponent is declaring his intention to actually bring the event about if the respondent fails to do what the proponent indicates. In the case of a warning, the proponent tells the respondent that the bad event will or may occur. But he does not tell the respondent that he (the proponent) will be the agency that makes it occur. Thus, in principle, the distinction between the speech act of making a threat and that of giving a warning is clear. In real cases in natural language discourse, however, many threats are of the type called indirect threats in order to give the threatener a route of denial. Such disguised threats are made to look like warnings on the surface.

Having defined the speech act of a threat, we might now ask how an inducement differs from a threat. First, we should note that the two actions have something in common. Both making a threat and offering an inducement involves the interests of the respondent. And in both making a threat and offering an inducement, the proponent has the goal of trying to get the respondent to take an action of some sort. In making a threat, the proponent is saying that he will do something that goes against the interests of the respondent unless the respondent complies by doing something else. When offering an inducement, the proponent offers something that is in the interests of the respondent. But it can be a positive or negative inducement. As the saying goes, it can be the carrot or the stick. A positive inducement is something the respondent would like to see come about. It represents an interest to him. A negative inducement is something the respondent would not like to come about. It represents something that contravenes his interests. A threat appears to be an especially negative kind of inducement that involves an event or outcome that the respondent would especially not like to happen. A threat also can be classified as a psychological form of inducement, because the event that the proponent threatens to bring about is often something that is fearful to the respondent. In practice, threats are often associated with fear appeal arguments under the category of the traditional informal fallacy of the *argumentum ad baculum*. To sum up, you could say that a threat is an especially serious form of negative inducement.

Now we come to the question of how the speech act of persuasion contrasts with these other two speech acts. This difference is a little hard to articulate, because persuasion seems so different in orientation from either of the other two speech acts. The main reason is that both threatening and offering an inducement are based on trade-offs of goods or services. Broadly speaking, goods and services that are traded off in inducements can be classified as "interests" of the parties to the transaction. Interests are often in the form of money or things that a price can be placed on, but they could also be things that would enhance the status or self-esteem of a person. An interest can be anything a person wants, or thinks he needs, or finds valuable to acquire and possess. Speech acts offering inducements or making threats are always based on interests. The proponent is trying to get the respondent to do something by appealing to his interests. Persuasion is an entirely different type of speech act. Offering interests, in the form of goods or services, won't work here. This type of inducement is not appropriate for persuasion. To persuade somebody to come to accept a proposition or to carry out an action, you have to give this person a reason to do it or accept it. This means you have to do two things. First, you have to offer the person some premises that he thinks are true or at least acceptable as opinions that can be taken to represent the truth of a matter. Second, you have to show the person a route from these premises to the claim you want to persuade him to accept, or to the action you want him to bring about. Trying to bribe the person or offering him inducements in the form of money or making threats, is a wrong or inappropriate means of persuasion. In fact, when we use the term "persuasion" in such a case, it has an ironic edge. For example, we might talk of gangsters "persuading" a shop owner to join their protection racket by threatening to wreck his shop. This speech act is one of threatening. It is a form of inducement, a negative one, but it is not really persuading in the sense represented in the two definitions of the speech of persuasion given above.

8. Negotiation Dialogue and Persuasion

Offering inducements and even making threats are normal parts of negotiation dialogue. Of course, they can sometimes be inappropriate or excessive, so that they are not helpful arguments. Making a threat in a negotiation dialogue, for example, is a high risk tactic. For a threat can appear to be an ultimatum to a respondent. He could respond by refusing to take any further part in the dialogue. But in a union-management dispute, for example, suppose that the union side declares, "If you don't raise benefits, the workers will be out on the picket line tomorrow!" The argument used here is definitely a threat. And it is not necessarily a bad or fallacious argument for that reason alone. On the other hand, making a threat as an argument in a persuasion dialogue would normally be so highly inappropriate that we would see right away that it was irrelevant. Suppose that during an ethics seminar on the topic of whether tipping is a good practice or not, one participant declares to another, "If you don't accept my view of the matter, I'll sit on your bag lunch!" This threat is not relevant as an argument in the persuasion dialogue on tipping. Of course, in this case, the threat would be so outrageously inappropriate that it would be more of a joke than an *ad baculum* argument of the kind that might seriously deceive anyone. But the point is that in a persuasion dialogue, making a threat is irrelevant. It just does not fit in as a normal sort of argument of the kind that makes the right sort of move to help the dialogue along. It is more of a disruption than a collaborative contribution. By the same token, offering an inducement, for example, a financial reward, as an argument during a persuasion dialogue also seems out of place, although it could be appropriate in a negotiation type of dialogue. These reflections about the *argumentum ad baculum* and about the use of inducements as arguments suggest several interesting hypotheses. They suggest that perhaps the speech act of persuasion is central to persuasion dialogue in a way that it is not central to negotiation dialogue, and that there may be a sort of asymmetry between persuasion dialogue and negotiation dialogue in this respect based on the speech acts used in these types of dialogue. But how well does this asymmetry thesis really stand up? For it would seem that persuasion is used as a form of argument quite often in negotiation dialogue, even though inducements and threats don't really belong very well in persuasion dialogue. These reflections call for some investigations into negotiation as a type of dialogue.

Like persuasion dialogue, negotiation dialogue begins with an issue. In persuasion dialogue, the issue is a conflict of opinions. In negotiation dialogue, the issue is how to divide up some goods or services that are in short supply and that both parties want. Each presently has something that the other wants. So they try to make an agreement on how to trade off. Because this kind of situation represents the basic issue in a negotiation, the normal form argumentation takes is as follows. Each side makes offers and tries to get concessions from the other side. It is not hard to see, therefore, that the normal kinds of argument moves made in a negotiation are different from those made in a persuasion dialogue. In a persuasion dialogue, one side tries to get the other to come to accept some claim, a proposition, as true. In a negotiation dialogue, the truth of the matter does not matter all that much, at least directly. What matters is whether the other side will make a concession in order to get what he wants.

In negotiation dialogue, persuasion of a certain sort does seem characteristic. By making you an offer, I am trying to "persuade" you to accept the division of goods or services that I have put forward. But the term "persuade" here is not used in the same sense as represented in the second definition of the speech act of persuasion given above. And literally, I am not trying to persuade you of anything in such a case. I am not trying to get you to accept some proposition as true by giving you reasons to come to accept it as true. I am only trying to "persuade" you to take action by accepting the offer I have proposed. The term "persuasion" as used here does seem appropriate, because I am trying to get you to change your mind, so to speak. I am trying to get you to change your initial position in the negotiation. But this is not persuasion in the sense that I am trying to get you to change your opinion. Whatever your opinions may be, negotiation is all about your interests.

And yet persuasion is often involved in negotiation dialogue. To see how, it is best to begin with an example.

Case 3: The Car Negotiation Example
Suppose I go to a car dealer and make an offer on a model I like to a salesman in the dealer's showroom. He replies that my offer is too low. I reply that I can get it for that price at another dealership that is closer to my home. I argue that getting the car serviced on the warranty would be more convenient at the other dealership. The salesman then argues that the service is better at his dealership. He gives a number of arguments to support this claim. His dealership has better mechanics. His dealership gives customers a free ride in their van during servicing of their vehicle. His dealership has a track record of taking good care of their customers. I reply to these arguments by saying that I have a friend who bought there, and he didn't get any free ride in a van when his car was being serviced.

One can see in this example that the dialogue, especially the latter parts of it, does seem to involve persuasion. There seems to be a conflict of opinions on the issue of which of the two dealers is better at servicing a vehicle. The salesman has presented several arguments that purport to show that his dealership is better. The customer has expressed doubt about the salesman's claim by offering an apparent counter-example to it.

The problem is to diagnose what has happened in a case like this. There has been a dialectical shift from one type of dialogue to another during the sequence of argumentation. The example started out to be a case of negotiation dialogue. The customer made an offer. The salesman refused it. But then at some point, the dialogue shifted to a persuasion dialogue about the issue of which dealership has a better maintenance service. However, there is another analysis that could be applied to the case. According to this analysis, the persuasion part is not separable as a type of dialogue from the negotiation part. According to the model of negotiation proposed by Fisher and Ury (1991, p. 4), the goal of negotiation is to reach a so-called wise agreement that not only meets the legitimate interest of each side, but also resolves conflicting interests fairly. Fisher and Ury advocate what they call "principled negotiation" as a method of reaching a wise agreement. Principled negotiation requires that the parties reach agreement based on some standards independent of the will of either side. As applied to the car negotiation example above, principled negotiation could mean that both salesman and customer could turn to some source of information or standard that is independent of the will of either. The two could then appeal to that independent standard to settle their disagreement about which dealer has the better service. It would appear that Fisher and Ury's analysis would not view the car negotiation example as exhibiting a shift from negotiation dialogue to persuasion dialogue. Instead, it would see the argumentation in the whole example as being part of the negotiation. On their analysis, the customer made an offer to the salesman. The offer was not acceptable, and so the bargaining appeared to be blocked. But the negotiation then turned to matters of service of the car. This could be seen as a turn toward at least the possibility of principled negotiation, because the issue of which dealership is better for service is an objective difference of opinions that could be settled by appealing to facts, or at least factual arguments.

Negotiation is a type of dialogue that is vital for multi-agent computer systems. An example from Chu-Carroll and Carberry (1995, p. 111; see also case 9.1) shows how negotiation is important in multi-agent planning and how such cases can very often involve other types of dialogue as necessary parts of the argumentation. In this example, the air-traffic control system in a country failed, and two neighboring countries, X and Y, negotiated to take over tracking and controlling all affected flights. To make the plan successful, the air-traffic controllers in countries X and Y had to negotiate with each other on which flights each would take. For example, when the controllers in the one country thought they were taking on too many flights during a busy period, they had to try to exchange these flights for others they could take on when they were not so busy. Chu-Carroll and Carberry proposed a computerized model of negotiation dialogue to represent agent communication in this kind of situation. But one can see that not just negotiation but other types of dialogue are involved as well. At first, the air-traffic control systems are engaged in a deliberation dialogue. They are attempting to find the best course of action so that all three countries can solve the problem of air-traffic control. But in order to conduct such deliberations in an intelligent manner, they will have to exchange information with each other. For example, the one group of controllers will have to tell the other when they are too busy to handle all the flights they are now assigned to control. They will also have to exchange information on matters such as which terminal is most capable of guiding which flights. Thus, information-seeking dialogue will have to be involved as well. Although it may be less obvious, persuasion dialogue will have to be factored into the mixture as well. For suppose the controllers for X and Y have a conflict of opinions on how many flights it is reasonable to expect the controllers in country Y to handle during a given time frame. To discuss and resolve this conflict of opinions, they must engage in persuasion dialogue. Chu-Carroll and Carberry have tacitly recognized the need for persuasion dialogue in this example by stating that there are intervals of argumentation in such cases where one agent needs to justify its beliefs to another agent.

One way to view the argumentation in this kind of example is to see the deliberation dialogue, the information-seeking dialogue, and the persuasion dialogue all as parts of the negotiation dialogue. Another way to see the argumentation is as a sequence of chained inferences that runs through a complex communicative context in which the negotiation dialogue is embedded in the other three types of dialogue. On this model, there are four separate types of dialogue involved, but each is embedded in the others. As the chain of argumentation proceeds, there is a shift from one type of dialogue to another. For example, the deliberation shifts to a negotiation. Then during the negotiation dialogue, there are some intervals where information-seeking dialogue occurs, and other intervals where persuasion dialogue occurs. In the example considered above, each of these shifts to information-seeking or persuasion intervals improves the quality of the negotiation dialogue. These shifts represent what are called embeddings of one dialogue into another. An embedding is a positive or useful kind of shift in which the one dialogue contributes to the goal of the other. Negative shifts are often associated with informal fallacies. For example, a shift from persuasion dialogue to negotiation dialogue in the making of a threat can be associated with the *ad baculum* fallacy.

Here then we have two ways of viewing negotiation as a process of dialogue. According to the Walton model, argumentation in negotiation is about goods or services that the two parties have or want. In a nutshell, it is about interests. In this model, an argument in a negotiation is not about what you should believe or accept as true or false. It is about maximizing your interests by reaching an agreement that gets enough of what you want while also giving the other party enough of what he wants so that he can accept the outcome well enough so that the agreement will last. According to the Fisher and Ury model, negotiation dialogue includes argumentation about what a participant should accept as true or false, independently of the will or interests of that participant. On this view, negotiation includes persuasion as a very important part of the negotiation process itself. Other exponents of both these views can be found in the literature. In a study of labor negotiations, Sycara (1990, pp. 217–219) identified many kinds of arguments that are commonly used in such negotiations and that seem to be familiar from the textbook accounts of informal fallacies. These include arguments such as appeals to socially sanctioned beliefs, appeals to self-interest, appeals to threats, and appeals to authority. The common use of such arguments in negotiations suggests that there is a strong element of persuasion dialogue in argumentation in negotiation dialogue. That is one point of view, at any rate. According to this point of view, persuasion attempts are an intrinsic part of the fabric of negotiation dialogue, and thus the two types of dialogue cannot really be separated as normative models of argument use. But according to the opposed view, persuasion dialogue is distinct from negotiation dialogue, and one primary reason is the centrality of the speech act of persuasion in persuasion dialogue. This is the view expounded in the system of dialogue typology put forward in Walton (1998b), but it has also been clearly expressed by Jon Elster, who identifies negotiation with bargaining and sees it as distinct from persuasion by rational discussion, or giving of reasons to support a claim. For example, Elster wrote, "Bargaining must be distinguished from attempts to reach agreement by rational discussion" (1989, pp. 50–51). He remarked that negotiation can be distinguished from trying to reach agreement by rational discussion on the grounds that certain forms of argumentation that are typical of negotiation are not allowed in trying to reach agreement by rational discussion. All that counts in rational discussion is "the power of the better argument."

The analysis of the speech act of persuasion put forward in the first and second definitions above can help to support my view and that of

Elster that persuasion dialogue can be seen as a normative model of argumentation that is distinct from negotiation dialogue. This view can acknowledge that negotiation dialogue often contains elements of persuasion dialogue. It can even acknowledge the thesis that persuasion dialogue is vitally important in helping negotiations along. It even posits an embedding of persuasion dialogue into negotiation dialogue, so that the dialectical shift from negotiation to persuasion dialogue can be positive and can contribute to the success of the negotiation dialogue. This sort of positive shift has been remarked on by Jacobs and Jackson (1983, 1992), in their work on divorce dispute mediation. They observed that a deadlocked dispute about child custody can sometimes be resolved by a shift from negotiation to persuasion dialogue. This can happen if the mediator turns the dialogue from the issue of who should get custody to a critical discussion on the issue of which parent would be the better caregiver. The transition, in such a case, is from a negotiation dialogue to a persuasion dialogue. But in this kind of case, the shift is a positive one that could resolve the deadlock reached in the negotiations. However, it need not follow that we should have to view negotiation dialogue as indistinguishable from persuasion dialogue. We can hold the two models of dialogue to be normatively distinct even though at any given point in a case of divorce mediation argumentation, it may be hard to determine whether an argument is part of the persuasion or the negotiation dialogue. What can now really help us in making a clearer theoretical distinction between the two types of dialogue, and in understanding better how each type works, is the analysis of the speech act of persuasion. We can see how this speech act contrasts with other speech acts, like making a threat, and how it is central to the way arguments work in persuasion dialogue. By contrast, we can then see how arguments work differently in other types of dialogue, such as deliberation and negotiation. Needless to say, the distinctions drawn above will remain highly controversial. There does seem to be a competing view holding that persuasion and negotiation, in particular, are so fused together in practice that any attempt to separate out the speech act of persuasion from the interest-based moves typical of negotiation is futile and misguided.

9. **Relevance and Argument Diagramming**

The first definition of persuasion above represented the notion of successful or completed persuasion. As such, it can be taken to represent the goal of the proponent in a persuasion dialogue. His goal is to prove his ultimate conclusion *A* by means of a structurally correct argument in which all the premises are commitments of the respondent. The goal of the respondent is to construct an opposed argument of the same kind that has the opposite of *A* as its ultimate conclusion (or in the case of the weaker kind of opposition, to throw doubt on the respondent's argument as being a successful act of persuasion). In a persuasion dialogue (Walton and Krabbe 1995), each party has an individual goal. These individual goals can now be represented as acts of persuasion, using the first definition of "persuasion." The persuasion dialogue, as a type of dialogue, also has a collective goal. According to Table 2.1 above, that goal is to resolve or clarify the conflict of opinions (or opposition) that is the initial situation of the dialogue. Thus the first definition represents the participant's ideal goal or aim in a persuasion dialogue. When examining individual arguments, in the study of fallacies and so forth, we are most often confronted with a single argument, or relatively short chain of argumentation, that is an act of persuasion, but does not come even close to realizing this goal. To see this kind of incomplete argument as "persuasion," the second definition must be applied. But to fit the two definitions together, as applied to any real case, there is a large problem to be confronted. How can we fit the short persuasion attempt in the given case to the ideal and final goal of the dialogue represented by the second definition?

For example, in the dialogue on tipping, Helen might argue that tipping has bad consequences. She might argue that tipping leads to misunderstandings that are socially awkward and embarrassing. Bob might agree that this is so. Helen then might contend that because these outcomes are bad, as Bob himself admits, tipping itself is a bad social practice that should be discontinued. Here we can see that Helen's argument is leading toward her goal in the dialogue of proving that tipping is a bad social practice. But by itself, this single argument is not very likely to reach that goal. Bob may admit that tipping sometimes leads to misunderstandings, and even that such misunderstandings are bad and can hurt people's feelings. But he may argue in reply that people need to overcome this problem by being more sensitive in how they tip. He may even argue that despite this reasonable argument against tipping, there are many more reasons why tipping is a valuable social practice that is worth preserving. Helen may then launch into a longer argument that tipping leads to such awkward and embarrassing consequences because of its underlying elitist nature. She might argue that tipping is just one aspect of the social inequality that is endemic to our society and that social inequality is the root cause of war and of all evil.

In this example, we see a typical case of a relatively small and local argument that is relevant in the dialogue on tipping because it has a place within a longer chain of argumentation in the persuasion dialogue. Helen's local argument that tipping leads to misunderstandings that are socially awkward and embarrassing is an act of persuasion. But it did not fulfil her ultimate goal in the dialogue of successfully persuading Bob that tipping is a bad practice, by itself. It was only one small argument in Helen's much longer and more complex chain of argumentation in the dialogue. And yet we can judge that Helen's local argument was relevant. It was dialectically relevant precisely because it has a genuine place in her longer chain of argumentation leading toward her ultimate conclusion in the persuasion dialogue. Thus Helen's local argument fits the second definition of persuasion. It can be classified as a persuasion attempt that was not successful, or wholly successful by itself but that has a place in Helen's longer chain of argumentation that (presumably) moves toward her ultimate conclusion to be proved in the dialogue. As this example shows, the problem is one of judging actual cases of argumentation to see whether persuasion, as defined above, can be said to fit the argument, as expressed in the text of discourse of a case.

The problem is one of defining relevance, in order to take a localized argument and embed it in a context of dialogue as part of a longer chain of argumentation. The local argument can be classified as a persuasion attempt only where it is set within such a wider dialectical context of use. The problem is how to judge whether the local argument is relevant in a wider context. If the wider context is that of a persuasion dialogue, and the local argument fits into the longer chain of argumentation aimed toward the proponent's goal of persuasion, as represented by the first definition of persuasion, then the local argument can rightly be classi-fied as an act of persuasion. The reason is basically to be found in the second definition of persuasion. The local argument can be a persuasion attempt that, while not successful in itself, is part of a longer chain of argumentation aimed toward the ultimate goal of persuasion dialogue. Thus certain dialectical methods are needed to make the definitions of persuasion applicable to real cases of argumentation. One is the method of argument diagramming, because it is the tool needed to identify the chain of reasoning used in a given case to try to argue for a conclusion. The other is the fitting of the local argument into a broader dialectical context of use through the notion of dialectical relevance. To judge an argument as dialectically relevant, you need to make an assessment where the argument is supposedly going, judging from the text and context of

the given argument. You need to first of all determine what ultimate conclusion the argument was supposed to prove in the dialogue. Then you
need to assess how far along the given argument went in that direction,
in light of the chain of argumentation it can be inserted into as one
part.

To test the given argument for relevance, the chain of reasoning in
the local argument needs to be extrapolated forward to see whether it
moves toward or reaches the ultimate conclusion to be proved in the
dialogue. A basic tool is the classification of dialogue types. An argument that is relevant in one type of dialogue may not be relevant in the
context of another type of dialogue. The classic case, as noted above, is
the *argumentum ad baculum.* The use of a threat might be relevant in a
negotiation dialogue. But suppose the very same threat is used as argument in a persuasion dialogue. In that context it may be irrelevant. And
indeed, as indicated above, threats tend to be visibly irrelevant in persuasion dialogue, where they are highly out of place. More subtle cases
concern the use of incentives that are not coercive but are interest-based.
They are the normal kinds of arguments used in negotiations, but they
too are not really relevant in persuasion dialogue. They don't fit the
requirement for the definition of a persuasion attempt, but they do fit
the kind of argument normally used in negotiation dialogue. How could
interest-based arguments even appear relevant in a persuasion dialogue?
The answer to this question takes us to the phenomena of dialectical
shifts and embeddings. If one type of dialogue is embedded in another, a
chain of argumentation crossing the shift can still be relevant in the first
type of dialogue, even when the argumentation has led into the other
type of dialogue. For example, as considered above, a negotiation dialogue might shift to a persuasion dialogue. But suppose the persuasion
dialogue is embedded in the negotiation dialogue. The persuasion inter-
val might actually be helpful to move the negotiation toward its ultimate
goal. For example, in the case of divorce mediation dialogue studied by
Jacobs and Jackson, the shift to persuasion dialogue might actually help
the negotiation dialogue. Thus even though there has been a shift to a
different type of dialogue, the argumentation in the persuasion dialogue
could be relevant. The reasoning is the embedding of the one type of
dialogue into the other.

Another tool needed to analyze real cases is the method of argument
diagramming. The argument diagram can be taken to represent the chain
of reasoning reconstructed from the discourse in a given case of an argument. An important part of the evidence needed to test for dialectical

relevance is the argument diagram. The argument diagram can give a view of the direction of the local argument by showing its conclusion and what premises lead into it and how. The diagram is an important part of the evidence needed to make a judgment of where the argument is going as part of a longer chain of argumentation that may or may not lead toward the ultimate conclusion to be proved in the dialogue. The ultimate conclusion is the end point that the local argument should be aiming toward. Is it going toward that end point or to some other end point? This question poses the problem of relevance. But by looking at the argument diagram, the direction of the argument at the local level can be visualized. Then, using a global viewpoint that takes into account the type of dialogue and the goal of argumentation appropriate for that type of dialogue, a match can be made between the local and global evidence.

Some cases of irrelevant argumentation, like many cases of the *argumentum ad baculum* cited above, are easy to diagnose. The reason is that in a persuasion dialogue, for example, the use of a direct and explicit threat is obviously inappropriate to meeting the requirements of the proper kind of persuasion argument that should be used. It may be that the *ad baculum* works not because it is deceptive, in that it seems relevant, but because it is a naked appeal to the interests of an arguer. Even if he knows that the threat is a bad argument in the persuasion dialogue, he still has to look out for his own interests and safety. Other cases of fallacies are more subtle, because the fallacious argument appears to be relevant but is not. Appeals to emotion, like appeals to pity or personal attacks, are often of this sort. They can be relevant in some cases. But they are also powerfully distracting. And hence they can have a persuasive effect, and may even seem to be relevant, when they are not. To judge individual cases, one should always ask which type of dialogue the argument is supposedly a part of. Then one should ask what the ultimate conclusion is to be proved in that dialogue. For example, in court, the defendant may launch a tearful appeal to pity. This argument could be relevant at the sentencing hearing after the criminal trial. But during the trial itself, the issue to be determined is whether the defendant committed the crime as charged. The argumentation here can be seen as a kind of persuasion dialogue in which the prosecution and the defense represent two sides that have a conflict of opinion. In that dialectical context, the appeal to pity may be irrelevant.

Cases of legal argumentation can be used to illustrate the typical kind of problem of relevance that one confronts in dealing with real arguments. For example, the prosecution may try to use an argument, and then the defense says, "Irrelevant." The judge, applying the rules of evidence, then has to make a decision. Is the argument relevant or not? It may be hard to say, because the trial may have started. Indeed, relevance of evidence is sometimes a hotly contested issue between the two sides, even at pre-trial hearings. The judge may not know, at this early stage, what the line of argumentation taken by one side or the other will be. The prosecuting attorney may even reply to the objection by countering, "If your honor will give me a little latitude, I can show where this line of argument is leading." What this kind of situation shows is that there can be two kinds of cases in which judgments of relevance or irrelevance are made. One is the kind of case where the line of argumentation on both sides has been completed and where the text of discourse of the whole argument is complete. For example, once a trial is over, a transcript of it can be examined. The other is the kind of case where the argumentation is incomplete. In this kind of case, we may only have a small text of discourse representing a local argument. The larger context of how the argument was used or where it led or may lead, may simply be unknown. In such a case, there is much less data. The best that may be possible is to give a provisional assessment of relevance.

Such matters of relevance are highly applicable to the problem of judging how the definitions of persuasion given above apply to actual cases of argumentation. How can we tell, in a given case, judging from the text and context of discourse, whether an argument is better classified as a persuasion attempt or whether it is better classified under the heading of some other type of speech act? For example, it might better be classified as the making of a threat or the offering of an inducement. There will be borderline cases. And in fact, many of the tricky borderline cases are precisely those identified with informal fallacies and other cases of deceptive argumentation tactics that have to do with subtly biased arguments and the like. What is most useful for assisting with the analysis and evaluation of argumentation in such cases are the clear definitions of the speech act of persuasion presented above.

10. **The Cognitive Component of Persuasion**

Once persuasion has been identified as a distinctive speech act, as above, we are in a better position to understand persuasion dialogue as a normative model of argumentation that is distinct from other types of dialogue, such as deliberation and negotiation. Of course, the speech act of persuasion is not all that goes on in persuasion dialogue. Asking a question is another important type of speech act in persuasion dialogue. But the speech act of persuasion is central to persuasion dialogue in that it typifies the main type of move that is so characteristic of what an argument is meant to accomplish in this type of dialogue. Most especially, identifying the speech act of persuasion gives us a clear basis for distinguishing between persuasion and other interest-based kinds of moves in argumentation that are influence attempts typical of negotiation. Understanding this distinction is important for analyzing informal fallacies, and centrally important to evaluating allegations of bias in argumentation. For one of the common arguments of this sort is the allegation that an arguer is biased because he has something to gain, or has an interest at stake in a discussion. This criticism has sting where two parties are supposed to be taking part in a critical discussion, for example, and one accuses the other of having something to gain by sticking to one side. For example, if two parties are having a critical discussion about an environmental issue, one may accuse the other of being a paid advocate of an industrial corporation. What is at issue in such a case is an alleged covert shift from persuasion dialogue to a kind of interest-based argumentation that could perhaps be identified with bargaining or negotiation. At any rate, a clearer understanding of the speech act of persuasion, and how it should work, can help us to analyze the argumentation in cases like these that are central to informal logic and the analysis of fallacies and common argument criticisms.

One issue that requires further commentary is the distinction between psychological persuasion and the speech act of persuasion as a normative notion. Some might say that it is the psychological notion of persuasion that is really important and that because the speech act of persuasion defined above is purely normative, it is of no real use in helping us to analyze how persuasion really works in argumentative discourse. A commonly held attitude is that empirical persuasion, measured by behavioral indicators, is all that really matters to any scientific notion of persuasion. In public relations and mass media, for example, what matters is whether an argument or persuasive technique really works. And that is, according to this widely held view, a matter that can be decided only by measuring how the target audience actually responds to the message by observable behaviors. What this view overlooks is the cognitive component of persuasion. But why should such a cognitive component be of any importance? The answer comes in the form of a hypothesis.

Hypothesis on the Cognitive Component of Persuasion (HCCP)
> When respondents find an argument persuasive, it is generally
> because they think that the argument is a reasonable one based
> on premises that they are committed to.

The HCCP provides a way of explaining how people are persuaded to
do things or to accept claims. It also provides a plausible explanation
of how sophistical (fallacious) arguments work as successful persuasion
attempts. The phenomenon to be explained is how people are led to
accept fallacious arguments. The basic explanation is that the respondent accepts the argument because it looks like a good one to him. The
basis of the explanation is the assumption that people are not just empty
receptors, to be persuaded by inserting propositions into the blank area.
People, whether they have studied logic or not, are already equipped
with a functioning apparatus for sorting the good arguments from the
bad ones. Whether they are persuaded or not in any given case very much
depends on this capability that the respondents are already actively using.
But they can be fooled. When they are fooled, according to the HCCP, it
is because the argument they have been presented with looks enough like
one of the good forms of argument they are familiar with to pass muster.

If this explanation of how fallacies work turns out to be a reasonable
one, it implies that the cognitive component of persuasion is extremely
important. To analyze, judge, or explain any persuasion attempt, and
see how it really works, you have to look at several factors, as indicated
by the first and second definitions of persuasion above. First, you have
to look at the structure of the argument as a chain of inferences and to
examine the form of argument at each step. Here you have to ask whether
the argument should be judged by deductive, inductive, or presumptive
standards. For example, if it is a presumptive argument, you then have
to identify its argumentation scheme, or form of argument. Second, you
have to look at the premises of the argument and judge whether they
are commitments of the respondent. Third, you have to look at where
the chain of argument is going. You have to judge whether it is relevant
by looking at the context of dialogue. These three factors represent the
cognitive component of the argument.

Of course, the empirical component is very important as well in any
analysis of how persuasion works in a given case of argumentation.
Nobody is denying that assumption, which is so well accepted in the
social sciences that there is really no need to argue for it. What tends
to be overlooked is the importance of the cognitive component. But if

the second definition of persuasion above is seen as a reasonable and useful one, the role of the cognitive component can be much better appreciated.

11. The New Definition of the Speech Act of Persuasion

Many of the problems arising from the attempts to study mass media argumentation turn on the central notion of persuasion. In the study of public opinion polls, the notion of the persuasive definition comes up again and again. The central purpose of mass media ads appears to be one of persuasion. In political rhetoric, the purpose of any argument seems to be centrally that of persuading the audience to come to accept some view or policy. Persuasion is also a central concept in speech communication, especially mass media and interpersonal communication, as well as in rhetoric. Thus it would be enormously helpful if persuasion could be defined in precise terms in multi-agent systems as an interpersonal speech act or communicative action. To construct such a definition has been the purpose of this chapter. Of course, such a multi-agent definition defines the speech act of persuasion as a dialogue exchange between rational agents. Thus it cannot be emphasized enough that the definition is not purely empirical. It has a rationality component. However, it has been argued in this chapter that this property is an asset, not a liability.

To begin to present a summary of the key ideas of this chapter, it is good to look back to the second definition of persuasion that was put forward in section 3. In light of the discussion of that definition that followed, a new, third definition can be formulated. This third definition meets all the objections that were raised concerning the second definition. The multi-agent structure is the same as that of the first two definitions. There is a proponent who is putting an argument forth, and possibly also making other kinds of moves in a dialogue with a respondent. The proponent is trying to persuade the respondent to come to accept a designated proposition A. To carry out the speech act of persuasion, the proponent should be guided by the following definition of the speech act of persuasion. It presents a recipe, so to speak, of how persuasion should be carried out in a multi-agent dialogue.

Persuasion: The Third Definition

The proponent persuades the respondent to accept a designated proposition A as true if and only if the proponent puts forward a chain of argumentation meeting the following requirements. First, each step, or single inference in the chain, is a structurally correct argument according to some appropriate requirements set out in the opening stage of the dialogue. Second, the premises of the argument are all propositions that are already commitments of the respondent in the dialogue or are propositions that he can tentatively accept or be gotten to accept by argument later in the dialogue. Third, the ultimate conclusion of the chain of argumentation, at the final step of inference, is the proposition A.

One key component in this definition is the notion of commitment. It is vital to draw a distinction, in using the definition, between commitment and belief, as the latter would be viewed in the BDI model. Another key component is the notion of argument chaining. The proponent cannot normally persuade the respondent by a one-step argument. The reason is that once the respondent sees that the conclusion follows from the premises, he will tend to reject at least one of the premises immediately. At least, this sort of reaction can be taken to represent the normal case. The respondent is strongly opposed to the conclusion in the typical case. Thus as soon as he realizes that the premises imply the conclusion, he also realizes that the negation of the conclusion implies that one or more of the premises must be false. Hence he will resist by finding any means to reject one of the premises. He will look for the weakest link in the argument. This principle is basic to all strategy of persuasion. It means that, for most practical purposes, the proponent needs a chain of argumentation. As the chain gets longer, the respondent tends to forget where it started out. It is this chain that makes persuasion realistically possible.

Another key component in the definition of persuasion is the assumption that there can be different kinds of arguments. We may assume that as well as deductive arguments, there are also inductive arguments, and a third type that could be called presumptive or abductive arguments. Each type of argument has its requirement for structural correctness. Deductive and inductive forms of argument have been thoroughly studied in logic. Presumptive forms of argument are represented by argumentation schemes. The study of these forms of argument is still at the exploration stage. But it is this third category that is the most important for the analysis of many common forms of argument used in mass media persuasion attempts, including appeals to fear and pity and *ad hominem* arguments. Each type of argument needs to be evaluated by its own standards for structural correctness. Agents in a dialogue sometimes dispute whether an argument is deductive or inductive, for example. Sometimes they will dispute whether the proponent originally meant the argument to be deductive or inductive, when he put the argument forth in the dialogue. Such disputes can be settled in individual cases only by examining the text of discourse and setting out requirements for structural correctness of arguments at the opening stage of a dialogue. What matters for the third definition of persuasion is that there should be structural standards of some sort in place.

Now it needs to be added that the third definition represents a persuasion attempt by the proponent in a dialogue. A successful act of persuasion is one where the respondent has agreed to all the premises, or the proponent has shown that he is committed to them. Then, by the standards for structural correctness, the respondent also becomes committed to the conclusion. Getting the respondent to become committed to the conclusion is the goal of the proponent's act of persuasion, and is what makes an act of persuasion successful. The following is the goal aimed at in persuasion.

Successful Persuasion: The Definition Based on the Third Definition

The proponent persuades the respondent to accept a designated proposition A as true if and only if the proponent puts forward a chain of argumentation meeting the following requirements. First, each step, or single inference in the chain, is a structurally correct argument according to some appropriate requirements set out in the opening stage of the dialogue. Second, the premises of the argument are all propositions that are already commitments of the respondent in the dialogue. Third, the ultimate conclusion of the chain of argumentation, at the final step of inference, is the proposition A.

To grasp this definition, one has to come to understand the role of retraction in persuasion dialogue. It should generally be possible for the respondent to retract a commitment. Retracting a proposition, once the other party has shown it is false or indefensible, is an important part of rationality. An arguer should be open-minded, and should not just stick dogmatically to his opinion, even when he is shown it is wrong. Thus it is a very important property of persuasion dialogue that retraction of commitments should be possible. On the other hand, a respondent should not always be free to retract, in any situation. If this were possible, then the proponent could never, at least realistically speaking, be capable of successful persuasion. Thus it is very important to make the distinction between a persuasion attempt and an instance of successful persuasion. The pair of definitions above attempts to make this vital distinction clear.

Now that we have defined the speech act of persuasion, we are in a much better position to confront the various problems of mass media argumentation that have proved so puzzling. Of course, a central and recurring one is the key notion of the persuasive definition. Within the field of speech communication, there is more and more interest in definitions as a topic of investigation, as it has become more and more evident how powerful definitions are as a way of framing an issue and controlling an argument. Having grasped the speech act of persuasion in multi-agent terms, we now have a much better chance of coming to understand how persuasive definitions work and how they should be evaluated.

In the dialectical models of argumentation outlined in this chapter, two parties interact with each other by taking turns to put forward arguments, ask questions, or perform other speech acts. Typically, the proponent tries to persuade the respondent. This model applies very well, for example, to the Socratic dialogue in which one party argues directly with another, trying to convince the other to accept some viewpoint. But what happens in cases where only one person argues with himself (playing devil's advocate), or in a case of legal argumentation in a trial, where many parties are involved? How can such cases be assimilated to the dialectical model? Another vexing kind of case is one where the speaker addresses a mass audience, for example, by designing a television commercial or by addressing an assembled audience in a speech. Govier (1999) posed this problem poignantly by titling one of her chapters "When They Can't Talk Back: The Noninteractive Audience and the Theory of Argument." One way to solve the problem is to consider how an argument stands up against some hypothetical questions or objections of a second party who does not really exist but is merely set up as a hypothetical construct. She sees carrying out this suggestion, however, as an important unsolved problem, and doubts that it can be solved with current resources. She writes that "to envisage a challenger who fits one's intended audience is virtually impossible in any case in which one's audience is a mass audience whose views are likely to be heterogeneous and largely unknown" (p. 187). This large theoretical problem will be posed even more pointedly in chapter 3, which concerns the kind of argumentation designed for a mass audience using propaganda. A clue to how to solve it by directing argumentation to the values of the audience to be persuaded was given in the Star Trek example, in chapter 1, section 9. But it won't be until chapter 9, section 4, that the problem will be taken up further, once some cases have been studied that will make the depth and importance of the problem more apparent.

3

Propaganda

A recurring problem for the normative analysis and evaluation of mass media argumentation is the use of the term "propaganda." One of the most common forms of attack on, or negative criticism of, rhetorical argumentation used in mass media is to label it as propaganda. What frequently happens is that arguments are automatically dismissed as irrational or fallacious, as soon as they are categorized as propaganda. This form of dismissal is especially evident in textbooks on logic and critical thinking, where forms of argument are frequently evaluated as fallacious using the term "propaganda." In this chapter, I critically question such a policy of automatic dismissal of arguments used in propaganda. I will seek out a better method of evaluating such arguments, so that evaluations can be supported or refuted on a case-by-case basis by employing clearly stated criteria that can be used to assess the textual evidence given in the particular case. This method could be called an evidence-based approach.

One of the thorniest problems is to define the term "propaganda" or at least to grapple with the contradictions that appear in its current usage. One of the results of this chapter is a proposed set of criteria for the identification of propaganda as a type of discourse. Ten defining characteristics (as well as several other typical properties) of propaganda as an identifiable type of discourse will be set out and argued for. A second task addressed is how mass media argumentation used in what is called propaganda should be analyzed. Some advice is given on how to analyze argumentation dialectically in propaganda and how to reconstruct certain types of arguments that are central to mass persuasion attempts commonly identified with propaganda. But the main problem addressed, and the most difficult one, is how to evaluate mass media argumentation used as propaganda. The term "propaganda" has such negative connotations that people tend to see only the arguments of their opposition as describable with this label, as if their own arguments could never be. The aim of this chapter is to get us over this one-sided or dismissive approach to evaluating arguments allegedly used as propaganda, in order to bring us to a dialectical perspective that takes a balanced but evidence-based approach.

This chapter ties in very closely with chapter 6. In chapter 6 a much broader approach is taken by analyzing the wider category of arguments based on popular opinion, including arguments that might fairly be considered as falling under the heading of propaganda and other kinds of arguments based on popular opinion that would not be considered propaganda. The general topic of chapter 6 is the form of argument called appeal to popular opinion, or *argumentum ad populum*, as it is called in the logic textbooks. Any argument based on a generally accepted opinion is covered in this broad category, including arguments based on public opinion polls and arguments based on common knowledge. However, there is one special subtype of this more general type of argumentation that specifically cites mob appeal arguments, or arguments directed to the enthusiasms of the multitude. This type of argument is closely related to the literature on propaganda, and the latter topic is scarcely comprehensible without dealing with it. It is therefore treated in this chapter. However, the reader must keep in mind that the more general type of argument traditionally called appeal to popular opinion will be analyzed in chapter 6, based on the assumption that the mob appeal type of argument often fitted into this category will have already been treated in this chapter.

1. Negative Connotations

According to the account of the origin of the term "propaganda" given in Ellul (1967), the term originally referred to a committee of church officials called the Congregatio de Propaganda Fide (Congregation for the Propagation of the Faith). The name of this committee continued as the name given to previous meetings of Pope Gregory XIII with three cardinals in 1572–1585, which had the aim of combatting the Reformation. It may be presumed that in this original meaning, the term did not have the negative connotations it has now, at least for the Catholics who originated the term. However, it is also reasonable to assume that it would soon have taken on negative connotations for the Protestants who became aware of what the word meant to the Catholics. The committee had the purpose of advocating a particular point of view, or taking one side, on an important issue of church doctrine. And it had an interest at stake in doing so. Thus it is easy to see how the modern, negative connotations of the word "propaganda" developed from this original use of the term.

Marlin (1989, p. 47) tells us that the word "propaganda" was used by the Allies during both world wars to characterize only the opinion-forming activities of the enemy, treating these so-designated enemy activities as composed mostly of lies. These practices left the word with strongly negative connotations. However, "here and there" in the literature on propaganda, according to Marlin, "one finds voices trying to rehabilitate the word for neutral usage." The negative connotations are so deeply entrenched, however, and the word is so charged with negative emotive connotations that the word itself is frequently used as a verbal weapon to attack views or arguments one is opposed to or wishes to condemn as not being rationally compelling. The strong negative connotations attached to the word "propaganda" imply that such discourse is both unethical and illogical. The ethical aspect implies intentional deception and manipulation of a mass audience. The logical or dialectical aspect implies that the argumentation used is not based on good evidence of the kind appropriate for a rational discussion, and instead is of an emotional and crowd-pleasing sort.

As Marlin noted, the word "propaganda," as used in the modern English-speaking world, still has the strong negative connotations set in place by its use in the two world wars. Politicians and bureaucrats would definitely avoid this term to describe their own public relations and promotional activities, using it only to describe those of their opponents. Generally, to describe any discourse or message as propaganda is to downgrade it by suggesting that the information content of the message, or its usefulness as reliable evidence, is suspect. The use of this word even suggests that the message referred to is intentionally manipulative and deceptive. For example, to describe a story in a newspaper or a televised report as propaganda would be to say that the story or report is not an objective presentation of the facts, not a balanced account of both sides of an issue. It would be classified as a biased argument with a spin that advocates some cause or particular viewpoint or interest. Generally, to say that something is propaganda is to say that it is the output of some interest group or organization that is pushing a particular viewpoint in a way designed to promote it to a mass audience.

But the negative connotations of the term are not universal. As Marlin (1989, p. 47) reminded us, Lenin and Goebbels did not mind its being used to describe their own activities of molding public opinions. The Russian usage seems to have persisted despite the Allies' use of the term in World War II to refer only to the enemy opinion-forming activities, presumed to be manipulative lies designed to deceive a gullible public that did not have access to free media. So the word has a mixed quality. It is generally negative in its connotations. The negative aspect seems to be at least partly logical in nature, suggesting that the discourse in question is somehow untrustworthy, deceptive, or not a kind of argumentation that is based on a balanced consideration of the evidence relevant to the issue being discussed. Also, there is a negative ethical implication to the effect that propaganda is intentionally manipulative, and involves lying or dishonesty of some sort. The implication is that this type of discourse masquerades as something else, that it is not what it appears to be on the surface, and hence that some kind of duplicity or pretense is involved in it.

Apart from ethical questions, these negative connotations of the use of the word "propaganda" raise some logical questions (logical in the sense of being questions of how to evaluate argumentation used in a text of discourse as rational or spurious, as correctly used or fallacious). What is propaganda as a type of discourse in which arguments are used for some purpose? And should the term "propaganda" be defined in an inherently negative way so that it is always bad or wrong? That is, should all arguments used in propaganda be judged to be fallacious or incorrect (or at least suspect or ill-supported) just because they were used for purposes of propaganda? Or should "propaganda" be defined in a neutral way that does not beg the question or foreclose the question of the worth of the arguments used in it?

Marlin (2002, pp. 18–22) has classified definitions of propaganda into three categories: negative, neutral, and positive. The positive definitions are quite rare. Most of the definitions offered fall into the two first categories of negative and neutral. Eight negative definitions are cited. The first definition says that the goal of propaganda is always to promote the interests of those who contrive it, instead of to benefit to the audience to whom it is addressed. The second definition also adds the characteristic of indifference to the truth, and defines propaganda as the management of opinions and attitudes by the manipulation of social suggestion. The third definition calls propaganda the attempt to control the behavior of individuals when the ends are considered unscientific or of doubtful value. The fourth definition defines propaganda as a means of gaining power by psychological manipulation of groups or masses. The fifth defines propaganda as any attempt by means of persuasion to enlist people into the service of one party to any dispute. The sixth definition defines propaganda as the systematic effort to manipulate other people's beliefs and attitudes or actions. The seventh definition focuses on corporate propaganda, referring to communication that has the purpose of bringing a target audience to adopt attitudes and beliefs chosen by the propagandist. The eighth definition defines propaganda as the advocacy of what we do not believe, as opposed to education, defined as the advocacy of what we believe.

Three neutral definitions are cited (pp. 20–21). According to the first, propaganda is dissemination of ideas, information, or rumor for the purpose of helping or injuring an institution, cause, or person. The second defines propaganda as the attempt to influence public opinion through the transmission of ideas and values. The third states that the real aim of propaganda is the spreading of information, whether true or false, good or bad.

Two favorable definitions are cited. The first is a wartime definition describing propaganda as a respectable name for the conveyance of information. The second describes propaganda as part of democratic education to promote active citizenship in a country by giving each individual a living conception of the community.

Of course, offering an abstract definition of a controversial word such as "propaganda" could be seen as using a persuasive definition (see section 3, below, and chapter 8) that makes the definition of propaganda itself a kind of propaganda. Even so, propaganda as a type of discourse does have certain characteristics that enable us to recognize it, or at least to use the word to make claims and criticisms in everyday conversations and in academic arguments. To claim that an argument is propaganda or is part of a discourse that may be described as propagandistic, is a common way of criticizing arguments or of evaluating them in a negative way that suggests that the argument is not based on reliable evidence or rational argumentation. By this means an argument can be attacked, suggesting that it may be rejected as logically unconvincing to a rational person.

But perhaps such common practices are naïve or not based on a form of evaluation that can be rationally justified by appeal to good evidence.

Even worse, perhaps such condemnations are prejudicial and fallacious. For perhaps propaganda is not inherently bad or illogical. Perhaps it has a purpose as an organized and methodical type of discourse that is recognizable as such. And perhaps argumentation in such a type of discourse ought to be evaluated in relation to the goals appropriate for such a use of arguments. The suggestion that propaganda may not be all bad, or not as bad as those who use the term in a negative way so often take for granted, may seem slightly scandalous. But until some clear account of what the term is supposed to mean is given, no way of throwing light on the issue is open.

2. **Public Discourse and Reason**

When an arguer addresses a mass audience using some form of communicative discourse to try to get the audience to accept a particular view or to support a particular policy, to what extent is such argumentation based on rationality? Many who have a negative view of rhetoric would say that such an appeal to emotions and crowd prejudices should not be described as any kind of rational argumentation. This ambivalence about the role of arguments that appeal to popular opinion will be made evident in chapters 6 and 7. But even without considering the ambivalent view of the logic textbooks on appeal to popular opinion, and the reservations about the role conventional public opinion polling in mass media argumentation, the same kind of ambivalence is expressed by those who have written about political decision making in a democracy.

Political issues should be decided by citizens engaged in public discourse with each other in a democratic and civil exchange of arguments, in the political theory of public decision making. This, at any rate, is the ideal of public discourse advocated by Rawls (1993). Primary components of this process of rational argumentation in public discourse, according to Rawls's theory (1993, p. 224) are "principles of reasoning and rules of evidence in the light of which citizens are to decide whether substantive principles properly apply," and rules that determine the kinds of considerations that can legitimately be appealed to in advocating a position or in voting on a policy. But where do such rules and principles come from? The answer given by Rawls is that we are to appeal to "presently accepted general beliefs and forms of reasoning found in common sense, and the methods and conclusions of science when these are not controversial" (p. 224). Part of this answer is evocative of the form of argument identified as *argumentum ad populum* in chapter 6. When arguing about laws and policies in public discourse, Rawls tells us, the duty of civility requires us to stay within the bounds of public reason. For Rawls, then, when a political speaker addresses a mass audience, to try to get them to accept some view she advocates or to support some policy she expounds, the ideals of public discourse require that the speaker should appeal to presently accepted general beliefs and forms of reasoning found in "common sense." But how should she do this? To get any answer here, we are driven back to reconsider issues related to the *argumentum ad populum* as a form of argument, taken up in chapter 6. Rawls appears to be of the opinion that an argument based on appeal to public discourse is not only a rational kind of argumentation. He seems to combine this assumption with the view that such an argument is useful in mass communication and can be successful in getting a mass audience to accept your view or to follow a policy you advocate.

These assertions are, of course, at odds with the traditional view that the *argumentum ad populum* is a fallacy, as expounded in chapter 6. Many would be highly skeptical about Rawls's claims and would say that viewing public discourse with a mass audience in his way is hopelessly optimistic. They would say that his view is a distortion of what really takes place in real public discourse, and would be hopelessly impractical as a method of getting a mass audience to do anything. The form of argument called appeal to popular opinion will be shown in chapter 6 to be reasonable under the right conditions. But is it reasonable when used by a mob orator to stir up emotions in a mass audience?

Among the skeptics at the other end of the spectrum from Rawls's view is that of Le Bon (1896), who argued that crowds think in images and are especially impressed by colorful images and marvelous stories, and that therefore crowds are not influenced by reasoning. Le Bon (p. 81) started from the premise, based on his observations, that crowds do not use logical reasoning to influence their actions and what they accept. From this premise he inferred that it would be a great mistake for a speaker who hopes to influence a crowd to use logical reasoning to try to persuade the crowd to do anything. Le Bon saw the public, or "the crowd," as he termed the mass audience, as irrational and driven by emotion. He drew the conclusion that what a mass media arguer needs in order to successfully influence the crowd is an appeal to emotion. Whether the appeal to emotion is logical or rational, in his view, matters very little or not at all.

We have shown that crowds do not reason, that they accept or reject ideas as a whole, that they tolerate neither discussion nor contradiction, and that the suggestions brought to bear on them invade the entire field of their understanding and tend at once to transform themselves into acts. We have shown that crowds suitably influenced are ready to sacrifice themselves for the ideal with which they have been inspired. We have also seen that they only entertain violent and extreme sentiments, that in their case sympathy quickly becomes adoration, and antipathy almost as soon as it is aroused is transformed into hatred.

According to Le Bon's account, the nature of the convictions of crowds is more like that of religious faith, or even religious fanaticism, than it is like that of reflective, balanced, logical thinking. Characteristic or the convictions of crowds, according to Le Bon (p. 83) are intolerance, fanaticism, and "whole-souled ardour" in the cause of an individual or in the service of a "victorious leader" who arouses their enthusiasm, and thereby becomes a guide to their actions. There does not seem to be much room for civil public discourse and rational thinking based on common sense, of the kind described by Rawls, in Le Bon's view of how the convictions of a mass audience can be influenced. The French writer Alexis de Tocqueville was also skeptical about the rationality of appeal to popular opinion as a form of argument in democratic politics. Tocqueville observed that popular opinion in political argumentation fluctuates rapidly in a way that is impossible to predict. He wrote (1966, p. 230): "All of the projects [of the majority] are taken up with great ardor; but as soon as its attention is turned elsewhere, all these efforts cease." This insight is even more valuable in an age of mass media. The attention span of the public seems to have become shorter and shorter. Something instantly becomes a public issue as all the media sources compete to give central attention to it, like President George W. Bush choking on a pretzel in January 2002. This story was on all the front pages and was the lead story in the news for one day. A few days later nobody was hearing about it. Another example was the disappearance of the Gary Condit story exactly at the time of the 9/11 attack on New York and the Pentagon. The reporting of news to the public goes in a disjointed way from one crisis or spectacular incident to another. This "snapshot" effect was observed by Yankelovich in his remarks on public opinion, discussed below in chapter 4. Reporting of news results in a disjointed sequence of public thinking, leaping from one attention-grabbing story to another. As Yankelovich observed, the public gets information in the form of a snapshot of the event, but there is not enough continuity to represent intelligent deliberation. Thus, Toqueville's view of public opinion in mass thinking is almost as skeptical as Le Bon's.

The views presented by Rawls and Le Bon represent the two extremes on how mass media argumentation influences popular convictions and attitudes. Rawls's viewpoint seems to represent a normative model of how public discourse is to be conducted in a democracy, if it is to be just and represent liberal values. Le Bon's account is more descriptive in nature, based on his own observations of how crowds behave. Le Bon was an astute observer of how convictions are led in a particular direction by the rhetorical arguments of leaders and popular orators. But even if the two views do not irreconcilably conflict, they are strongly opposed in certain ways. Suppose Le Bon is right about how argumentation in popular discourse actually works in influencing mass audiences. Surely, it follows that an account such as that of Rawls, which assumes a fairly high level of rationality in public discourse, is hopelessly impractical, idealistic, and out of touch with how mass conviction works and can be altered. Suppose, on the other hand, that Rawls is right that his model of public reason is a good method for conducting the civil exchange of arguments in a democracy. Then surely it follows that cynics who pander to the worst instincts of crowds by engaging in Le Bon's methods of dramatic appeal to emotion are engaging in the very sort of irrational demagoguery that most threatens a democracy. The two opposed views represent an interesting problem that can be posed in the form of a dilemma. Can a speaker engage in a rational kind of deliberation or persuasion dialogue with a mass audience, say, in an election campaign or a political speech? And is this kind of rational *argumentum ad populum* necessary for public discourse in a democracy? Or does public discourse influence a mass audience only by appealing to emotions and popular enthusiasm in a way that makes it a deceptive, myth-making, or distorted type of argumentation that is logically suspect or even fallacious?

3. Appeal to the People Revisited

One aspect of propaganda is that, by its very nature, it is designed to reach and influence a mass audience and, as such, is a kind of technique that must appeal successfully to the emotions, commitments, and enthusiasms of the crowd to win acceptance for a conclusion. The fact that propaganda is an "appeal to the people" as a type of argumentation makes it inherently suspicious to logicians. Indeed, it is shown in chapter 6 that the so-called appeal to the people has traditionally been treated by logic textbooks as a fallacious type of argument. Examples from two of the leading introductory textbooks will indicate how this type of argument has generally been treated in logic as a fallacy.

Chapter 6 will concentrate on the *ad populum* argument and its variants. The type of appeal to popular opinion argument in which a premise is "Everyone accepts this proposition" is one variety of the argument, but there is also another one, sometimes called the "mob appeal" type. The distinction between the two types was drawn by Hurley (1994) in his popular logic textbook, *A Concise Introduction to Logic*. According to Hurley (1994, p. 120), the "indirect approach," or "appeal to the people," variant of the *argumentum ad populum* has the following basic structure as an argument: You want to be accepted/included in the group/loved/ esteemed. . . . Therefore, you should accept XYZ as true.

The indirect approach can be classified as a subtype of the more general *ad populum* argumentation schemes defined in chapter 6, section 4, an indirect type of appeal. By contrast, in the "direct approach" (p. 119), the arguer directs his or her appeal to the individuals in the crowd, as a mass audience. According to Hurley's account, as quoted below (p. 120), the contrast is that in the direct approach, each person feels united with the crowd, and anyone who fails to go along with the conclusion accepted so enthusiastically by the crowd risks the loss of the security of acceptance by the crowd. Thus the two arguments are connected. But the direct approach is identified with crowd-pleasing rhetoric directed to the mass audience.

The direct approach occurs when an arguer, addressing a large group of people, excites the emotions and enthusiasm of the crowd to win acceptance for his conclusion. The objective is to arouse a kind of mob mentality. This is the strategy used by nearly every propagandist and demagogue. Adolf Hitler was a master of the technique, but it is also used with some measure of success by speechmakers at Democratic and Republican national conventions. Waving flags and blaring music add to the overall effect. Because the individuals in the audience want to share in the camaraderie, the euphoria, and the excitement, they find themselves accepting any number of conclusions with ever-increasing fervor.

The direct approach is not limited to oral argumentation, of course; a similar effect can be accomplished in writing. By employing such emotionally charged phraseology as "fighter of communism," "champion of the free enterprise system," and "defender of the working man," polemicists can awaken the same kind of mob mentality as they would if they were speaking.

Hurley does not consider the possibility that the appeal to the people argument could be reasonable (non-fallacious) in some instances. The appeal to the people is classified by Hurley (p. 116) as a fallacy of relevance. This categorization means that the appeal to the people is a fallacy because it fails to be relevant as an argument. This analysis allows that the premises of such an argument can be psychologically relevant to the conclusion, making the conclusion seem to follow from the premises. But it denies that they are logically relevant, in the sense that they "provide genuine evidence in support of the conclusion." Hurley's citing of Hitler as a propagandist who was a master of the technique of appeal to the people seems to make "appeal to the people" sound particularly despicable. The choice of example seems to be based on the assumption that propaganda is inherently wrong as a form of argumentation, because it is based on the appeal to the people as an underlying argument. The assumption seems to be that propaganda is something that contains, or is based on, the fallacious argument called "appeal to the people."

Other leading textbooks have reaffirmed this approach. Copi (1982, p. 104) defined *argumentum ad populum* as the attempt to win popular assent to a conclusion by arousing the emotions and enthusiasms of the multitude, rather than by appeal to the relevant facts. He went on to link this fallacious type of argument with the use of propaganda.

This is a favorite device with the propagandist, the demagogue, and the advertiser. Faced with the task of mobilizing public sentiment for or against a particular measure, they will avoid the laborious process of collecting and presenting evidence and rational argument by using the shortcut methods of the *argumentum ad populum*. Where the proposal is for a change and he is against it, he will express suspicion of "newfangled innovations" and praise the wisdom of the "existing order." If he is for it, he will be for "progress" and opposed to "antiquated prejudice." Here we have the use of invidious terms with no rational attempt made to argue for them or to justify their application. This technique may be supplemented by displaying the flag, brass bands, and whatever else might serve to stimulate and excite the public. (p. 104)

Copi went on to criticize the "twentieth-century advertiser" in particular, as a "huckster" and "ballyhoo artist" who has elevated the *argumentum ad populum* "almost to the status of a fine art" in designing commercials that sell "day-dreams and delusions of grandeur" (pp. 104–105), as will be noted in chapter 6. Copi, like Hurley, classified such *ad populum* arguments as fallacious on the grounds that they commit fallacies of relevance (p. 98). Like Hurley, Copi (p. 99) saw the failure as one of a failure of logical relevance, masked by a psychological relevance that makes such an argument seem persuasive and correct.

Now the basic assumption that propaganda uses, or is even based on, the *argumentum ad populum* because it does address a mass audience does seem to be true. Propaganda does try to persuade a mass audience to accept a conclusion based on premises that are popularly or widely accepted, and it does typically work by exciting the emotions and enthusiasms of the crowds. If propaganda is based on this fallacious kind of irrelevant argumentation, surely that explains both why propaganda is negatively evaluated from a logical point of view and why it contravenes rational standards of argument. But there are grounds for doubt about this explanation. According to the analysis in chapter 6, below, at least some kinds of *ad populum* arguments are not inherently fallacious and can sometimes be reasonable. To clarify the question, it is necessary to reconsider the grounds on which the logic textbooks condemn *ad populum* arguments as fallacious.

One of these is that *ad populum* arguments appeal to emotions, specifically the emotions and enthusiasms of the crowd. But is the use of emotional appeal in itself sufficient grounds for judging an argument to be fallacious? I have argued previously (1994) that use of emotional appeal does not necessarily mean, by itself, that an argument is fallacious. In the following chapters, we will see that appeals to emotion can often provide good grounds for presumptively accepting a conclusion on a default basis. This means that in the absence of the hard information needed to conclusively resolve the issue, the argument can function in a dialogue such as a deliberation as a way of steering conduct toward a prudent line of action based on practical reasoning.

Another reason *ad populum* arguments are often classified as fallacious is that they pander to the crowd by drawing on premises that are popularly accepted. As Copi (1982, p. 105) warned, "popular acceptance of a policy does not prove it to be wise [and] general assent to a claim does not prove it to be true." According to this account, *ad populum* arguments are based on premises that are commitments of the mass audience, and therefore they are not rational arguments based on evidence that is factual and has been verified. But is this factor, by itself, a sufficient reason for judging all *ad populum* arguments to be fallacious? The answer is no, according to the analysis presented below in chapter 6, because endoxic arguments, arguments based on popular opinions or that have premises that express widely held assumptions, are not necessarily and in themselves fallacious. Also, arguments addressed to a specific audience, and based on the commitments of that specific audience as premises, are not necessarily fallacious either. It depends on how those premises are used in an argument in a specific case, whether the premises are subject to doubt and critical questioning in the discussion, and which other kinds of arguments and evidential considerations are used alongside these *ad populum* arguments. Once again, as long as the *ad populum* arguments are not taken as conclusive or as the only basis for arriving at a conclusion, they can have a legitimate role in shifting a weight of presumption to one side or the other in a rational discussion.

The main ground Hurley and Copi bring to bear in classifying *ad populum* arguments as fallacious is that of relevance. On both their accounts, *ad populum* arguments are said to be fallacious because the premises of an appeal to a mass audience or a crowd are psychologically relevant to its acceptance of a conclusion but are not logically relevant. To be logically relevant, they must provide good evidence to support the conclusion.

But are premises based on popular opinions, or on the enthusiastic convictions of a crowd, always logically irrelevant to a conclusion? It would seem not. As will be shown in chapter 7, in public opinion polls of the kind commonly used to predict election results, poll-based appeals to popular opinion can be reasonable when they have the following form. The premise is the statement that the majority, or such-and-such percent of respondents polled, accept proposition A (such as believing that someone is the better candidate for office). The conclusion that proposition A is true is rationally justified as a reasonable presumption with a certain weight of likelihood – for example, the proposition that so-and-so will win the election. In many cases, polling is quite a good way to judge public opinion or to help set social policy. The use of the poll to draw an inference, as shown below in chapter 7, is not an inherently fallacious form of argumentation. In fact, in many arguments commonly used in everyday conversational exchanges and deliberations, the fact that a proposition is widely accepted is rightly taken as a reasonable (but not conclusive or irrefutable) and relevant premise for provisionally accepting that proposition as plausible. As has been emphasized so often above, such an argument needs to be evaluated in a dialogue framework. It needs to be seen as subject to further questioning, before hasty inferences are drawn from it to other propositions.

Much depends here on what is meant by "logically relevant." A proposition based on crowd appeal or popular acceptance would not be logically relevant in a scientific discussion, say, in physics or chemistry. But it could be logically relevant in an argument used in a court of law or in a business meeting about advertising strategy in marketing a product, as shown below in chapter 4. Dialectical relevance depends on the purpose of the discourse the argument in question is being used to contribute to. If the purpose of a speech is to mobilize the country for war or to persuade an audience to support a cause like protecting the environment, appealing to the commitments of the audience or even to its enthusiasm may be relevant. It may be necessary and appropriate in order to convince them that a particular course of conduct would be wise and should be accepted as a policy. In the right setting, an appeal to mass enthusiasm to get support and commitment for a proposed policy or course of action can be suitable rhetoric.

Our tentative conclusion (which will require more support) is that propaganda is based on an appeal to the people type of argument, especially the so-called direct type. The problem is with the leap from that premise to the conclusion that propaganda must be wrong or fallacious for that reason alone. The urge to take this leap seems to stem from what has become the routine assumption that rhetoric directed to a mass audience is inherently illogical, deceptive, or full of trickery. This pervasive assumption seems hard to combat. As shown in chapter 1, the negative attitude toward rhetoric has itself become a popular opinion. But once that assumption is seriously questioned, the need to look at propaganda in a different normative light becomes apparent. The characteristic that propaganda is a form of mass media argumentation should not, in itself, be regarded as sufficient for drawing the conclusion that all propaganda is irrational or illogical or that any argument used in propaganda is for that reason alone fallacious.

4. The Dialectical Viewpoint on Propaganda

Propaganda is itself such a negative term that any attempt to redefine it runs the risk of being labeled as a persuasive definition of the most questionable sort. In public opinion, propaganda is just something bad, and it is very hard to argue against a firmly entrenched public opinion in a philosophical or intellectual discussion. But having introduced dialectic as a normative framework for argument analysis and evaluation in chapter 1, can we apply it now to a discussion of propaganda? Can we play devil's advocate, and argue that when used in an appropriate dialectical setting, argumentation that could be classified propaganda could be reasonable? It all depends, of course on what one means by "reasonable." Rationality, as argued in chapter 1, must always be judged according to some standards. Traditionally in logic, arguments have been evaluated as valid or invalid according to semantic standards. But recently, pragmatic or dialectical standards of the kind outlined in chapter 2 have been developed to also evaluate how arguments are used in different types of conversational contexts. In such a dialectical framework, each type of dialogue has its goal, and an argument is successful (or used correctly) to the extent that it contributes to the chosen conversational goals. This pragmatic framework has also been used to investigate informal (and formal) fallacies in Walton (1995), where an argument is judged to be used incorrectly or inadequately if it fails to contribute to a given conversational goal. Within such a framework an argument is said to be used in a fallacious way, in a given context of conversation, if it hinders or even blocks the fulfillment of the goal of the conversation (often by the use of deception, by seeming to be used correctly). So how does propaganda fit in? Evidently, it is a type of persuasion, to get action, judging from the characterizations considered so far. But also, as made evident in the discussions of Rawls, it has to do with public deliberation in a democracy. Thus deliberation would seem to be part of it. As Le Bon showed, it also has to do with mass appeal crowd rhetoric, suggesting perhaps an eristic aspect. Somehow, the kind of mass appeal argumentation characteristic of propaganda combines these dialectical elements.

In chapter 2 the six types of conversational frameworks – called types of dialogue – were identified. They are especially basic to evaluating argumentation of the kind typically used in everyday conversational arguments. To review, these are eristic dialogue, persuasion dialogue, deliberation, inquiry, information-seeking dialogue, and negotiation. Each goal-directed type of dialogue provides a conversational framework in which a given argument can be normatively evaluated as used correctly or incorrectly to contribute to the goal of a type of dialogue the participants are presumably engaged in. Of course, each argument in a given case needs to be evaluated in light of the text of discourse from which the argument can be reconstructed and identified. Eristic dialogue –the quarrel being the leading subtype – is the type of verbal exchange where each party has a grievance and "hits out" at the other party to try to humiliate him or her. The quarrel is often an angry, emotional exchange, and as the saying goes, it generates more heat than light, and is not much of a friend to logic. This observation is evocative of some of Le Bon's observations on propaganda as an emotional appeal to the mass audience, mobilizing the crowd to "hit out" aggressively. In persuasion dialogue, each participant has the goal of getting the other party to become committed to a particular proposition, based on arguments using only premises the other party is already committed to. The key concept is that of an arguer's commitment. The problem with the direct or mob appeal type of *ad populum* is how the mass speaker can appeal to the audience as a whole group or argument community, rather than just targeting single individuals as respondents. In the inquiry, the goal is to prove a particular proposition (or disprove it, or prove it cannot be proved, or prove it cannot be disproved) based on premises that are verified (known to be true). The inquiry uses cumulative argumentation of a kind that is so well established that no propositions in the chain of reasoning ever need to be retracted. At least that is the goal (ideally) of the inquiry type of dialogue. Thus, the inquiry seems to have little to do with appeal to popular opinion, for, as Tocqueville pointed out, mass public opinion is inherently unstable. In information-seeking dialogue, one party tries to get some information that the other party possesses but that the first party lacks. This type of dialogue is relevant to propaganda that is so often presented in a news format. In the negotiation type of dialogue, the goal is to "make a deal" – to come to a division of some goods, services, or interests that are in short supply. Each party tries to get a share of the goods that represent what is most important to her, while leaving the other party enough of a share of what is important to him so that he does not feel cheated. Negotiation dialogue is not about searching for the truth of a matter or about rationally convincing the other party that a particular proposition is true or false. It is simply interest-based bargaining. This type of dialogue also seems relevant to propaganda, which often seems to be based on advancing interests and not on getting to the truth of a matter.

5. Persuasion and Propaganda

The ultimate goal of propaganda is to get the respondents to take a particular course of action. Many definitions of "propaganda" postulate that the goal of propaganda is to change the respondents' beliefs or to persuade the respondents to accept some proposition as true (or false). But these goals, although they are typically part of propaganda, are secondary to the ultimate goal, which is always (as a matter of practical politics) to get the respondents to do (or abstain from doing) something. These secondary goals are always means to the ultimate end of propaganda, which is action or compliance with action.

Thus propaganda involves rhetoric. For as indicated in chapter 2, the purpose of rhetoric is persuasion (Wenzel 1990, p. 81). But how is propaganda related to dialectic? Is the speech act of persuasion a kind of argument move used in propaganda? And could propaganda be seen, or judged normatively, from a viewpoint of persuasion dialogue? In persuasion dialogue, the proponent's goal is to use the commitments of the respondent as premises in order to persuade the respondent to also become committed to some particular proposition he previously had doubts about accepting. This process of persuading a respondent to accept some particular proposition as true is tied in with how propaganda is used. And therefore, many conclude that from a dialectical point of view, propaganda can be defined essentially as a type of persuasion dialogue. But it certainly is a peculiar type of persuasion dialogue. Many would say it is a degenerate or false (pseudo) persuasion dialogue used to try to influence a mass audience.

But the aim of propaganda is not just to secure a respondent's assent to a proposition by persuading him that it is true or that it is supported by propositions he is already committed to. The aim of propaganda is to get the respondent to act, to adopt a certain course of action, or to go along with and assist in a particular policy. Merely securing assent or commitment to a proposition is not enough to make propaganda successful in securing its aim. Whether or not an audience really believes a particular viewpoint or accepts it as true, the aim of propaganda is to get them to go along with a policy or program in a more practical sense, by taking part in it and by allowing it to be implemented as a plan of social action.

This way of defining propaganda has important implications for the issue of whether propaganda is inherently bad, deceptive, or against truth. For if you see propaganda as a type of persuasion dialogue, then once you note its indifference to the truth, you then can pinpoint its bad aspect as being a defective kind of persuasion dialogue. For participants in persuasion dialogue are supposed to have a regard for the truth of a matter. This is particularly crucial in a critical discussion, where participants are not supposed to ignore matters relevant to the issue of the discussion. This is certainly true in the critical discussion type of persuasion dialogue described by van Eemeren and Grootendorst (1987, 1992). Hence propaganda, once seen as a species of persuasion dialogue, is easily seen as inherently defective, because it ignores or even suppresses relevant evidence on the issue being argued when such an ignoring is convenient to its purpose. But if you don't see propaganda as a type of persuasion dialogue, it may be less easy to convict it as being inherently negative or critically defective in nature. Thus, from a dialectical point of view, it is useful to at least initially view propaganda as persuasion dialogue of a sort.

If the goal of propaganda is to get the respondent to act in a certain way, then ignoring evidence on whether certain propositions are true or are relevant to accepting them as true is not necessarily a deviation from or a subverting of the goal of the dialogue. Defining propaganda as a kind of action-getting dialogue, as opposed to a persuasion type of dialogue, it is harder to condemn propaganda as being inherently negative in nature. Its indifference to the truth may no longer necessarily be a failure or critical defect of propaganda that makes it inherently bad or deceptive. It could be that propaganda is indifferent to truth because finding the truth of a matter is simply not its purpose. It shouldn't be ethically condemned for failing to pay attention to some aim that is not central to its purpose as a type of discourse.

On the other hand, it is clear that persuasion is typically an important part of propaganda and that much of its method involves persuasion. And it does seem that, descriptively speaking, one of the main means used in propaganda to get an audience to act in a certain way is to use persuasive argumentation targeted to their commitments. The goal is to get them to accept or to adopt a favorable attitude to certain propositions they may have doubts about. Propaganda is in this respect comparable to the discourse of commercial ads, such as those used on television. The purpose of the ad seems mainly to get the viewers to buy more products. Try talking to representatives of the advertising firms that make these ads, and suggest to them that the ads should use rational persuasion to convince the viewers that the product is good or better than those of the competition. They will dismiss this account of the purpose of commercial advertisements as both naïve and too narrow. Sometimes the ads are evidently designed to rationally convince the potential buyer that the product has certain good or useful features or is a good buy. But more often the strategy of the ad is simply to draw attention to the brand or to generate a favorable ambience associated with the brand, by using visual images to arouse emotions.

Similarly, the goal of propaganda is basically to get compliance for action, or action itself, and surely its success or failure ought to be judged by this criterion. Persuasion by logical reasoning designed to rationally convince the audience is not necessarily involved – although it could be used in some cases – even though persuasion of a sort is involved as part of the *modus operandi*.

Propaganda then is a mixed type of dialogue that does not fit any of the six normative models of dialogue in chapter 2 exactly. It seems to be a distinctively different type of discourse altogether, even though it can directly involve elements of at least five of the six types of dialogue noted. Propaganda is best seen as a type of goal-directed discourse in its own right that has ten essential, identifying characteristics. As such, it can function in its own right as a normative structure in which arguments can be evaluated as used correctly or incorrectly (provided the other normative models of dialogue are also used) in a given case. Like deliberation dialogue, it is directed toward recommending a course of action; like persuasion dialogue, it works by calling on the commitments of the audience to gain its acceptance for a standpoint; and like eristic dialogue, it is aggressively partisan and emotional.

6. Characteristics of Propaganda

Below, ten essential characteristics of propaganda as a mode of discourse are set out, followed by a discussion of some other incidental characteristics.

1. Dialogue Structure. Propaganda has the form of a dialogue (communicative discourse) between two participants. The one party, who can also be a group, or a person representing a group, is called the proponent and is the speaker or sender of the message. The other party, called the respondent, and who is generally a mass audience of people, is the receiver of the message. Typically, the proponent is the active participant, while the respondent is a passive receiver of the message sent out by the proponent. But this asymmetrical relationship is not characteristic of all cases of propaganda. In some instances, the respondent group does engage in a bilateral dialogue exchange by responding positively or negatively to the proponent's message, or even by questioning or criticizing it – information that the proponent can use as feedback to craft her message more persuasively. Also, propaganda has a dialogue structure in that the argumentation of the proponent is based on what she takes to be the commitments of the respondent. The goal of the argumentation is to alter the convictions or actions of the proponent in a particular direction or toward a particular view different from the one the respondent already has.

2. Message Content. The content of the proponent's message is an argument, expressed in a verbal discourse and/or in other means of altering convictions that are not verbal in nature. The message can be purely verbal, as in a speech, but it can also be pictorial. Or it could be a mixture of these, as in the case of a news reporter commenting on videotaped clips. Propaganda frequently involves props, such as drums and flags, and it may also use music or drama or be conveyed in a dramatic format, such as a film or a novel. In some cases, propaganda can

be conveyed by objects such as coins or statues or even by costumes and settings that express the values of a particular life-style or social class.

3. Goal-Directed Structure. Propaganda is essentially goal-directed as a type of dialogue exchange. The proponent's goal is to get the respondent to carry out a particular action or to support a particular policy for action. This purposive aspect of propaganda is so marked that it is frequently described as "manipulative" in nature. As well as there being a goal for the proponent, against which the success or failure of the proponent's argumentation can be evaluated, there is also a general goal for propaganda as an institutionally recognizable type of dialogue. The general purpose is to support the existence, aims, and interests of a particular regime, organization, viewpoint, or interest group. Frequently, the purpose of propaganda is to support the interests of a country or a political party, government, or regime that directs the affairs of the country. But other groups or individuals, such as religious groups, political action groups, or advertisers, can also engage in propaganda.

4. Involvement of Social Groups. Propaganda is not just any argumentation meant to persuade or to get action. The respondent is a mass audience. And while the message may be delivered by an individual speaker, she always represents some broader agency or organized group that has interests or views that binds its members together.

5. Indifference to Logical Reasoning. The goal of propaganda is to move a mass audience in a certain direction, and its success or failure as argumentation used in a context of discourse should be judged in relation to how well (or badly) it performs in fulfilling this purpose. If methods of logical reasoning are useful for this purpose, then they should be used in propaganda. Thus propaganda is not, as a structure of discourse, either for or against using logical reasoning and relevant evidence. If appeals to emotion, of a kind that would be judged dubious or even fallacious by logical standards of good reasoning, work better than rational evidence to achieve the goal of argumentation used in propaganda, then such appeals are appropriate and should (normatively speaking) be used by good propagandists.

6. One-Sided Argumentation. Propaganda is a kind of advocacy dialogue that uses partisan argumentation to advocate one side of an issue and to present the arguments in favor of that side as strongly as possible. Propaganda is not an attempt to rationally deliberate on the wisdom or prudence of a course of action by looking at all the alternatives and weighing them judiciously or fairly. Neither is it an attempt to critically discuss an issue by openly considering all the arguments on both sides. Instead,

it is inherently one-sided as a type of discourse in which argumentation is used.

7. Involvement of Persuasion Dialogue. The primary goal of propaganda is to get an audience to support the aims, interests, and policies of a particular group, by securing the compliance of the audience with the actions being contemplated, undertaken, or advocated by the group. The goal of the propagandist then is not just to persuade or "re-educate" the audience to change their beliefs. It is also to gain their commitment to the extent that they will act on the basis of the new viewpoint they have come to accept or to take part in or support actions in line with or justified by this viewpoint. So persuasion is involved, but the speaker's goal in propaganda is more than just to change the beliefs of the audience. The proponent's fundamental goal in propaganda is to move the masses to action (to go to war, to buy a product, etc.), to comply with action, or to accept and not oppose a certain line of action. But persuasion is involved in a secondary but essential way, because the means used to get action, or support for action, is that of persuading the audience to become committed to a particular point of view that the audience did not accept (or did not fully embrace) before.

8. Justified by Results. Because its central purpose is to get action, propaganda as a socially organized activity is justified by the results it is supposed to achieve (both normatively and, in fact, by its defenders, in particular instances). In fact, propaganda is justified by the supposed value of bringing about a particular outcome said to be necessary for a good end, such as public safety or the saving of human lives in war. Propaganda is generally justified by citing a danger to the group, and then stressing that the adoption of a particular point of view is needed to combat or guard against that danger. Such a justification balances the costs of engaging in one-sided or even deceptive argumentation against the danger or loss of life that might result from an open-minded rational discussion that might turn up good arguments for the other side. The justification of propaganda is, in this respect, similar to the justification of lying in ethics, illustrated by case 3.6 below. Propaganda tends to be justified, as a matter of fact, in terms of its consequences, by those who try to justify or excuse its use. But also, from a normative point of view, propaganda ought to be justified by such a use of argumentation from consequences, for its goal is to lead to action.

9. Emotive Language and Persuasive Definitions. An essential part of all propaganda is the use of emotively charged words and phrases that make the advocated viewpoint take on a highly positive coloration, and any opposed viewpoint take on a highly negative coloration. For example,

supporters of an advocated view may be called freedom fighters, while supporters of the opposed viewpoint are designated as terrorists. A whole new vocabulary may be invented, and all kinds of pejorative words and phrases may be used to denote the opposed viewpoint. Another characteristic of propaganda is the use of persuasive definitions, as defined by the theory of emotive meaning of Stevenson (1944). This theory will be outlined, developed, and extended to mass media argumentation in chapter 8. Now it can be seen as applicable to propaganda as a type of argumentation. According to Stevenson's theory, the purpose of a persuasive definition is to engender a favorable or unfavorable attitude toward something by changing the descriptive meaning of the word for that thing while leaving the evaluative meaning the same. How persuasive definitions are so characteristic of propaganda can be already appreciated by reviewing some illustrative examples given in a popular logic textbook. Hurley (1994, p. 92) offered the following two examples.

Case 3.1

"Abortion" means the ruthless murdering of innocent human beings.

"Abortion" means a safe and established surgical procedure whereby a woman is relieved of an unwanted burden.

Case 3.2

"Liberal" means a drippy-eyed do-gooder obsessed with giving away other people's money.

"Liberal" means a genuine humanitarian committed to the goals of adequate housing and health care and of equal opportunity for all of our citizens.

Persuasive definitions tend to be deceptive as used in argumentation (and objects of suspicion, from a logical point of view) because, as Hurley (p. 92) pointed out, they conceal the approving or condemning of something by masquerading as an honest assignment of meaning to a word. Thus there is a very close resemblance between the deceptive technique of propaganda and the deceptive kind of tactic used in putting forward a persuasive definition in argumentation.

10. Eristic Aspect. Propaganda has a structure of argumentation like that of the quarrel, or eristic type of dialogue. It postulates a dichotomy for the audience: "We are the good guys. If you are not for us, you must be against us. All those opposed to our view are the bad guys." Often the words "fight" or "struggle" are used in propaganda. The implication is that any means required to fight against the "evil" or danger posed by the "enemy" is justified. Propaganda is most visible and has been most studied

as used in war. In time of war, the participants become caught up in an emotional attitude of hate and bitterness that is not conducive to what Thouless (1942) calls "calm thinking" of the kind that dispassionately weighs the evidence on both sides of an issue. Even when used outside war, propaganda often paints the picture of an emergency or danger of a kind that provokes fear and panic. The circumstances are portrayed as like that of a war, where a "fight" is needed to combat the danger facing the group.

Another characteristic of propaganda (Marlin 1989, p. 46) is the phenomenon of orchestration, meaning that it manipulates different media over time to produce a cumulative message. Other characteristics associated with propaganda cited by Marlin are misuse of statistics, manipulation of opinion polls, photomontage techniques, and the use of psychological techniques of persuasion. Misuse of opinion polls by advocacy groups will be studied in chapter 7. Propaganda is known to use psychologically effective techniques, such as visual imagery, repetition, massed crowds, and symbols of group identification, to create a climate of acceptance for its message. Propaganda is also known to often use suggestion in place of or to supplement explicitly verbalized arguments for a conclusion (Thouless 1942, p. 65). Thus, suggestion and implicature are vitally important modes of argumentation in propaganda.

These additional characteristics are not essential to propaganda, but only typical of it, whereas the first ten characteristics listed above are all essential for a text of discourse in a given case to qualify as propaganda. This definition is not meant to be purely stipulative in nature but is meant to represent, within the limits of any abstract philosophical theory, the conventionally accepted view of propaganda as a familiar kind of discourse. You could say it is a persuasive definition of "propaganda" as a type of discourse, partly characterized itself by using persuasive definition. But I believe that the circularity or reflexivity of the definition can be defended and rationally justified. Because it has been argued here that persuasive definitions are not inherently fallacious, it is also possible to argue for the claim that a persuasive definition of "propaganda" is possible and legitimate. What is the purpose of offering a definition of "propaganda"? Primarily, it is meant to be part of a normative model of a type of argumentation familiar in a kind of conversational discourse known to us in examples of mass media argumentation. The definition is primarily dialectical, in that it relates to norms of conversation. The normative model is meant to be used in a helpful way to identify, analyze, and evaluate argumentation used in particular cases in a given text of discourse.

7. Is Propaganda Necessarily Dishonest or Irrational?

One approach has been to capture the negative connotations of the word "propaganda" by defining it as a type of discourse that expressly has the purpose of going against or circumventing critical thinking of the kind used in a rational discussion of an issue, based on good evidence and information. This type of definition makes propaganda inherently negative, illogical and/or deceptive in nature, on the grounds that it is opposed to rational discussion and logical evaluation of arguments. The definition given by Marlin (1989, p. 50) is of this kind.

PROPAGANDA = (def.) The organized attempt through communication to affect belief or action or inculcate attitudes in a large audience in ways that circumvent or suppress an individual's adequately informed, rational, reflective judgment.

This definition is very helpful in capturing several important features of propaganda, but in light of the approach proposed here, it goes questionably far in defining propaganda as inherently negative on grounds of its being opposed to informed, rational argument and discussion. According to Marlin's definition, the purpose of propaganda includes the circumvention or suppression of informed, rational, and reflective judgment. But there are grounds for questioning such a negative way of defining "propaganda."

Thouless (1942, p. 71) has discussed the issue of whether the word "propaganda" should be defined in a negative way that makes it contrary to the aims of logical thinking. He argued that if "propaganda" means any attempt to influence attitudes or opinions of a group, it does not follow that propaganda is necessarily dishonest or irrational. To support this point, he cited a case where a true statement is made as a propaganda claim.

Case 3.3

Men's opinions may be changed by telling them a perfectly true fact that was previously unknown to them. Thus a statement that British fighting aeroplanes have shot down thirteen German bombers with a loss of seven to themselves may serve the ends of propaganda by creating confidence on our side and alarm and despondency in the enemy (if he hears it). Yet it may be perfectly true. This is one honest and reasonable way in which propaganda may influence opinion; by giving new and true information. (p. 71)

In this kind of case, propaganda presents a statement that is both true and informative to the audience. In such a case, the propaganda is not dishonest, deceptive, or against the aims of rational discussion, because informing the audience of a true statement has propaganda value. Case 3.5 provides a counter-example to the thesis that propaganda should be defined as inherently negative, in the sense of always being against informed, rational judgment or always consisting of lies or deceptions.

However, there is another sense in which propaganda does seem to be against informed, rational, and reflective thinking of the kind characteristic of a critical discussion that takes into account all the relevant information on an issue. Propaganda selects out the facts it presents to an audience, and although it may present some true statements, it may ignore other true and relevant statements that lack propaganda value, even though they are relevant, in a logical sense.

As Thouless put it, "The difficulty is that not all truth has propaganda value." He uses the following case to illustrate the point.

Case 3.4

Let us suppose that there were two air battles in one of which the enemy losses were heavy and our own were light, while in the other battle our own losses were heavy and the enemy's were light. If our own news service chose to tell us only about the first battle while the enemy news service only reported the second, there would be a certain (not very important) sense in which both sides were telling the truth. Neither side would be telling the whole truth, and it would no longer be honest propaganda. This is a very simple example of what is meant by "selection" of the facts, perhaps the commonest of all the devices used by propaganda which is intended to mislead. (p. 71)

In this case, reporting the outcome of the one battle has propaganda value to one side but not to the other. Whereas reporting the outcome of the other battle has value only to the other side. Thus both sides are telling the truth in their propaganda reports. The fault lies in the selectivity – both sides are giving a biased account.

In case 3.4, what makes the propaganda at odds with a balanced critical discussion, or a presenting of information that tells the whole truth, is the selectivity type of bias evident in the discourse. It is not that the propaganda lied or was deceptive in reporting what was not true. The problem, from a point of view of informed and rational thinking, was that the propaganda showed evidence of a bias, by ignoring those facts that had no propaganda value or would even have had propaganda disvalue. And this aspect does seem to imply that propaganda is against the aims of a rational discussion based on an informed assessment of the facts. The conclusion implied is that propaganda is necessarily irrational or dishonest in the sense of being opposed to the critical and informed rational discussion of an issue.

But now the question is raised whether all bias is necessarily bad bias, in the sense of being bias that is dishonest or contrary to the aims of logic and reasoned discussion and argumentation: Blair (1977) argued that not all bias is of the kind that could be called "bad bias" and that in many cases, bias is normal partisanship or advocacy, of the kind that is expected in a certain type of case. I have previously defined dialectical bias in argumentation as one-sidedness of an argument (1999b). Such one-sidedness, exemplified in arguing to support one's own point of view in a critical discussion, is normally expected in that type of dialogue. Advocacy is required for the dialogue to be successful, and is not a sound basis (by itself) for condemning the given argument, used in a particular case in that context, as logically defective or fallacious. Where bias does become what could be called bad bias, from a logical point of view, it occurs in the kind of case where the argumentation is supposed to be balanced, in the sense of considering the evidence on both sides of an issue, but where the argumentation is only one-sided. It is in just this kind of case that fallacies of relevance tend to occur, that is, cases in which an argument is supposed to be part of a balanced type of dialogue, such as a critical discussion, but is really being advanced in eristic fashion. In such a case, the problem is that the argumentation is not supposed to be exclusively one-sided. Such an argument can be said to be appropriate and useful as part of a quarrel. From that point of view, it could be productive in getting both sides to express buried grievances. But it is not a productive way of taking part in a critical discussion, where openness to both sides is essential. From a point of view of persuasion dialogue it could be counter-productive.

It is in just this kind of case where a dialectical shift has occurred of the kind that makes an argument appear (psychologically) to be relevant when it (logically) is not. And this explanation of fallacies of relevance pinpoints exactly the problem of evaluating arguments used in propaganda. If a discourse is supposed to be propaganda, and if the audience is aware that the discourse is of this type, then no deception or irrelevance need be involved. This can hold true even if the speaker uses arguments that appeal to the commitments and enthusiasms of the people by using emotional language slanted to one side of a cause, or even persuasive definitions that involve emotive connotations of words and phrases. However, if such a discourse purports to be a critical discussion, a rational deliberation on the issue, or some other type of dialogue requiring standards of argumentation, the evaluation could be quite different. If the argumentation uses emotional mass appeals that are inappropriate or non-contributing to the goals of that type of dialogue, then it could be correctly judged to be irrelevant. It may be psychologically relevant but dialectically irrelevant to the goals of the dialogue that the participants are supposed to be engaged in. It could reasonably be judged to be fallacious on that basis, from a dialectical point of view.

It follows then that propaganda is not in itself irrational or deceptive, in the sense that arguments in it should always be judged as critically defective, not based on good evidence, fallacious, or whatever. The key to the dialectical evaluation of propaganda is in the deception and in the dialectical shift. It is the mismatch between appearances conveyed to the mass audience by the proponent and the reality of the proponent's argumentation. The basic fault is one of irrelevance in argumentation. Propaganda is a type of discourse in which arguments can be justifiably dismissed as logically defective on grounds of irrelevance where there has been an illicit dialectical shift from some other type of dialogue that is supposed to represent a balanced account of two sides of an issue. The shift is to a purely one-sided attempt to engage in a kind of mass appeal to emotion to push in a one-sided way to gain the commitment of an audience to accepting a particular conclusion. Typically, this is an eristic type of dialogue in which the proponent has adopted the strategy of engaging in a "fight" to get action. It also often involves the reality of a negotiation type of dialogue in which the proponent is engaged in interest-based bargaining. The underlying reality is that the proponent is only putting on a superficial display of considering the arguments on both sides of the issue.

According to our proposed analysis and definition of propaganda so far, then, there are not sufficient grounds for concluding that propaganda is inherently irrational or deceptive as a type of discourse. But one key factor remains to be carefully considered.

8. Openness to Contrary Evidence

The eristic and one-sided characteristics of the argumentation used in propaganda raise further questions about the closed nature of propaganda as a type of discourse. As noted in describing the eristic characteristic of propaganda, a dichotomization typically occurs, and the words "fight" and "struggle" are often used. One of the properties of the quarrel as a type of dialogue is that the one side being advocated is never really open to defeat. Any argument that presents good evidence for the other side will be deflected by any means possible, instead of admitting that it makes a good point. Propaganda also has a biased manner of treating the evidence, indicating a lack of openness to arguments on both sides of an issue. Thus the question is raised whether propaganda is essentially a closed type of discourse that never judges an argument on the basis of the evidence that is brought forward to support it.

To begin with, it is evident from instances of propaganda that it does have a way of interpreting a situation that conforms to the viewpoint being advocated. A good case in point was found by Thouless (1942, pp. 72–73) in an article, "Germany and the Law at Sea," in the *Sunday Times* of December 24, 1939.

Case 3.5

The writer described how a British fishing trawler was sunk by a German submarine; the boats were stated to have been shelled while they were being lowered, the submarine afterwards going away. Here we have a typical atrocity story. If the shelling of the boats was deliberate and not accidental and if the submarine went away intending to leave those who were in the water to drown, this can properly be condemned as wicked and cruel behavior. The article also reported, however, that the submarine came back, picked up survivors out of the water, took off their wet clothing, and gave them hot drinks and blankets. That surely would seem to an impartial observer to be a good and kind action. It might, in fact, arouse some doubt as to whether the earlier atrocity story was not perhaps based on inaccurate observation.

The matter is not, however, so simple to the propagandist. The writer of the article says: "This sort of thing makes it clear that the German submarine commanders, while acting with true German ruthlessness, are also acting in accordance with a carefully prepared plan designed to impress upon the world that Germany is, in fact, employing chivalrous and humane methods despite the well-established and widely known facts to the direct contrary." So it appears that if the Germans are ruthless to their enemies, they are showing their ruthlessness; if they are kind to their enemies they are carrying out a plan to conceal their ruthlessness.

Thouless described the argumentation in this case as similar to that used by the handwriting expert in the Dreyfus trial, where Alfred Dreyfus was accused of giving military secrets to his country's enemies. When the handwriting on the document in evidence resembled that of Dreyfus, this was taken as proof that he wrote the document. But when other aspects of the handwriting on the document differed from that of Dreyfus, the differences were taken to prove that he had disguised his handwriting. So it was a case of "Heads I win, tails you lose." This kind of argument represents a persistent twisting of the evidence so that it always comes out only one way.

Case 3.5 shows how propaganda has a tendency to interpret a situation in such a way that the evidence presented always supports the advocated viewpoint and goes against the opposed viewpoint. What seems like it should be exactly the right sort of empirical evidence to support the other side is somehow cleverly interpreted in a way that it comes out looking like positive evidence supporting the advocated view instead. This twisting of evidence phenomenon in cases of propaganda raises questions about the verifiability and falsifiability of arguments used in propaganda generally. It suggests that argumentation used in propaganda is never really open to refutation, even by clearly opposed evidence. What one may conclude is that propaganda is an inherently closed type of dialogue, like eristic dialogue, that never really admits defeat, even when good evidence supporting the opposed view has been presented. What reinforces this conclusion are certain aspects of examples of propaganda that are often cited, such as Nazi propaganda, communist propaganda, or any political kind of argumentation meant to promote a cause in which the world is divided into converted believers and enemies. Another type of discourse that fits the description in some cases could be called religious preaching rhetoric of a kind designed for conversion of unbelievers and reaffirming the beliefs of the faithful. In this kind of rhetoric, there is no middle ground. The arguments are one-sided, and the dialogue may appear open, but there is no possibility that the proponent will ever admit defeat. A good argument for the other side will always be repelled or discounted, and that outcome is determined in advance. These cases represent a kind of argumentation that could in some cases be called fanatical. They are fanatical in the sense that the argumentation represents the proponent's ideological view of things that is not really open to refutation by means of rational arguments citing factual or verifiable evidence. These fanatical kinds of discourse always twist the evidence to support the one side exclusively, exhibiting a closed kind of attitude that I have called hardened bias. The bias is not only a one-sided argumentation but a pattern of argument that is relentlessly one-sided in a predictable way.

But is propaganda inevitably one-sided, exhibiting this pattern of hardened bias as a type of discourse? It seems that it is not. For often propaganda is most effective when it pretends to be balanced, to admit contrary evidence, and to present true statements in a reporting format. To make such a pretense effective for an audience, it has to admit some true statements and to acknowledge some evidence that does not support the point of view being advocated. Hence this twisting of evidence, while it is a typical feature of propaganda, is not so constant that it makes propaganda exhibit the hardened form of bias as an essential characteristic. Propaganda has a tendency to interpret evidence in such a way that it supports the advocated viewpoint, but it also often makes a pretense of being impartial, which requires an admitting of some evidence that may support the opposed viewpoint.

9.)eceptiveness and Relevance in Propaganda

Bernays (1923, p. 212) distinguished between education and propaganda by defining the former as "the advocacy of what we believe" and the latter as "the advocacy of what we do not believe." This definition makes propaganda a species of lying, that is, of advocating as true something one does not believe is true. Certainly, it makes propaganda deceptive in a way that makes it an insincere or dishonest kind of advocacy. But is propaganda necessarily insincere or deceptive in this way? It would seem not, for it is possible to put forward propaganda for a cause the propagandist believes in, and not all propaganda consists in saying what is false or what is known or believed to be false.

What then does the deceptiveness of propaganda consist in? The deceptiveness of propaganda is not just due to the conveying of statements that are known or believed to be false, which is really more of an accidental feature of it. The deceptiveness is due to the format within which propaganda is typically presented. For example, the news reports in Nazi Germany mixed factual reporting in with the lies and distortions to enhance the credibility of the message reported. The audience may well have been aware that what was presented to them was propaganda – that is, biased advocacy of a cause – but its presentation in the news format set in place an expectation that the function of the discourse was to report the news. Thus the deception, the clever illusion that is at the basis of propaganda as an effective kind of advocacy, is the expectation of the audience concerning the type of discourse that is supposedly being engaged in. Because it is placed within a format, like news reporting, propaganda of this kind is designed to look like information-seeking dialogue. The appearance presented is that information is being reported to the mass audience through the media. Information-seeking dialogue normally (or at least supposedly) has a balanced format of reporting facts. Thus, propaganda in such a setting is not likely to be so easily dismissed as simple partisanship and promotion deliberately used to get compliance to action by appealing to emotions and working on the audience psychologically.

So the explanation of the deceptiveness of propaganda that makes it a kind of discourse that can be used effectively for persuasion to a course of action is the dialectical shift, or change from one type of dialogue to another. By invoking a context familiar to the audience, expectations are put in place that one particular type of dialogue is being engaged in. But the reality is that a quite different sort of dialogue is being engaged in (unilaterally, and generally without the other side knowing about the real purpose of the discourse).

It is exactly this kind of dialectical shift from one type of dialogue to another that underlies the evaluation of the logic textbooks of the *argumentum ad populum* as a fallacy of relevance. In itself, there is nothing logically fallacious about appealing to enthusiasms of a crowd or to popular beliefs, if you are trying to get a mass audience to accept a conclusion they did not accept before or to commit to a policy of action. But such an argument would be irrelevant, and could be fallacious on such grounds, because the speaker was supposed to be engaged in convincing the audience with rational arguments that presented all the available evidence on both sides in a calm and dispassionate way. So the question of relevance depends on an assessment, in a given case, of what the speaker was supposed to be doing in the given situation. The question is one of what type of dialogue she was supposed to be engaged in (as known or reasonably presumed in a given case).

The next question is whether this kind of deceptiveness, which is associated with the failure of dialectical relevance, or relevance of use of arguments in a purposive context of dialogue, is essential to propaganda. Does it have to be present for a given instance of discourse to qualify as propaganda? The answer is that it does not. If it has already been made clear at the outset that the purpose of an advertisement is to sell a product or that the purpose of a speech is to rouse crowd enthusiasm to support a cause, there need not be any deception to try to pretend that the discourse is supposed to be a critical discussion of the issue or a balanced deliberation on what could be the prudent course of action. Such an advertisement or speech could be described as propaganda, because it is based on an appeal to the people and has all the other characteristics of propaganda, but the arguments used in it could be dialectically relevant. In such a case, then, an argument that appeals to the people to sell the product or to get support for the cause could be dialectically relevant within the discourse (in relation to the goals for this type of dialogue). There has been no dialectical shift, no failure of relevance, no deception, and no fallacy.

To judge the dialectical relevance of an argument used in a particular case, a critic has to look at the direction the argument is taking. Then he must identify the goal of the type of dialogue the participants are supposed to be engaged in. Then he must ask whether the argument could (actually or potentially) be used to contribute to that goal. For example, if the discourse is supposed to be a critical discussion, an argument used in that discourse is dialectically relevant if it could be used to help resolve the conflict of opinions at issue in the discussion. This can be done by supporting (or refuting) the point of view on one side or the other of the conflict. Advocacy in a critical discussion is not inherently wrong.

The question is thus raised: when is an argument dialectically relevant as used in propaganda (assuming there has been no dialectical shift from another type of discourse)? As expressed in the seventh characteristic of propaganda as a type of discourse, the goal of propaganda is to get an audience to support the aims, interests, and policies of a particular group, by getting the audience to act in compliance with these aims and interests. The goal of propaganda, somewhat like that of negotiation dialogue, is to try to get the audience or respondent to serve the interests of the person or group who is arguing. Any argument used in propagandistic discourse to contribute to the goal is dialectically relevant. Thus the relevance involved in assessing propaganda as a type of discourse is an instrumental kind. To say that an argument is relevant in this sense is not necessarily to say that it is a perfectly good argument in every respect. It is not to judge it as a rational argument that successfully furnishes evidence supporting the conclusion that a proposition is true or false, or that a course of action is a practically reasonable thing to do, or that to assent to it is a wise policy. An argument also has to meet other requirements to receive this accolade, as shown in chapters 1 and 2.

10. Evaluating Argumentation in Propaganda

The ten characteristics set out in section 6 above give a rational critic a means of identifying discourse as propaganda in a given case where a text of argumentative discourse has been presented. Of course, such an identification is bound to be subject to dispute, because arguers are often very much opposed to their discourse being labeled as propaganda, and may have a lot to lose by such an identification. But the ten defining characteristics at least give relatively clear criteria that may be used to support this identification. The second task is the analysis of argumentation in a context of use in propaganda, to try to find missing premises required to support arguments. The third task is that of evaluating the argumentation. This task has proved the most controversial and confusing. These three tasks characterize the evidence-based approach to argumentation in propaganda advocated in this chapter.

On the evidence-based approach, propaganda is not necessarily against informed, rational, reflective judgment or logical thinking on an issue, in the sense that its goal is opposed to these ways of thinking. Instead, its goal is to get the desired action by any persuasive means. If logical thinking and informed rational judgment work for that purpose, then propaganda can or will use these means. But if these means don't work, then propaganda will use other means that can or do work, including myths, stories, symbols, group loyalties, group-oriented appeal to the people, popular enthusiasms, visual imagery, and any techniques of persuasion that are psychologically effective. All these ways of arguing can be dialectically relevant in propaganda, and therefore *ad populum* arguments or appeals to the people, the kind of arguments typically used in propaganda, should not be evaluated as irrelevant and fallacious per se.

Our attitudes toward propaganda are highly ambivalent. It is a much more common type of discourse than is generally recognized, no doubt partly because people are given to the verbal practice of describing only the opposed viewpoints as propaganda, while refusing to admit that their own arguments could be so categorized. But it is a type of discourse that can be justified, or at least excused, on instrumental grounds, despite this aversive attitude. Propaganda comes under the heading of what Garner (1993) calls "convenient fictions," or stories that are useful for getting people to do things and, in particular, for running a state or country. Such convenient fictions have been advocated and justified by philosophers. Garner (p. 89) cited Plato's advocacy of the noble lie, the kind of convenient fiction in the form of a "caste-fixing myth" used by the rulers to convince the various classes, such as the guardians, that their role is a noble one.

Convenient fictions are also used in Buddhist philosophy, such as the tradition that when understanding is reached, the Buddhist doctrine can be discarded as something only provisionally needed to get there. Justification of the use of convenient fictions is similar to the kind of justification cited for some instances of lying in moral philosophy. For example, Garner cited the case of the Lotus Sutra where a father tells his children a lie in order to save their lives.

Case 3.6

In chapter three of the Lotus Sutra a parable is offered to support the practice of using expedient devices. The parable, told by the Buddha to his disciple Sariputra, is about a wealthy lord who has placed his children in a huge but run-down house that catches fire. The children are occupied with their toys, to which, we are told, they are addicted. When the father cries to them about the fire, they pay no attention, so busy are they with their play. Finally the desperate father hits upon the expedient of telling them that just those toys they most love are outside the door waiting for them. This they hear and understand, and immediately scamper to their safety. (p. 91)

In this case, the father lied to save the lives of his children, and our inclination is not to condemn the lie, at least not as wholly wrong, in the dangerous circumstances. Instead, we see it as an act that, while deceptive, was necessary to save lives, even at the expense of telling the truth. Hence it can be ethically justified.

Propaganda is not necessarily lying, as we have seen. But it is a use of argumentation that is not directed toward the truth of a matter. To justify its use, for example, in time of war, the danger of putting forward balanced arguments that fairly and dispassionately consider all the evidence on both sides of a question is cited. In particular, the danger may be the loss of life that may result by giving information or encouragement to the enemy. Propaganda is an instrumental type of discourse that is justified (appropriately) by the use of argumentation from consequences. Such arguments are not necessarily fallacious, but care is needed to watch for dialectical shifts in using them.

Certain aspects of propaganda are commonly associated with it, but by themselves do not define it or enable a one-step evaluation of it. Propaganda associated with the use of *argumentum ad populum* in appeals to crowd enthusiasm is often condemned in the context of teaching courses on logic and critical thinking. But such dismissive one-step condemnations (as noted in section 3) tend to be more reflexive than thoughtful. Propagandistic discourse sometimes takes the high ground of pretending to be a rational discussion of an issue, by portraying the opposition as being illogical, deceptive, or dishonest. But this is not an essential property of propaganda, even though it is a characteristic of the quarrel. Propaganda is not inherently deceptive or illogical, but once discourse has been identified as propaganda, it is wise to be on guard to realize that it is not a critical discussion or rational deliberation of the kind that openly examines arguments on both sides of an issue.

Thus some skepticism toward arguments used in propaganda is justifiable and prudent, from a logical point of view of critical thinking. As a normative framework of the use of argumentation of the kind that is worthy of rational assent on the grounds that it provides evidence to support a view, propaganda is not much a friend of logic. It has a kind of dialectical relevance that represents only an instrumental use of argumentation, somewhat like that of negotiation dialogue or eristic dialogue.

The best critical attitude to take toward propaganda is not to dismiss every argument used in it as critically defective, of no value as an argument, or even fallacious. For such an argument may be based on good evidence, and may be a form of reasoning that is rationally compelling. The evidence-based approach recognizes that the argumentation in this type of discourse as a whole is a biased kind of advocacy. It is specifically designed to be persuasive, to get action, and to push for the one side of an issue in as strongly partisan a manner as possible (or is useful for the purpose of getting a particular action). On the evidence-based approach, the best attitude to adopt concerning any argument said to be propaganda is one of careful skepticism, but not one of routine or holistic dismissal with respect to the arguments in the discourse.

On the other hand, if the discourse is supposed to be that of a balanced critical discussion or other type of dialogue that requires a balanced consideration of the arguments on both sides of the issue, then a different evaluation of it as argumentation is called for. Propaganda is an extremely inappropriate and inefficient method of argumentation to fulfill the goals of this type of dialogue. If the propaganda pretends to be one of these other types of dialogue, but covertly and systematically takes the one-sided approach characteristic of propaganda (as defined above) as a type of discourse, then the argumentation should be evaluated as demonstrably irrelevant, on grounds of there being an illicit dialectical shift. The deceptive tactic used here is the device of the concealed shift from one type of dialogue to another, and this is in fact the very type of tactic so often (but not always) used by propaganda to gain credibility. As shown above and in chapter 6, in some cases, the appeal to the people can be evaluated as a fallacious argument. But the evidence required to support the charge must be based on an assessment of the purpose of the discourse the argument is supposed to be part of, as compared with the way the argument has been put forward in the text of discourse of the case. This evidence can then be used to support (or refute) a charge of dialectical irrelevance in a given case.

So once something is identified as propaganda in a given case, that is not the end of the story. The job of evidence-based evaluation of the argumentation (and especially the assessment of dialectical relevance) remains to be done. This job of collecting, analyzing, and evaluating the evidence in a given case is actually quite hard work. It is much easier to use "propaganda" eristically as a negative emotive term to dismiss an opponent's views and arguments peremptorily. The problem with this approach arises when one's own arguments are thoughtlessly dismissed as propaganda.

4

Appeals to Fear and Pity

Appeals to fear and appeals to pity are two types of argumentation widely used in the media in political debates and advertising by advocacy groups, public relations firms, governments, and corporations. Johnson (2000, p. 269) has emphasized that mass media rhetoric, to be effective, needs to take the human emotions, in particular, fear and pity, into account. Both types of rhetorical argumentation can have a tremendous emotional impact on a mass audience, when presented in the right way. Mass media argumentation as a persuasive effort involves strategic maneuvering based on advocacy, audience adaption, and presentational devices, which are used to resolve a difference of opinion in one's own favor (van Eemeren and Houtlosser 1999b, 2000, 2001, 2002). On the other hand, both kinds of arguments are so well known to be subject to exploitation and manipulation that they have been traditionally classified in logic as fallacious. Recently, it has come to be recognized, however, that the traditional blanket condemnation is not warranted (Walton 1994). Appeals to emotion should be generally recognized as having legitimate standing as being, under the right conditions, reasonable arguments carrying some weight in shifting a burden of proof in a balance of considerations case where exact calculation of the outcome is not a practical possibility. But if appeals to fear and pity are sometimes rational arguments, how can we strike the right balance between recognizing their rhetorical power and the logical defects they admittedly have in some instances? The key is to probe beneath their rhetorical uses as strategically persuasive rhetorical tools to their underlying dialectical structure that makes them rationally persuasive.

In this chapter, it is shown that the key to understanding how appeals to fear and pity work as persuasive arguments can be discerned using the dual process model of persuasion (O'Keefe 1996). According to this model, there are two routes to persuasion, a central and a peripheral route. The central route requires an elaboration of the rational argumentation in the mass of evidence in a case. But appeals to fear and pity offer a short cut to a mass audience by suggesting a peripheral route. The short cut, using heuristics that appeal to fear and pity, may suggest leaping to a conclusion prematurely but is not inherently wrong or fallacious. Applying this dual process model in a helpful way requires grasping the subtle relationship between the rhetorical and dialectical routes of argumentation underlying both types of argument. To meet this requirement, a structure of practical goal-directed reasoning as a deliberation process is presented. Knowledge of this structure is shown to explain how appeals to fear and pity can be judged to be rhetorically persuasive and to explain how the dialectical task of evaluating real arguments of these kinds in particular cases can be judged to be reasonable or fallacious. Once we see more deeply how these appeals work both rhetorically and dialectically, by grasping how they function as persuasive arguments in a multi-agent framework of practical reasoning, it can be shown how, and to what degree, they are sometimes more persuasive than they should be in media argumentation.

1. Appeals to Fear and Pity in Mass Media

A classic example of the appeal to pity in mass media argumentation is the Nayirah case, summarized below (Walton 1997b, ch. 5; and Marlin 2002, pp. 194–200). An atrocity story that was covered widely in the news media in 1990, Amnesty International was the source named as confirming its authenticity (Marlin 2002, p. 196).

Case 4.1

Just after the invasion of Kuwait by Iraq in August 1990, there was a meeting of the United Nations to deliberate on the question of whether to respond with military force if Iraq did not pull out. At the meeting a videotape was shown, among other presentations. The videotape showed a fifteen-year-old girl identified only as Nayirah, who tearfully testified that she had seen Iraqi soldiers take babies out of incubators in a hospital and leave them to die on the cold floor. The story had powerful appeal and was widely publicized in the mass media, supported by an Amnesty International report on the incident. In January 1991, the U.S. Senate voted to go to war against Iraq. But then in March 1991, it was revealed that Nayirah was the daughter of a member of the Kuwaiti royal family and that there was a public relations campaign connecting Kuwaiti financing with the presentations made to the U.N. and the U.S Congress. The New York firm of Hill and Knowlton was paid over ten million dollars for persuading the public that the atrocity took place, funded by a group called Citizens for a Free Kuwait. Subsequent investigations also found no evidence that the incubator story was true.

This example is interesting for many reasons. It shows how powerful an appeal to pity can be in the mass media. The videotape was so effective because it supplied just the right emotion-arousing ingredients to attract the sympathy and fuel the indignation of the American public. It shows how this form of argument can be powerfully deceptive when used at the right moment in a developing situation. It can be seen as typical of how atrocity stories are used to try to get a reluctant nation to go to war. The technique takes the form of an appeal to pity that tugs at the heartstrings.

But how should we evaluate the appeal to pity in such a case? In this particular case it appeared that the story Nayirah told was simply false and that the mass presentation was a public relations technique used to persuade by those who paid for it and stood to gain by it. It seems like a pretty bad argument. It was intentionally deceptive, and it was based on a lie. But are appeals to pity inherently wrong, deceptive, or fallacious? The answer appears to be no. Whether this form of argument should be criticized as inappropriate or even fallacious seems to depend on the context. During a criminal trial, for example, it may be questionable if the defendant appeals to pity when the issue is whether he is guilty or not of the charge. But during the post-trial sentencing stage, it might be legitimate for the defendant to throw himself on the mercy of the court, using an appeal to compassion as his form of argumentation. There has been a tradition in Western culture of treating emotional appeals of any sort as questionable, suspicious, or even irrational. But many charitable appeals to raise funds for medical research and treatment of diseases or to aid victims of poverty are frankly based on appeal to pity. Often the appeal is visual and quite graphic. Do we want to condemn all such instances of mass media argumentation as fallacious, deceptive, or irrational? Such a policy probably goes too far in a negative direction. As even Aristotle acknowledged, appeal to pity is a form of argument that is central to rhetoric.

McClurg (1992) has used argumentation on both sides of the gun control issue to illustrate emotional appeals in rhetoric. He argues that such appeals are not always fallacious, however, in a democratic society where political action rightly depends on persuasion, and persuasion depends on rhetoric. However, McClurg uses the following case, among many others, to show how bad rhetoric can take the form of fallacies. This particular argument in the gun control debate appeals to both fear and pity at the same time.

Case 2.2

> In arguing against the Brady bill, Representative Barbara Vucanovich, a Republican from Nevada, invoked the tragic episode of serial murders that occurred in Gainesville, Florida, in the summer of 1990. She posed the following query: "If the Brady bill were law, who knows how many more young women would be dead in Gainesville because they had to wait to protect themselves." Then, in almost the same breath, she urged her fellow representatives "not to let their judgments be clouded by the antigun lobby's emotional banter." (pp. 65–66)

McClurg evaluates this case by commenting, "Conjuring up the nightmarish image of defenseless coeds being butchered by a mad killer was a blatant attempt to use emotion to generate opposition to the Brady bill" (p. 66). McClurg sees the emotional appeal as fallacious because the argument is weak and questionably relevant. But however the argument in this case is evaluated, it certainly is an excellent example of an appeal to pity and fear combined into one argument. This kind of case is common in cases of political rhetoric. The problem of having an objective framework in which such arguments can be fairly and reasonably evaluated requires not just concentrating on the fallacious cases, however. Because in other cases the same kinds of emotional appeals can be reasonable arguments, the prior problem is to determine the right conditions under which such an argument can be correct and reasonable. But what are the right conditions? To answer this question, it is shown in this chapter that we need to consider multi-agent communication structures containing sequences of means-end reasoning in which agents have dialogues about their goals and about the actions required to achieve these goals.

The first thesis argued in this chapter is that arguments appealing to fear and pity share an underlying inferential structure that can be modeled by Aristotelian practical reasoning. The second thesis is that such arguments are neither deductive nor inductive in nature. They are defeasible arguments that shift a burden of proof onto the side of a respondent in a multi-agent dialogue. Their proper function in a dialogue is to carry a certain weight, or occupy a ground, in a dialogue on a contested issue in which there is uncertainty and on which exact knowledge cannot directly or conclusively be brought to bear. In light of these two theses, recommendations are made on how to analyze and evaluate appeals to fear and pity. Once an objective framework is set in place for seeing how such an argument can be correctly used to make a legitimate point in a given case, then the analysis can be extended to achieve a solid basis for understanding and dealing with the fallacious cases.

2. Appeals to Fear

The fear appeal argument is currently recognized within the social sciences as a distinctive type of argument format used by those in the business of changing public opinion and attitudes through the mass media. Fear appeal arguments are currently in vogue with advertisers, corporations, public relations firms, and government agencies – all the powerful organizations that use the media to mold public opinion. Fear appeal arguments are typically used on issues of heath and safety. One ad tells smokers they will die an excruciating death if they do not quit smoking. An ad for Trojan-Enz, Inc. shows a man with a serious expression talking about the need to use condoms. He relates that he has heard the Surgeon General's warning about the new severe threats of venereal disease (LaTour and Zahra 1989, p. 62). Another warns teenagers that their teeth will decay if they do not brush them properly. An ad for American Express Travelers Checks shows a couple on vacation victimized by a robbery and left in a state of shock and desperation (LaTour and Zahra 1989, p. 62). In another ad for the Lifecall System, an elderly woman falls and pushes the "panic button" worn around her neck. Paramedics and physicians are shown responding to the medical emergency. In an anti-smoking ad, a woman reaches for her cigarette, and then puts the filter end into a small hole at the base of her throat. She inhales deeply, and a message comes on the screen, "The tobacco industry denies that nicotine is addictive." The message is that the woman has lost her vocal chords to cancer, exposing the lie of the tobacco industry (Allossery 1999).

The much-publicized ad that started all the interest in fear appeal ads was the famous Grim Reaper ad produced by the National Advisory Committee on AIDS in Australia in 1987. The ad portrayed a skeletal, black-shrouded, skull-headed figure carrying a scythe. This figure was shown throwing bowling balls that knocked down a series of typical Australians, including a housewife, a baby, a footballer, and a little girl. The message was that all members of the community, and not just homosexual males, were at risk from AIDS. The general perception was that the ad was successful (Morgan 1987). Following this perception, use of fear appeal ads has become highly popular. Government agencies in Canada, for example, produced the following fear appeal ads. A man at a bar is shown squeezing a bunch of cigarettes over a beer glass. As a brown goo oozes into the glass, a voice-over intones the message that arsenic, cyanide, mercury, lead, and other chemicals in cigarettes form a "lethal brew" that kills 40,000 Canadians every year. In another ad, a baby in a crib is gasping for air as smoke drifts under the door and into the room. In one much-shown ad, teenagers are pictured drinking at a party, and their car crashes as they drive home. The boy who drove the car tries to follow the stretcher as his girlfriend is taken away in an ambulance. In the next scene police officers appear telling the girl's mother that she is dead.

Fear appeals are not only used in advertising and in public safety messages. They are also widely used in political debates, and particularly by advocacy groups in rhetoric designed to influence legislation on public policy issues. Three excellent cases of the use of fear appeal arguments on the gun control issue by the National Rifle Association have been cited by McClurg (1992, p. 67). The first used graphic pictures and a series of rhetorical questions.

Case 4.3

> After the 1992 riots that followed in the wake of the jury's decision to acquit most of the police officers charged with using excessive force against motorist Rodney King, the NRA employed a four-page advertisement to boost membership by shamelessly exploiting the fear and horror generated by images of the violence. The advertisement, featuring color pictures of looters and burning buildings, asked: "Must your glass be shattered? Must your flesh and blood be maimed? Must your livelihood be looted? Must all you've built be torn down? . . . What will it take before you stand up with the one group that will *stand for no more?*"

A second ad depicted a woman's mangled locket under the headline, "Your mother just surprised two burglars who don't like surprises." A third ad showed a high heel shoe with the heel broken off, and read, "He's followed you for two weeks. He'll rape you in two minutes." These ads all have a factual basis, and the fears they appeal to may not be at all unreasonable. Yet one can't help having the impression that one is being manipulated somehow in a questionable way by the ad. On the other hand, the NRA should have the right to present the strongest and most persuasive possible arguments to represent their view, and to try to get others to accept it. So we are perplexed by these appeals to emotion and frustrated by the problem of finding an objective way of evaluating what is reasonable or unreasonable about them. If we had some objective way of judging such arguments, it would be a powerful tool, for both logic and rhetoric.

Social scientists have conducted many empirical investigations of fear appeal arguments to try to see how they work to change behavior and attitudes with experimental subjects. The general perception is that fear appeal arguments do work, but not everyone agrees. Some think that such arguments are inherently negative and that positive ones work better to persuade an audience to take action (Tripp and Davenport 1988). The empirical work has not been very conclusive, mainly, it seems, because fear appeal arguments have a cognitive component that is not well understood. Three main theories or models have been formulated to try to explain how fear appeals work in modifying behavior. According to the drive theory, in a fear appeal, there is a so-called drive, or bodily state that leads to activity, that moves a subject toward reduction of fear (Dillard 1994, p. 297). According to Rogers (1983), the drive theory had to be abandoned because it failed to show a direct relationship between the drive (fear) and attitude change. The parallel response model cites two independent systems at work in fear appeals: fear control, which is seen to work in a way similar to drive theory, and danger control, which involves changing the circumstances to reduce the danger (Leventhal 1970). In Leventhal's parallel response model, fear control and danger control are seen as two simultaneously operating variables, rather than as sequentially related (Leventhal 1971, p. 1211). A criticism of this model is that it does not predict how the subject will reason in choosing the one response or the other. According to the protection motivation model, response to a fear appeal depends on three factors: (1) the perception of the severity of the danger, (2) the probability of occurrence of the danger, and (3) the belief in the effectiveness of the subject's coping response (Rogers

1983, pp. 157–158). This third factor refers to how well the subject feels she can cope with the danger, given her existing resources. The protection motivation model sees the subject as a kind of rational calculator. Because it stresses the cognitive aspect so much, some critics say it has lost sight of the "fear" in fear appeals (Tanner, Day, and Crask, 1989, p. 269). While all three models have been valuable in bringing out different aspects of fear appeals, none has been regarded as altogether successful in predicting experimental outcomes.

In the logical tradition, fear appeal arguments have been treated under the category of the *argumentum ad baculum*, which includes the use of threats and force in argumentation, as well as fear appeals. The early textbooks typically cited use of force, but most of the logic textbooks in the first half of the twentieth century featured examples of threat appeal arguments. These are arguments in which the proponent actually makes a threat to the respondent in order to try to get the respondent to accept her conclusion. The speech act of making a threat requires the proponent conveying to the respondent the message "If you don't accept what I propose, I will see to it that a cited harmful outcome (to you) comes about." The speech act of making a threat goes beyond the speech act of warning in that the proponent actually commits herself to (undertakes) bringing about the harmful outcome, if the recommended action is not carried out. As stated above, most of the older textbooks regard threat appeal arguments as the central instances of the *argumentum ad baculum*. But the trend in the more recent textbooks is to include and emphasize fear appeal arguments under this category as well. Fear appeal arguments, by definition, do not rest, as part of the argument structure, on the making of a threat by the proponent.

Both fear and threat appeals appear to be practical kinds of arguments that address the self-interest or personal safety of the person to whom the argument is addressed. Fear appeals, in particular, postulate a state of affairs that is perceived as a danger to the respondent. Then the fear appeal argument recommends an action as an indicated way of avoiding the danger.

3. Appeals to Pity

Like fear appeals, appeals to pity have been widely used by public relations experts in commercial ads and initiatives of various kinds. Most visibly, Third World children are shown in order to solicit food or charitable contributions. Typically, a TV ad or letter features a particular child who is evidently starving or in some other kind of distress. The appeal then directs the reader or viewer to send a check or credit card number, to the organization. I personally receive a steady stream of these ads in the mail. On January 23, 2002, I received a brochure from World Vision.

The World Vision Example

On the cover of the brochure was a large photograph of a child's distraught face, accompanied by the words, "Let my heart be broken with the things that break the heart of God." Inside the brochure, the same child's picture was reprinted, with three other pictures of faces of small children, two said to be from Africa and one from Peru. The message inside the brochure read as follows.

World Vision's founder, Bob Pierce, wrote those words more than 50 years ago. It was during the Korean War, and he was deeply moved by the suffering of war orphans he saw there. Back home, he couldn't forget those little ones. He began recruiting friends and relatives to help them. That's how World Vision was born. And today, caring people sponsor over 1 million needy children around the world through World Vision. Will you join them today? As a sponsor, you'll help provide things like clean water, schools, clinics and agricultural training that will help lift your sponsored child, his/her family, and community out of poverty. For a dollar a day, you can help change a child's life forever. To start your sponsorship, just return the coupon below. You'll receive information and a photograph of a child who needs your help. Let your heart be broken. Sponsor a child today.

At the bottom of the brochure was a form to be filled out, asking for a credit card number or a check. The appeal to pity in this ad is based on a formula common to many of these ads. A prominent photograph, usually of a child who appears to be in distress, is supposed to evoke an emotional reaction on the part of the respondent. The premise is, "Here is something bad, a problem that needs to be solved." The recommended solution is to send money. This form of the appeal to pity appears to be quite legitimate, on the ground that if people are to be persuaded of the urgency of the need, telling the story of a particular child is probably the most graphic way to convey the appeal. Whether the solution recommended is the right one, or one that will really solve the problem, is of course something that should be examined. Before sending money, it would also be appropriate to ask critical questions about the agency sponsoring the ad and to have some assurance that they really spend a reasonable proportion of the money received on helping those individuals said to be in distress. There is much more that could be said about the technique of appeal to pity used in these ads. One assumes that the technique is effective in collecting money, because such ads are so very common. However skeptical one might feel about them, though, it would not be justified to declare that the appeal to pity used in them is a fallacious argument. Thus the problem is posed in a sharpened form. When is an appeal to pity fallacious and when is it not fallacious? Assessing each case individually could be a non-trivial task.

A method for helping the reader to distinguish, on a case-by-case basis, between the fallacious and non-fallacious uses of this argument is presented in Walton (1997b). The fallacious uses of appeal to pity have been widely illustrated in the traditional treatment of the *ad misericordiam* fallacy in the logic textbooks. It is not hard to appreciate why this type of argumentation has been classified as a fallacy. Its use as an effective courtroom tactic is well known to pleaders. Appeal to pity has frequently been exploited with amazing success as a deceptive tactic of argumentation, even in ancient trials, so notoriously that its traditional treatment as a fallacy is well warranted. It can be a powerful form of argument, as all lawyers know, and it can be used in a manipulative way to influence the decision of a jury.

The analysis in Walton (1997b) used a case study method to examine uses of appeals to pity and compassion in real arguments, in order to classify, analyze, and evaluate the types of arguments used in these appeals. One case studied was that of the Jerry Lewis telethon for muscular dystrophy, which was much criticized by activists for the rights of the disabled on the grounds that Lewis exploited pity by televising pathetic images of the "tortured bodies" of disabled children to raise money. In the Nayirah example, outlined above, the appeal to pity was instrumental in Senate deliberations that led to the invasion of Kuwait by U.S. forces. In another classic case, a student argued that if his professor didn't give him a passing grade, he would be deported, and then shot. As evidence of how widely accepted the use of appeal to pity by students has become, one professor found the following complaint on one of his student evaluations: "Not once, when grading an exam, has the instructor shown mercy, or signs of heart." This remark is interesting in suggesting how legitimate the appeal to pity is perceived to be as a basis that should be used for evaluating assignments.

The problem with many cases of use of appeal to pity by students is that the emotional appeal is put forward as a reason for changing a grade or a deadline, even when there is no basis on the merits for making such a change. The suggestion is that the professor should take action to avert an allegedly harmful outcome, even though the action would not be justified in light of what the professor should do as a fair grader. A fair grader is obliged to judge academic work on the merit of the work in her discipline. Each case needs to be judged on its individual merits, but the problem is that in many cases, appeals to pity are weak and poorly substantiated as logical inferences, yet pressed forward in an aggressive and emotionally powerful presentation that is designed to overwhelm the critical judgment of the respondent.

One fault often cited in logic textbooks is failure of relevance. But in some cases, appeals to pity can be relevant, yet still fallacious because they are exploited to have a much greater impact than should properly be the case. The successful use of such arguments for purposes of persuading an audience often has to do with the timing of the argument at the opportune moment in presenting a larger body of evidence. If the case hangs in the balance, a strategic use of appeal to pity just at the right moment can tilt the burden of proof enough toward one side to make a big difference in the outcome of the case. But relevance in the dialectical sense appropriate for evaluating argumentation depends on the context of use of a given argument in relation to some kind of communicative exchange. As noted above, in a debate on matters of public safety, appeals to fear or pity – for example, in gun control rhetoric – could be relevant. The reason is that the proponents or the opponents of a gun control bill should properly use the arguments that will persuade the public to come to accept their view of the matter. Emotional arguments, such as appeals to fear or pity, are in fact often the most highly persuasive on matters of public debate. In principle, then, such arguments should be regarded as relevant, unless it can be shown in specific cases why they are not. The reason is that in public deliberations on what to do on a social issue, the ramifications are so complex that neither party can have any claim to know the truth of the matter. It is a matter of using good judgment to weigh the relative strengths and weaknesses of the argumentation on both sides. That is the way it should be in a democracy.

The problem of how to evaluate appeals to pity, and accord each its proper weight in a case, seems to be a formidable one. The first step is to get some grasp of the structure of the reasoning used in this kind of appeal. Because, presumably, appeals to pity can be reasonable arguments in at least some cases (even if they tend to be weak arguments by themselves), the place to begin is to describe the kinds of premises used in such an argument, and the kind of conclusion they are used to support. It will be the thesis of this chapter that such arguments have the conclusion that the person to whom the argument was directed should carry out a recommended course of action. The premises support such a claim by appealing to the interests or goals of that person, and alleged facts about his circumstances.

4. The Respondent-to-Dialogue Problem

Many mass media rhetorical arguments, including those that appeal to fear and pity, do not appear to fit the dialogue format outlined above as a model for evaluating argumentation. In the types of dialogue outlined above, the argumentation was composed of an exchange of connected question and reply moves between the proponent and the respondent. In some of the examples, this sort of dialogue exchange was evident. For example, in the gun control case, a debate was ongoing. And in the Nayirah example, when the video was presented in the U.S. Congress, the context was also that of a debate. But in the examples of fear appeal ads, the role of the respondent is questionable. The ad was targeted at a mass audience. No single respondent was meant to be the receiver of the message. And if there was any dialogue, it appears to be curiously one-sided. The proponent broadcast the message or paid to have it sent out by the media. But the audience did not then reply and start a dialogue. The message just went out. The audience presumably saw the presentation and was presumably influenced by it in some manner. Maybe all it did was influence many of them to turn to a different channel. But the message can be presumed to have had some sort of effect. There the dialogue (if it was one) ended. The audience never had a chance to raise questions, to criticize the argument in it, or to verbally respond by agreeing or disagreeing with it. So what kind of dialogue is that?

In contrast to some cases of argumentation, in which the proponent and the respondent are clearly identified, rhetorical mass media arguments tend to be diffuse as a class. They often seem to share many characteristics with comparable arguments used to influence a single respondent, or a smaller, more precisely defined group of respondents. But that contrast by itself is perhaps the first characteristic of mass media arguments. They are diffuse, in that they are not aimed at a specific respondent. Instead, they are aimed at a mass audience at a national or even international level. They may even be attempts to influence an audience or readership that continually changes over time. Some readers who may be strongly influenced by the argument may not even have been born at the time the argument was expressed in writing. At that point, others who were influenced by it may be long dead. Thus mass media arguments are diffuse in this respect. It may be problematic to define who the respondent is or was meant to be.

As noted in chapter 2, section 10, Govier (1999, ch. 11) expressed this problem very well in the title of her chapter, "When They Can't Talk Back: The Noninteractive Audience and the Theory of Argument." She was very skeptical about solving this problem using dialectical models of the kind presented in chapter 2 when she wrote that envisioning a challenger who fits one's intended audience is virtually impossible when addressing a mass audience, given that its views are likely to be "heterogeneous and largely unknown" (p. 187).

Blair (1998) was the first to formulate this problem, when he complained that in cases where the audience is unknown, cannot talk back, cannot be responded to, and has unknown characteristics, the current dialectical models of argumentation are stretched out of shape. Krabbe (1998) replied to Blair's complaint by suggesting that in such problematic cases that differ from the primary model, the other party or parties in the dialogue have to be envisioned as participants who are discrete and hypothetically present, and thus able to ask questions or make objections. Govier, however, remained highly skeptical about this sort of response. She argued that when the views of the audience are not specifically known, appealing to a hypothetical notion of audience to whom an argument was directed is not generally useful to decide matters such as the acceptability of premises, the acceptability of missing premises, the sufficiency of the reasoning, or other matters like burden of proof that are important for argument evaluation. This response seems to split dialectic and rhetoric apart, because audience is a fundamental component in rhetorical argumentation.

This difficulty of matching the dialogue model to cases of mass media argumentation where the audience can't talk back could be called the respondent-to-dialogue, or RTD problem. The problem is that there appears to be no real dialogue interaction, or only a partial one at best in such cases. A dialogue has five basic components (Hamblin 1970, 1971). It has two participants, usually called the proponent and the respondent.

The two participants take turns making verbal moves (speech acts). And the resulting pairs of moves produce an orderly sequence. There are rules governing each move, telling us whether a move was appropriate or not, as a response to the prior move. And finally, at each move, propositions are inserted into or deleted from the commitment set of the participant who made the move (and possibly from the commitment set of the other participant as well). In the fear appeal ads cited above, for example, it is unclear whether these five components are present. There certainly was an initial move by the proponent, in the form of the argument put forward in the ad. And therefore we can't really evaluate the argument using the conventional methods of the new dialectic. But it is doubtful whether the other four components of a dialogue were present. There was some target audience; that is presumed by the construction of the ad. But the target audience was merely a device that the ad presenter used to aim the argument in the ad. If the ad was broadcast in the media, then of course there was a real audience, or group of viewers. But this was a diffuse group that changed each time the ad was aired. Could this set of persons be the "respondent"? It seems hard to say. The problem is that they can't really continue the dialogue by asking the ad presenter critical questions.

Because of the RTD problem, it is hard to see how the fear appeal ads fit the dialogue model. And thus it is hard to see how they could ever be analyzed as fallacious arguments on the dialectical model. The best that could be done to try to get a match is to portray the mass media argument as like the commercial ad in involving a hypothetical kind of dialogue interaction. We can say that the proponent had a target audience in mind when he designed the ad. The ad was intended to be persuasive. It was aimed at getting a group of respondents to carry out a designated action or to come to accept some particular proposition as true. Thus it seems reasonable to say that the argument was used as a persuasion attempt. Something like what might be called a speech act of persuasion was central to the function of the argument. If the arguer was trying to persuade the audience, he had to try to anticipate the audience's response to it. And presumably it was the anticipation that guided the construction of the argumentation in the ad. This hypothetical dialogue interaction can be better understood by bringing in the notion of an agent.

Suppose we look at the proponent and the respondent in a dialogue as agents. Both have the capability to carry out actions. Both have the capability for practical reasoning. Both have an ability to understand how sequences of actions go in common situations. Thus, the one can be seen as having the ability to anticipate how the other might normally be expected to react in a situation familiar to them both. If one is fearful of a dangerous situation, then perhaps the other is likely to be as well. Agents are also familiar with common forms of argumentation. Thus an agent can base his argument on anticipating how another agent is likely to react to an argument. The ability to anticipate an objection or question and to deal with it in advance in a dialogue is called *prolepsis* in classical rhetoric. Using prolepsis, an agent can use advance strategy to deal with objections he reasonably expects to be felt by his respondent or audience, even before the respondent has voiced that objection. In other words, an agent has the capability of making up a strategy of argumentation when dealing with another agent. If this is right, then perhaps mass media argumentation can be viewed usefully in dialectical terms. The strategic interaction could at least be seen as based on a dialogue interaction between agents. But what is an argument strategy, in the new dialectic?

The examples of the use of appeals to fear and pity in mass media in this chapter show that the proponent who designs the mass media message has a certain strategy in mind. Each example is a crafted argument used by an argument presenter to try to persuade a mass audience. According to the new dialectic, the argument should be analyzed by seeing its presenter and the mass audience as two participants engaged in a dialogue. This approach requires some way of formally representing the notions that the participant is capable of carrying out a strategy of argumentation, and also has the capability for deception. Such capabilities are based on anticipation by one dialogue partner of the expected moves of the other party, and also on the use of an organized attempt to exploit this anticipation by making tactical moves in advance. The problem is to figure out how the current systems of formal dialectic can be extended to take these capabilities into account and to model them in a way that is useful for analysis and evaluation of argumentation and fallacies.

An approach that could be considered would be to broaden the notion of a participant in a persuasion dialogue, or other type of dialogue, by thinking of each participant as having properties of an agent. An agent is an entity that has the capability for action. An agent also has goals. He can modify his actions when he sees their consequences. Using feedback and the capability for practical reasoning, the agent can change his actions and make the sequence of actions move closer to his goals. The same properties can apply to verbal actions in a dialogue. In a deliberation dialogue, for example, an agent can alter his plan of action once certain undesirable aspects of these actions are pointed out to him. An agent can also anticipate the expected plausible moves of another agent with whom he is engaged in dialogue, and change plans to fit in with these anticipated moves. In the current systems of formal dialogue recognized in argumentation theory, a participant in a dialogue is seen as a simple unanalyzed unit with a set of statements (commitment set) attached. A participant makes moves according to the dialogue rules. But is such a participant capable of carrying out strategies of argumentation based on anticipation of the moves of the other participant?

Planning is a field of artificial intelligence in which strategies take the form of sequences of actions (Wilensky 1983). There is also the notion of a partial strategy used by Hamblin (1987) in his work on the logic of imperatives. Can these notions of action strategies of agents be transferred to dialogue theory for argumentation? A strategy in a dialogue could perhaps be seen as a device that a participant uses to anticipate the plausible future moves of the other participant in the dialogue. Putting all these components together could give us a way of modeling mass media appeals to fear and pity as a form of argumentation fitting the dialogue framework. But many aspects of the model are, so far, unclear and not very plausible. The central point is that both the arguer and the audience can be seen as agents engaged in a dialogue type of interaction in which one anticipates the reaction of the other to an argument. The anticipation or *prolepsis* is an essential part of the argumentation strategy, and the part that makes the argumentation possible to analyze in a dialectical format. What makes the strategy possible, in turn, is the capability of both agents to engage in practical reasoning.

5. Simulative Reasoning

Simulation theory is important in psychology, biology, and cognitive science as a hypothesis to explain factors of human and animal behavior that would otherwise be hard to understand. In an experiment (Premack and Woodruff 1978), a chimpanzee was shown a film of an actor trying unsuccessfully to reach for some bananas dangling overhead. The chimp was then offered a choice among several pictures that showed what the actor's next move could be for getting the bananas. The chimp chose a picture of the actor moving some crates underneath the bananas. The experimenters took this choice to represent the best, or most practical move, as a way of getting the bananas in the situation pictured. What hypothesis could account for the outcome of this experiment? Simulation theory explains the outcome by postulating an act of imagination on the part of the chimp. On this explanation, the chimp imagines itself trying to reach for the bananas. It is presumably familiar with this kind of problem from its own experience. So the chimp, according to the theory, sees itself dragging some crates under the bananas. Thus the chimp can grasp the correct solution, even though it is the actor, not the chimp, who is now seen as being in that kind of situation. If simulation theory is a good hypothesis, it shows that animals as well as people are capable of reasoning about the reasoning of another practical agent.

Gordon (1986) used the example of strategic thinking in chess as a dialogue model to show how simulative reasoning is used when one person tries to anticipate the reactions of another person. He began by observing that chess players report that they often visualize the chessboard from the opponent's point of view. In this act of empathy, a chess player visualizes his pieces on the board as being his opponent's pieces, and the opponent's pieces as his. Is a chess player, in performing this act of simulative reasoning, trying to imaginatively duplicate the actual beliefs or feelings of the other player, or only trying to put himself strategically into the position of the other player? Probably, both kinds of simulation are involved. Of course, strategic simulation is the more important one. But the player should also take into account any patterns of play or habits or special strategic preferences of the other player that he knows about.

How should simulative reasoning be defined? In the definition of Goldman (1995, p. 189), "simulation" means "pretending to have the same initial desires, beliefs, or other mental states that the attributor's background information suggests the agent has." Goldman's definition of simulative reasoning represents the belief-desire-intention approach. But there is an alternative: the commitment-based approach based on practical reasoning as a model. On this model, the secondary agent who performs the simulation proceeds by understanding the problem faced by the primary agent. The secondary agent can then use this shared practical knowledge to grasp the actions that he saw the primary agent take in order to take steps to solve the problem.

Collingwood (1946) adopted a commitment-based approach in his theory of historical explanation as reenactment. He gave the example (p. 283) of a historian studying the edict of a Roman emperor called the Theodosian code. Collingwood posed the historian's task as one in which the historian tries to see this problem as the emperor saw it himself. Of course, the historian cannot be in the emperor's real situation. But what he can do is to study the details of the past era and try to put himself in the mind of the other person in the distant past, and reconstruct the problem faced by that other person. Collingwood described the process as one of reenactment. To perform a reenactment, the historian must go through roughly the same process of thinking the Roman emperor did. Only thus can the historian come to understand the reasons why the emperor came to the particular solution of the problem that he in fact came to. Dray (1964, 1995) explained this process of simulative reasoning as one of problem solving based on the capability for goal-directed deliberation. The secondary agent must "enter the practical deliberations" of the primary agent by understanding the purposes the primary agent had, and the means that he thought he had at his disposal as he saw the facts at the time (1964, pp. 11–12). Collingwood's theory of history as reenactment was also shown by Martin (1977) to be based on simulative practical reasoning. According to Martin's interpretation of Collingwood's theory, the secondary agent can only reenact the actions of the primary agent because both are agents, and therefore share the capability of practical reasoning. Building on Collingwood's insights into historical explanations, it is possible to define simulative reasoning in a commitment-based approach built on practical reasoning. This approach is not based on a psychological notion of empathy in which the secondary agent tries to recreate the primary agent's actual beliefs or intentions. It is based on the shared practical reasoning capabilities of the two agents. The agents must be seen as rational agents.

According to the commitment-based definition, simulative reasoning involves two rational agents. A rational agent is an entity that is capable of reasoning, but also capable of collecting and using information, including information about the actions of another agent. This information can include feedback, when one agent sees the consequences of its own action on another agent. Simulative reasoning is a form of dual agent reasoning in which one agent is reasoning about the reasoning of another agent. In simulative reasoning the one agent used his own capability of reasoning as the basis of his reasoning about another agent's reasoning. Simulative reasoning can also be reflexive, meaning that an agent can reason about his own reasoning. Reflexive or single-agent simulative reasoning is called autoepistemic reasoning in artificial intelligence. Moore (1985, pp. 78–79) illustrated autoepistemic reasoning with the example of an agent giving his reasons for his belief that he does not have an older brother. The simulative reasoning in this example can be displayed as follows.

If I did have an older brother, I would know about it.
I don't know of any older brothers.
Therefore, I must not have any older brothers.

This example of autoepistemic reasoning has the form of argument traditionally known in logic as argument from ignorance (*argumentum ad ignorantiam*). Although it was long thought to be a fallacy in logic, the argument from ignorance is a common and often reasonable form of argument in everyday thinking (Walton 1996).

Using simulative reasoning is required in successful persuasion dialogue. It is not unique to mass media persuasion. But here it has special features, because the respondent is not a single individual but a mass audience composed of many individuals who may think very differently about any issue or problem. But recognizing the importance of simulative reasoning is the key to solving the problem of coming to understand how dialectical argumentation and rhetorical argumentation are related.

6. The Dual Process Model of Persuasion

The problem in many of the cases cited above is that the decision to be made involves a complex deliberation in which there is a large mass of evidence on both sides. But then when the emotional appeal to fear or pity is made, it is so powerful that it suggests simply disregarding all the other evidence and following an impulse. The impulse is to give in to the powerful emotional appeal of the moment. That is why, in some of these cases, the appeal to emotion is so compelling. In the student's appeal to pity case, for example, the professor is supposed to judge and evaluate the student's performance by the evidence of his work in the course. But when the student tearfully appeals to pity, she suggests that he forget all that relevant but complex evidence. Instead, her appeal suggests that he go by how he feels at the moment. As the Nayirah case shows, the strategy is in the timing. Timing of an argument is especially important if the mass of evidence on both sides is balanced. The emotional appeal, coming at the right time just before the decision is to be made, may tilt the balance one way or the other. Appeal to fear and pity function in this way as shortcut arguments. There is a mass of evidence that needs to be weighed and thoughtfully considered on both sides of an issue. When the appeal to fear or pity comes along, it suggests, "Why bother?" Instead, the impulse is to go for the short cut, the emotional appeal of the moment. This kind of appeal is especially powerful to a respondent who doesn't understand the larger body of relevant evidence in a case or who doesn't care about it. The option given is to just go with your emotions of the moment and put all the other evidence aside.

The short-cut pattern can be explained by the dual process model of persuasion of O'Keefe (1994, pp. 61–62). In this model, what is called "elaboration" is systematic issue-relevant thinking about the matter in hand. The model hypothesizes that in some cases, receivers of a persuasive message will engage in extensive elaboration, while in other cases, receivers display relatively little elaboration. Part of the reason for the disparity in cases might be that receivers don't understand the message. Another part might be that they just can't bother to make the effort required. Thus according to the dual process model, there are "two routes to persuasion." Central route persuasion involves careful examination of the information and arguments in a message, and careful thinking about them. Peripheral route persuasion is characterized by low elaboration, and using instead a simple decision rule to come to a conclusion. An example of peripheral route persuasion would be the kind of case where the message receiver likes the message sender or finds him credible, and simply accepts the message for this reason.

The dual process model of persuasion can help to explain how emotional appeals work. The appeal to fear or pity is based on the simple decision rule indicated by the argumentation scheme. The appeal to pity follows this decision rule. If the respondent can supposedly help this person who is in such a pitiable state by means of compassionate act X, then compassionate act X is indicated as the right action to take. The conclusion is to help this person by carrying out action X. The appeal to fear follows this decision rule. If the respondent wants to avoid fearful outcome X, he should comply by carrying out recommended action Y. The conclusion is to carry out action Y. Both decision rules are simple and require little elaboration to act on. What makes these appeals so powerful is that they are so inviting. They suggest that instead of worrying about all the complex body of arguments and evidence that is required for direct route persuasion, there is an option. The alternative is to take the route of peripheral persuasion by giving in to the emotional appeal now before you. Especially if the mass of relevant evidence requiring elaboration is complex and difficult to understand or evaluate, or if it appears to be balanced on two sides, making a decision difficult, the alternative being offered may be very attractive.

Jackson (1994) has probed more deeply into the question of why fallacies are persuasive than has most of the literature, which has tended to concentrate on the question of why fallacies are incorrect arguments. To explain why fallacious arguments can be persuasive, she has stressed the importance of simplifying strategies called heuristics used by the receiver of an argument (p. 105). For example, an audience might use a credibility heuristic when the audience goes by characteristics of the source, in judging an appeal to expert opinion, in place of examining the evidence supporting what the source says. Why do people tend to use such a heuristic? There may be many reasons. They may be unable to evaluate the evidence. After all, if one is not an expert in the given field, it can be very hard to understand what the expert is saying. Or they may be unmotivated. It may in fact be a lot of work to try to probe critically into the reasons given by the expert. Hence it is understandable why, in so many cases, the heuristic offers a short cut that is easy to take. The alternatives that are available may be very difficult. They may require a lot of elaboration and work. They may even seem so difficult as to be impossible. And following the heuristic, or short-cut rule, is not inherently unreasonable as a mode of argument processing. In many cases, it might lead to the right conclusion. Hence using the heuristic, and choosing the peripheral route of persuasion over the direct route, can be very attractive.

These observations and theories suggest a basis for helping to explain how appeals to fear and pity in mass media arguments are persuasive. They put in place for the receiver a simple heuristic that can be very attractive under the right conditions. Looking through a mass of evidence on a complex issue can appear to be difficult, or even impossible to the respondent. He may be confused or uncertain about the issue. The issue may involve complex scientific knowledge that the respondent can't be confident about or even claim to understand very well. Furthermore, the mass of arguments on both sides of the issue may appear to be deadlocked. On the other hand, an appeal to fear or pity has immediate emotional impact. It is a short cut, and perhaps a very attractive one at that. If a decision has to be made right away, the appeal to fear or pity commands attention right now. It can loom over complex matters of evidence that may appear more remote.

7. The Structure of Appeals to Fear

On the subject of whether or when fear appeal arguments should be evaluated, the logic textbooks have fallen into a presumption that they generally are fallacious. But especially when we see examples of fear appeal arguments used by governments for purposes of public health and safety, people do not see these arguments as fallacious. Because they are offered for a good purpose, the presumption is that these arguments are legitimate, and should not be judged to be fallacious (certainly not, in general, at any rate). In many cases, this presumption appears to be quite reasonable. So a problem is posed. Which criteria should we use to evaluate fear appeal arguments, so that in particular instances, we can tell which are fallacious and which are not? The first step in this endeavor is to analyze the logical form of fear appeal arguments.

Once many cases of the fear appeal argument have been observed and studied, it becomes apparent that certain basic properties of the structure of the argument are common to them all. The fear appeal argument has two basic premises. The first premise presents a state of affairs that is dangerous to the respondent, and is often called "threatening." It represents a harm to the respondent, in the sense of something that is very much against the respondent's personal goals and interests. Such goals, in a fear appeal argument, typically have to do with the respondent's bodily preservation and safety. The outcome represented is something the respondent (presumably) wants to avoid. The second premise cites a recommended course of action such that if the respondent takes it, he will avoid the disastrous outcome stated in the first premise. The conclusion is that the respondent should take the recommended course of action. To judge whether such an argument is reasonable or not in a given case, the multi-agent structure of the dialogue in the case needs to be considered.

In the fear appeal ads used by the NRA, cited above, the dangerous situation portrayed is that of young women being killed by a serial murderer because they had to wait to buy a gun and were unable to defend themselves. The recommended course of action is not to vote for or support the Brady bill or other policies advocated by the "antigun lobby." The reason is that these policies delay the buying of a gun to be used for self-defense. The emotional appeal of this argument is conveyed by visual imagery. In McClurg's words, it conjures up "the nightmarish image of defenseless coeds being butchered by a mad killer." But the basic structure of the argument is practical in nature. To prevent this fearful outcome, the audience is directed to follow a designated policy or course of action. The issue is whether to support the Brady bill or not. The fear appeal argument carries probative weight in shifting the burden of proof to the one side on this issue.

The structure of the fear appeal argument is not deductive in nature. Even if the respondent accepts the premises as true, it does not follow that he would be inconsistent not to accept the conclusion. Instead, the conclusion posits a recommended course of action, and to preserve his goals of safety and preservation of life within the situation as presented by the first premise, the respondent is urged to take the designated course of action. But the respondent may have other goals that have priority. He may think of possible alternatives to the recommended course of action. He may doubt that the harmful outcome will affect him, or there may be other reasons why he is not convinced he should take the recommended course of action. The type of inference involved in the fear appeal argument leaves a respondent a number of escape routes. But if he does accept the premises, it puts some pressure on him, facing him with the unpleasant conclusion of the argument unless he can find a weakness in it perhaps afforded by one of these escape routes. The logical problem is to figure out what all the escape routes are, so that the cognitive structure of how the fear appeal argument as a kind of logical inference can be understood.

As can be verified by examining the cases cited above, fear appeal arguments generally have a particular way of putting forward the two key premises. One premise relates to the health or safety of the respondent. It postulates a state of affairs that is harmful and potentially dangerous to the health or safety of the respondent. It conveys that message not in abstract way but by presenting a graphic picture of the disaster that might occur to that respondent – the danger that threatens his health or safety. The other premise cites a specific course of action presented as a way of preventing this disaster state. The conclusion indicates to the respondent that he should carry out the action cited in the second premise. This type of argument has the basic structure of an Aristotelian practical inference. Such an inference has a goal premise, and a second premise citing an action that is supposedly the best, or the recommended way of achieving the goal. The conclusion then states that the respondent ought (practically speaking) to carry out the designated action. But the way the premises and conclusion are presented to the respondent is typical of the fear appeal argument. Some state of affairs is indicated that represents a real danger to the particular respondent, or is generally thought to do so. This state of affairs must really represent a danger to the respondent, in that it must undermine or defeat some goal that is highly valuable to him. Then the argument presents a way out of the danger.

The various ways the respondent can argue his way out of having to accept the conclusion are represented by the five kinds of critical questions he can ask. He may have other goals that have priority over personal safety. He may know of more effective or less costly ways of averting the danger. He may think there are harmful consequences of carrying out the recommended course of action. He may think that the dangerous outcome is inevitable anyway or that he can't do anything about it. In social science terms, he may not have a "coping mechanism." If any of these ways out seem plausible to the respondent, the proponent's fear appeal argument is defeated.

In cases of fear appeals on the gun control issue used by the NRA, one should examine each case on its merits, and weigh the whole body of evidence, asking critical questions. The fears that the NRA appeals to by presenting scary ads may not be all that irrational. In fact, the basing of the appeals in the ads on real events is a large part of what makes them powerfully persuasive as arguments. But the danger is that a mass audience will be strongly influenced by the emotional appeals in the ads without really thinking about the complex issue of gun control in a more practical way. According to the dual process model of persuasion, receivers of a persuasive message may go for the short-cut solution instead of engaging in the extensive elaboration required to think through the problem. In this case, the solution is not all that easy. Making it easier for everyone to have handguns so they can defend themselves personally may not be the answer. Certainly, some critical questions should be asked about that proposed solution to the problem. On the other hand, simply declaring the ads fallacious because they appeal to fear is to go to the other extreme. Instead of immediately either accepting or rejecting the argument expressed in the ad, the rational approach would be to think critically about the practical aspects of the proposal being advocated. The basis for such a critical assessment should be the structure of the practical reasoning in the case, along with an accompanying set of critical questions. This is the framework that should define relevance and that should determine the weight of the ad as an argument that is weak or strong.

8. The Structure of Appeals to Pity

With respect to their underlying reasoning structure, appeals to pity are very much like appeals to fear. The appeal to pity rests centrally on a graphic display, often presented visually to the respondent. Baby seal pups may be shown visually, or the proponent may cry and whimper while presenting the verbal part of the plea. The tactic is to make an empathetic link-up with the sympathy of the respondent by presenting a state of affairs that is especially distressful to him. Then, as with the fear appeal argument, a way out, in the form of some recommended action, is offered. The conclusion is that the respondent should take this recommended course of action. But the problem with many appeals to pity is that the suggested way out may be an easy solution to a problem that may be complex. Again, as shown by the dual process theory of persuasion, a message receiver may opt for the short-cut solution instead of going through the proper process of elaboration required to weigh all the evidence in a case. Any problem of practical reasoning tends to be complex, because all probable consequences, and all relevant practical aspects of the case, need to be taken into account. One needs to take the whole body of evidence into account. If much of that evidence is not yet in, it may be better to wait before taking action.

In the student appeal kind of case, some actual hardship of the student may be relevant, but it needs to be considered in light of the whole body of evidence in the case. If the student has clearly failed the exam, the professor may sympathize when the student says that his parents will be unhappy or that he needs the course to graduate. But these factors by themselves may not carry enough weight to justify giving the student a passing grade, if the exam results do not justify such action, or even go strongly against it. The student who puts on a tearful display to try to get action anyway is engaging in a sophistical tactic.

In cases of visual appeals to pity in charitable pleas for funds, two aspects need to be emphasized. One is that, in principle, the appeal to the emotion of pity is not by itself fallacious. The tactic of showing a picture of a starving child or presenting some comparable pity-inducing display, surely should be (in general) regarded as a legitimate means of trying to get action. The second factor, however, is that practical questions about means and ends need to be asked by the critical thinker. One question is whether the means recommended (sending money) will in fact alleviate the pain or harmful situation depicted in the appeal. In the case of starving children, for example, one needs to ask whether sending the money to the relief agency, as requested in the plea, will actually get food to the children.

Two other basic critical questions are whether the premises of the practical inference in a given case are in fact true. Both questions involve looking into the particulars of a case. Asking whether the conditional (second) premise is true or is well supported in a given case is a factual question that involves seeing the particular situation and getting an assessment of what is possible and practical in that situation. The problem with many charitable uses of the appeal to pity is that the respondent to whom the appeal is presented is not in a position to observe the situation for himself. It is hard for him to assess whether, if he sends the money, the pitiable situation presented in the ad will actually be made better by that money. The situation is in a far-off country that the respondent is not familiar with. If he brings about state of affairs *B*, the sending of money, will that action be sufficient or a necessary part of some sufficient condition for the outcome of alleviating the starvation (or other bad outcome featured in the appeal)?

Increasingly, in recent years, empirical grounds for doubting the conditional premise in the argumentation of many such appeals to pity have been brought forward. According to Maren (1998), an aid worker and journalist for twenty years in Africa, food solicited by aid appeals frequently goes to the militia of the local warlord, who uses it to feed his troops and to buy weapons and ammunition for them. The main beneficiaries of the food aid are the very people who caused the problem in the first place and who use it to continue fighting and creating new scenes of starvation. According to Maren, in Zaire after the Rwanda genocide, the relief food was commandeered by the very same people who planned the massacres. Similar situations in the Sudan and Somalia are cited, where warlords used the food aid to continue the fighting. According to Maren, "Hunger is political, and fighting it requires moral commitment on a higher level than writing a check" (p. 13). The problem is that the images of hunger broadcast an emotional, visual appeal that is hard for many to resist, because it is easy to write a check, and the respondent hopes something will be done, even though he lacks information about the specifics of the situation. Such appeals to pity have been very successful in the past, and continue to be. But critical questions are appropriate, especially when information comes in of a sort that raises suspicions about the probable consequences of actions.

The problem with many appeals to pity is that a short-cut solution is offered that may make the respondent feel good when action is taken, but may not be a realistic approach to doing anything effective about the problem. The dual process theory explains how the short cut invited by an appeal can look very attractive compared with the work of elaboration required to collect all the evidence and think rationally through all that evidence in a case. It is hard to resist such a short-cut appeal. To question it, or to forbear in any way from taking immediate action, may present an appearance of being insensitive or uncaring. The problem, once again, tends to be that information about the specifics of the case may be lacking.

The children may be alleged to be starving in a foreign country where the viewer does not really know what is going on. In fact, information on the situation may be carefully monitored and controlled by those in power who have something to gain by the influx of foreign aid. As with the fear appeal argument, the practical evaluation of the argument should depend on asking relevant critical questions appropriate for the case.

In the case of the debate on the Brady bill, in which the Gainesville serial murders were cited as the basis of an appeal to pity and fear, the problem is not that the argument is completely worthless or entirely irrelevant. The real problem, as noted by McClurg (1992, p. 66), is that from a practical point of view, it is implausible that a handgun waiting period would have had any appreciable effect on the tragic events in Gainesville. At any rate, this practical question is the critical question that should be asked in evaluating the fear appeal argument used in the speech.

9. **Multi-agent Structure of Both Types of Argument**

Having now revealed the practical reasoning structure that is common to both fear appeal and pity appeal arguments, I proceed to the second thesis. This thesis is that the evaluation of both types of argumentation is inherently dialectical in nature. This is a second respect in which the two types of argumentation have the same underlying structure. Both are contextual, and to analyze either type of argument, you need to grasp the purpose it is supposedly being used for, as part of some goal-directed conversational exchange. In other words, the recommendation is that the best way to evaluate appeals to fear and pity is within the multi-agent framework of an orderly dialectical exchange between two agents, called a proponent and a respondent. These arguments can be used for various purposes in various types of conversation exchanges (dialogues). But when they are reasonable arguments, the context is normally one where the proponent is trying to persuade the respondent to carry out some recommended action. The practical inference is put forward by the proponent in order to argue that some particular course of action is prudent for the respondent. This means that the respondent ought to carry out the cited course of action if he has the goal cited in the premise, and if his situation is as described in the other premise. It means that the designated course of action is being said to be a practically wise one for the respondent. He should do it if he wants to preserve his interests in the given situation, as both agents see it. It doesn't mean that the respondent actually will carry out the recommended action or that he must carry it out, as a matter of logical necessity. It means only that the designated course of action is being proposed by the proponent as the right or the prudent thing for the respondent to do, if he wants to avoid the harm, or make the gain cited in the major premise of the argument. All such arguments depend on what is taken to be the actual situation the respondent finds himself in, and of course, any estimate of such circumstances of an agent is constantly subject to changes and revisions. Mistakes are possible, and even quite likely, in any realistic case. So the conclusion rests only on a tentative basis that is subject to corrections and updating as new information comes in.

In such cases, the best way to evaluate the argumentation in a given case is to look at the practical inference put forward by the proponent as shifting a burden of proof, or burden of rebuttal, onto the side of the respondent. If the respondent accepts the premises, he must either accept the conclusion or raise one of the appropriate critical questions that cast doubt on the proponent's argument. Once the respondent has raised a critical question, the burden shifts to the proponent's side. Either she must answer the question adequately or the original argument defaults. If she does answer the question adequately, the burden shifts back. The respondent must then accept the conclusion or ask another critical question. Once the respondent runs out of critical questions in a dialogue, he must then accept the practical inference as practically binding on him. However, if the situation changes, and new information comes in to the dialogue, the re-asking of a critical question may be prompted, and the dialectical cycle begins once again. If the question is not properly answered, the inference defaults.

In other words, the bindingness of the practical inference in a given case depends on the so-called closed world assumption. The closed world assumption means that the respondent's goals are fixed, and the information accounting for the respondent's situation is regarded as complete, meaning that all the facts are known, and no new facts will come in (Reiter 1987, pp. 158–162). In any real situation, the closed world assumption is precisely that – an assumption. As such, it may have to be given up. And that is why practical reasoning is best seen as being generally a defeasible kind of reasoning that is subject to default. What we know about our circumstances is always changing, but we can artificially close the dialogue for practical purposes. Otherwise, taking prudent action would not be possible, in cases where it is wise to stop discussing or researching the problem and act now. So we can close off the multi-agent dialogue and draw a conclusion on the basis of what we know now about the situation, even though we realize that this conclusion may have to be altered. In the future, new circumstances may crop up that call for a new plan or a new decision on how to proceed.

Fear and pity appeal arguments need to be seen from this multi-agent dialectical viewpoint, to fully understand how they work and how they should be evaluated in particular cases. The first part of the argument is the proponent's putting forward of a practical inference, targeted to the goals and the situation of the respondent. The proponent puts forward an argument that describes a situation that evokes (a) the pity of the respondent for some third individual or group or (b) the fear of the respondent for his own safety, health, or well-being, and/or that of those near to him. Mass media is tailor-made for this kind of appeal, because of the emotional impact of an audiovisual presentation. Suffering seal pups that look to viewers like babies can be shown being clubbed to death with baseball bats. A horrific automobile crash can be presented, in which a car full of happy teenagers smashes into another vehicle and its occupants are shown dying, mutilated, and covered with blood. Such presentations, especially when targeted to specific audiences, have a much greater effect than any purely verbal argumentation would have. Then, following up the visual presentation, a message may be broadcast citing the recommended action to avoid the state of affairs so forcefully presented. The viewer is advised to send money to the animal welfare fund or to give the car keys to someone else before going to a party. The message is (presumably) clear: this is what you should do to avoid or stop the horrible situation pictured in the ad. The NRA fear appeal ads use graphic images that evoke the horror of women being murdered or raped. Then they, somewhat implausibly, cite "anti-gun" policies as the problem.

The next part of the argument to be assessed is the reaction of the respondent. The argument will be unpersuasive unless certain conditions are met. One is that the state of affairs presented must really evoke the emotions of the respondent, by being tailored to the specific situation and presumptions of the respondent. The fear appeal ad may be targeted to the elderly, for example, who may have a fear of crime or a fear of being in a medical emergency without being able to call for help. Or it may be targeted to women, who have a fear of stalking or rape. Second, the action recommended must be seen as relatively easy to carry out, so that the harmful situation presented is thought of as greatly overwhelming the cost or effort of carrying out the designated action. For example, when presented with the horrific sight of baby seals being clubbed to death, the designated response is relatively easy for many viewers – all you have to do is to write a check and send it to the address indicated. Once again, on the dual process model of persuasion, the solution offered by the argument is attractive because it offers a short cut. It looks easy compared with the work that would be required to deal with the whole mass of relevant evidence in a complex case. To engage in elaboration of the practical reasoning in a case, other critical questions may need to be considered. No better, more effective, or easier way to correct the harm should be evident. The harm must really be seen as a harm. It must be something that the target audience really fears or that evokes a strong feeling of pity in that audience. There should be no conflict with other goals of the respondent audience. For example, if the viewers make their living from seal hunting, the appeal to pity may not be persuasive.

10. When Are Appeals to Fear and Pity Fallacious?

Fear appeals, of the kind represented by the televised and newspaper or magazine ads considered above, are based on the premise that the fearful state presented really does represent a danger to the target audience. For example, it is assumed that AIDS or venereal disease really does represent a danger to teens. Or it is assumed, to cite another case, that drinking and driving really is a dangerous combination. Or it is assumed that being brutally murdered or raped is a potential danger. One might be tempted to argue that the appeals to fear or pity in such cases are fallacious because the premise they are based on is false or unwarranted. But in all these cases, the premise is in fact true, or at least represents an assumption that is quite reasonable. There seems little reason to doubt that the outcomes warned against are dangerous. In fact, these premises are generally accepted as true by the general population and the experts, and they are probably not in question for the teenagers who are the target audience for the ads. Nor is there real reason to say that these assumptions themselves are unwarranted or are the basis for judging fear appeal arguments to be fallacious. Indeed, it is one of the requirements for the success of such an appeal that the danger not be perceived as being exaggerated, or "hyped," by the respondent. For this reason, and because many of the ads examined above are perceived as having a socially commendable and worthy purpose, the use of the fear appeal arguments in most of the cases examined above should not be seen as "fallacious." In many cases, the arguments thus based on appeals to fear and pity can be quite reasonable.

Of course, one could always critically question the fear appeal ad in such cases, asking whether preventing the fearful outcome cited can really be accomplished by the means advocated. But in many of the kinds of cases examined above, there is little real doubt on that score. In other words, in evaluating fear appeal arguments, a lot depends on the background knowledge or information that the audience, and even the general population, is presumed to have. The same is true of appeals to pity in the kinds of ads considered above, including the charitable type of appeal for aid. Much depends on our knowledge or information of the specifics of the case. The problem with many of these appeals, as has been noted, is that such knowledge – for example, of the situation in a foreign country – may be lacking. But even if this is true, it seems a stretch to call the appeal to pity fallacious. What we should say, perhaps, is that it is premature or weak, because it is based on insufficient evidence of the kind that should properly be required to support this kind of practical reasoning.

What about the cases of the NRA appeals cited by McClurg? He sees them as fallacious, on the ground that they are irrelevant. Our diagnosis was somewhat different. Looked at as arguments used by the pro-gun side in the gun control debate, they can be seen as dialectically relevant arguments used to give reasons not to support the Brady bill. But once critically examined, the arguments seem weak and implausible, on a practical basis. Once the underlying structure of practical reasoning on which they are based is made explicit, its weakness as a practical argument becomes apparent. They are open to so many appropriate critical questions, that as they stand, they are unconvincing. The reason McClurg judges these arguments to be fallacious is that they evoke such strong emotions of pity and fear, using graphic visual images that are irrelevant. But is the use of graphic visual images to evoke strong emotions of pity and fear inherently irrelevant or fallacious? I think not, where decisions about practical actions or political policies are being deliberated, and I think the bulk of the casework analyzed in this chapter supports that thesis.

What should be said about the conditions under which fear and pity appeal arguments can properly be said to be fallacious? This question depends on what is meant by the term "fallacy." This issue has been discussed in relation to appeals to pity in Walton (1997b), but as noted above, Jackson (1996) has added a new dimension to it by bringing in the factor of argumentation heuristics. These discussions show how arguments that appeal to fear and pity typically offer a short-cut solution to a complex problem. In light of these discussions, and of recent work on the fallacies, a hypothesis may be ventured: the use of an appeal to pity or fear should be judged to be fallacious or not on how open the argument presentation is to critical questioning of the kind appropriate for the practical reasoning used in the case. Consider the appeal to fear and pity used by Barbara Vucanovich to argue against the Brady bill, citing the serial killings in Gainesville. As noted above, the argument that these tragedies could have been prevented by not having a waiting period to buy guns is somewhat implausible. It may be acceptable to advocates of the pro-gun lobby, but those open to the opposed point of view could ask many pointed critical questions about the practical reasoning basis of the argument. But a weak argument is not necessarily a fallacious argument. Grounds come in for judging the argument in this particular case to be fallacious when Vucanovich followed up by urging her fellow representatives not to "let their judgments be clouded by the antigun lobby's emotional banter." This added flourish is quite amusing because of its inconsistency in condemning the very type of argument just used. But it has a more serious function as well. It attacks the other side in a way that is meant to be distracting and to cover up the faults of the emotional appeal put forward just before. It is a way of sealing off the argument and preventing the asking of appropriate critical questions by trying to shift the burden to the opposing side. Thus we can see in this argument the use of an argumentation strategy designed to get the mass audience to opt for the short-cut solution and to shut their minds to engaging in further practical reasoning.

The hypothesis I put forward now is that appeals to fear and pity should be judged as fallacious or not in particular cases by analysis of the strategy of persuasion used by the proponent. Such a strategy should be analyzed by examining not only the proponent's strategy, but also the expected response of the respondent. The respondent should ask critical questions. A fallacious argument is designed to prevent this possibility in advance. Appeals to fear and pity should be judged to be fallacious only in cases where the appeal has been put forward by the proponent in such a way that the presentation of the argument gives evidence of a strategy used to prevent the asking of the appropriate critical questions by the respondent. The evidence for such a claim of fallaciousness is to be sought in the text of discourse of the dialogue as far as information has been given in the particular case at issue. What you have to look for is evidence that the proponent has pressed ahead too strongly so that the respondent's ability to pose the relevant critical questions has been precluded in advance of any actual response. There are some grounds for finding some evidence of this sort in the Vucanovich case, and it is these grounds that should be cited as the right evidence for the claim that the argument in this case is fallacious. In the Nayirah case, the video portraying the appeal to pity was part of a public relations campaign designed to get support for a cause. That it was advocacy does not necessarily mean that it should be judged to be fallacious. That it was based on a false premise also does not, by itself, mean that the appeal to pity was fallacious. But how was the argument used in context? It was used in deliberations in the United Nations and in the U.S. Congress. Its timing as a presentation in both cases was such that it probably had an influence on the vote on the question of whether to take action. In that context and at that time, apparently it was not questioned. It was seen as just another piece of evidence or another consideration to take into account. But it was highly successful as a strategy of argumentation because of its timing. It was introduced at just the right moment to be influential. It was only later that an investigator uncovered its use as a deliberately crafted tactic of persuasion. By then, the ad had done its work of influencing the deliberations.

The important thing is that a distinction should be made between two kinds of evaluations of fear and pity appeal arguments. One kind of evaluation is that the argument is critically weak, meaning that it is not supported well enough by the evidence given. The other is that the argument, as used in the given case, is more than just weak but is fallacious. This second sort of criticism should be regarded as a strong kind of charge. It needs to be backed up by the right kind of evidence, and the claim that a particular appeal to pity or fear is fallacious needs more than just evidence to show that the given argument is open to critical questioning. It has a dialectical aspect, because it needs to reveal the strategy of the proponent as a means of influencing the respondent.

Some would say that fear and pity appeal arguments are fallacious because they are manipulative. The fear appeal ad is cleverly crafted by public relations experts ("spin doctors") to graphically portray a scene that will move the target audience to action. For example, trying to get teenagers to use condoms may cleverly portray some danger that really is fearful to teens. It is true that this tactic is a kind of manipulation. But many would defend it by pointing out that abstract rational argumentation may not work with teens, while certain kinds of graphic, emotional appeals may change their behavior. Thus just evidence of being manipulative should not be enough to support a claim that an appeal to fear or pity is fallacious. The manipulativeness has to be of the sort that is part of a tactic to suppress the rightful asking of critical questions in a dialogue, especially critical questions of a sort directed to the practical reasoning basis of the argument. Fallaciousness, so conceived, is a dialectical matter, relating to how an argument has been put forward in a dialogue. Openness to critical questioning is vitally important in a persuasion dialogue. The timing in the Nayirah case was the factor that delayed the asking of critical questions.

We are supposed to live in a democracy where advertisers can use all kinds of persuasive tactics in the media, and it is up to the consumer to judge for herself whether to accept the argument or not. The question here pertains to the context of dialogue in which such ads are used in the media. The producer of the ad and the individual viewer are not literally having a dialogue, because the viewer does not reply to the ad, in a dialogue in which the producer of the ad gets that immediate feedback. Thus the RTD problem is a constant in attempting to evaluate mass media appeals to fear and pity. Nonetheless, there is a kind of dialogue involved (in our abstract sense of the term), because the producer of the ad is making an argument that is directed to a specific respondent audience. The ad is meant to be persuasive, or at least to get action on the part of the viewer. The viewer watches the ad, and then either accepts the conclusion by taking the recommended course of action or does not. It can be seen that the producer of the appeal is using a strategy of persuasion. By examining the discourse of a case, we can often reconstruct that strategy, and evaluate it using the dual persuasion model. So there is a kind of dialogue exchange in the process, even though it is an abbreviated one. And it makes sense to evaluate the argument from the normative perspective of its use in a context of dialogue, as advocated in thesis two above.

5

Ad Hominem Arguments in Political Discourse

The *ad hominem*, or personal attack, argument is now highly familiar in politics, especially in the use of negative campaign tactics in elections. This form of argument has been studied previously in the argumentation literature, but it has some special features of interest as a mass media argument strategy. In this chapter it is shown how it has some features comparable to appeals to fear and pity when it is used in mass media as a device of persuasion. This chapter brings out the multi-agent structure of the *ad hominem* argument as used in rhetorical argumentation, by showing how the proponent mounts a successful strategy in this form of argumentation. It is shown how he or she must use prolepsis by probing into the commitments of the respondent and configuring them in a certain way prior to the attack. These insights into the multi-agent structure of the *ad hominem* reveal how the proponent must collect evidence proactively, and then use this evidence to attribute a plan to the respondent. The aim is not just to reveal how to use such a tactic of personal attack in the mass media. The analysis is meant to be helpful to both voters and political campaigners, giving them a better understanding of how to deal with rhetorical *ad hominem* arguments by identifying, analyzing, and critically evaluating them.

The *ad hominem* argument is not a new phenomenon in American political discourse. A pamphlet was circulated telling of Andrew Jackson's "youthful indiscretions." In the 1860s, Northern newspapers attacked Lincoln's policies by attacking his character, using the terms "drunk," "baboon," "too slow," "foolish," and "dishonest." Steadily on the increase in political argumentation since then, the *argumentum ad hominem* has been carefully refined as an instrument of "oppo tactics" and "going negative" by the public relations experts who now craft political campaigns at the national level. It has been so prominently used in the major political campaigns, debates, and ads of the past few years that there has even been a reaction against it – a feeling that we have gone too far in this direction and that some kind of restraint is needed.[1] But there has been no evidence of such restraint in the argumentation used in recent campaigns. The norm is even more visible use of negative campaign tactics, and the acceptance of the character issue as relevant. Personal matters that were once "off limits" for media reporting are now probed into, using opposition research, and routinely drawn on in attack ads. The abundance of these *ad hominem* arguments in current political discourse provides much interesting material for studying how to evaluate the strengths and weaknesses of this type of argument. In this chapter, two specimens that pose some interesting problems have been selected for study. How does the *ad hominem* argument really work as a way of molding public opinion, why is it so often so effective, and how can it be defended against? How can it be evaluated as a clearly identifiable type of argument, with some kind of objective standards, in a way that can be applied to particular cases?

The best way to approach this problem is to study some actual cases in a detailed analysis. The problem posed by one case studied in this chapter is that the argument looks like an *ad hominem* argument, but on closer inspection, it is arguable that it is not an *ad hominem* argument at all. The case in question is a fairly short and relatively self-contained segment of dialogue from the televised impeachment trial of President Bill Clinton in February 1999. The other case is even more typical of so many *ad hominem* arguments currently in use in political discourse. It is an *ad hominem* attack on Al Gore in the "Election Notebook" article in *Time* magazine in 1996. It also has some special features that turn out to be quite interesting in advancing our knowledge of how the *ad hominem* type of argument works in political argumentation in a democratic system where mass media reporting is a big factor. The Gore case is simpler, and more nicely illustrates key features of the circumstantial *ad hominem* argument. So it is presented first.

---

[1] A range of cases, from ancient times to the present, is studied in Walton (1998a).

1. Classifying the Types of *Ad Hominem* Argument

The *ad hominem* argument has a long history of being treated as a fallacy in logic textbooks. Hardly anyone questioned the general assumption that this type of argument can be routinely dismissed as fallacious until Johnstone (1952, 1959) pointed out that many famous philosophical arguments are *ad hominem* arguments of a kind that do not appear to be fallacious. Johnstone was the first to seriously question what had become a generally accepted tradition in logic of taking for granted that *ad hominem* arguments are fallacious. The assumption was that not much care was needed in evaluating individual cases of the *argumentum ad hominem*, because all instances of it are fallacious. Johnstone put this assumption sharply into question by citing cases of what not only appear to be *ad hominem* arguments in philosophical discussions, but that also appear to be, on the whole, quite reasonable arguments. Certainly, these cases could not any longer be brushed aside as fallacious just on the grounds that they fit the form of argument described as *ad hominem* in the logic textbooks. By showing that the *ad hominem* argument could be reasonable in some cases, Johnstone opened up the real problem to be solved: how can we tell on the basis of evidence in a given case whether a specific *ad hominem* argument is reasonable or fallacious? This question poses the problem of evaluation.

Prior to the evaluation problem in dealing with *ad hominem* arguments, there is an identification or classification problem. The textbook accounts indicated that there are different types of *ad hominem* arguments. The problem was how to classify these different subtypes, and generally how to define the *ad hominem* as a distinctive and identifiable form of argument. Many subtypes of *ad hominem* argument have been shown to have distinctively different forms as arguments. In Walton (1998a), five main types of *ad hominem* argument are defined. These subtypes are the abusive (direct) *ad hominem*, the circumstantial *ad hominem*, the bias *ad hominem*, the poisoning the well subtype, and the *tu quoque* subtype. Each subtype has a well-defined form as a recognizable type of argument. There are also many other kinds of arguments associated with *ad hominem* arguments that are not themselves *ad hominem* arguments. These arguments are easily confused with or misclassified as *ad hominem* arguments. The previous lack of any standard system of classifying all these various forms of arguments has stood in the way of any serious study of the *ad hominem* argument. Now that problem, at least to some encouraging extent, has been solved. But the problem of refining and extending the systems of classification (Lagerspetz 1995; Walton 1998a) still exists. Other resources for identifying and evaluating personal attack (*ad hominem*) arguments have been developed by Johnstone (1952), van Emeren and Grootendorst (1984, 1995), Brinton (1985, 1995), Walton (1989a, chap. 6), and van Eemeren, Grootendorst, and Snoeck Henkemans (1996), Krabbe and Walton (1993). The method for identifying and evaluating *ad hominem* arguments worked out in Walton (1998a) uses a set of argumentation schemes (forms of argument) for each distinctive subtype of *ad hominem* argument recognized, and a set of appropriate critical questions matching each scheme. Because each different type of *ad hominem* argument needs to be evaluated differently, the question of how to identify the type used, when confronting an argument in a given case, is highly significant. But reality being what it is, there are borderline cases where it is very difficult or even impossible to tell whether a given argument presented in a text of discourse is one type of *ad hominem* argument or another. Or it may even be hard to tell whether it is an *ad hominem* argument or not. This is the problem Hamblin (1970) called "pinning down" the fallacy in a given case.

In the direct, or so-called abusive, type of *ad hominem* argument, the proponent argues that the respondent is a bad person and that therefore his argument should not be accepted as being as plausible as it was before. There are several background presumptions. One is that there are two parties, called the proponent and the respondent. Another is that the respondent has put forward some particular argument, that has some initial degree of plausibility. Another is that the respondent is assumed to have some ethical qualities of character, like honesty and integrity. When the proponent says that the respondent is a bad person, he means that the respondent has displayed some negative ethical quality of character, like dishonesty or hypocrisy. At any rate, these are all the properties of the direct *ad hominem* as a type of argument. The following is the argumentation scheme for the direct, or so-called abusive, form of the *ad hominem* argument – called the ethotic type of *ad hominem* argument in Brinton (1985) and Walton (1998a). The variable *a* stands for an arguer, and the variable α stands for an argument.

Ethotic (Direct, Abusive) Ad Hominem *Argument*
     a is a person of bad character.
     Therefore, *a*'s argument α should not be accepted.

An *ad hominem* argument in a particular case is evaluated in relation to, in the first place, whether it meets the requirements for the scheme and, in the second place, how it manages critical questions. The fallacious cases are the ones where critical questioning in a further dialogue exchange is suppressed. But in principle, both types of *ad hominem* arguments can sometimes be reasonable.

The *ad hominem* argument can be a reasonable way of questioning an arguer's credibility by throwing doubt on his character (for veracity, in particular), and using that allegation to throw doubt on whether his argument has much weight in supporting its conclusion. But this type of argument can be used wrongly if the claim is that the arguer's conclusion is absolutely wrong (or indefensible), as opposed to the weaker claim that it is open to critical questioning. In other words, the *ad hominem* argument is a relative one, but runs into difficulty as soon as it becomes an absolute claim that the proposition advocated by the arguer is false. In evaluating cases, the critical thinker must watch out for words such as "certainly" and "must," which rule out the possibility that a claim is true (or false).

2. The Circumstantial and Other Types

What is important to notice when initially approaching any particular case study is that the circumstantial type is different from, but also related to the direct, or so-called abusive type. The circumstantial type essentially involves an allegation that the party being attacked has committed a practical inconsistency, of a kind that can be characterized by the expression, "You do not practice what you preach." Then this allegation of inconsistency is used as the basis for launching a direct, or personal, *ad hominem* type of attack to the effect that the person attacked has a bad character and that therefore her argument is bad or should not be taken seriously. So the distinction is that the direct *ad hominem* does not require an allegation of circumstantial inconsistency of the kind that the circumstantial type does. The circumstantial *ad hominem* argument, unlike the direct one, is always based on an allegation of inconsistency. The proponent alleges that the respondent is committed to some kind of inconsistency, and then uses that allegation as a springboard to argue that the respondent's argument is not plausible. Typically, as just noted, the allegation of inconsistency takes the form of an argument to the effect that the respondent "does not practice what he preaches." The classic case is the smoking example. In this case, the parent argues to her child that he should not smoke, because smoking is unhealthy. The child replies, "What about you? You smoke. So much for your argument against smoking!" What is going on in this case is that the child observes an inconsistency – the parent argues against smoking, but the parent herself smokes. Citing this pragmatic inconsistency the child rejects the parent's argument. The smoking case is tricky to evaluate. On the one hand, the child is right to note the pragmatic inconsistency, and to question the parent's credibility as a spokesperson for an anti-smoking argument. On the other hand, the child may be over-reacting by rejecting what may be a good argument against smoking.

The form of the circumstantial *ad hominem* argument has been presented as follows in Walton (1998a, p. 219). As above, the lowercase *a* stands for an arguer, and the Greek α stands for an argument; the uppercase *A* stands for a proposition.

Circumstantial Ad Hominem *Argument*
1. *a* advocates argument α, which has proposition *A* as its conclusion.
2. *a* has carried out an action or set of actions that imply that *a* is personally committed to not-*A* (the opposite of *A*).
3. Therefore, *a* is a bad person.
4. Therefore, *a*'s argument α should not be accepted.

When this form is applied to the smoking case, it may not seem that the subconclusion 3 really applies to the case. After all, is the child really claiming or asserting that the parent is a bad person, as part of the argument? Although no such assertion is explicitly made by the child, it can be inferred as a non-explicit part of the argument. For, presumably, the reason that the child is rejecting the parent's argument against smoking is that the child sees the parent is a smoker, and then draws the inference that the parent is not sincere in what she advocates, based on the perception of the inconsistency. For the argument to make sense, there needs to be an implicit conclusion drawn by the child that the parent lacks some kind of personal ethical quality, such as sincerity or integrity. Whatever we might call it, the quality of character involves a consistency between a person's principles and her personal actions. At any rate, assuming that the child's argument in the smoking case has this component, it can be classified as an instance of the circumstantial *ad hominem* type of argument. If it lacks this component, it would be classified in Walton (1998a, p. 251) as an argument from pragmatic inconsistency, but one that is not a genuine type of *ad hominem* argument (in the narrower sense in which *ad hominem* is a personal attack argument).

The example below is a summary of a newspaper article that appeared in the *National Post* (October 14, 2005, p. A10).

The Sealers Example

Rocco DiSpirito, a New York chef and best-selling food author, made famous as the star of the NBC reality show *The Restaurant*, wrote a public letter supporting a campaign by the U.S. Humane Society to end the Canadian seal hunt. The article quoted Mr. DiSpirito as saying, "Most of the seal clubbers [in Canada] are also snow crabbers. By refusing to use Canadian or Canadian-sourced snow crab in our restaurants, we can make a very vocal statement against the seal hunt." The Humane Society had been lobbying for an American boycott of Canadian seafood, especially snow crab from Atlantic Canada, advocating the boycott as an economic tactic to stop the seal hunt. Many American restaurants and seafood wholesalers had joined the boycott, pledging not to buy Canadian seafood. Newfoundland fishermen in the sealing industry replied by arguing that DiSpirito was a hypocrite for calling the seal hunt inhumane while serving *foie gras* made from the engorged livers of force-fed geese in his restaurant. This practice was officially banned in some European countries and California, where the humane society condemned it. Frank Pinhorn, managing director of the Newfoundland-based Canadian Sealers Association, was quoted as saying, "He's an absolute hypocrite, a man of double standards." Earl McCurdy, president of the Fish, Food and Allied Workers Union in St. John's was quoted as saying, "I think somebody who lives in a glass house shouldn't throw stones. It shows the hypocrisy of these celebrities, who know nothing about the seal hunt. . . . if he wants to serve *foie gras* in his restaurants, that's fine with me, but he shouldn't pass judgment on us." John Grandy, senior vice-president of the Humane Society, defended the chef. He was quoted as saying, "Absolutely the society is opposed to *foie gras*, but this issue is about seals, and a man of his distinction and abilities, who is simply appalled at the brutal destruction of these seals, well, *if* we can use him on the seals issue, we're happy to do so."

The argument in this case is partly based on an implicit use of appeal to popular opinion, because it argues that the practice of serving Canadian snow crab should be condemned for the reason that several states have already banned it. But the central argument in the example is a circumstantial *ad hominem* attack. The sealers argue that the chef is a hypocrite for condemning sealing as inhumane, while his personal activities as a chef support practices, that are just as inhumane. They argue that he does not practice what he preaches. The basis of their argument is the cited practical inconsistency between the position that the chef advocates and his own actions. They use this argument as an attack on the chef's credibility as an arguer whose arguments should not be taken seriously on the issue of humane treatment of animals. The argument suggests that the chef is hypocrite when he is more interested in publicity, and perhaps in promoting his career, than in the ethical issue.

The bias type of *ad hominem* argument is also an attack on an opponent's credibility. In this type of attack, the proponent argues that the respondent is biased, or has shown some sort of bias, and argues that the respondent's argument should therefore not be taken to be as plausible as it might have appeared before. Bias of this sort can be shown by a number of indicators, such as having something to gain or being strongly committed to a viewpoint (Kienpointner and Kindt 1997). Bias is not always a bad thing in argumentation. How bad a bias is, in a given case, depends on the type of conversational context the argument was used in. The same argument if used in an editorial column might be quite okay, but when used in a news report could exhibit a kind of bias that rightly opens it to criticism. At any rate, the bias type of *ad hominem* is different from the direct and circumstantial types. It focuses not on character or on an inconsistency but on the bias an arguer is alleged to have shown in her argument.

The fourth type of *ad hominem* argument is the poisoning the well type. In this type of attack, the proponent alleges that the opponent is strongly committed to some position in a rigid and dogmatic way. It is concluded that he can never be trusted to judge an argument on its merits, in an open-minded way, and will always push instead for the side of his preferred position. The classic case (Walton 1998a, p. 15) is the attack on Cardinal Newman, in which it was alleged that as a Catholic, he always reverted to the Catholic position on any political dispute on any subject, and therefore could never be trusted to take an open-minded view of a matter. Newman replied that such an attack, if taken seriously, meant that he as a practicing Catholic could never really take part in any political debate on any issue with any credibility.

The fifth type is the *tu quoque*, in which one party replies to an *ad hominem* attack by attacking the attacker, using another *ad hominem* argument. There are strong elements of the *tu quoque* in the *ad hominem* attack in the sealhunt example. However, there are general problems classifying the *tu quoque* as a type of argument. There is much confusion in the textbooks sorting out this type of argumentation from other types, such as the two wrongs argument and the guilt by association argument (Walton 1998a, pp. 233–240). There are also other subtypes of *ad hominem* argumentation, such as the situationally disqualifying subtype, that are hard to classify (Krabbe and Walton 1993). These problems can be bypassed in the cases that follow, for the main concern will be with the ethotic and circumstantial subtypes.

All five subtypes of *ad hominem* arguments are personal attack arguments in which one party, called the proponent, attacks the person of the second party (the respondent) in a dialogue in which both parties are arguing about something. The basis of the argument is that the proponent is attacking the credibility of the respondent, and then using this proposed lowering of credibility to argue that the latter's argument should be reduced in plausibility value. One assumption is that the respondent has put forward an argument and that this argument has only a certain degree of plausibility or worth of acceptance as an argument. Another assumption is that this plausibility value can be raised or lowered by consideration of the person, or personal characteristics of the respondent, as a participant in argumentation. Yet another assumption is that both parties have something that could be called personal credibility that also can be raised or lowered in the course of argumentation. The final assumption is that a lowering of the personal credibility of an arguer can result in a lowering of the plausibility value of the argument that the arguer has put forward. All these interconnected assumptions are parts of the structure needed to evaluate *ad hominem* arguments. So it is not difficult to see that the *ad hominem* is a complex form of argument in its own right, with many components that require an analysis that goes well beyond the traditional structures of deductive and inductive logic.

What consideration of the *ad hominem* argument does is to bring the notion of the person, or the arguer as person, into logic. Of course, this intrusion has traditionally been resisted. Logic is seen as an abstract and formal science of propositions and truth values. But to get any kind of useful and workable way of analyzing and evaluating *ad hominem* arguments, the notion of the arguer as a person, or as an entity with credibility and properties of character, must be taken into account. Many in traditional logic might be reluctant to take such a step, because it would broaden the subject of logic into the whole area of persons, seeming to make logic subjective in way that is inappropriate and even dangerous.

3. Argument from Commitment

Ad hominem arguments have become a special subject of concern in media reporting political argumentation, as noted in the introductory section of this chapter. One example is the revealing case study of an election campaign in which the *ad hominem* argument was the decisive instrument of victory for an underdog candidate (Cragan and Cutbirth 1984). But since that time, *ad hominem* has been used even more effectively and commonly by politicians, raising much concern about negative campaigning and attack ads. Although *ad hominem* arguments have been around for a long time and are now used more than ever, the problem of how to deal with them in a critically balanced way is a matter of concern for public discourse in a democracy. What is needed is a method or normative framework that a consumer of political rhetoric can use to critically evaluate these arguments.

In the case described and analyzed by Cragan and Cutbirth, Adlai Stevenson, the son of the presidential candidate Adlai Stevenson, was criticized in an election campaign for the governorship of Illinois on the grounds that he belonged to an all-male Chicago club. Stevenson overreacted to the criticism by complaining that he had been treated as "some kind of a wimp." Once this comment appeared in print, his opponent, who at that point was behind in the race, made much use of the so-called wimp factor. He portrayed Stevenson as a kind of fussy patrician who had claimed he only belonged to this club because he couldn't find any other decent place to eat lunch. Stevenson lost, and the perception was, according to Cragan and Cutbirth, that the *ad hominem* "wimp factor" argument was the instrument of his defeat.

The historical origin of the *ad hominem* argument has been something of a mystery, and its beginning as a clearly identified type of argument has generally been attributed to Locke or Galileo (Finocchiaro 1980). However, recent historical research has traced its roots back through the treatises of the middle ages to Aristotle. One root passage (Nuchelmans, 1993, p. 37) is the reference to *peirastikoi logoi*, or arguments designed to test out or probe a respondent's knowledge, by examining views held by that respondent (*On Sophistical Refutations*, 165a37). Another root of the historical development of the "argument against the person" is the more often cited passage 178b17, in which Aristotle contrasts directing a refutation at an argument with directing a refutation against the person who has put forward that argument. Because there are two roots, however, the textbook treatments of the *ad hominem* have been ambiguous and confusing.

The type of *ad hominem* argument that is the concern of this case study is the personal attack type, defined above. The other type is portrayed by Locke in his *Essay*, in a neglected passage fully quoted in Hamblin (1970, p. 160). Locke describes this type of argument as pressing "a man with consequences drawn from his own principles or concessions." This type of argumentation is called "argument from commitment" (Walton 1998a). Barth and Martens (1977) see the *ad hominem* fallacy as best analyzed on this Lockean model, as being basically the same as argument from commitment. But I have argued (1998a) that these are two distinct types of arguments and that although argument from commitment is a subpart of the personal attack type of *ad hominem* argument, it is not the whole argument. At any rate, the reader should be aware that terminological confusion about the *ad hominem* is, and continues to be, a serious problem. The circumstantial *ad hominem* argument is a subspecies of a more general form of argument called argument from commitment. It is vitally important to distinguish between the two. However, the whole history of the subject has been terminologically clouded, especially since Locke's influential remarks (Hamblin 1970, p. 160), by the fact that *ad hominem* argument has prominently been taken to be equivalent to argument from commitment.

Argument from commitment has the following form, where *a* is an arguer and *A* is a proposition (Walton 1996, p. 56).

Argument from Commitment

> *a* is committed to proposition *A* (generally, or in virtue of what she said in the past).
> Therefore, in this case, *a* should support *A*.

This is illustrated by the following example (Walton 1996, p. 55).

> *Bob*: Ed, you are a communist, aren't you?
> *Ed*: Of course. You know that.
> *Bob*: Well, then you should be on the side of the union in this recent labor dispute.

In this particular case, it may be that Ed is on the management side. But if so, he will have to offer some explanation why he is. Otherwise, given his commitment to communism generally, there is a presumption that he would normally tend to side with the union on labor disputes. So we see that argument from commitment is defeasible. It creates a presumption in favor of drawing a certain inference. But the inference is subject to default in the face of new information that might come in regarding the particulars of the case.

Now the big issue is whether the circumstantial *ad hominem* (or possibly the other forms as well) is the same thing as argument from commitment, or whether they are two different types of argument. I have argued at length (Walton 1998a) that the two types of argument are different, basically for two reasons. One is that that all *ad hominem* arguments are personal attack arguments, but because it is not the case that all arguments from commitment are personal attack arguments, it follows that some arguments from commitment are not *ad hominem* arguments. To really understand the *ad hominem*, as a clearly defined type of argument with a distinctive structure, you have to begin with analysis of character as a moral concept that has a role to play in the dialogue structure of argumentation. In any genuine *ad hominem* argument, including the circumstantial subtype, one party makes a personal attack on the moral character of another in order to criticize the other party's argument.[2] The other reason is that circumstantial *ad hominem* arguments are always based on an allegation of inconsistency, as indicated above. It is this alleged inconsistency that is the central characteristic separating them from the other subtypes of *ad hominem* arguments. But not all cases of argument from commitment make an allegation of inconsistency, as shown by the Bob and Ed case above.

From a viewpoint of argumentation theory, it is vital to be clear about the distinction between the circumstantial *ad hominem* argument and argument from commitment. But it is very easy to confuse the two, from a practical point of view. One reason is that the circumstantial *ad hominem* is a subspecies of argument from commitment. Another is that argument from commitment is very often a lead-in or prior argument to the use of the circumstantial *ad hominem* argument. In individual cases, it may be hard to tell exactly where the one form of argument changed into the other. Before argumentation theory can advance much further as a field, these problems of argument classification need to be sorted out. One of the reasons there has been so little advance for so long must surely be the conflicting definitions of the *ad hominem* argument and its various subtypes in the logic textbooks.

As noted above, the *argumentum ad hominem*, or personal attack argument, has been traditionally treated as a fallacy in logic. But recent research in argumentation cited above shows that, in many cases, as used in conversational arguments – including ones in political

---

[2] The best analysis we have of the role that character plays in reasoning goes back to the account of Aristotle, through the concept of practical reasoning or practical wisdom (*phronesis*), as shown in Garver (1994). So, in more ways than one, the genesis of the *ad hominem* is to be found in Aristotle.

argumentation – *ad hominem* arguments are not fallacious. This research has shown that while some personal attack arguments can definitely be judged fallacious, many others are quite reasonable (when evaluated in the appropriate context), while still others should be evaluated as weak (insufficiently supported) but not fallacious. As shown in this case study, the real function of an *ad hominem* argument (when properly used) is to attack an arguer's credibility in order to criticize the argument she advocates.

Before going any further, it is necessary to remind ourselves of some considerations on multi-agent argumentation from chapters 1 and 2. A multi-agent structure of argumentation always involves two parties (in the minimum case) in a dialogue. An *ad hominem* argument is the use of personal attack in a dialogue exchange between two parties, where the one party attacks the character of the other party as bad in some respect, and then uses this attack as a basis for criticizing the other party's argument. An argument is *fallacious* if it is a special baptizable (Johnson 1987) type of argument that is used in such a way by one party in a dialogue exchange that it blocks or interferes with the collaborative realization of the goal of the type of dialogue that the two participants are supposed to be engaged in (Walton 1995). Thus, there is a difference between a weak argument that is open to critical questioning and a fallacious argument. The general point is that a fallacious argument has to be worse than just weak, or unsuccessful in fulfilling a burden of proof. A fallacious argument is a tricky, deceptive sophistical tactic, used to try to get the best of a speech partner in a way that is inappropriate as a collaborative contribution to the dialogue exchange. At any rate, let us now go on to examine two cases. The first one is a classic case of the use of the circumstantial *ad hominem* argument in political discourse. The second appears to be somewhere on the borderline between argument from commitment and circumstantial *ad hominem* argument.

4. The Gore Case

This case comes from *Time* magazine's "Election Notebook" of November 18, 1996 (p. 16), where *Time* gave out "Campaign 96 Awards" to "recognize outstanding achievements by politicians, their relatives and their hecklers." Two of the awards are directly quoted below.

THE SLIGHT-INCONSISTENCY MEDAL: To Al Gore, who left not a dry eye in the house at the Democratic Convention as he described his sister's death from

smoking-induced lung cancer. Gore failed to mention that for some years following her death, his family continued to grow tobacco and that he continued to
accept campaign money from tobacco interests.

THE MOST NAUSEATING SPIN: Gore explained the above by saying, "I felt the
numbness that prevented me from integrating into all aspects of my life the
implications of what that tragedy really meant."

No author of the "Election Notebook" was given. The page simply appears
as an editorial column, with accompanying pictures (including one of
Gore, in a speech-making pose).

   To classify the type of dialogue that the argument of this case belongs
to, one would have to say that it is an editorial page of a sort, as opposed to
a news story. The intent of the entries on the page could be described as
ironic and satirical in nature, but each of the entries definitely has political content, in the sense that it is an argument expressing a particular
political viewpoint. Each entry is an editorial comment with a particular
"spin," or opinion, expressed. So the function of the discourse can be
classified as one of political commentary, which is partisan in nature, as
opposed to an information-seeking or news-reporting type of dialogue.
In the case above, for example, a point of view is expressed in an argument for only one side of an issue. It is different in type from a newspaper
report on politics, where there would be an expectation that the views of
both sides would be represented or, at any rate, that the reporting would
not be exclusively one-sided.

   The argument used in this case is an instance of the argumentation
scheme for the circumstantial type of *ad hominem* argument, as can be
shown by examining its components and how they are put together to
support the conclusion. First, Gore's speech about the death of his sister
from lung cancer is cited as showing that he has advocated the proposition
that smoking is a very bad thing – something he is strongly against – in a
way that expresses his emotional stand against it in the strongest possible
terms. But then the argument goes on to say that Gore "failed to mention"
two key facts. One is that his family continued to grow tobacco after
the death of his sister. The other is that he continued to accept money
from "tobacco interests." The actions cited in these two statements clash
with what Gore is reported to have said in his speech. This clash takes
the form of a pragmatic inconsistency, from which the reader draws the
conclusion by implicature that Gore could not have sincerely meant what
he (so tearfully) said in his speech. The conclusion suggested is that he
must be a hypocrite, in the sense that he does not really mean what he
says. He passionately pours out his personal emotions against something,
but then, in his actions (which he "failed to mention" in his speech), he

actually supports and contributes to the production of this very thing he condemned so strongly.

Could there be an explanation for such a contradiction? The editorial actually gives one, but it makes Gore sound even more insincere. So the third part of the argumentation scheme for the circumstantial *ad hominem* is set into place. The reader draws the conclusion that Gore must be a "bad person" – that is, in this case, a hypocrite who recommends values and policies in his political speeches that are the direct opposite of his personal policies, as revealed by his own actions. This kind of inconsistency can be explained away, in many cases. But in this case, the implied argument seems to be air-tight. To seal it up even further, Gore's (presumed) reply offers even further evidence of his insincerity. The ultimate conclusion, the fourth stage indicated in the argumentation scheme for the circumstantial *ad hominem,* can then be drawn by the reader of the editorial. What is suggested is that Gore's tearful speech was a mere rhetorical flourish and that, because he is such an insincere man, you can't really trust or accept anything he says in politics.

To analyze the argument in this case, the first step is to confirm the classification above of the argument in the case as an instance of the circumstantial type of *ad hominem.* The allegation made is that Gore's actions and his arguments are pragmatically inconsistent – the two things clash, one being the opposite of the other. Also suggested by Gricean implicature from this inconsistency, as noted above, is that Gore's arguments against the use of tobacco products are not sincerely meant. The idea is that he says one thing but does another, so "actions speak louder than words." The personal attack element of the argument is the suggestion that Gore is hypocritical – that his argument is only political posturing and is not expressing a conclusion he really accepts personally. In this sense the circumstantial *ad hominem* leads into, and is built on, a personal attack of the ethotic type.

But exactly how is the personal attack drawn by Gricean implicature from the circumstantial contradiction that is posed by the argument? The alleged practical inconsistency arises from the clash between the following two propositions.

1. Gore, in a speech, tearfully described his sister's death from smoking-induced lung cancer.
2. For some years following his sister's death, Gore's family continued to grow tobacco and he continued to accept money from tobacco interests.

From proposition 1, the implication is drawn that Gore is strongly against smoking. The fact that his tearful description of his sister's death was part of a political speech implies that this description was relevant politically. In other words, presumably Gore included it in such a public speech because he was sending a message to the American public that smoking is a bad habit, that he is against smoking, and that the public generally ought to be against smoking. But then proposition 2 says that Gore, after his sister died of smoking-induced lung cancer (and the timing is very important to the *ad hominem* argument), personally accepted money from tobacco interests and his family profited from growing tobacco. But how exactly does this connection imply a contradiction that reveals hypocrisy?

Now there is, of course, a well-known connection between the growing of tobacco and the habit of smoking. Growing tobacco is a necessary means for smoking. We all know that cigarettes are produced from tobacco and that the normal way of manufacturing cigarettes has the growing of tobacco as one of its most important parts. So if anyone is sincerely against smoking, it would be highly questionable for that person not to be against the growing of tobacco. The close connection between smoking and tobacco makes the advocating of both propositions 1 and 2 by the same person highly questionable. It cries out for an explanation. And in the absence of one, the conclusion implied (by implicature) is that this person is the worst sort of hypocrite, even going so far as to exploit the death of his sister to move an audience for political gain. The implications of the inconsistency make Gore out to be not only a scoundrel, but ridiculous as well. So as an *ad hominem* attack, the argument is a powerful one indeed.

The picture presented of Gore, where he appears in a rhetorical pose with a visibly caring and passionate look on his face, adds to the ridicule invited by the argument. The idea of a speaker looking this sincere and acting in such a hypocritical way, suggesting a scurrilous opportunism and absurdly insincere posturing, is an irony that is funny, in just the way that the ironies satirized by Voltaire and Molière were funny. They depict a rogue who can sell things to gullible and unsuspecting buyers of his products or ideas by saying all sorts of ridiculous things that he does not believe at all. And yet he says them with the greatest apparent sincerity. It is somehow very ironic and hence comical to people that the respondent pays rapt attention to this absurd performance. The sincerity apparently expressed by both parties makes for a highly amusing dialogue. Whatever is at the bottom of it, the humor in this sort of *ad hominem* attack is a powerful part of its effectiveness.

5. The Battalino Case

The Battalino case occurred on February 6, 1999, day 16 of the senate impeachment trial of Bill Clinton, a day in which several important witnesses were interviewed, including Monica Lewinsky and Vernon Jordan. In the late stages of the hearing, manager Jim Rogan, with little time left, made one last point, in response to two previous arguments that had been used by the Democrats. One is a case of the idea of proportionality of punishment. The other is the argument that everybody lies about sex, therefore perjury should be minimized in a case of this sort. To counter these arguments, Rogan cited a case in which attorney and Veterans Administration doctor Linda Battalino admitted having sex with a patient, Ed Arthur, in her office in June of 1991. Dr. Battalino had asked Arthur – a veteran who had served two tours of duty in Vietnam and was suffering from post-traumatic stress disorder – to come to her office. She announced that she had "feelings" for him, and then performed oral sex on him. She then began a four-month intimate relationship with him. In 1992, Arthur sued her for sexual harassment, and Battalino denied in court that anything of a sexual nature had taken place in her office. But Arthur had tape-recorded about twenty-five hours of conversations with her that proved she had lied under oath. Jonathan F. Mitchell, the lawyer for the fraud section of the Justice Department's Criminal Division, prosecuted the case against Dr. Battalino. She lost her medical and legal rights to practice, resigned her position, was fined, and was sentenced to six months of imprisonment under electronic monitoring. The case had been reported in *The Boise Weekly* in 1991, but was not widely known until it was discovered by the media in 1998 in response to the question of perjury in the Lewinsky case.

In questioning Battalino, Rogan drew explicit comparisons to the case of Bill Clinton and Monica Lewinsky. In the following sequence of questions and replies, quoted from the CNN.com transcript, he showed that the two cases are alike in central respects. The key difference he drew out is that Battalino was not treated with leniency by the Clinton Justice Department.

ROGAN: Dr. Batta –
BATTALINO: Battalino.
ROGAN: Battalino. Your case intrigues me. I want to make sure I understand the factual circumstances. You lied about a one-time act of consensual sex with someone on federal property.
BATTALINO: Yes.

ROGAN: Is that correct?

BATTALINO: Absolutely correct.

ROGAN: And this act of perjury was in a civil lawsuit, not in a criminal case.

BATTALINO: That's also correct. And that –

ROGAN: In fact, the civil case eventually was dismissed.

BATTALINO: Correct.

ROGAN: Yet, despite the dismissal, you were prosecuted by the Clinton Justice Department for this act of perjury, is that correct?

BATTALINO: That's correct.

ROGAN: What I want to know, Dr. Battalino, during your ordeal, during your prosecution, did anybody from the White House, from the Justice Department, did any members of Congress, did any academics from respected universities, ever show up at your trial and suggest that you should be treated with leniency because everybody lies about sex?

BATTALINO: No sir.

ROGAN: Did anybody ever come forward from the White House or from the Justice Department and urge leniency for you because your perjury was only in a civil case?

BATTALINO: No.

ROGAN: Did they argue for leniency because the civil case, at which you committed perjury, was ultimately dismissed?

BATTALINO: No.

ROGAN: Did anybody from the White House ever say that leniency should be granted to you because you otherwise did your job very well?

BATTALINO: No.

ROGAN: Did anybody ever come forward from Congress to suggest that you were the victim of an overzealous, sex-obsessed prosecutor?

BATTALINO: No.

ROGAN: Now, according to the *New York Times* they report that you lied when your lawyer asked you at a deposition whether "Anything of a sexual nature" occurred. Is that correct?

BATTALINO: Yes, that's correct.

ROGAN: Did anybody from Congress or from the White House come forward to defend you saying that that phrase was ambiguous or it all depended what the word "anything" meant?

BATTALINO: No sir. May I just – I'm not sure if it was my lawyer that asked the question, but that is the exact question that I was asked.

ROGAN: The question that you were asked that caused your prosecution for perjury?

BATTALINO: That's correct.

ROGAN: No one ever asked if that phrase itself was ambiguous, did they?

BATTALINO: No.

UNIDENTIFIED JUDGE: Does the gentleman yield?

ROGAN: Regrettably, my time is limited and I will not yield for that purpose. Now Doctor, you lost two licenses, you lost a law license . . .

BATTALINO: Well I have a law degree, I was not a member of any bar.

ROGAN: Your conviction precludes you from practicing law?

BATTALINO: That's correct, sir.

ROGAN: You also had a medical degree?

BATTALINO: That's correct.

ROGAN: You lost your medical degree?

BATTALINO: Yes. I am no longer permitted to practice medicine either.

ROGAN: Did anybody from the White House or from Congress come forward during your prosecution or during your sentencing and suggest that rather than you suffer the incredibly difficult punishment of no longer being able to practice your profession, perhaps you should simply just receive some sort of rebuke or censure?

BATTALINO: No one came to my aid or defense, no.

ROGAN: Nobody from the Justice Department suggested that during your sentencing hearing?

BATTALINO: No.

ROGAN: Has anybody come forward from the White House to suggest to you that in light of circumstances as we now appear to see them unfolding, you should be pardoned for your offense?

BATTALINO: Nobody has come, no.

(END VIDEO CLIP)

ROGAN: That's how the Clinton administration defines proportionality and punishment. Mr. Chief Justice, we reserve the balance of our time.

Toward the end of the sequence of dialogue quoted above, Battalino replied, in answer to Rogan's questions, that because of her conviction, she was no longer allowed to practice either medicine or law. Driving his point home, Rogan also had her admit that nobody from the White House or Congress came forward to suggest that she should only "receive some sort of rebuke or censure" instead of the harsher punishment she received. The intended parallel to the Lewinsky case is highly evident at this point.

Rogan's argument is clearly an argument from analogy. He is comparing the earlier case of Battalino's perjury about an act of consensual sex on federal property with the Lewinsky case. But the argument is more than just an argument from analogy. It would appear that it can also be classified as an instance of the circumstantial *ad hominem* argument. What has been shown above is that it is characteristic of this form of argument that one party attacks another party by arguing that the first party "does not practice what he preaches," and then uses this allegation of inconsistency to undermine the first party's prior argument. Rogan's argument can be so classified, provided it can be analyzed as putting forward the following premises and conclusions.

Premise 1: Clinton lied under oath about an act of consensual sex in his workplace, but argued that he ought to be treated with leniency.

Premise 2: In an earlier case where a woman lied under oath about
an act of consensual sex in her workplace, Clinton [in the form of
his justice department] prosecuted the case, and did not treat the
woman with leniency.

Conclusion: Clinton did not practice (in the earlier case) what he now
preaches (in this case).

The secondary conclusion Rogan's argument leads to, based on the first
conclusion above, is that Clinton's argument for leniency in his own case
is not worth much. Clinton, according to Rogan, has argued that he
ought to be treated with leniency on various grounds. One is the idea of
proportionality. The other is that everybody lies about sex, and that min-
imizes the perjury. But the fact is that the Clinton Justice Department,
when faced with a similar case, did not show leniency when prosecuting the case. The ultimate conclusion that Rogan's argument implies is
that Clinton's own actions belie the sincerity of his argument. He wants
leniency for himself, but did not give it to someone else in the same situation. It would seem then that, at least on the basis of this brief outline of
what is taken to be its main structure, Rogan's argument fits into the form
of argument identified above as that of the circumstantial *ad hominem*. But
is this circumstantial *ad hominem* argument really the one that Rogan is
putting forward in the impeachment trial? The first problem is to identify
the argument, before going on to attempt to analyze or evaluate it.

6. Classifying the Argument in the Battalino Case

In attempting to identify, analyze, or evaluate any real argument, there
are always many uncertainties, questions of interpretation, and rough
edges. And so it is with this case. Some may be inclined to doubt, for
example, that Rogan really meant to make a circumstantial *ad hominem*
type of argument. There are four interrelated grounds for doubt that call
for discussion. These are all based on considerations that have a basis in
the text and context of discourse of the case.

   The first consideration is that Rogan is arguing against prior arguments
for leniency and for the principle of proportionality. Citing the Battalino
case could be directed just at attacking these arguments rather than at
attacking Clinton personally. After all, Rogan was only citing a precedent –
a similar case. Citing of precedent is not an *ad hominem* form of argument,
at least not necessarily. And the case was from a trial that took place
six years before Clinton's impeachment trial. It's not like the smoking

case, where the problem was a conflict between what was argued and what was presently being done. Maybe Rogan was just arguing that there was no leniency in this other case. And if the ruling in that case can be defended as reasonable, there should be no leniency in this case. This argument is not an *ad hominem* argument, but just an argument from precedent.

Another ground for doubt concerns the person who is the subject of the argument. The point is that the Battalino case was prosecuted by "the Clinton Justice Department," to use Rogan's terms. It was not prosecuted by Clinton himself, as the prosecuting attorney in the case. Nor is it Clinton himself who is making the plea for leniency in the impeachment trial. It is his attorneys who are pleading for leniency on his behalf. So it is not the same person who put forward the arguments in the two allegedly similar cases. So Rogan's argument is therefore not really a circumstantial *ad hominem* after all. The main problem here is that Clinton was governor at the time, so it was "his" justice system that prosecuted the Battalino case. But he may have had nothing to do with it, directly. He may even have strongly disagreed with the judgment in the case, but may not have been able to intervene, or thought it inappropriate to do so. Maybe he didn't even know about the case.

The third ground for doubt is that if Rogan's argument is a personal attack (*ad hominem*) argument on Clinton, this aspect of it is not stated explicitly. On the surface, the argument seems to be an argument from commitment of the following form.

Premise 1: Nobody from the White House, the Congress, or the Clinton Justice Department argued for leniency in the Battalino case.
Premise 2: The Battalino case was an instance of perjury relating to an act of consensual sex in the workplace.
Conclusion: All those indicated are committed to non-leniency in cases of perjury relating to acts of consensual sex in the workplace.

The upshot of this argument from commitment is that these people should be committed to non-leniency in this case too. Therefore, they should prosecute Clinton without leniency – they should be on the side of impeachment. But this argument from commitment is not, by itself, an *ad hominem* argument. The doubt then is whether Rogan is making an *ad hominem* attack on Clinton at all. Maybe he is just putting forward an argument from commitment, and we are just reading into the text that there is an *ad hominem* argument there.

There is a form of argument called argument from pragmatic inconsistency (or say one thing, do another) identified in Walton (1998a, p. 218).

Argument from Pragmatic Inconsistency

   a advocates argument α, which has proposition A as its conclusion.
   a has carried out an action or set of actions that imply that *a* is personally committed to not-A (the opposite, or negation of A).
   Therefore *a*'s argument α should not be accepted.

I argue that this type of argument should not be classified as a species of *ad hominem* argument. The reason is that it lacks the premise to the effect that *a* is a bad person. But if the implication that *a* is bad person is there, the argument then becomes an *ad hominem* argument. For example, if in using argument from pragmatic inconsistency, the arguer says that *a*'s actions represent his true commitments, and the conclusion is drawn that *a* is deceiving us, or that *a* is a hypocrite, or something of that sort, then the argument is a genuine *ad hominem*. In short, the general problem posed by the third ground for doubt is whether Rogan's argument is really an *ad hominem*, or whether it is only an argument from pragmatic inconsistency (but not one of the *ad hominem* type).

The fourth ground for doubt relates to Rogan's intentions. We, as critics in this case, do not really know what Rogan's intentions were in citing the prior Battalino case. Rogan never uses the expression *ad hominem*, or any equivalent expression. And he does not appear to come right out anywhere and claim that Clinton is bad person, or that Clinton is a hypocrite, or anything of that sort. Maybe, then, he didn't really intend to attack Clinton with an *ad hominem* argument at all. Maybe he merely meant to cite the difference between the two cases, and leave it at that. Or maybe, as suggested above, he was only using argumentation from commitment, but stopping short of a full *ad hominem* argument of the kind that essentially involves personal attack. After all, if Rogan didn't really intend to attack Clinton personally, how can we fairly classify his argument as a circumstantial *ad hominem*, a personal attack argument?

I believe that each of these four grounds for doubt has some evidence to support it and that each argument merits discussion. But I also think that all four can be adequately replied to, based on the textual and contextual evidence given in the Battalino case text of discourse quoted above. Let's start with the fourth one. The basic point to be made here is that when we evaluate an argument in a given case, we don't need to prove what the arguer's intentions really were in that case. For example, it has been held that because a fallacy is an intentional deception, in order to prove that fallacy was committed in a particular case, it has to be shown that the arguer had an intent to deceive. But Govier (1987) has rejected this view as a form of psychologism. To show that an argument is fallacious in a given case, according to Govier, you do not need to prove intent. But you do have to show that a kind of strategy was involved. What you need to prove is that it is an instance of one of the types of argument that can be used fallaciously and that in this case it has been used in a way that falls into a certain pattern as an argumentation strategy. Carrying out such a task of evaluation does not require proof that the arguer actually had guilty motives or an intent to deceive.

7. Evaluating the Argument in the Battalino Case

After the passage quoted above, the impeachment hearing went on to discuss Monica Lewinsky's prior testimony. No reply to Rogan's argument on the Battalino case was made, nor was the case discussed any further. So we don't really know what impact it had on the trial, if any. Nor do we know how Clinton's defenders replied to it. Rather than speculate on such matters, the more interesting dialectical task is to try to analyze and evaluate the Battalino case as an argument. In particular, it is interesting to try to evaluate the *ad hominem* argument that is apparently contained in it. Should it be judged to be a reasonable *ad hominem* argument or a fallacious one? Or does it lie somewhere between these extremes?

One reply to the argument is that it is not relevant, because the Battalino case took place over twenty years before the impeachment trial. Clinton could have changed his views since then. And anyway, he was only remotely related to the case and was not himself the prosecutor. Therefore, it could be argued, the relevance of the Battalino case to the impeachment case is tangential and minimal. Against this argument is the argument for relevance. The two cases are quite similar. Both involve prosecution of a case of consensual sexual relations in a federal government workplace between a powerful person and someone who was dependent on or in a subordinate position to the offender. The Clinton policy has been strongly against sexual harassment in all forms, both then and now, and presumably this policy has not changed. So the Battalino case would seem to be quite relevant to the one under consideration in the impeachment trial. It seems to be possible at least to make a strong case for relevance.

An *ad hominem* argument should be evaluated in light of how it can respond to critical questioning in the type of dialogue to which it was put forward as a contribution. I have presented (1998a, pp. 224–225) six critical questions corresponding to the circumstantial type of *ad hominem* argument.

1. What are the propositions alleged to be practically inconsistent, and are they practically inconsistent?
2. If the identified propositions are not practically inconsistent as things stand, are there at least some grounds for a claim of practical inconsistency in the textual evidence of the discourse?
3. Even if there is not an explicit practical inconsistency, what is the connection between the pair of propositions alleged to be inconsistent?
4. If there is a practical inconsistency that can be identified as the focus of the attack, how serious a flaw is it? Could the apparent conflict be resolved or explained without destroying the consistency of the commitment in the dialogue?
5. Does it follow from *a*'s inconsistent commitment that *a* is a bad person?
6. Should the conclusion be the weaker claim, that *a*'s credibility is open to question, or the stronger claim, that the conclusion of α is false?

The analysis above shows which two propositions are alleged to be practically inconsistent. So the first critical question, and with it the second and third, can be answered. Of all six critical questions, the one that is hardest to answer affirmatively is question 5. The main problem in this case is that Rogan never explicitly states, in so many words, that Clinton is a bad person or that the Clinton administration is unethical – for example, that they are liars. The best we can say is that the implication that the Clinton administration has been less than forthright is suggested by what Rogan says. The best evidence that the latter is drawing such a conclusion, or trying to get the audience to draw it, is his last statement: "That's how the Clinton administration defines proportionality and punishment." This remark has an edge of irony to it, suggesting that the Clinton administration has not been forthright about how they define proportionality and punishment. Hence there is evidence that Rogan's argument is *ad hominem*, but it is not conclusive. So here we are back to the classification problem again. Evaluation of the argument as weak or strong must depend on how it should be classified. Is it *ad hominem* or merely an argument from pragmatic inconsistency?

Judged as an argument from pragmatic inconsistency, Rogan's argument is reasonable, and not fallacious. It is quite a strong argument, because of the close similarity of the two cases. But it is subject to critical questioning. If the opposing side had wished to reply to it, it could have found several weak points in it to question. It could have shown, for example, that the people who prosecuted that case may be people different from those who now argue for leniency. They could have argued that the earlier case took place twenty years ago, and used that to question its relevance or to argue that the situation has somehow changed. There are various avenues of critical questioning open. But as things stand, Rogan's argument looks persuasive. It simply asserts that the Clinton administration prosecuted without leniency then, but is all for leniency now. This apparent inconsistency by itself, even without using it as the basis of an *ad hominem* attack, is a fairly persuasive. It indicates that the Clinton administration's argument for leniency is somehow dubious, because it conflicts with what was advocated in a previous case, where the administration prosecuted without leniency. This argument by itself is sufficient to sow legitimate doubts in the minds of an audience.

8. Implicature and Innuendo

Rogan's argument, when judged to be *ad hominem* argument, is a genteel and indirect one. He does not come right out and call the Clinton administration names, saying they are liars or hypocrites. His pointing out the inconsistency on how they have treated the two cases is used only to suggest that the administration's argument for leniency and proportionality is not very credible. With respect to critical question 6, then, the answer is that Rogan is claiming only that the credibility of the Clinton administration is open to question. He is not making the stronger claim that the conclusion of the Clinton administration's argument is false. He is arguing that the administration's stance on prosecuting for perjury in the Battalino case has shifted to the opposite in the Lewinsky case. What he is saying is that they may argue for leniency now, but when their interests were not at stake, in the earlier case, they did not prosecute with leniency. This argument suggests that the Clinton administration is just arguing this way because it is in their interests to do so. They are not arguing that way because they really believe the argument or are committed to it.

But now notice we have come to the point where we are discussing an argument that was only suggested by the text of discourse in the Battalino case, not explicitly stated. We are getting into the area of suggestion, implicature, and innuendo. Is that legitimate? Can we attribute arguments on the basis of what was suggested in a case, as opposed to what was explicitly stated? The answer is yes. If we are to understand and evaluate fallacies, we must deal with innuendo and suggestion. For it is the very factor of innuendo that makes many an *ad hominem* argument so powerful and so difficult to refute.

To analyze arguments based on implicature, innuendo, and indirect speech acts, contextual assumptions about collaborative conversation in the form of so-called conversational postulates or ethical rules of polite discourse (Grice 1975; Johnstone 1981) are very important. In many cases of rhetorical arguments of the kind studied in this book, the speaker or writer sets up suggestions in the form of inferences that will be drawn by a mass audience when the message is broadcast to them. In the most persuasive kind of commercial ad or political message, the speaker does not come right out and say what he means. Instead, he draws a picture in the form of a sketch with missing parts and lets the audience fill in the missing parts. This way, the members of the audience have a creative role. They use their own initiative to draw the invited conclusion. And the speaker has plausible deniability. If confronted with having made a damaging or controversial allegation, he can deny that he meant to say anything like that at all. Plausible deniability works because the speaker does not state the conclusion himself. The audience generally draws this conclusion not by deductive or inductive reasoning but by a process of suggestion or innuendo.

Dascal and Gross (1999) have shown how the Aristotelian framework of rhetoric in Perelman and Olbrechts-Tyteca (1969) and the Gricean pragmatic theory of conversational interaction can work together well as tools to study forms of argumentation, such as *ad misericordiam* and *ad hominem*. They showed how such forms of argument, even though traditionally viewed as fallacies, can be modeled as reasonable forms of rhetorical persuasion based on *pathos* and *ethos*. When such arguments are used, typically a speaker suggests a conclusion that the hearer then draws by implicature within the Gricean framework of a collaborative talk exchange. A Gricean conversational implicature is an inference drawn by one party in a conversation based on what another party has previously said in the conversation, using rules governing how both parties should contribute collaboratively to the conversation.

Grice (1975, p. 65) used the following example to illustrate how a conversational implicature is drawn. The participants in the conversation are represented by variables, *A*, *B*, and *C*, after Grice's notation.

Suppose that *A* and *B* are talking about a mutual friend *C*, who is now working in a bank. *A* asks *B* how *C* is getting on in his job, and *B* replies, "Oh quite well, I think; he likes his colleagues, and he hasn't been to prison yet." At this point *A* might well inquire what *B* was implying, what he was suggesting, or even what he meant by saying that *C* had not yet been to prison. The answer might be any one of such things as that *C* is the sort of person likely to yield to the temptation provided by his occupation, that *C*'s colleagues are really very unpleasant and treacherous people, and so forth.

In this case, *A* draws the conclusion that *C* is a not a very honest or trustworthy person. By what process does the speaker set up the message so that A draws this inference? Grice's explanation is that when the speaker is seen to violate a conversational rule, the hearer will recognize that the violation is intentional. The hearer will then draw an inference that the speaker is indirectly trying to convey a message. Of course, the message has been conveyed covertly without the speaker actually asserting that *C* is dishonest. Thus, as Grice noted, the hearer may actually ask the speaker what he was suggesting.

How is the conclusion communicated by the speaker drawn by the hearer in cases of Gricean implicature? As noted above, it is not by deductive reasoning or by inductive reasoning based on probability and statistics. It is based on expectations set in place by the speaker's actual message and by the conversational context in which the speaker put forward the message and the hearer received and understood it. Calling on a term used in artificial intelligence, the process of reasoning could be described as an inference to the best explanation. The best explanation the hearer could give of what the speaker said, and why he said it (his goals or intentions), is that he was intentionally violating a conversational rule. Thus, to grasp how implicatures work, we need to understand more about conversational rules. Grice calls these rules conversational maxims, formulating the following four conversational maxims (1975, p. 68).

Maxim of Quantity: Make your contribution as informative as is required for the current purposes of the talk exchange.
Maxim of Quality: Try to make your contribution one that is true.
Maxim of Relation: Be relevant.
Maxim of Manner: Be perspicuous.

The first two maxims are self-explanatory, but the other two need to be explained a bit. The maxim of manner, although about clarity, may not seem clear at first. Grice explained this maxim by means of four injunctions: (1) avoid obscurity of expression, (2) avoid ambiguity, (3) be brief, and (4) be orderly. He explained relevance by stating the rule that one should expect a speech partner's contribution to be appropriate to immediate needs at each stage of a conversation (p. 68). Thus, for example, if a question has been asked by one speech partner at the last move in a conversation, the next move made by the other speech partner should be relevant. It should be a reply to the question, or at least a response that addresses the question. Making an unrelated remark, like "It's a nice day," would be irrelevant. Thus relevance has to do with fitting into the connected sequence of proper moves in a dialogue. The maxims all need to be understood in light of a more general principle that governs all conversations or collaborative goal-directed dialogues: "Make your conversational contribution such as is required, at the stage at which it occurs, by the accepted purpose of the talk exchange in which you are engaged" (p. 67). Grice called this principle the cooperative principle (*CP*).

Grice (p. 69) showed how the *CP* is used, along with conversational maxims, in explaining how the implicature is drawn in the case about *A*, *B*, and *C* above. First, it is apparent to *A* that *B*'s statement that *C* hasn't been to prison yet is not relevant to the rest of the conversation. What could explain this irrelevance? A plausible explanation is that *B* may be intentionally violating the *CP* by "flouting" (Grice's term) the maxim of relevance. Does this mean that *B* is opting out of the conversation by being intentionally uncooperative? That is one explanation, but *A* has no further evidence that *B* is really opting out of the conversation, as *B* appears to be cooperative in other respects. As an alternative explanation of what has occurred, *A* can try to make what *B* says relevant. How could *A* do that? Well, the fact known to both speech partners is that *C* is working at a bank. The expected or normal outcome of some dishonest practice in that situation would be *C*'s going to jail. From *B*'s remark that *C* has not gone to jail yet, *A* can draw the conclusion that what *B* is suggesting is that *C* is not entirely honest or trustworthy. One can see already how imputations of this sort are the standard tools of innuendo and so-called smear tactics of the kind used in negative campaign tactics.

Another example from Grice (p. 71) can be cited. Asked to write a letter of reference for a student who is applying for a job in philosophy, a professor writes, "Dear Sir, Mr. X's command of English is excellent, and his attendance at tutorials has been regular, Yours, etc." As we all know, this kind of letter would be interpreted by the reader as conveying the message that Mr X is not a strong candidate. The writer of the letter has not gone on record as saying so explicitly, but that message can be inferred indirectly from what he wrote. Grice explains this phenomenon by appeal to a conversational postulate he calls the Maxim of Quantity (p. 68), which states that a contribution to a conversation should be neither more nor less than is required. Because the writer of the letter is saying too little, we search around for an explanation. He knows that more information is wanted, and because X is his student, he must have that information. The only plausible explanation that seems to be left is that he thinks that Mr. X is not a strong candidate.

What this case shows is that when a message is conveyed indirectly by innuendo, the receiver gets the message because of background assumptions that are not stated but are known to the speaker and hearer. In this case, the two parties are engaged in an information-seeking dialogue, and both understand that there are conversational postulates governing this collaborative kind of dialogue. What is not said, taken together with the conversational postulate, suggests a particular conclusion or message that the receiver draws by inference.

Many of the most powerfully effective *ad hominem* arguments are cases where the proponent does not come right out and assert that the respondent has done something bad or has exhibited some character flaw. Instead, the proponent only says that she has heard rumors to this effect and that although she does not believe these rumors herself, nevertheless that is the word going around. Another way of mounting the attack is to say that the allegations were "leaked" by a source who is close to the proponent but who does not want to be identified. These ways of putting forward an *ad hominem* argument remove the requirement of burden of proof and leave room for plausible deniability. This type of *ad hominem* argument is often much more effective, because it can raise suspicions and doubts that can be highly damaging, and impossible or extremely hard to disprove. It does not really need to be proved in order to be effective. For example, if put forward just before an election, the respondent may have no time to effectively rebut this form of argument.

Rogan's argument is one of these tricky ones used as a tactic to evade burden of proof. It is an *ad hominem* argument, but one based on suggestion. That should not be taken as meaning that it is a bad argument or a fallacious one. For many of the most persuasive arguments work that way. For example, some facts may be cited, or a story told, or an inconsistency pointed out, but the ultimate conclusion to be drawn may never be explicitly stated. Even so, the audience may be quite capable of drawing it themselves. And when they do so, they may find it acceptable.

The tricky, and therefore especially interesting, tactic exhibited by this case is the conjunction of the two propositions used as a dual basis for supporting the one side of the alleged pragmatic inconsistency. The conjunction is composed of the following two propositions.

> P1: For some years following his sister's death, Gore's family continued to grow tobacco.
>
> P2: Gore continued to accept money from tobacco interests.

As shown above, the allegation made in P1 is quite a weak and questionable basis for an *ad hominem* argument. We don't blame people for things that members of their families do. So unless there is some further link to be established here, P1 is not much of a basis for an *ad hominem* argument that shows that Gore is a bad person. The real basis of the *ad hominem* argument is P2. While a lot of other politicians probably also accepted money from "tobacco interests" at the time Gore was alleged to have done so, still, his having done this does clash with his speech about his sister in a way that strongly supports the *ad hominem* argument used against him.

So the trick in this case is to combine a weak but persuasive basis for an *ad hominem* argument with a stronger basis. The stronger basis, by itself, does not seem all that impressive (probably because all politicians were engaged in pretty much the same practice at the time). But when combined with the weaker one (that somehow looks more impressive when combined with the stronger one), the effect is considerable. The argument, as a whole, succeeds in making Gore look quite ridiculous. This *ad hominem* argument is revealed as quite weak from a critical point of view, once it is analyzed as above. But it is highly persuasive when you first encounter it, without really thinking about it too much. At least, it would certainly be persuasive to those who are cynical about politicians to begin with or to those who already suspect that Gore is selling a kind of superficial rhetoric to support his own interests and those of his allies. To the extent that a reader has these cynical attitudes, she is likely to find the *ad hominem* argument used in this case easy to accept.

10. Evaluating the Arguments Rhetorically and Dialectically

In the Battalino case, there was a question about whether the argument really was *ad hominem* as opposed to a mere attempt to smear a person by attacking his character, instead of his argument. The same question also needs to be raised in the Gore case. Is the argument really *ad hominem*, or is it just a slur against Gore's character? For it is a requirement of an argument being an *ad hominem* argument that it be a personal attack used to detract from the argument of the party being attacked (Walton 1998a). Calling someone a bad name, for example, is not necessarily an *ad hominem* argument. An *ad hominem* is not just any slur on someone's character. It must be one used to try to refute or attack that person's argument by attacking the credibility of the arguer for that purpose. It is a matter not of the actual intention of the attacker but of how the argument is being used in a given case.

In this case, then, we need to ask what argument of Gore's was the attack on his character, by way of the alleged circumstantial conflict, being used to refute? Presumably, it was his passionate speech. This speech, if relevant to politics at all, was a message to people against smoking. Was the *Time* segment (as quoted above) then meant to be an attack against smoking? Could you say it sent a kind of pro-smoking message? Presumably not. That does not seem to be what the editorial was about. And if not, the question is whether the editorial really contains an *ad hominem* argument at all.

I believe there is something more in this question than many commentators might initially be inclined to think. In a way, the editorial is, I believe, a kind of pseudo *ad hominem* argument that is being played as much for its entertainment value as for its serious political content as an argument. But on the other hand, there is enough of an element of counter-argument there to serve as a basis for classifying the editorial as containing a circumstantial *ad hominem* argument. The basis for this classification is that Gore's speech as a whole is being attacked by the argument in the editorial, even though no details of the speech are given in the editorial itself. But the speech is recent news, and readers of the editorial are presumably aware of the contents of the speech. And therefore there is some basis for classifying the *Time* segment as an *ad hominem* argument. Yet that basis only allows such a classification as conditional and partial. A subtler analysis of the argument would be that it is used to attack Gore's personal *ethos* in a way that makes amusing material for an editorial comment, while posing as an *ad hominem* argument, and thereby making the editorial seem more legitimate as political commentary. So the interesting point is that the argument is a borderline *ad hominem*, one that has all the elements of this type of argument except (arguably) one. In this respect it is comparable to the Battalino case.

The Gore case looks like a pretty typical example of the circumstantial *ad hominem* argument as used in political discourse. And in certain respects it is. The allegation of pragmatic inconsistency is there, and use is made of it to mount a personal attack on the character of a politician. But some factors of the context of dialogue in which the argument was used need to be observed. It is not the more typical kind of case of one politician attacking the policy or argument of another in a political debate, for example, with a negative ad in an election campaign, of the kind studied by Pfau and Burgoon (1989). Instead, the argument in this case is an ironic commentary on an editorial page of a major national news magazine by an anonymous author. The purpose is somewhat unclear. It may be more of an attempt to stir up controversy or to amuse readers who are cynical about politicians, than it is an attempt to attack Gore's political position or some specific argument he has advanced. But it very definitely has a strong *ad hominem* component. It has been argued above that this case should, on balance, be classified as an instance of a circumstantial *ad hominem* argument.

Looking at the Battalino case as a media message, it is hard to judge what real impact it had on the impeachment proceedings or on the television audience that it also reached. There appeared to be no further discussion of this particular argument in the subsequent proceedings of the impeachment trial. Searching through *Newspaper Abstracts* on March 1, 1999, I could not find any further media commentary on the case. However, there was media commentary before the impeachment trial on how the Battalino case had originally come to public attention. Clinton's lawyers had complained that nobody had ever been criminally investigated for perjury in a civil case about sexual conduct. Monica Lewinsky's lawyer had said on *NBC Today* in February 1998, "I challenge you or any of the pundits on the air to find me a case of civil perjury that has been pursued criminally at the federal level in the last 100 years." A search for legal cases then turned up the Battalino case, among others. So by February 1999 when the impeachment trial was under way, the Battalino case was known to the public. Rogan simply took advantage of it as the basis for one of the arguments he used in the trial.

Looking at the argument dialectically, in the context of the impeachment proceedings, what thrust did it appear to have in the debate? From a narrow perspective, its thrust seems to be against leniency. If the Clinton justice system was not lenient in the Battalino case, then on the basis of argument from commitment, that would seem to be a good reason to be against leniency in this case.

But maybe the argument had a much broader import. The Clinton position, on the whole, is open to circumstantial *ad hominem* attack, because of the strong stand taken in the past by the Clinton administration on a case of a sexual relationship between someone in a position of power and someone in a position of dependency on that power. They have tended, in general, to support the strong prosecution of such cases. Citing the Battalino case not only reminds us of that commitment, but also excludes possible ways out by stressing the similarity between the Battalino and the Lewinsky cases. Both were consensual, both took place in a government workplace, and both involved a subordinate relationship in the hierarchy. By citing the Battalino case, therefore, Rogan mounted quite a broad sort of attack on the whole Clinton administration, as well as on the president in particular. Rogan argued that, on fundamental principles, the Clinton administration had always been strongly in favor of prosecuting such cases. But then, when it affected one of their own, they turned around and used arguments like the principle of proportionality to argue against prosecuting the case strongly. This argument, then, is a form of circumstantial *ad hominem* argument that has a broad sweep. It attacked Clinton, his administration, and even the Democratic party as a whole, arguing that they don't follow their own principles. This was an attack on alleged hypocrisy that was potentially very powerful, not only in the impeachment trial, but as addressed to public opinion by way of television.

One way to evaluate Rogan's argument is as an argument from analogy between the situation of Battalino and that of Clinton. The comparison between the two cases holds up persuasively in many relevant respects, as argued by Rogan. You could counter this argument by pointing out other relevant respects in which the two are dissimilar. For example, Battalino was a physician and Arthur was a patient in her care, whereas Clinton was president and Monica Lewinsky was an intern in his office. Using this kind of comparison, you could argue that Rogan's argument from commitment is weak. So just because the Clinton administration was not in favor of leniency in the Battalino case, it does not follow (according to this way of evaluating the argument) that they have to be against leniency in the present case. This is one way to evaluate the argument, but it misses the point, in certain important respects, because its real thrust is not just an argument from commitment. The real thrust is found in Rogan's closing remark, "That's how the Clinton administration defines proportionality and punishment." The thrust of the argument is that the Clinton administration's real view of proportionality and punishment in a case of perjury to conceal an improper sexual relationship is revealed or defined by its actions in the Battalino case. Contrasting their actions in that case with their argument for proportionality and leniency in this case suggests that their argument is not sincerely meant. What is suggested is that they do not really believe or support his argument themselves and that they use it not because they really accept it, but only because it supports their interests.

So the real thrust of Rogan's argument is missed if it is just seen as an argument from analogy or an argument from commitment. It is both, but its strongest impact is as a circumstantial *ad hominem* argument that is used to suggest that the supporters of the argument do not themselves sincerely believe it, as is revealed by their own actions. Assuming that Rogan has gotten the details of the Battalino case right, this circumstantial *ad hominem* argument is a reasonable one. Its weak points have already been noted. The weakest part of the ad hominem argument is that "the Clinton administration" is treated as a single stable group that is the arguer in both cases. But on the whole, as a circumstantial *ad hominem* argument, Rogan's argument is a reasonably good one. It is weak in certain respects, but it is not one that should be judged fallacious.

From a dialectical and rhetorical perspective, comparing the two cases is interesting. In the Battalino case, there was an actual dialogue between the two leading participants. In the Gore case, there was little real dialogue. Although Gore's reply to the argument was printed, the way it was done made his case look even worse. The Gore case was typical of what we so often see in argumentation in political and commercial ads. The argument is a short message in the print or broadcast media with some visual material. What is visible is mainly the proponent's side of the argument in the form of an *ad hominem* or other type of argument, such as an appeal to fear or pity. The problem, as noted in chapter 2, is that we don't see the dialogue because we see little evidence of the respondent's argument or point of view. The ad seems to be a one-shot message sent out by the proponent or presenter to the mass audience. Where is the dialogue? But if you compare the Battalino and Gore cases, it is evident that there is the same kind of multi-agent dialogue implicit in the Gore case that was more visible in the Battalino case. In both cases, the same type of circumstantial *ad hominem* was used. The structural and dialectical similarities are highly evident, once both cases have been analyzed. Thus these cases bring out very well how even the short political or commercial ad of the kind so typically used in rhetorical persuasion attempts has a multi-agent dialectical structure. The key is to be found in the proponent's argument strategy. The strategy builds on the anticipated reaction of the mass audience, and the argument is directed to this reaction. Such an argument is thus devised as a response to anticipated critical questioning by a respondent. Or at least an argument in an ad can be analyzed in this dialectical fashion. And when it is so analyzed, a lot of interesting features come out. One can get a much better idea of how the rhetorical argumentation works as a persuasion attempt. One can also get a good idea of how to react to such an argument or counter it in a reply. Of course, each case is unique. But in this chapter it has been shown how the *ad hominem* argument has a distinctive dialectical structure.

6

Arguments Based on Popular Opinion

In the kinds of media arguments examined so far, including those classified as appeals to fear and pity and as *ad hominem* arguments, the argument is partly based on and directed to popular opinion. In the type of argument called *argumentum ad populum*, as defined in chapter 3, the proponent tries to get the respondent to accept an opinion or perform an action because that opinion is accepted by the popular majority. Of course, much of what we do we learn by watching or following others. And there is a powerful urge not to be singled out or left out of the group. Thus, as already shown in the analysis of propaganda in chapter 3, this form of argument can psychologically be very powerful. But from an evidential point of view, it would appear to be extremely weak. For just because a large number of people accept some proposition, it does not follow that the proposition is true. We have all long been taught that such an inference is erroneous. We are all aware that science has proved many popularly accepted beliefs to be false. How then should one evaluate an appeal to popular opinion? Could there be some legitimate grounds for accepting such an argument in some instances, or is the commonly accepted view in logic right that this type of argument is fallacious?

There is a tendency to swing to extremes in evaluating arguments based on appeal to popular opinion. As shown in chapter 3, traditional logic textbooks have portrayed the *argumentum ad populum* as a fallacy. Yet many arguments used in media ads are based on appeal to public opinion as a means of marketing commercial products. If these arguments are patently unreasonable, why do they appear to work so well as persuasive strategies? This question poses a number of fundamental puzzles about arguments used in mass media ads and appeals. To study the question through actual examples, three cases of commercial ads are featured in this chapter as focal points of the investigation. One part of the problem is to identify the argumentation schemes (forms of argument) for the various species of *ad populum* arguments involved. Another part of the structure turns out to be dialectical, referring to the conversational context in which a pair of speech partners reason together in a collaborative goal-directed exchange. When both structures have been integrated, an answer to the question of how to evaluate these arguments can be given. The answer is furnished by building an objective structure for evaluating these arguments that does not swing, without any objective basis for judging cases, to the one extreme or the other.

In this chapter a deeper insight into media arguments based on popular opinion is attained by studying the dialectical nature of these arguments, something not well appreciated in the past and only now being uncovered in the work of Freeman on argumentation containing presumptions and commonly accepted premises. According to Freeman (2005, p. 311), there should be a presumption for common knowledge for acceptance of a statement that is in accord with what is accepted as normal, usual, or customary in public discourse. Use of such presumptions as premises in an argument based on common knowledge should be acceptable dialectically under the appropriate dialectical and rhetorical constraints, even though such arguments are fallible and can be fallacious in some instances. The rationale behind the careful and balanced use of such premises in argumentation, it will be argued in this chapter, lies in the concession of them tentatively for purposes of rational persuasion and deliberation.

1. Influencing the Mass Audience

Many of the appeal to pity and appeal to fear arguments studied in chapter 4, as well as the *ad hominem* arguments studied in chapter 5, are obviously attempts to influence a mass audience using rhetorical argumentation. In the Nayirah case, for example, the argument was basically a public relations strategy designed to win public sympathy for a cause. The use of fear appeal arguments to try to get teenagers to stop smoking or to engage in "safe sex" were clearly rhetorical strategies designed to influence a particular target audience. Those who design such ads are well aware that they are trying to reach a well-defined mass audience. The targeting to a specific mass audience is a vital part of the strategy of the ad. If you think of it, this aspect of such an argument is dialectically peculiar.

The intended respondent of the argument is not a single person but a group of identifiable respondents who may be expected to have particular opinions about lots of things, including the issue that is the subject of the ad. What these ads have in common is their being attempts to influence public opinion, or what might be called popular opinion. An ad might be targeted to a specific demographic group, or it might be just an attempt to influence public opinion generally, to make the general climate of opinion more accepting of a particular viewpoint or policy. In some of the arguments we have examined, the directing of the argument toward influencing public opinion is obvious. In other cases, this aspect of it is concealed beneath appearances. The argument may look on the surface as if it was directed to a single respondent, but beneath the surface it may also be directed to a wider audience. Such observations led us to the respondent-to-dialogue (RTD) problem in chapter 4. In this chapter we examine arguments that in many instances are aimed to influence popular opinion, but are also based on premises that appeal to popular opinion.

In many of the cases examined so far there has been a split respondent effect. From one point of view the argument appears to be directed to a particular respondent. The message is directed toward the commitments of a particular respondent. From this point of view, the argument can be analyzed by dialectical methods. For example, in the Gore case studied in chapter 5, the argument appears to be directed toward Al Gore as respondent. And the argument was based on what were taken to be the commitments of Gore expressed in his speech. However, it is also possible to look at such an argument from a different point of view. From a rhetorical point of view, the argument is directed toward public opinion. In the Gore case, the article was printed in *Time* as a kind of editorial comment. The author of the article was not (of course) actually arguing with Al Gore. He was writing a kind of ironic comment on Gore's speech. From this rhetorical point of view it is possible to see the argument as an attempt to influence public opinion. Of course we all know that such an article is highly political in nature. It's not just an abstract critical discussion about the issue. It's really an *ad hominem* attack designed to influence a mass readership in a political context. The split respondent effect represents this duality in the argument. On the one hand, dialectically, the argument appears to be directed toward a specific respondent. On the other hand, rhetorically, there is a strategy to influence public opinion. Examined from a second point of view, the argument is a mass influence attempt. Its real thrust is that it interacts politically with the readers of

Time. It assumes that these readers are already somewhat familiar with Al Gore as a political figure and that they have certain opinions about the tobacco issue.

The existence of the split respondent effect throws light on the RTD problem explained in chapter 4. It shows that arguments used in the mass media, although they are based on a kind of dialectical format, are rarely as simple as they may appear when looked at from a dialectical point of view. For mixed with that dialectical point of view, there is also a rhetorical point of view. From the rhetorical point of view, the argument is aimed at public opinion. It is also somehow based on public opinion. There seems to be a feedback process at work. The argument assumes that the audience will be somewhat informed about an issue and that they will already have some opinions about it. On the other hand, while the argument uses this input as premises, it also has a conclusion that is directed toward the public audience.

The aiming of any argument at a mass audience raises many questions about appeal to popular opinion as a type of argument. Evidently, the proponent of the argument has to try to enter into the thinking of the mass audience to judge what its views are and how the audience is likely to think about a particular issue. How can this act of empathy be carried out? In the case of a single respondent, as we have seen, the proponent of an argument in a persuasion dialogue must base his argument on the commitments of the respondent, or what he takes to be these commitments. This act of empathy, as noted in chapter 1, seems to involve something like a skill of examining how the respondent has argued in the past to try to judge where he stands on a certain issue now. But how is a comparable act of judgment to be carried out in a case of mass media argumentation? Presumably, the proponent must have some knowledge of where the public stands on a certain issue at some point in time, as a situation has developed. Presumably, the proponent must also be able to judge how the public would be likely to react to or to draw conclusions from new developments that are reported in the mass media news. This "news" in the form of incoming information is always changing.

What is involved in such mass media influence attempts is a feedback effect. The proponent bases his argument on what he takes popular opinion to be at any given point. Then as developments change and new information comes in, the proponent must also try to get some notion of how public opinion has changed on the issue. There are all kinds of ways of gathering this information. Some are sophisticated methods, such as using public opinion polls or focus groups. Others are simpler, such as reading newspaper reports or editorials that convey some sense of the public mood or feeling about an issue. As this information comes in, the proponent will need to change his argument to take the latest developments into account. There is a parallel with the normal case of a two-person persuasion dialogue. In this type of case, the proponent will change his argumentation as he becomes more aware of how the respondent is reacting in the dialogue. In the mass media case where the argument is directed to popular opinion, the proponent will similarly have to update and refashion his argumentation as the public reactions to it become evident. Thus some aspects of the way persuasion dialogue works dialectically in the normal kind of case will transfer over to cases of mass media arguments directed to public opinion. But quite a bit will change, because of the special nature of the mass audience. The mass audience may be thought to have commitments, but they are not commitments in the same sense as the commitments of a single respondent with whom one is engaged in dialogue. The mass audience has what is called public opinion or popular opinion. Appeal to popular opinion is a special form of argument in its own right. It needs to be seen as having special characteristics that make it unique as a type of argument. As I will show, it has a distinctive argumentation scheme, or at least there are a group of argumentation schemes that collectively represent its form as an argument.

2. Appeal to Popular Opinion as an Argument

The *argumentum ad populum,* or appeal to popular opinion, can be roughly expressed (subject to refinements below) as having the form, "Everybody accepts proposition *A*, therefore *A* must be true." We tend to be quite suspicious of such arguments, saying, "Just because everyone believes it doesn't mean it's right." In traditional logic, the *argumentum ad populum* is classified as a fallacy. But many arguments in both public and private spheres of discourse are based on premises that express what is supposedly public opinion (Childs 1965; Herbst 1993). Such arguments are often assumed to be reasonable, or at least to have some standing, especially in a democratic political system (Freeman 2005). As Hamblin (1970, p. 44) noted, "it is not clear from the name (*argumentum ad populum*) that it does not consist of the purest valid reasoning, and only an anti-democrat could unhesitatingly assume the contrary." Thus there is ambivalence about appeal to popular opinion as a form of argument. Although our logic books condemn it as fallacious, common examples of its use seem to indicate that it can often be reasonable, especially in certain contexts, such as political argumentation. According to the model of appeal to popular opinion presented in my book (Walton 1999a), this form of argument should be evaluated by using argumentation schemes that apply to particular cases.

In mass media rhetorical arguments of the kind so commonly used in democratic politics, public opinion is probably the most important factor in the success of any argument. In a free market economy, rhetorical argumentation in mass media ads to sell products must, of necessity, be based on an appeal to popular opinion. If any such argument misreads public opinion at any given point in time, it is quite likely to be a failure. Of course, the conventional wisdom is that empirical techniques, such as public opinion polling, can be used to determine what public opinion is on an issue, at any given time. Although polls can be extremely useful, especially in election campaigns, the poll by itself will not necessarily tell a strategist how to craft a successful appeal to popular opinion. Chapter 7 takes up the question of drawing conclusions from public opinion polls. Prior to approaching the question of polling as a method of judging public opinion, it will be useful to examine some examples of mass media arguments based on appeal to popular opinion as a form of argument.

The purpose of this chapter is to extend my analysis (Walton 1999a) by applying it to cases of appeal to popular opinion of the kind found in media argumentation, especially the kind used in commercial advertisements of various kinds found in the media. Appeals to popular opinion are frequently the argumentative basis of ads built on a claim that a product is "number one" or is the best selling or most widely used product. Uses of appeal to popular opinion in such ads not only are very common in the media, but also are often featured as examples of fallacious arguments in the logic textbooks and critical thinking manuals. When you scan some of the most widely used logic textbooks treating the subject of informal fallacies, you don't have to go far to detect ambivalence. As noted in chapter 3, Hurley (2000, p. 124) classifies the *argumentum ad populum* as an informal fallacy, and cites examples like the following one: "Of course you want to buy Zest toothpaste. Why, 90 percent of America brushes with Zest." But then, if you look on the back cover of Hurley's textbook, you see an ad beginning with the following sentence: "The clearest and most accessible logic text available today, Hurley's *Concise Introduction to Logic* is used by more students and instructors than any other throughout North America." What is remarkably evident here is this very ambivalence. In this chapter, a way of dealing with the basis of this ambivalence is sought. It is argued that once its basis is analyzed and clarified, arguments that appeal to popular opinion as used in commercial ads can be evaluated in an objective way. It will be shown how such arguments can vary from strong to weak to fallacious, depending on various logical and contextual factors.

3. Cases in Point

Many common cases of arguments used in commercial ads fit into the *ad populum* category. For example, consider the following advertisement for Microsoft Office 97 Pro, found in the *Wall Street Journal* (January 15, 1999, p. B3). This case could be called the Microsoft Office case.

Case 6.1

> *The world's most popular office suite . . .*
> **Microsoft Office 97 Pro with Bookshelf Basics**
> Get FREE Internet access through MSN for a full month!
> Special Price for WSJ readers!
> Limit of 5 per order!

This ad gives the reader several reasons to buy Microsoft Office 97 Pro. One of these reasons is that it is said to be the world's most popular office suite. But why is that a reason to buy it? First, the inference is suggested that if so many people have bought it, it must be a good product. But what backing supports this inference? Just the fact that so many have bought it doesn't make it good. After all, these people could be mistaken. But there is a further consideration. If all these people have bought it, and are using it, presumably those who are using it must have found it to be good, and recommended it to other people. Behind the brute fact of all these people using the product is the assumption that if it is now the most popular office suite, it got that way because more and more people who used it (presumably) found it good, and that led to more and more people using it. At least that is the usual way these things tend to work. So, in other words, backing up the sheer appeal to popularity is the assumption that so many are continuing to use the product because it is thought to be a very good product, perhaps even the best product available. In this case, then, we can see that while the appeal to popular opinion argument may not carry much weight in its own right, it is bolstered by other supporting argumentation that is not explicitly stated but is there in the background.

Another example – it could be called the rave pants case – shows how the *ad populum* argument is the basis of advertising and sales strategy in the marketing of products.

Case 6.2

> According to a report in the *Wall Street Journal* (Kravetz 1999, p. B1), jeans with superwide legs that drag on the ground – called "rave pants" – were a hot fad with teenagers in 1998. But in 1999, the trend changed rapidly when teenagers moved to slimmer, non-denim pants. Clothing manufacturers were left with warehouses full of wide-leg denim inventory. Their marketing strategy is to try to judge what is popular, and then manufacture a lot of that popular product. But sometimes they are wrong. And inevitably, because trends among teenagers may change very fast, even a guess that was right may become wrong at some point. According to one manufacturer (Kravetz 1999, p. B10), the strategy is not to leave "too much hanging on one style's popularity" and to try to make a certain number of right marketing choices, even though not all styles will be "winners."

Media marketing is a process of intelligent guessing. In such cases, corporations are drawing inferences from premises about popular opinion. But the form of the argument is not the same as that of the pop scheme.[1] They are not arguing that something is a good course of action because it is accepted or adopted by a lot of people. They are not saying that the popular practice in question is a good thing or a bad thing. They are drawing a conclusion about how to act based on popular opinion, or popular tastes, preferences, or actions – like buying a lot of wide-leg jeans. Thus they are using argumentation based on popular opinion. But this appears to be different from the kind of argumentation represented by the pop scheme. The problem is, then, that this kind of case appears to be on the borderline with respect to the usual form displayed by appeal to popular opinion arguments. The question is whether this marketing strategy type of argumentation is a species of appeal to popular opinion argument or not. And if not, the question is how the two types of argument are related.

One can easily see that the rave pants case is similar, in certain respects, to the Microsoft Office case. For example, the producers of rave pants

---

[1] The usual form attributed to appeal to popular opinion arguments, called "the pop scheme" is "Everybody believes proposition *A*, therefore *A* is true."

may have used the argument in their 1998 ads that rave pants are the most popular among teenagers who are supposedly the leaders regarding what's trendy. Such an advertising strategy would be comparable to the ad used by Microsoft saying that their software is "the world's most popular office suite." Both marketing strategies are based on an appeal to popular opinion, although the one appeal is different from the other – the latter being more of an appeal to fashion or trendiness than the former.

Commercial ads often sell a product by claiming that this product is "number one," or the best-selling product in the market. The problem is that two competing products in the same market may claim to be "number one." Bayer aspirin is "number one," but so is Tylenol. Nobody is "number two." How can it be possible that two competing products in the same market are both "number one"? According to a consumer's report ("The Microscope" 2000, p. 2), the situation is like the Grammy awards. It depends on what category you are in. The Benylin ad reads: "Thank you for making BENYLIN Children's Cough Syrup the #1 pharmacist recommended brand in the Children's Cough Medication Category." The Dimetapp ad reads: "Kids everywhere thank you from the bottom of their taste buds. We thank you too for making us number one in the children's cold remedy category." It may not be clear to consumers what the difference is between these two categories. Both cold remedies sound like "number one." But before a pharmacist recommends any cold remedy, she would probably ask the consumer specific questions, and recommend a different product for a different category of ailment, like a sore throat or a cough. Thus both products could be "number one," or the most recommended product, each in a different category. The fallacy in such a case is one of lack of proper qualifications. The consumer is likely to be confused and draw the wrong conclusion. Seeing the expression "number one" in the ad, the conclusion may be drawn that the product is the most popular (best selling) cold remedy. But that conclusion may be erroneous.

In the first two cases, the *argumentum ad populum* seems to have a basis as a reasonable argument, when placed in context. If you are advertising a product, then one way to do it is to argue that your product is "number one." If a lot of people are using the product, then that finding does not seem to be a bad reason for recommending it. Of course, the premise could be false. The ad could simply be lying. But if it is not, then why shouldn't you be allowed to use the popularity of the product as the basis of an *argumentum ad populum* in an ad? The third case, in contrast, clearly does involve some sort of fallacy or tricky deceptive tactic used to confuse the consumer. What then is the difference between the apparently reasonable cases (or ones that seem reasonable, even though there can be doubts and reservations about exactly how to analyze them), and the apparently fallacious cases?

4. The Form of the Argument

What really is the logical basis of arguments based on appeal to popular opinion as used in commercial ads? Why is it that in judging such arguments we tend to swing to extremes, either just accepting them without thinking there are further questions to be asked or treating them with suspicion as superficial or even fallacious? To answer these questions, the form of the *argumentum ad populum* needs to be more carefully identified. Then it needs to be shown how to evaluate arguments of this form in a specific context like that of commercial advertising. Both problems can be solved by a dialectical method of analysis. What is required is a dialectical structure that can accommodate this form of argumentation, as well as the appropriate responses to its use in specific cases.

The analysis presented in this inquiry is based on the kind of structure of argumentation now called dialectical (Rescher 1977; van Eemeren and Grootendorst 1984, 1987, 1992, 1995, Blair and Johnson 1987; Walton 1998b, 1999a; Freeman 2005). This term refers to a structure in which two speech partners reason together in a goal-directed collaborative conversational exchange (Grice 1975). The two parties take turns making contributions to a goal-directed conversation (Walton 1998b) that has rules determining how it is appropriate to reply to each type of move made by the preceding speaker (Hamblin 1971). Each argument in a given case is evaluated, not only as having a specific form, but also with respect to how the argument was used as a contribution to the type of dialogue. The participants have to agree at the outset on what type of dialogue they are supposed to be taking part in. Once this agreement has been reached, the argument can be evaluated as correct or incorrect on the basis of whether it contributes to moving the dialogue forward or not.

Part of the problem with analyzing and evaluating arguments based on popular opinion is that they don't fit the usual structures of formal logic. They don't seem to be deductive, and although they are often based on polling techniques that use statistical methodology, they don't seem to be any straightforward kind of inductive argument either. They fall more into a third category of argument now called abductive, or inference to the best explanation, a type of argument that works by presumption but that defaults in some cases. Part of the problem, then, is to identify the logical form of arguments based on public opinion.

Part of the problem is also to define this type of argument as a class of arguments that has various subspecies and variants. Appeal to popular opinion seems to be a subclass of arguments based on generally accepted opinions, which could include appeals to generally accepted scientific opinions as well as to public opinions of the kind estimated by polls. Polling itself is another whole area of interest and controversy within argumentation theory. Polls look precise, but they are based on shifting sands of wording that often contains suggestions and implicatures that are hard to quantify and that change over time, or with different audiences (Yankelovich 1991; Crossen 1994). Much in polling also depends on the exact structure of the question – whether it is an open or closed question, and so forth (Campbell 1974; Moore 1992). Social scientists have even measured how subtle variances in the wording of the question in a poll can have highly significant outcomes on the response gotten when the poll is run to a respondent group (Schuman and Presser 1981).

Another problem is that the term "popular opinion" is equated with or confused with the term "public opinion." But the latter term is highly ambiguous and is used in different fields to mean different things (Herbst 1993). Sometimes this term is used to refer more strictly to the outcome of a poll. Other times it has more of an ethical meaning, suggesting that if something is the generally accepted thing to do, it represents a standard of what you should do, or otherwise you are somehow in the wrong. The term "popular opinion," widely used in logic textbooks, is more negative, suggesting a certain trendiness that might be superficial (Walton 1999a), automatically indicating an argument that is fallacious.

The form of the argument most commonly cited by the logic textbooks under the heading of appeal to popular opinion bases the conclusion that a proposition is true on universal acceptance of that proposition. This form of argument is really one special type of appeal to popular opinion argument, which is called in my book (1999a) the "pop scheme."

Pop Scheme

Everybody believes proposition A.
Therefore A is true.

Variants on the pop scheme have even been identified by the textbooks. Nolt (1984, p. 289) distinguished between a "factual version" and a "prescriptive version," where A is a proposition and x is an action.

Factual Version
Believing that A is popular.
Therefore A is true.

Prescriptive Version
Doing x is popular.
Therefore x is permissible (or should be done).

All three forms of argument are clearly of the abductive and defeasible type. Just because everybody believes A to be true, it doesn't necessarily (or perhaps even probably) follow that A is true. The proposition A might be false even though the premise is true and the argument has the above structure. Or just because x is popular, it doesn't necessarily follow that x should be done. Such arguments are abductive because they single out one proposition or action by inference to a preferred explanation of a situation, but do not categorically rule out other competing explanations beyond all doubt. Because the pop scheme type of argument is abductive in nature and is subject to defeat in some cases, it might be better to rephrase its logical form in terms of acceptance rather than truth, as follows.

Abductive Pop Scheme
Everybody accepts A.
Therefore A is acceptable tentatively (but subject to default).

This version of the argument begins to look fairly reasonable, depending on what theory of abductive inference might be used to give it a structure. But even so, the argument looks pretty weak.

Case studies of the appeal to popular opinion type of argumentation (Walton 1999a) have shown that in most cases where this type of argument is used, it is not in the simple form outlined above. In many cases, for example, it has the following form.

Group Pop Scheme
Everybody in group G accepts proposition A.
Therefore A is true (or acceptable).

Much here depends on which group is referred to. For example, if the group referred to is a group of scientific experts in a domain of knowledge into which proposition A falls, the argument may be quite strong. This observation leads to a general hypothesis called the bolster thesis: appeals to popular opinion, while fairly weak on their own, are frequently strengthened by combining them with another supportive form of argument, like an appeal to expert opinion.

Some cases are not as strong as those bolstered with an appeal to expert opinion, but not as weak as an appeal to popular opinion that stands on its own. For example, cases of the following form of argument are relatively common: "All civilized countries view torture as an unacceptable method of interrogation. Therefore torture is an unacceptable method of interrogation." This argument is more than just an unbolstered appeal to popular opinion, but is quite as strong as an appeal to expert opinion. Presumably, the basis of it is that people in these countries have themselves deliberated about torture, and their consensus is based on the outcomes of this intelligent deliberation.

An important aspect of the argumentation used in the commercial ads cited in the cold remedy case is the combination of appeal to popular opinion with appeal to expert opinion. Physicians and pharmacists have expertise in health care products, such as cold remedies. Thus, for example, if it is claimed in an ad that most doctors recommend this product, the argument used is appeal to expert opinion. Appeal to popular opinion is often combined with, and supported by, appeal to expert opinion. In my 1999a book (p. 223), the *bolster thesis* was put forward. Appeal to popular opinion is generally a weak type of argument that gets most of its plausibility from being bolstered up through support from other arguments it is combined with in practice. If a cold remedy, for example, is said to be "number one," this expression may be taken to mean that it is the most popular product with consumers. By itself, this argument only gives a consumer a weak, but possibly persuasive reason for buying this product. If most people use the product, then that may be some indication that the product is well established and that many people find it satisfactory. Of course, these people could be wrong. They could just be buying it because of brand recognition, or even because the ads for it have been persuasive. But if the expression "number one" is taken to indicate that the product is the one most recommended by experts, such as physicians, that aspect would bolster up the reasons that a consumer might have for selecting that product over competing ones.

The Microsoft Office case seems to fit the prescriptive version of the pop scheme best, rather than the factual version. The buying and using of Microsoft Office is cited as the reason why you (the reader of the ad) should buy Microsoft Office. But notice that the case does not quite fit the prescriptive version. What the ad is presumably trying to do is simply to get action – to get readers to buy the product. This appeal is different from arguing to the conclusion that action *x* is permissible or should be done. The ad is perhaps arguing that the reader should (in some sense) buy Microsoft Office, but not in the sense that buying Microsoft Office is permissible. What is the ad really arguing in a case like this? This is a perplexing question that has never really been resolved. Further analysis below throws some light on it.

5. Fallacious Appeals to Popular Opinion

Traditional logic textbooks have worried about the potentially fallacious exploitation of arguments that appeal to popular opinion on various grounds. So-called mob appeal rhetoric can be exploited by a skilled speaker to whip up the emotions of a mass audience to win consent for a cause or a proposed course of action (Engel 1976). Such an appeal might be extremely effective in persuading the audience rhetorically even if it presents little or no real evidence to support the conclusion advocated, or even if it is one-sided, biased, and propagandistic. An appeal to emotion can be rhetorically strong even if it is logically very weak, in the sense of presenting relevant evidence that supports the conclusion that is supposed to be proved. It is presumably for this reason that appeals to emotion have been treated with distrust and skepticism in logic.

Another reason for distrusting appeals to popular opinion as arguments is that popular opinion seems so often to favor the trendy and superficial. What's "in" seems to exert powerful pressures to conform. Often when something is currently accepted as the new way to do things, it can be hard to be against it. Going against what is currently accepted as the "politically correct" mode of conduct may be found offensive. What is important about public opinion, or popular opinion, in argumentation is that if you can appear to have it on your side, a presumption in favor of your side is lodged in place. And it may be hard for the other side to dislodge it. In North America, and probably in other cultural settings as well, having public opinion on your side performs an important legitimating function in argumentation. It doesn't just mean that most agree with your view. It also means that your view is the right one, because it is the accepted one right now. How is this kind of argumentation, in turn, legitimated or justified? The idea seems to be justified on the basis of an assumption that could be called "progress." It is the idea that morality is constantly improving and becoming more enlightened. What appears to follow from this assumption is that the latest moral viewpoint must be more enlightened than any previous one. If you do not follow the dictates of this viewpoint, negative language may be used to describe your conduct or viewpoint, like "racist" or "sexist."

An example would be attitudes about war, the military, and self-defense. During the Vietnam era, any kind of military action was popularly held to be very bad. It was identified with "violence" and seen as an unnecessary event caused by the military-industrial complex for its own profit and advancement. Probably, the same view was representative of popular opinion between the two world wars. During these periods, in any argument, the premise that military engagement of any sort is bad and unnecessary was easy to accept and hard to oppose. The assumption appeared to be that now that "peace" and "non-violence" were recognized to be such important values, anyone could see how barbaric and uncivilized past generations had been when they went to war. Anyone who tried to go against this popular opinion by arguing that there have been just wars that were necessary to fight, for a good purpose, would find this a very hard line of argumentation to make headway with. Indeed, anyone who tried to argue along such lines would quite likely be demonized as a bad person and labeled with a pejorative term. In the public opinion climate of this time, any argument of such a person could be easily dismissed as "wrong-headed" or even uncivilized.

The thing to notice about this kind of public opinion is that it changes with changed circumstances, and with how these circumstances are perceived. For example, look at some old newspapers and magazine articles written during World War II or World War I. The language makes clear that the enemy is demonized, even dehumanized, and that our own soldiers are heroes. The assumption is that the war is necessary and that all steps must be taken to support those engaged in fighting it. It is very difficult to be a pacifist, as Bertrand Russell found. Your freedom of speech will be highly limited. You find yourself in jail or under careful supervision. Such a climate of opinion is not too surprising, when you consider that lives are at stake. Any intellectual who speaks out for the enemy cause, or appears to, will find his words exploited by that enemy for propaganda purposes. Morale is very important in war, as Napoleon said. Loss of morale leads to loss of life. So public opinion not only does change, but is constantly changing. In some circumstances, it can change very fast.

What these various grounds for doubt about arguments based on popular opinion suggest is that it is best to see such arguments as abductive and open to critical questioning. While they can have their right uses, they can also have their wrong uses, or abuses. In some cases, they carry a lot more weight than they really should, and it is good to be somewhat suspicious about them. This viewpoint on arguments based on public opinion fits in well with the analysis of their logical form given above. As abductive arguments, they can be reasonable in some cases when used to support a conclusion. But that support should not be regarded as final and complete – as closing the issue beyond further questioning. Instead, it should be seen as tentative and subject to challenge. It may nevertheless carry some weight of evidence in support of a conclusion.

The best approach to evaluating arguments based on premises that claim to express public or popular opinion is to see them in a dialogue structure. A proponent puts forward such an argument as presumptively acceptable, subject to possible objections by the respondent. If the respondent can make no relevant objection, or cannot propose appropriate critical questions, the argument is tentatively lodged in place in the dialogue as acceptable. If the respondent poses an appropriate critical question, the argument defaults until the proponent can adequately answer the question. Such arguments are best seen as dialectical, in the sense that they need to be evaluated in a dialogue framework. The idea of systematically criticizing arguments based on popular opinion in a dialogue format may come as a novelty to many people today. But it was quite familiar to ancient Greek philosophers, such as Plato and Aristotle.

6. *Endoxa* in Greek Dialectic

As shown in chapter 1, Aristotle's notion of dialectic was built around the concept of the *endoxon,* or reputable opinion, accepted by the many and the wise. What is characteristic of dialectical argument, according to Aristotle, is that it is based on premises that are *endoxa,* statements that are generally accepted, by both the many and the wise. Jonathan Barnes (1980) translated *endoxa* as "reputable" statements, meaning that they have a certain standing among both the general public and the experts. Aristotle's view on this matter is very interesting, for two reasons especially. One is that his view is quite contrary to the one that was so widely accepted for so many years afterward. This is the view that appeal to popular opinion is a fallacious argument. Another, as indicated in chapter 1, is that Aristotle had done something remarkable by tying in the appeal to popular opinion with dialectic. You could even say that Aristotle's doctrine of the *endoxon* is revolutionary in logic. It shows that appeals to popular opinion, far from being always fallacious as arguments, are essential to dialectic, as well as to rhetoric.

What was essential to Greek dialectic was the notion of using popular opinion as premises in a sequence of inferences that led to contradictions and other absurd propositions that are either problematic or known to not be true (Evans 1977). The form of logical reasoning used is that of *reductio ad absurdum*, which has the following form. First, you start with a set of premises that act as assumptions. Then, using a chain of valid inferences, you derive a conclusion that you know to be false. You could know this because it is a contradiction, or for a variety of other reasons. For example, the proposition might be so problematic or seem so absurd that you think it could not possibly be true. But now, by deductive reasoning, it follows that at least one of the original premises must be false. This principle of reasoning was relied on in the Socratic *elenchus*, the technique of question and answer examination used by Socrates in the Platonic dialogues (Robinson 1962). Socrates begins by asking a respondent a question. The answer assented to by the respondent may represent some widely accepted popular opinion. But then, by asking a series of further questions, Socrates shows that the original answer leads to some absurdity or contradiction. The outcome is that the respondent is revealed not to have been as knowledgeable as he initially appeared to be. So Greek dialectic was based on an initial premise of popular opinion, or widely accepted opinion. But its aim was destructive. It reduced such widely accepted opinions to absurdity, showing them to be problematic or even contradictory.

Nevertheless, both Plato and Aristotle felt that dialectic was a valuable art and that it had positive, beneficial consequences (Barnes 1980). However, what exactly the purpose of dialectic was supposed to be, and what were seen as beneficial consequences, is problematic (Devereux 1990). It appears that the Greeks thought it was very valuable to discover the limitations of what you know or think you know. They seemed to think that knowing you do not know something is itself a valuable kind of knowledge in some cases. Socrates made a great point of disclaiming that he himself had knowledge. His wisdom, he often maintained, was that he knew his own ignorance, unlike the experts he often questioned using the techniques of dialectical argumentation (Kennedy 1963). Thus any art that could show a person how and why many of the popular opinions he uncritically accepted are open to doubt could be extremely valuable. It may not be possible to have knowledge, at least scientifically proven knowledge, about many of the ethical, political, and other accepted opinions we have. But if we can come to understand our lack of knowledge about such things, we may be in a much better position to deal with them rationally. We don't need to become complete skeptics, but a little skepticism can be healthy. It can show us how to make a rational decision between two opposed opinions on a balance of evidence without being dogmatic. Even though we realize we may be wrong and are in a sense ignorant, we can still choose an intelligent opinion, even though we realize it may, in the end, turn out to be wrong.

In other words, the Greeks were ambivalent about public or popular opinion. They seemed to think it was not altogether worthless and that it could act as a legitimate kind of premise to assume for purposes of logical reasoning. On the other hand, it is clear that they thought it fallible, or apt to be wrong in some cases. They even thought that, in many cases, it could be proven to be false, although it initially appeared to have been true. But note that even though the process of dialectic is one of refutation of public opinion, the Greek view still presumed its worthiness. For after all, why bother to take such elaborate steps to demonstrate that public opinion is dubious or problematic, unless it seemed to be true in the first place? In other words, by making public opinion a worthy target of dialectical argumentation, the Greek view implied that public opinion does have a certain standing as a viewpoint to be taken seriously. It may not have the same standing as a proposition that has been proved scientifically to be true. But it is something that can be presumed to be true for purposes of discussion, or possibly for purposes of tentatively adopting a policy or course of action under uncertainty. This level of acceptance is indicated by Barnes's use of the term "reputable" to translate *endoxon*. An *endoxon* is a proposition that can be tentatively accepted as true in a discussion or deliberation, as long as there is awareness that it might be false. It has a dual aspect. It can temporarily be accepted in order to move matters ahead, but it should also be seen as open to doubt. It should be seen as possibly subject to legitimate criticism in the discussion that follows, and therefore as something that might have to be given up later in the discussion. The most celebrated practitioner of the criticism of generally accepted opinions was, of course, Socrates, the gadfly of Athens. He freely criticized many beliefs held dear by the public of the time and, interestingly, paid the ultimate penalty for engaging in this kind of philosophical activity.

7. Public Opinion as Informed Deliberation

An abductive argument is an inference to the best explanation. If the public accepts some particular proposition as true at some given time, it does not necessarily follow that this proposition is true. The public could be wrong. But if the public accepts this proposition as true, we can ask why they accept it as true. It could be that the best explanation is that the proposition really is true. Of course, there could also be other explanations. The public might have strong interests in thinking this proposition is true, for example. Thus public opinion can provide a premise to support an abductive inference. On the other hand, such an inference should be seen as subject to challenge and criticism. And yet it may have a certain standing as a reasonable inference. It seems it is possible to engage in a critical kind of dialogue with a public opinion, and challenge the thinking on which that opinion is based. This dialectical view of appeal to popular opinion as a kind of argumentation is holistic. It suggests that public opinion is not just an isolated proposition of the form "The public opinion is such and such an opinion" that stands or falls on its own. Instead, public opinion is better seen as representing a kind of thinking, or as the outcome of that thinking, in a process of argumentation.

The pollster Daniel Yankelovich (1991) has advocated such a holistic view of public opinion as representing a kind of train of thought. His criticism of public opinion polling is that it represents only a snapshot of a single instant of public thinking that is dynamic and evolves over time, as an issue develops and more becomes known to the public about it. Yankelovich saw public opinion as a process of deliberation, in which a problem is posed or an issue formulated, and then various solutions to the problem are tried out, as more and more information becomes known to the public about the issue. Yankelovich sees this process as one of intelligent deliberation, in which the public becomes more informed and educated about an issue, as reporting on it and discussion of it proceeds in the media. To really understand public opinion, according to this view, you need to see how it evolves over time as the process of intelligent deliberation on an issue progresses. The public can be seen as an agent, confronting a problem. As new information is presented to the public through the mass media, a process of deliberation is under way. Solutions to the problem are considered and weighed.

The way of viewing public opinion proposed by Yankelovich makes public opinion appear to be the outcome of a process of intelligent thinking. But that outcome changes over time, as an opinion is retracted and qualified or a new opinion is formed. What kind of reasoning is used in this thinking, and what kind of thinking is it? If we could answer these questions, and find out what kind of logical structure is the basis of this thinking, it would give us a new way of evaluating appeals to public opinion as a kind of argument that can be weak or strong. The answers proposed here follow the typology of dialogues set out in chapter 1. The kind of thinking that very often occurs can take various forms, but two are very common. One is that of deliberation on some problem (Hitchcock et al. 2001). The other is the persuasion dialogue, or critical discussion of some issue in which there is a conflict of opinions (van Eemeren and Grootendorst 1992). In deliberation, the most common thread of reasoning is goal-directed reasoning that seeks to find some course of action that is a prudent way to solve a problem, as outlined in chapter 2. In the persuasion dialogue or critical discussion, there is a conflict of opinions, and all kinds of relevant arguments on both sides are expressed, listened to, and weighed against each other.

Yankelovich was surely right that in many cases, public opinion arises as important on issues where some sort of practical problem is posed that affects a lot of people in some way and that requires action of some sort. For example, suppose there is a huge flood one year, and many homes and businesses are destroyed. In the aftermath, the citizens who live in the area discuss what measures should be taken to prevent such an event from having such bad consequences in the future. One school of thought proposes building a huge dike around the city. Critics of this proposal argue that building such a dike would be too expensive and that it is dubious whether it would really be very effective anyway. Another school of thought proposes moving the city center to a different location. Critics of this proposal argue that the new location is almost as likely to be flooded, that it would cost much more to rebuild in this area, and that it would be a less convenient location for traffic and for proximity to the river. In such a case, engineers and many other experts will be asked to give their opinions, and these opinions will be made known to the public. The most important form of argument in such cases is the appeal to expert opinion, identified as an argumentation scheme in chapter 1.

What form of reasoning is used in such deliberations, and how does it take the form of a dialogue? It is Aristotelian practical reasoning of the form described in chapter 2. When public opinion is embedded in the kind of dialogue called the deliberation (Hitchcock et al. 2001), the form of reasoning used is that of practical reasoning. As shown in chapter 2, in each case a chain of practical inferences can be identified. Matching each practical inference is a set of five critical questions. Using the practical reasoning model, answers can be given to the questions posed above. Practical reasoning is goal-directed, and it moves toward a conclusion that states an action. On this model, the public is seen as a group of agents trying to solve some practical problem, or trying to judge how best to proceed in a situation that requires some decision on a form of action or inaction. Practical inferences are put forward as arguments, and critical questions are asked about them. Hence the deliberation takes the form of a dialogue in which arguments are put forward and then critically questioned.

Dynamic information-based argumentation is a key feature of practical reasoning. As new information comes in, the agent can be aware of this incoming data, and that will change his or her reasoning. Agents need to be seen as entities that can perceive the consequences of their actions, and then modify their conclusions based on what they have seen. This aspect of agent reasoning is called feedback. Through trial and error, agents can improve their skills by seeing both the positive and negative consequences of their actions, and modifying their output accordingly. Thus practical reasoning is contextual. Agents, over time, receive more and more information about what is happening in a situation, and will be constantly modifying their conclusion – or changing their minds, you might say – as this new information comes in. What was the right conclusion in one situation gets rejected in favor of a different conclusion as the situation changes. This input of information can be seen as a form of dialogue between the agent and sources of information. The agent receives this information passively, but also needs to be constantly evaluating it, judging how to take it into account as a basis for action.

The dialectical framework for evaluating an appeal to popular opinion, or any of the types of mass media argumentation so far considered, is more complex than might have been initially thought. There is an embedding of a persuasion dialogue into a deliberation dialogue. The attempt to persuade, and the strategy behind it, need to be considered at the point that they enter into the sequence of public deliberation in a given case. The public must be presumed to have knowledge about the domain of the problem being considered. This knowledge must be seen as changing as new information comes in and as the process of deliberation proceeds through its various stages. But, as shown below, there are still more questions about mass appeal ads as arguments.

8. A More Careful Basis for Evaluating Cases

Evaluating these three cases requires making an assessment of what the context of dialogue is supposed to be in each case. It is one thing to evaluate an appeal to popular opinion in a critical discussion of an issue. For example, the use of an appeal to popular opinion in an ethical discussion on euthanasia could be criticized on various grounds. But it is quite another thing to judge an appeal to popular opinion in a commercial ad for a product like jeans, computer software packages, or cold remedies. Clearly, it would be a mistake to hold the argumentation in a commercial ad to the standards required in a philosophical argument. But then an important question arises. Exactly what type of dialogue is a commercial ad? Is the purpose of an ad to present information? Some would argue that, but it seems a naïve view. A more realistic view is that the purpose of an ad is to get the viewers to buy the product. But what kind of dialogue is that? What is its appropriate mode of argumentation? Is the goal to persuade the viewer to think that the product is good? Or is the goal simply to get action? Is the dialogue a kind of deliberation exchange in which the ad is designed to use the viewer's presumed goals to get him or her to think a particular course of action well advised? Maybe none of these interpretations is accurate. Some ads seem designed to gain brand recognition. The aim is to associate the brand with something the consumer knows or feels warmly about.

I do not believe that any of these questions have been answered or that the literature on fallacies has even addressed them much or considered them deeply. Until they are answered, a full and objective evaluation of appeals to popular opinion arguments in commercial ads is not possible. But even before getting to this stage of evaluation, many more questions about the form of appeal to popular opinion arguments need to be addressed. Studying these questions of logical form, in relation to the kinds of cases cited above, can prepare the way for the analysis of commercial speech in ads.

The argument in the Microsoft Office case is an appeal to popular opinion, but it does not appear to fit any of the argumentation schemes cited above. The argument has the form, "Microsoft Office is the world's most popular office suite, therefore it is the one you should buy." Or at least, that is a rough first approximation to its form. As noted above, this argument derives most of its strength from being bolstered by implicit supporting argumentation. The assumption is that Microsoft Office is the most popular product in its category because the people who have bought the product have found it useful. What should be said about evaluating this kind of argument? In the main, used in the context of a commercial ad, the argument is reasonable. Of course, the premise that most people are using Microsoft Office could be false. And the assumption that people continue to use it because it is a useful product or the best in its category could also be false. The argument could be weakly supported or have other faults. But there appears to be no good reason to judge the argument as fallacious. After all, it simply says that this product is the most popular, and then leaves the consumer to draw his or her own opinion from that assertion. Presumably, the purpose of the ad is to get people to buy the product, or at least to give them some reason to do so. This kind of argument comes close to fitting the prescriptive version of the pop scheme. The premise is that buying this product is popular. The conclusion is that the consumer should buy this product. Or, at least, the conclusion is that the consumer has a reason for buying the product. It is a weak reason, but one that is bolstered.

Does the "rave pants" type of case fit the form of the prescriptive version of the pop scheme? It appears that it does not. The reason is that the conclusion of the prescriptive version of the pop scheme is that the action in question is permissible or should be done. But in the rave pants case, that does not seem to be the conclusion of the inference drawn by the clothing manufacturers when they attempt to devise a marketing strategy. The conclusion they draw is not that buying rave pants should be done or is permissible. It is that teenagers will probably continue buying rave pants. Or maybe it is the conclusion that we, the manufacturers, should increase production of these pants. The conclusion is an action, a proposition about what is permissible or what should be done.

In my opinion, this type of case is problematic, and the problem is not easily solved. It is on the borderline of being an argument based on appeal to popular opinion. So you can argue one way or the other, that it fits the scheme for this type of argument or it does not. It fits in certain respects, but not in all. My opinion is that the argument used in the rave pants case does not fit the pop scheme exactly. All kinds of conclusions may be drawn from a premise that expresses popular opinion. Politicians, for example, may take actions based on what they assume to be popular opinion. Business organizations may take actions on the basis of what their marketing analysts tell them about popular practices, beliefs, or trends at any given time. That does not mean, in such cases, that those who take the actions are making any claim about such beliefs being true or about whether such actions should be done. Part of the problem resides in the meaning of the term "should" in this context. Does it have ethical connotations or does it only express the so-called prudential ought? This inherent ambiguity is an important aspect of the problem.

If we interpret the conclusion of the prescriptive version of the pop scheme as expressing any kind of ethical "should" or "ought," then clearly the rave pants case does not fit the pop scheme. But even if we can interpret the conclusion of the pop scheme as representing a more narrowly prudential "should," it would still appear that the rave pants case does not exactly fit the pop scheme. The reason is that in the rave pants case, the action in the premise is not the same as the action in the conclusion. The rave pants case has something like the following form.

> Wearing (or buying) rave pants is popular.
> Therefore, we should make lots of rave pants.

The conclusion here is not an ethical "should." And the action cited in the premise is quite different from the action cited in the conclusion. The line of argument here appears to be complex, and to run roughly as follows.

> Wearing (or buying) rave pants is popular.
> Therefore, there is a strong market for rave pants.
> We can profit from this market by making more rave pants.
> Therefore we ought to make more rave pants.

This argument is a sequence of practical reasoning. The third proposition in the sequence expresses a goal, namely, making profits from manufacturing a type of product the company is equipped to produce. The conclusion expresses a prudential "ought" to carry out a specific course of action.

Once this kind of argumentation is spelled out in more detail, we can see how, even though it is based on appeal to popular opinion (or actions), it is different from the kind of argument represented by the pop scheme. The question then is whether it should be classified under the heading of appeal to popular (or perhaps public) opinion. On this question, there is room for argument. But whatever the outcome, what is important to recognize is that the argument in the rave pants case does not fit what is often taken to be the form of the appeal to popular opinion type of argument, the pop scheme. The more general lesson is that a premise expressing popular opinion or popular action can be used to draw all sorts of different kinds of conclusions. Not all such arguments necessarily fit the mold of the pop scheme.

An *ad populum* argument can be fallacious in many ways (Walton 1999a). There is no single error or tactic of deception characteristic of this fallacy. The basic form of the argument can be bolstered in various ways, resulting in various related forms of argument. Each of these forms can be exploited or abused in various ways. In the cold remedy case, one of these argumentation tactics is revealed. The illusion of being "number one" in a broad product category can be fostered by using questionable polling methods, as shown in more detail in the next chapter. Such methods apply only to a more specific category, not to the wider category. For example, the product appears to be "number one" as a cold remedy, but in reality, the claim made is that it is the most popular product in some special category, such as sore throat medications for children. The fallacy here can be classified as one of neglect of qualifications (*secundum quid*). But it is used in conjunction with an appeal to popular opinion, bolstered by the use of appeal to expert opinion. Aspects of the fallacy could be classified in various ways. But the prominence of the use of the expression "number one" in the ad indicates that it is a species of appeal to popular opinion that is centrally involved. Such phenomena of crossovers and bolstering among different argumentation schemes are common in the fallacy world. In this case, then, even though appeal to popular opinion is, in principle, a reasonable form of argument as used in commercial ads, there are specific reasons why this instance of its use is fallacious.

9. Viewing the Public as an Agent

What have these ads shown us about the dialectical nature of mass media appeals to popular opinion? When there is a split respondent effect, how can the public audience be seen as a respondent? The answers to these questions require a realization that the structure of dialogue in typical mass media arguments is complex. On the one hand, the proponent of the argument is engaged in a persuasion dialogue. He is trying to persuade the public, or some mass audience designated as part of the public, to change opinion on an issue or to come to accept some policy for action. Persuasion dialogue is involved. But at the same time, the mass audience or the public needs to be seen as a group that is engaged in deliberation on how to solve a problem or take action on some issue. So deliberation dialogue is involved. At the same time, the public, presumably informed by the media, is changing its deliberations as the situation develops and as more becomes known about the particulars of the problem. So information-seeking dialogue is involved. It is in fact typical of practical reasoning in deliberation that it is based on incoming information that the agent collects and then applies to the problem. The mass audience or the public, informed by the mass media, can thus be seen as an agent engaged in deliberation, but also influenced by persuasion and by incoming information that can change the perception of the problem. Several types of dialogue are therefore involved, one type of dialogue being embedded in the others.

There can be multiple contexts of use in which appeals to popular opinion should be evaluated, depending on the particulars of the case. Commercial speech is not a basic type of dialogue in its own right. It can involve different kinds of dialogue. But deliberation, as noted above, has turned out to be one extremely important context. The best way to judge appeals to public opinion used in the context of deliberation is, as Yankelovich has advocated, to see the public as an agent thinking in a way comparable to that of a single individual.[2] As shown by the practical reasoning model in chapter 1, an individual called an agent is said to have goals, and to carry out actions based on those goals. An agent is any entity that has goals and that can autonomously carry out actions based on these goals and on information. An agent can be a human being or a machine. As shown in chapters 1 and 2, one agent communicates with another agent in deliberation dialogue. Or in a case where a person deliberates in solitary fashion, he or she may be viewed as two agents taking part in a dialogue. First, he or she proposes a plan of action, and then he or she plays the role of devil's advocate by criticizing the weak point in the plan or even attacking the plan and proposing an alternative. According to Yankelovich, the public, or a whole group of people designated as a "public" of voters or citizens, may be seen as thinking as an agent. In other words, the public is presumed to have certain goals, and the public is also taken to have certain information on a particular issue at any given time. This information is constantly changing as a news story breaks. Consequently, as Yankelovich pointed out, public opinion will change over time, in accord with how the public sees the situation developing at any given time. The model is to see the public as one big agent that is deliberating on what to do and what to think in relation to some problem or issue currently regarded as newsworthy. This view of the public as agent in a deliberation dialogue shows how dialectical methods can be applied to appeals to popular opinion.

But is viewing the public (or a mass audience) as an agent a simplification? Surely, the public, or a mass audience, is a heterogeneous collection of individual agents who have all kinds of different views on

---

[2] The philosophical question here is whether deliberation represents the way of thinking of a single individual or whether deliberation is better represented by seeing two parties (or a group) deliberating together. Current opinion in multi-agent technology is that both views need to be represented. In the literature on argumentation theory (Walton 1999a), the group model is primary, but the single agent model can be accommodated by seeing the agent as adopting the pro and then the contra viewpoint concerning a decision on what to do.

any given issue. Subsets of these individuals will almost always disagree about an issue. So, yes, viewing the mass audience as an agent is a kind of hypothetical construct or dialectical device that will generally not match the reality of the actual beliefs of the individuals in the group. Nevertheless, it is a useful construct for the purposes of understanding mass media argumentation. For a mass media argument must be built on what van Eemeren and Grootendorst (1984) called "common starting points" in a discussion. These represent propositions that are not at issue in a given discussion. They may not be provable, but neither party disputes them. Thus both parties are willing to accept them, or at least not to challenge them, in order to focus on the issue that they really disagree about and want to resolve. Thus the proponent of the successful mass media argument is the speaker or writer who can grasp what the mass audience is plausibly thinking about the issue, given that he shares a common understanding with them and has the same information as they possess on what is happening in relation to current developments on the issue. By these means, the successful mass media arguer can base his appeal to popular opinion on what he takes to be the commitments of the mass audience to whom he directs the argument. Of course, he can be wrong about these commitments. But because both he and the mass audience can be thought of as agents, both have the capability for practical reasoning. Both can be expected to draw similar conclusions from the same set of facts. It is this shared capability for practical reasoning, based on shared information about what is happening and a shared perception of the problem to be solved, that provides the dialectical foundations of an appeal to popular opinion.

10. Evaluating Appeal to Popular Opinion

Logic textbooks in the past have routinely denounced appeal to popular opinion as a fallacious type of argument. From a viewpoint of someone teaching skills of critical thinking, one can easily appreciate this negative attitude. The importance of public opinion polls tends to be overestimated by many who take for granted that polls are a scientific and reliable method of judging what public opinion is on an issue. Polls appear to be scientifically exact, and in some ways they are. But they are biased by nuances in question wording and structure that are not measured by the numerical figures typically given when reporting the poll outcome in the media (Crossen 1994). Therefore the results of a poll purporting to convey public opinion on an issue should be subject to critical questioning. Too often such polls are highly questionable. As shown in the cold remedy case, claiming a product is "number one" may seem to be based on a poll. But the poll may have been conducted by the company trying to sell the product. If no information is given about the real basis of the poll, consumers have no way of evaluating whether the poll was accurate and unbiased. If you don't know the actual wording of the question used, you have no basis for accepting (or criticizing) the appeal to popular opinion based on that poll. Where there is a simple choice to be made, and no slipperiness about the wording of the question, as tends to be the case in U.S. presidential election polls, the polls have proved to be accurate. But it appears to be widely taken for granted that public opinion polls on all kinds of social issues and commercial products are equally accurate. This faith in the accuracy of public opinion polls is now shaken by the use of political push polls, in which the question asked is loaded to support (or attack) a particular platform or candidate. Some push polls even use loaded questions to attack a political opponent with innuendo and false rumors. Looking at the wording of the actual question used in a poll, and critically examining the language of the question, should become a required part of judging the worth of a public opinion poll. But in commercial ads, the bare claim that one's product is "number one," despite its lack of backing, may still be effective in getting the consumer to pick one brand over another in a fast decision made in the supermarket.

These quite legitimate reservations about polling as a method of determining public opinion will be given many more grounds in chapter 7. But there is also an opposite tendency, once one has adopted a critical attitude, to throw all appeals to popular opinion out as worthless. This reaction is a mistake. What has been shown above is that many appeals to popular opinion that are useful arguments that are rational in guiding an agent toward prudent action in a situation of imperfect knowledge. The argument, though it should be subject to critical questioning, may perform a legitimate and important role in an intelligent deliberation about what to do or which product to buy. In many cases, it seems that the model of deliberation is most helpful to understanding how appeals to popular opinion are used as arguments, and how they should be evaluated. In the case of commercial ads, such the Microsoft Office case, the cold remedy case, and the "rave pants" case, the purpose of the argumentation is evidently to get consumers, or significant numbers of them, to take action of a certain sort. The most useful way to evaluate such cases is to see consumers as engaged in deliberation on what to do. The argument used in the commercial speech is designed to influence this deliberation and guide it toward a particular, recommended course of action.

In other cases, the goal may be simply to find out what public opinion is on some issue. For example, a poll may be designed to find out which candidate the voters prefer, and to what extent. In this kind of case, no argument is (necessarily) presented. The goal may be only to find information. However, even here, argumentation may be involved. For example, in a push poll, the attempt is to influence voters for or against a candidate, and not merely to find voter preference. Also, even in legitimate polls, the finding of the poll may be used in argumentation. For example, polls are often used in campaigning to make the other candidate appear to be losing ground.

What lessons can be drawn from the above analysis of the reasoning structure of arguments based on public opinion? The main lesson is that we need to steer between the extremes of condemning such arguments as fallacious and seeing them as somehow sacrosanct. They are highly fallible arguments that change quickly with the advent of new information. No wonder then that they often appear to be superficial. As Yankelovich (1991) rightly pointed out, they are commonly based on a poll that picks out one instant in a changing sequence of deliberations. The media are no doubt partly responsible for this superficiality. A problem is posed, it becomes a public issue, the media have a feeding frenzy on it, and then public discussion ceases as the media move on to the next hot issue. Intelligent public deliberation on the issue never really has a chance to get started. However, the media are not the only culprits. The public attention span seems to prefer "sound bites" and short commercial-type coverage of issues. That does not allow for much depth of intelligent deliberation based on gathering and assessing of information, including practical and realistic consideration of the consequences of actions. Emotional appeals have a powerful impact on public opinion when pictures of baby seals being clubbed to death are shown. But the longer term consequences of banning the seal hunt may not be considered by public opinion, once the issue is no longer hot. Public relations experts know how to exploit the opportune moment to champion a cause, to swing public opinion one way or the other. Once a conclusion to take some form of legal or government action is lodged into place, it will tend to stay in place for some time. Once the issue disappears from the media spotlight, further intelligent deliberations, that take new information into account, simply fail to take place. Experts in manipulating public opinion know very well how to exploit this bureaucratic inertia effect.

For all these reasons, appeal to popular opinion should be seen as a weak and fallible form of argumentation. Nevertheless, it should have some standing as a basis for intelligent action, especially in a democratic system of government. The word "intelligent" is the key, however. A lot should depend on how informed public opinion is on an issue, and what stage the deliberations are at. Appeal to popular opinion is best seen as a shaky form of argument that is strongest when bolstered by allied forms of argument. If an appeal to popular opinion is based on good information – for example, on appeal to expert opinion – it can be a much stronger form of argument. Even when it is based simply on intelligent deliberation on an issue, it can be quite a strong form of argument. In the absence of such supportive forms of argument, it tends to be weak, but can still be a premise that is some part of an argument that is a basis for taking prudent action. Much should depend on the specifics of the form of the argument and the context of how it was used in a dialogue. Thus, once again, in order to grasp the structure of media argumentation in any depth, we are brought back to analyzing the dialectical argumentation structure it is based on.

7

Fallacies and Bias in Public Opinion Polling

Social statistics are needed to conduct intelligent public deliberations and set social policies in a democracy. But activists, the media, and private agencies can and often do use "mutant statistics" as tactics to manipulate public opinion. They can and often do convince people that even the most implausible claims are true by twisting the question wording in a poll (Best 2001, p. 4). But if such polls are based on scientific statistical methods, how is it that their results can be deceptive, misleading, and even deployed fallaciously to support bad arguments? One of the main problems is the use of natural language questions in the polls, containing words and phrases that have emotive connotations that subtly lead respondents toward one answer or away from another (Campbell 1974). This spin factor introduced by the wording of a question is not measured by any indicator of the numerical reliability of the poll typically published alongside the poll findings (Clark and Schober 1992). It is widely recognized that there are biases in scientifically accurate poll results due to the wording of questions used, and that inferences drawn from these biased polls can often be fallacious (Pinto, Blair, and Parr 1993). Critics such as Warnke (1990) and Crossen (1994) have pointed out that exploiting biased language deceptively to twist poll results in a desired direction has become a widely used technique in advertising, cause advocacy, and political push polls.[1] Polling is based on the respect of the public for the

---

[1] Feld (2001) remarked that there is little consensus in the political community on what a push poll is. However, he quoted (p. 37) a definition proposed by the National Council on Public Polls in 1995. According to this definition, a push poll is "a telemarketing technique in which telephone calls are used to canvass vast numbers of potential voters,

accuracy of a poll that has been carried out using statistical methods of sampling. But as polls have been more visibly abused, it has become more obvious that the outcomes of polls are also based on unmeasured factors and that these factors can easily be manipulated to deceptively puff up an argument based on a poll. The result is that the public has begun to lose faith in the polls (Witt 2001), and it is necessary for us to critically question media polls to judge their reliability.

Using eleven paradigm examples, this chapter analyzes fallacies that arise from question wording in polls. Included are the fallacies of inappropriate and concealed use of persuasive definitions, the fallacy of use of a broad definition to inflate a statistical result, the fallacy of meaningless statistics, the fallacy of using an atypical example in place of a definition, the fallacy of question structure bias, the fallacy of dichotomous questions, and the fallacy of a double negative in question wording. Fallacies are especially deceptive in polls because of the misleading appearance of objectivity encouraged by the ways polls are typically presented. The persuasive spin on the question is concealed by the objective appearance of the announced poll result, especially when it is presented with a numerical calculation of the probability of error. These fallacies point to a deeper problem in evaluating bias in the questioning used in polls. How can it be measured, or determined exactly, whether a question in a poll is biased or to what degree it is biased? It is argued that the best approach to the problem should combine dialectical methods of argumentation theory with empirical methods of measuring response effects.

1. Definitions and Sampling Surveys

Many of the most common inferences from sampling to statistical conclusions encountered in everyday media arguments are based on polls. Polling is a type of sampling procedure that Young describes as having five steps.

> Polling involves five basic procedures – usually carried out in the following sequence: first, questions are written and organized into questionnaires; second, a sample is selected to represent the population to be surveyed; third, designated respondents are interviewed; fourth, answers given are statistically analyzed; and, fifth, results are interpreted and conclusions reached. (Young 1990, p. 47)

> feeding them false and damaging 'information' about a candidate under the guise of taking a poll to see how this 'information' affects voter preferences." The real intent of a push poll is not to provide information but to "push" the voter away from voting for one candidate and toward voting for the other candidate.

In many polls, the sequence is straightforward. In the simple cases of survey sampling methodology so often cited in statistics textbooks, there may seem to be no real controversy about how the key terms should be defined. When making a sampling estimate of the proportion of black and white balls in an urn, there is normally no real problem of saying clearly whether a given ball is black or white, or of trying to determine clearly what counts as a black ball or a white ball. But when drawing a generalization about marital compatibility or sexual abuse or mental health, it is a lot more problematic to determine what exactly counts as a positive or negative instance of these concepts. The problem in these cases is one of definition. Not only are concepts such as these vague, but any attempt to offer a precise definition becomes arbitrary, conveying a spurious impression of accuracy. Moreover, terms like these are highly controversial, and any definition is at risk of taking up one side of a controversial issue.

As a result, the definition used in a statistical survey on such an issue is inevitably what Campbell (1974, p. 15) calls a "friendly definition," one of several contending definitions that the pollster can choose to accept. A friendly definition is often stipulated by introducing some precise criterion, so that it is clear what counts as fitting the defined term. But the use of a stipulated definition inevitably introduces arbitrariness. "Marital compatibility," for example, may be defined by a married couple who do not divorce over a period of ten years. Such a stipulated definition need not intentionally be a persuasive definition of the kind that uses emotive terms to incline to one side or another on some controversial issue (Stevenson 1944). But still, it might have implications that would induce some to see it as persuasive. Some might say that the definition is too wide in certain respects, while others might say it is too narrow. Either way, the result of the poll could be misleading, because if the term "marital compatibility" is used in announcing the results of the survey, anyone reading the results will interpret this term in its ordinary, conventional meaning. Thus inevitably, the survey result will have a bias, and its apparent precision is misleading. The following example of a persuasive definition is given by Hurley (2000, p. 98).

"Football" means a sport in which modern day gladiators brutalize one another while trying to move a ridiculously shaped "ball" from one end of the playing field to the other.

This example may not be typical of a persuasive definition, but it conveys the idea of how such a definition works. In this case, the definition puts a negative persuasive spin on the term "football" by its use of negative emotive terms. Persuasive definitions are not always wrong, because terms in natural language often have an argumentative spin. But where the definition is part of a concealed tactic of persuasion used to manipulate the users of a poll, it is appropriate to speak of the *fallacy of the inappropriate persuasive definition* in polling. As will be shown in chapter 8, persuasive definition (Stevenson 1938) is a complex notion, however, posing a problem that has never really been solved in logic. Logic textbooks tend to be very suspicious of persuasive definitions, but they generally stop short of declaring them to be fallacious per se. A fallacy can arise, though, when the outcome of a poll is treated as a precise statistical result based on a persuasive definition. While drawing an inference from sampling is an exact method of reasoning in certain respects, once friendly (persuasive) definitions enter the picture, the methodology of the inference is no longer exact. It may appear exact, but an element of arbitrariness and/or bias has entered that the appearance of statistical accuracy conceals. The incorporation of a friendly definition will mean that the exact conclusion drawn from a poll (using measures of statistical accuracy) is not as well justified as it may seem to be.

Statistical surveys are routinely used to make all kinds of practical decisions on government policy. For example, government agencies use survey data on issues like poverty and unemployment to justify and promote political policies. One problem is that the generalizations drawn from these surveys have an aura of scientific objectivity. So if any other presumption conflicts with the findings of the survey, it will be discounted as wrong. The fact that the poll itself is an inference based on untested, nonnumerical, and non-objective assumptions built into the definitions of the properties being surveyed tends to be concealed. The concealment is even less visible when the poll result is announced with a numerical confidence level giving an exact margin of error. When polls are used as a basis for political deliberation, for example, their results are typically announced by the media without giving any information about the definitions of key terms that were the basis of the questioning methodology. The fallacy lies not in the use of a persuasive definition per se, but in the concealment of the persuasive spin introduced into the poll results by the use of a concealed persuasive definition. Here the *fallacy of the concealed persuasive definition* is a very real danger.

Statistical figures that measure the unemployment rate are constantly being used in political deliberations and media discussions on issues of whether to cut the deficit. But how do the statisticians define "unemployed person"? How actively does a person without a job have to be in looking for one, to count as unemployed? A puzzle for years has been why the unemployment rate is so much higher in Canada than in the United States. One factor that may be significant is the different way Canadian and U.S. officials define "unemployed person." If people say they are looking for work, but do nothing more than read job ads, Canada counts them as "unemployed," whereas in the U.S. such people are classified as being "out of the labor force altogether" (Little 1996, p. Bl). The difference in definitions could be quite significant for a reported outcome of employment. But media reports of unemployment figures typically give no information about how "unemployed person" was defined in the survey. Such figures can make it appear superficially that unemployment is much higher in Canada than in the United States, but any real basis for comparison would have to take definitions into account.

Campbell (1974, pp. 18–19) has outlined the "bewildering and contradictory" estimates of unemployment in the United States that have been tabled by many agencies over the years. According to his account, estimates differ primarily because of differences in the definition of "unemployed person" used by the various agencies (p. 19). By introducing an all-embracing official definition, the Bureau of Labor Statistics has supposedly put an end to all such differences of opinion. But as noted above, there is no reason to think that their definition is any more justifiable than the different (and conflicting) definitions used by other countries. In such cases, the definition chosen could be wider or narrower, depending on what the polling agency chooses. This latitude leaves plenty of room for advocacy. Advocates of a cause will tend to go for a broader definition. This common tactic in cause advocacy could be called the fallacy of broadening a definition to dramatize a problem (Best 2001). The idea is to broaden the definition in order to include more cases under it, and thereby to get bigger statistical outcomes that appear to support the cause. The following example was presented by Best (2001, p. 39).

Case 7.1

Suppose we want to define sexual violence. Certainly our definition should include rapes. But what about attempted rapes – should they be included? Does being groped or fondled count? What about seeing a stranger briefly expose himself? A narrow definition – say, "sexual violence is forcible sexual contact involving penetration" – will include fewer cases than a broad definition – for example, "sexual violence is any uninvited sexual action." This has obvious implications for social statistics because broad definitions support much larger estimates of a problem size.

A comparable problem is posed by a definition that is either too broad or too narrow. Either kind of definition, when used in a poll, will lead to misleading result. But activists promoting a cause will generally try to work with a definition that is as broad as possible, because this approach will yield statistical figures that make the problem appear wider, and thus more severe. And as we all know, statistics about the extent of a problem are often used by activists to get public support for the cause. There are two fallacies in such cases that need to be identified. One is the converse of the other. The first could be called the *use of a definition that is too broad to inflate a statistical result*. The other fallacy is the *use of a definition that is too narrow to deflate a statistical result*. However, using a definition that is too broad or too narrow in a statistical poll is not itself a fallacy, because this sort of mistake is inevitable in nearly all cases.

Any income criterion of poverty inevitably fails to be accurate to cover all cases. As Campbell (1974, pp. 17–18) showed, over the years different agencies have used varying definitions to produce official counts of persons living in poverty. These statistics have ranged from 30 million (1964) to 40 to 50 million and to one zealous claim of 80 million. The problem is that not only is the term "poverty" vague, but it is not possible to give a non-arbitrary definition of it, by a precise numerical criterion, that would fit all situations, and circumstances in different locations. Inevitably, then, any definition that is precise has a certain bias or spin on it. Relief agencies and poverty advocates find it hard to resist using broad definitions to inflate their statistics, feeling that the cause justifies the means. The defense of this tactic is expressed in the rhetorical question, "If it helps the poor, so what?" Here we have the danger of using a precise definition that is promoted on the grounds of its precision but is arbitrary and is far too broad. What is fallacious is the illusion produced by the use of a statistic that appears precise but has been inflated through the tactic of defining a term too broadly. Part of the problem here is concealment, because how to define "poverty" is highly controversial. Persuasive arguments can be marshaled on both sides of a social and political issue. Thus the concealment introduced by employing a definition implicitly is a highly misleading and deceptive tactic. Questioning is suppressed.

On the other hand, the danger of not defining a vague term used in a sampling survey can rightly be classified under what is called *the fallacy of meaningless statistics* (Seligman 1961). This fallacy is the use of a precise figure as the outcome of a statistical survey based on a vague term for which no precise definition is provided and for which no non-controversial definition could be provided. Seligman gave the following classic political case case as an example (p. 146).

Case 7.2

> Attorney General Robert F. Kennedy stated, "Ninety percent of the major racketeers would be out of business by the end of the year if the ordinary citizen, the businessman, the union official, and the public authority stood up to be counted and refused to be corrupted."

Without definitions of terms such as "major racketeer" and "stood up to be counted," the figure of 90 percent is meaningless. The fallacy here arises not from using a definition that is persuasive, too broad, or too narrow, but from not defining the terms at all. Of course, any attempt to define such terms non-arbitrarily would be difficult at best.

Another typical example was given by Campbell (1974, p. 26).

Case 7.3

> An author asserted that he had studied the food intake of more than 50,000 men and women and found, to his own astonishment, that in one group of 4,500 cases, 83 per cent were found to be overweight while undereating. Moreover, only 17 per cent were found to be overweight because they overeat. These facts might have seemed astonishing to the reader as well as to the writer if the latter had only been more clear about what he was calling "overweight," "undereating," and "overeating." If the actual criteria used were no more precise than the description given in this article, then the 17 and 83 per cent figures are worthless. Either way, the reader of this particular article is left poorly informed.

Too often, no information is given about how key terms were defined when statistical results of surveys are announced in the media. A persuasive definition, even if we don't agree with it, can at least be questioned or criticized. But if no definition at all is given, it would not be reasonable to accept the claim at face value. All one can do is to ask the right critical question. In this case, the right critical question is how to define the terms the poll was based on. In the absence of an answer, the presumption should be that a precise statistical outcome based on a vague term that has not been defined is a mismatch. Such a mismatch conveys a spurious aura of scientific precision that justifies the allegation that the argument commits the fallacy of meaningless statistics.

Crime figures are a constant source of disputable claims and statistical fallacies used to manipulate public opinion. People are personally affected by what appears to be a growing crime rate, but the statisticians keep saying that crime is going down. Are the figures all that reliable, given that there has been so much change over the years in how crimes are reported, how they are defined as crimes, and how the areas in which crimes are tabulated (like cities) have changed in size? For example, in 1991, arson offenses in Canada took an unusual 20 percent jump from previous levels. But coincidentally, in July 1990, amendments to the Criminal Code broadened the definition of "arson" to include such things as mischief fires, instead of restricting it to cases of willfully setting fires to specific types of property ("Changed Law Fuels Statistics" 1992, p. A3). Could it be that the sudden increase in arson statistics can be attributed to the definition? It certainly is a possibility, suggesting how the unqualified use of crime statistics can be misleading. "Stats wars" in which competing definitions are evaluated and criticized by both sides on an issue can actually be beneficial. The reason is that they bring out these concealed problems and controversies about definitions of key notions that are vital in forming public policies in a democracy. Fallacies arise when the problems about definitions of these terms are concealed by advocates, who present the finding as a scientific poll that is objective and cannot be critically questioned. The fallacy is employing the definitions in a deceptive way by trying to conceal its persuasive aspect.

2. Question Wording and Emotive Bias in Polls

Polling, like all statistical generalization procedures based on sampling, looks objective and precise. Indeed, it is, in certain respects, provided the sequence of the five steps of polling shown in section 1 above is followed. But the definitions of key terms used to generate the conclusion are subject to the problems and fallacies covered in this section. These problems arise at the first stage of the sequence. As noted above, one of the most problematic stages in the construction of a poll is the phrasing of the question. The question is typically phrased using natural language words or phrases that are not defined but have a meaning to the respondents. And the emotive terms in natural language not only import a bias, they can lead to the various fallacies cited above. The problem of question wording effect is much more significant than it appears to be. An apparently small or insignificant variation in the words chosen to appear in a question can have a large effect on the statistical outcome of the poll.

Some of the fallacies of polling cited in the preceding section arose from faulty definitions that were too broad, too narrow, or had other faults. But fallacies and problems of bias can also arise where a term has not been defined at all. Such a problem may arise because the term has a hidden emotive impact that puts a spin on the outcome of the poll. But the poll user or reader may not be aware of this hidden bias at all.

Stevenson warned about the emotive use of language and persuasive definitions (1938, 1944). He distinguished between the descriptive (cognitive) meaning of a term and the emotive meaning, which refers to how people react emotionally to the use of the term. The problem is posed by the fact that many words used in natural language discourse have built-in positive and negative emotive connotations or spin. For example, the terms "bureaucrat" and "public servant" have almost identical literal meanings, but they have very different emotive meanings. "Bureaucrat" expresses resentment and disapproval, while "public servant" expresses respect and approval. This emotive difference between terms that appear to be equivalent can conceal a persuasive element in many statements and questions. Yet such persuasive elements often function as arguments supporting one side or the other of an issue. The following simple example of how emotive meaning can act as the basis of a persuasive argument was presented by Stevenson (1944, p. 141) in the form of a dialogue.

A: He had no right to act without consulting us.
B: After all, he is the chairman.
A: Yes, but not the dictator. He violated democratic procedure.

The term "dictator" works as a negative emotive word in this dialogue, while the term "democratic" works as a positive emotive term. Both terms have emotive connotations. When the person in the dialogue is described as a dictator, it implies that he did something wrong that we should condemn. When a procedure is described as democratic, it is implied that it is good, a procedure we should approve. Many terms used in everyday language have positive or negative emotive meaning, and words used in polls are no exception. When such words appear in a question in a poll, this will have a so-called question wording effect (response effect), meaning that it will influence the statistical outcome of the poll one way or the other. One question wording effect relates to the positive or negative connotations of equivalent words chosen in a question. What may superficially appear to be an equivalent word may have different connotations for respondents. Hence an apparently slight rewording of a question may result in a dramatic difference in a poll outcome. The reason is that the two terms may have the same cognitive meaning, but have very different emotive meanings.

You might think that public support for welfare would be equivalent to, or roughly the same as, public support for the poor. But a national survey in 1985 showed that only 19 percent of people said that too little was being spent on welfare, while 63 percent said that too little was being spent on assistance to the poor (Moore 1992, p. 344). The difference of 44 points is a statistically significant one in the outcomes of the two polls, even though they appeared to be asking pretty much the same question. The researcher conjectured that the word "welfare" has negative connotations of welfare fraud for many respondents, while the term "assistance to the poor" has positive connotations of providing equal conditions and care of the people (Moore 1992, p. 344). Because of this variance in the connotations of words chosen, the variance in poll outcomes was huge.

Howard Schuman and Stanley Presser did an experiment in 1940 to study the question wording effect of changing "forbid" to "allow" when the question of whether the United States should forbid speeches against democracy was put to a sample of respondents. For a detailed account of their research on wording of questions in polling, see Schuman and Presser (1981). The two questions in this particular experiment were the following:

(Q1) Should the U.S. forbid public speeches against democracy?
(Q2) Should the U.S. allow public speeches against democracy?

Forty-six percent of respondents said "no" to Q1, but only 25 percent said "yes" to Q2, according to the account of this experiment given in Moore (1992, p. 334). This impressive outcome difference of 21 percent was produced just by altering a single word in the question.

Schuman and Presser also tested the effect of a forbid/allow substitution in the question of whether the government should forbid the showing of X-rated movies, but the outcome here was only a 4 percent difference in the responses of the two groups polled. The lack of consistency between this outcome and the previous one Moore described (p. 335) as "dismaying." According to Wheeler (1990, p. 203), the Gallup poll makes it a practice to include the specific wording of all questions used in a poll, whereas Harris does not. Wheeler noted (p. 203) that, according to Harris, including the wording of questions would take up too much space. But the result of not including this information is that a reader of the Harris survey has no real way of evaluating the reasoning that the poll is based on. As Wheeler puts it (p. 203), a reader of the poll in the media has to "take it on faith" that the pollster has evaluated the results correctly. The reader lacks information necessary to evaluate the inference made by the pollster when he reports a trend or opinion, based on a question or a series of questions asked of a sample group of respondents.

In other cases, the problem is not just due to the wording of a question, but to emotive spin introduced into the poll precisely because of this failure. This kind of fallacy occurs where a key term is not defined at all but is represented in the argument by an example that serves as a paradigm. But it is a paradigm that has an emotive impact on how the poll outcome is taken, because the paradigm twists the meaning of a key term in a certain emotive direction. Thus in this kind of case, there is a bias relating to definitions in the argument, even though the term in question has not been explicitly defined. Best (2001, p. 39) comments on a television news story that tells about a child who was beaten to death.

Case 7.4

> Relatively few cases of child abuse involve fatal beatings; comparatively mundane cases of neglect are far more common. But defining child abuse through examples of fatal beatings can shape how we think about the problem, and child-protection policies designed to prevent fatalities may not be the best way to prevent children from neglect. Whenever examples substitute for definitions, there is a risk that our understanding of the problem will be distorted.

In this kind of case, the problem is not that the definition is biased or misleading. The problem is that no definition has been given. The example given presents to the reader or audience a paradigm that functions as a definition, or functions in place of a definition. The problem is partly a failure to give a definition, and partly using an example that acts as a definition. This kind of case is very common, because the media like to use emotionally dramatic and extreme examples to make a story more exciting to viewers or readers. Also, advocates of a cause like to feature such shocking and atypical examples because it makes the problem seem more urgent. A shocking and disturbing example can be used as a call to action, a call to rally the public to support the cause. This kind of fallacy could be called *the fallacy of using an atypical example in place of a definition*.

These problems are exacerbated in media reports of polls. Commonly, in media reports of polls, the exact statistical finding of the poll is stated, but the questions used to generate the conclusion are not. Unless you can see the actual wording used in the conclusion drawn, however, accepting the inductive inference used to get to this conclusion would not be justifiable. If you don't know the actual wording the poll question used, you are not in a position to tell whether any of the above fallacies may have been committed or not. You simply have no way of knowing. What this implies is that many of the poll outcomes cited in the media to support arguments or claims are worthless as evidence until critical questions about the wording of the question are asked and answered. In terms of the five stages of polling cited above, these problems arise at the fifth stage. The problem may not be with the poll itself, at any of the first four stages. The sampling procedures, for example, may be impeccable. The problem can arise at the stage where an inference is drawn from the poll results. Polls are often used by advocates of a cause or by the media to create an interesting story line. The poll outcome is used to draw a conclusion by means of an inference. But often this inference is drawn in a distorted and biased way, because the exact wording of the question in the poll, or the definition of a controversial term, is not even reported to the readers. The problems here are not in polling itself but in the use of polls by advocates, the media, or other parties. Even this distinction is tricky, however. In some cases, the media or the advocates conduct the polls themselves. Thus a key critical question to ask is, "Who conducted the poll?" If the pollster is a reputable company, you can be assured that some standards of proper sampling have been met. But if the poll was conducted by the media or by an advocacy group, there are no guarantees that any standards have been met.

3. The Structure of the Question

How can a method be provided that would detect these biases and fallacies by objectively evaluating question wording in polls? There is a literature on the logic of questioning in logic (Harrah 1984), and there has been some work on studying question methodology in cognitive science (Graesser, Bommareddy, Swamer, and Golding 1996). There are also resources in argumentation theory on the structure of asking questions in dialogue (van Eemeren et al. 1996). The solution to the problem recommended in this chapter is based on all these resources.

In some polls, the problem is not just in the wording of the question but in the structure of the question itself or in the order in which a sequence of questions is presented. Pinto et al. (1993, p. 156) cite the use of questions like, "Mayor Smith is running for re-election. Are you in favor of her candidacy?" There are several problems here that could easily be overlooked. One is that the question is posed in a positive direction. It doesn't ask, in a more balanced way, whether the respondent is for or against the candidacy of Mayor Smith. Another problem is that the question is prefaced with a statement, and this statement alludes to Smith's experience as mayor. So the placing of the question after a statement puts the question in a context that gives it a certain spin. There is also an imbalance, as Pinto et al. note, because the question does not mention the other candidates. These subtle factors of the structure of the question can produce effects that are difficult to measure in assessing the worth of a poll. This fallacy is committed when the options offered to the respondent are improperly limited or biased by the structure of the question. It could be called the *fallacy of question structure bias in polling.*

Roper (1990, pp. 230–231) cites what he calls a "yea-say effect" when a question used in a poll is posed in one direction only. As an example of such "unidirectional" phrasing, he contrasts the question "Do you admire Ronald Reagan?" with the more balanced question, "Do you admire Ronald Reagan, or don't you think very highly of him?" There is a tendency of respondents to agree with a statement rather than to disagree with it, especially if the statement is one on which the respondent lacks strong opinions. Hence the unidirectionally phrased question is more likely to elicit a response in favor of Reagan than the bidirectional question. According to Roper, the more a question involves a subject "on which knowledge is hazy or about which people have not thought widely," the wider is the margin of agreement over disagreement. Thus unless the pollster knows whether the respondents have knowledge about a particular question, or have thought about it much, the response effect of choosing a unidirectional versus a bidirectional question cannot be known or calculated. And the effect of asking a unidirectional question can be a bias or error due to the wording of the question. Here the pollster needs to understand not only the structure of the question, but which structure is appropriate for the respondents, given what the respondents know or don't know about the subject. In other words, there is a dialectical aspect here that has to do with the communicative relationship between the pollster and the polled. The pollster must know (or try to anticipate) what the respondents know or don't know about the subject of the poll.

The problem cited by Roper is similar to the problem of leading questions in law. Sometimes leading questions are admissible in law, but if a question is leading in a bad or problematic way, the judge is supposed to not admit it. Similarly in polling, any question will have a tendency to lead the respondents toward one answer or another. If the question is a good fit, its bias may not be a big problem. On the other hand, if the question is phrased in a wrong way for the respondents, it could lead to a large bias in the outcome of the poll that may not be evident to the poll users.

Another kind of response effect was discovered by Howard Schuman, in a study done in 1950, commenting on a 1948 study of American attitudes toward American and Soviet journalists. Schuman was interested in the differences among ways of ordering a series of questions put to a group of respondents in a poll. The following summary of Schuman's findings is from Moore (1992, pp. 337–338).

Case 7.5

Form A in the 1948 study asked respondents, "Do you think the United States should let communist newspaper reporters from other countries in here and send back to their papers the news as they see it?" Form B reversed the situation, by asking, "Do you think a communist country like Russia should let American newspaper reporters come in and send back to America the news as they see it?" When the question about communist reporters was asked first, people's great distrust of communism at the time led to overwhelming rejection, with only 37 percent saying communist reporters should be allowed to report news from America. But when the communist reporter question was asked second, after the question about whether American reporters should be able to report the news from Russia (which people overwhelmingly supported), then support for communist reporters to report from America went up to 73 percent, a jump of 36 percentage points.

Schuman interpreted these results as showing two different sentiments of the public (Moore 1992, p. 338). In Form A, a negative sentiment to communism and communist reports is shown, in accord with the cold war mentality of the time. In Form B, the sentiment shown is one of fairness or reciprocity. When the American reporter's question is asked first, it puts a context in place in which the next question evokes the issue of fairness or reciprocity. So it is not just the structure of a single question itself that needs to be considered. The place of the question in the series of questions in a questionnaire can be very important in judging inferences based on polling. Part of the problem here is the use of emotive terminology. The fallacies and biases associated with the persuasive functions of natural language terms have already been discussed above. What is new here is the bias introduced by the structure of the question. These problems have to do with the logical form of the question. What is needed to cope with these problems is some knowledge of the different kinds of questions. Below it will be noted that there are various systems in logic and cognitive science that classify different types of questions. Each type of question has a different structure. But it is not just the structure of the question itself that needs to be considered. The place of the question in a context of dialogue also needs to be taken into account. It is for this reason that it will be argued below that we need a dialectical analysis of not only questions themselves, but how these questions function in a context of dialogue.

In other cases, the problem is one of confusion of the respondents because of an unclear question. Often this is due to the ambiguous wording of the question. For example, in cases where a question is expressed in a negative form, it may be hard to interpret what the answers "yes" and "no" really mean. What one person thinks is the meaning of a "yes" answer may be the same as what another person thinks is meant by a "no" answer. Payne (1951, p. 22) gave the following example of this kind of problem in a poll.

Case 7.6

It can happen that different people will read directly opposite meanings into the same words. Let us imagine a community where feeling runs very high on a proposed referendum to sell the city zoo to a meat packer for use as a slaughterhouse. Then we ask the citizens, Do you think that the sale of the zoo to the meat packer should go through, or not? Both those who answer "No" and those who answer "Yes" could mean the same thing. Those saying "No" would probably mean that the zoo should not be sold, while those saying "Yes" might mean that the sale should "fall through."

Adler (1994, p. 56) cites the case of a 1992 Roper poll that phrased its question with a confusing double negative, coming out with the result that 22 percent of Americans say the Holocaust may not have happened. When the question was re-worded in a 1994 poll, the result was that only 1 percent doubted the Holocaust. In cases like these, the structure of the question is confusing, and though respondents may answer the question, they don't really know what it means. Confusing polls of this kind are based on an error that could be called *the double negative fallacy of question wording*.

Roper (1990, 231) polled one half of a sample of respondents on the double-negative statement, "It is not true that women don't make as good executives as men do", and polled the other half on the positive statement, "Women make as good executives as men do." The results (p. 231) were as follows.

Case 7.7

In the case of the double negative statement, 50 percent agreed, 42 percent disagreed, and 7 percent didn't know. In the case of the straightforward statement, a large 87 percent agreed, only 10 percent disagreed, and just 3 percent didn't know.

The difference of outcomes here is a response effect that indicates confusion of the respondents caused by unclear wording. This type of error is different from a bias that artificially tilts the responses to one side rather than the other. But even so, it can result in a response effect. Even if people are confused or don't know the answer to a question, the structure of the question encourages them to guess or pick the answer that seems most likely to be wanted or to represent something like their viewpoint, as far as they can guess. Poll questions are typically designed to solicit a yes or no answer. But for various reasons, giving a yes or no answer may not be realistically possible, or may be simplistic or otherwise not representative of the respondent's real thinking. An answer is called for anyway, and many people will give one. But the fallacy of false dichotomy will be treated below as a special fallacy in its own right.

What is needed to cope with these fallacies arising from the structure of questions used in polling is, to begin with, a classification of the different types of questions. Some attempts to construct such classifications have been made in logic (Harrah 1984). But the effort has mainly been directed toward syntax and semantics. To deal with the kinds of fallacies cited above, the response of the respondent to the poll question, and also the reactions of the users of the poll, need to be taken into account. It is encouraging to see that some normative work of this kind is being done using computational models of human question answering. Graesser, et al. (1996) developed a computer program called QUEST that specifies the cognitive strategies that humans use when they answer survey questions in different categories. In QUEST sixteen different types of questions are represented. Some of the main types, with examples, are the following (Graesser et al. 1996, p. 148).

> *Verification*: Are you a citizen of the U.S.?
> *Disjunctive*: Are you male or female?
> *Quantification*: How many children do you have?
> *Definition*: What does it mean to be bonded?
> *Causal Antecedent*: Why is my tooth hurting?
> *Goal Orientation*: Why did you move to Memphis?
> *Instrumental*: How did you move to Memphis?

Note that in the QUEST classification system, there can be different types of why-questions. Different kinds of why-questions are important in the field of logic called formal dialectic, which uses formal models of dialogue to study fallacies (Hamblin 1970). It is argued below that the best way of analyzing fallacies of questioning in polling is through the use of such formal dialectical models of argumentation.

4. Forcing an Answer

As noted in the previous section, the structure of the question used in a poll is of a kind that is meant to narrow down the range of responses to definite outcomes that can be counted up in a numerical manner. This structure may not only introduce a bias by encouraging the respondent in one direction rather than another, but it may also impose a definiteness on an issue that is not really appropriate or consistent with what the respondent really thinks about it. The outcome of the poll in such a case may impute a definiteness that is not really there. So the sampling procedure used to get the poll result could generate an outcome that is highly misleading. This sort of fallacy is commonly known as *the fallacy of false dichotomy*. It is also sometimes called "the black and white fallacy" or "the fallacy of simplistic alternatives." This fallacy is quite simple. It is the fallacy of falsely representing a range of choices as solutions to a problem or answers to a question as being only two, when in reality more than two solutions or answers should be considered. The more general fallacy is one of limiting the options unfairly, even where more than two choices may be involved. This could be called the *fallacy of forcing an answer*. For example, only three answers might be allowed, when four are really needed to permit a satisfactory response to the question. This fallacy is familiar to all of us who have struggled to answer a multiple-choice question that allows no "none of the above" answer. This kind of fallacy of questioning is already familiar in logic as the fallacy of many questions. In ancient philosophy, it was called the fallacy of the horns. For example, one person asks another person whether he has stopped abusing his aged father. Whether the second person answers "yes" or "no" to this dichotomous question, he admits to having abused his aged father.

One solution to this fallacy sometime proposed is to use open as opposed to closed questions in a poll, as indicated by the following examples.

Closed Question: Do you think the government is doing a good job of dealing with inflation, or not?

Open Question: What kind of job do you think the government is doing in dealing with inflation?

The open question is preferable to the closed question, because it leaves a range of permissible responses open, instead of narrowing them down to two, as in the closed (yes-no) question. Always using open instead of closed questions would eliminate the fallacy of false dichotomy, or certainly make it less severe.

But the practical problem is that, given the nature of polling as a quantitative, statistical undertaking, there is a need to get the questionnaire in a form whereby numerically it can be tabulated by counting up the answers. This limitation means that in practice, the open question, of the type above, for example, has to be reduced to some sort of closed or multiple choice question, with only definite answers allowed, of a kind leading to definite results that can be counted. So the open question ultimately has to become a closed question of some sort. For example, the open question above might become the following multiple choice question.

Multiple Choice Question: What kind of job do you think the government is doing in dealing with inflation: (a) good, (b) fair, (c) poor?

Putting in a fourth opinion, "None of the above" is possible, but may not make for a very exciting outcome. The polls, especially those used by the media, are specifically designed to get a newsworthy outcome. Also, in political polling, it is often appropriate to ask a simple yes-no or two-choice question. For example, there may be two candidates X and Y in an electoral race, and the poll best designed to find public opinion needs to ask, "Are you going to vote for X or Y?" as the appropriate question. Thus it is unrealistic to think that simple dichotomous questions can be eliminated in polling. They need to be seen as sometimes appropriate. What is needed is a method of judging when such a question is inappropriate or fallacious. It is naïve to think that there is any simple syntactic or semantic way of devising a useful method of this sort. The method has to examine the subject matter of the poll, and then ask whether the question is appropriate to the subject matter. Such a method would be useful, because this fallacy is so common.

If given a yes-no question or another type of multiple choice question that admits of only a small list of choices as answers, many people, as noted above, will opt for one choice or the other, even though they don't know the answer to the question. The results of such a poll could be quite consistent, in the sense that subsequent polls putting the same question would get the same statistical result. Payne (1951, p. 17) stated the problem succinctly, by way of an example.

With straight faces we might start our interviews among the general public by asking, Which do you prefer, dichotomous or open questions? We might be surprised at the proportion of people who would soberly express a choice. Their selections obviously would not be meaningful in the desired sense. Yet, it would be incorrect to assume that their answers were entirely meaningless or haphazard. People might vaguely think that they understood us but not knowing the first term might choose the second in high proportions. And in passing, we might forecast that repeated experiments with the same question would probably give closely duplicating results. Stability of replies is no test of a meaningful question. The more meaningless a question is, the more likely it is to produce consistent percentages when repeated.

Would it be a good guide to rational deliberation on a question if we used the results of a poll based on this type of question? No, it would not, because the poll is not telling us correctly what the opinion of those polled really is. But citing the results of such a poll in an argument could sound impressive. The problem, in such cases, is not just the running of the poll itself, but how the outcome is reported in the media.

When the results of a poll are given with an exact numerical figure representing the margin of error, many people think that this number represents how accurate the poll has been in correctly ascertaining the opinion of the population group. In other words, the figure is taken to refer to the probability that the poll might be wrong in drawing the conclusion that a group of people have a particular opinion. But that is not what the figure represents at all. The figure represents the probability that when the same poll is run with another sample group of respondents, it will come up with the same statistical results. So in other words, the margin of error is the probability that the poll has not picked out the respondents by a sample that is adequate. The margin of error figure represents the accuracy of the sampling method. The figure says nothing at all about whether the poll is really accurate in the sense that its conclusion represents the real opinions stated. It says nothing at all about the wording used in the question in the poll or about how key terms in the question were (or were not) defined. So, as Payne points out, even if this figure is very high, showing that the poll agrees with the results of repeated trials, it could still be that the poll is biased, or for other reasons does not give a true picture of what the respondents think. Wheeler (1990, p. 203) pointed out that the polls should make an attempt to filter out respondents who don't know anything about an issue. People are naturally reluctant to admit ignorance, and a respondent may even be quick to give a yes or no answer just to keep the poll interview from taking up more of their time. Wheeler noted that newspaper polls on issues do not generally give information on this filtering out factor, and this omission is an important defect in enabling a reader to evaluate any inference drawn from such a poll.

Very rarely do they reveal whether people who know nothing about the issue were filtered out of the sample. It makes little sense to ask people how they feel about the president's policy on deregulation of natural gas prices if they have not previously considered the matter; a surprisingly high percentage of the population does not think about such questions. Indeed, the pollsters ought to be reporting less on whether the people support or oppose a given policy and more on whether they have even thought of it. There should also be much more done in the direction of showing intensities of opinion, measuring how deeply people care about a given issue. (p. 203)

The problem is that conflicts of opinion on controversial issues are much more interesting to the media than detailed information on a question like the deregulation of natural gas prices. For the outcome of an opinion poll to be exciting and newsworthy, it should represent a dramatic conflict that suggests struggle and urgency. Hence there is a natural tendency to puff up the results of a poll by asking questions that are more likely to yield a provocative outcome.

Polls inflate and dramatize people's real opinions by forcing a respondent to make up his or her mind, frequently by asking a yes-no question, on an issue where the respondent may not have arrived at a decision. This speeding up of the decision process to get a definite answer is described by Crossen (1994, p. 106). It is a pollster's business to press for an opinion whether people have one or not. "Don't knows" are worthless to pollsters, whose product is opinion, not ignorance. That is why so many polls do not even offer a "don't know" alternative. If someone volunteers a "don't know" (and studies have shown many people will guess an answer rather than volunteer their ignorance), the interviewers are often told to push or probe. In choices among candidates, those who say they are undecided might be asked how they lean. The result is that people seem more decided about issues and candidates than they are. Thus the fallacy of false dichotomy is rampant in polling. But the solution to the problem is not obvious. In some cases, dichotomous questions are appropriate. Public opinion polls are generally good at predicting the outcome of an election, mainly for one reason. When a person votes, he or she also has to make up his or her mind, and vote one way or the other (although polls have been wrong, as in the 1992 general election in Britain, where they wrongly predicted a Labor victory). But on an issue requiring deliberation, where people have not made up their minds, or on a question that the respondents know little about, a public opinion poll can be misleading, suggesting a definite opinion on one side or the other of an issue where none exists. In these kinds of cases, the use of a dichotomous question produces a misleading result. Many cases are of this sort, and so the problem is how to use proper questions that give the respondent the right amount of latitude to give an answer that represents what she really thinks about the issue.

Not only do pollsters tend to resist asking questions with a "none of the above" option, but in reporting the results of a poll, the people who were undecided may not even be reported as part of the sample. Wheeler (1990, pp. 196–197) cited a case in point.

Case 7.8

> During the 1972 presidential campaign, for example, George Gallup reported, "The Democratic Party currently holds a marginal lead over the GOP, 53 to 47, as the party voters believe they can better handle the problem they consider to be most important." In a year when there was great disenchantment with the candidates in particular and politics in general, it was preposterous to think that everybody preferred one party or the other. Indeed, that was not what people had told Gallup's interviewers. Only 34 percent had thought the Democrats were more competent, compared to 28 percent who favored the Republicans. The largest group, 38 percent, either said that there was no difference between the two parties or did not express any opinion. That figure may well have reflected the

> alienation and apathy in the country. Gallup, however, simply discarded it, arbitrarily allocating half of the group to the Democrats and half to the Republicans!

In this case, even though there was a "none of the above" option offered to respondents, the published results of the poll simply neglected to mention this part of the finding. The result is one that looks to a reader much more significant and interesting than it really is. Presenting dramatic poll results in the media seems harmless enough, if the issue is not all that significant. But if the same practices are tolerated when it comes to matters of social and public policy in a democracy, the biased poll is more than just a mischief. It can lead to poor decision making on issues that involve large amounts of money and even human life.

As Schuman and Presser pointed out, in order to devise appropriate questions that do not force an answer wrongly from the respondent in a poll, the pollster must know what the respondent does or does not know. There has to be empathy and dialogue between the two parties. The pollster has to try to look at the question from the respondent's point of view. The only way to deal with fallacies of dichotomous questions and forcing answers in polls is to get access to the questions asked, and then ask yourself, "Could I have answered that question?" The general method of dealing with such fallacies is to ask the critical question, "What question was used in the poll to get the reported result?" But if the poll, as reported, does not even tell the reader the exact question asked, then the reader (or poll user) simply has no way to judge the worth of the argument or claim based on the poll. The problem in such a case is that the asking of appropriate questions has been effectively blocked. Thus the fallacy is one of blocking off the dialogue that is needed to make sense of and to properly evaluate an argument. In the use of polls by advocacy groups, this tactic of blocking off dialogue is all part of the strategy.

5. Use of Polls by Advocacy Groups

Precisely because statistical polls do so heavily influence government and political deliberations in a democracy, advocacy groups have now undertaken to use statistics to get more funding for causes by showing that a problem is much worse than anyone thought. As Best (2001, p. 40) pointed out, activists "couple big statistics based on broad definitions with compelling examples of the most serious cases." What is typical of many cause advocacy arguments is that they combine both techniques to puff up the dramatic urgency of the problem in order to get public support in a call to action. Thus this familiar method of advocacy commits two fallacies at the same time. Inflated figures on poverty, abuse of women, and other issues where advocacy groups have made exaggerated claims based on polls have been the subject of much critical scrutiny in recent years. At one point, *Time* reported that four million women are assaulted by a domestic partner every year. *Newsweek* reported that two million women are beaten by husbands, ex-husbands, and boyfriends every year. Both figures were based on polls, but subsequent polls contradicted these large numbers, raising many questions about the questions asked and words used in these questionable polls (Adler 1994, p. 57). The use of such polls is felt to be ethically justifiable on the grounds that they draw public opinion in support of a worthy cause. Advocacy groups even see the questioning of these statistics as an unjustified attack on their goals, using the argument, "If they can save even one woman from being battered, they don't see the harm" (Crossen 1994). This use of argumentation from consequences is, in effect, an attempted ethical justification of the use of biased polling techniques to influence public opinion for social and political purposes.

Use of slanted questions in political opinion polls to make a candidate look good or bad has become so common that it has been given a widely used name, "push polling."[2] Kesterton (1995, p. A24) presented the following example.

Case 7.9

> Push polling: A deceptive political telephone tactic that aims to sway, rather than survey, the opinions of voters. For example, people in Colorado last year were asked: "Please tell me if you would be more likely or less likely to vote for Roy Romer if you knew that Governor Romer appoints a parole board which has granted early release to an average of four convicted felons per day every day since Romer took office."

Push polling has become a widely used technique of argumentation for political and advocacy purposes. It is meant to deceive. Such polling is widely regarded by professional polling organizations as unethical, but there is little agreement on what should be or can done about the practice (Feld 2001). Push polls show that asking critical questions about the

---

[2] See note 1 at the beginning of the chapter.

question wording of a poll is by no means purely an academic exercise. Anyone who is trying to influence public opinion by using such a tactic is likely, as part of the tactic, to try to deflect critical questions about the structure and wording of the question actually used to obtain the poll results. Typically, media reports do not include any information of that kind. The best defense against such fallacious tactics is to promote public education on how to critically question polls and arguments based on them.

It is typically not possible to get answers to critical questions about methods used in polling from media reports, or from an arguer who has used a poll to support his claim, because the poll result is quoted as part of an argument in the media. To judge the worth of the argument it is vital in such cases to ask who did the polling, and whether they are a reliable organization. But even reputable polling organizations have been known to make serious mistakes. Even worse, there is growing concern that reputable polling agencies can have an active agenda of advocating the particular view or interests of a group that stands to gain or lose by the poll outcome. In Canada, academics criticized a 1993 study by Statistics Canada on violence against women, based on the polling methods used by StatsCan (Mitchell 1995). Critics argued that StatsCan distorted the picture by using only women as respondents and asking leading questions to elicit the desired answers. This controversy has raised questions about the reliability of StatsCan as an objective collector of scientific data, as opposed to being a government agency controlled by advocacy groups that have an active interest in using statistics to promote their goals.

It is fair to classify the use of push polling by political parties and government agencies as a species of propaganda. Propaganda is the use of a one-sided advocacy argument, biased to push for one side of an issue. It is disguised to look like an objective collection of data, or an argument that takes both sides of the issue into account in a balanced fashion, in order to influence mass opinion or to get action for a cause. It is fair to say that misuse of polling has become an instrument of propaganda on a wide scale in the Western democratic countries. In making public policy decisions in a democracy, it is very tempting for advocacy groups to use polling as an instrument to influence opinion. Because it employs statistical sampling methods, polling appears to many to be a purely objective kind of inductive inference that is only "reporting the facts." However, in many cases, this appearance of objectivity is an illusion. The persuasion aspect of the wording of the poll is deceptively concealed under the guise of scientific accuracy.

One problem that has frequently been observed in polls used to estimate public opinion on complex political issues of the day is the presence of internal contradictions in their results. According to Susan King, quoted in Cantril et al. (1990, p. 379), these contradictions tend to recur where polls are routinely used to measure public opinion on certain political issues.

Case 7.10

> Contradictions occur because these are very complicated issues. For example, whereas there may be strong registration of public feeling about government regulation in general – a broad majority of the public is opposed to additional government regulation, and thinks there is too much government presence in the private sector – when you ask specific questions, almost all the polls reflect a sizable majority in favor of health and safety regulation, particularly in the areas of air and water quality, workplace safety, and consumer product safety. These questions always elicit around 74, 75, 76 percent positive response.
>
> As an example of the contradictions, take a Harris poll in May of 1978, at the time the Consumer Protection Agency was under consideration. Fifty-eight percent of the respondents indicated that they were in favor of the creation of such an agency and 28 percent opposed it. Sixty-nine percent said that creation of such an agency was long overdue, and about 65 percent agreed that the consumer couldn't fight big business alone and needed a government agency to help protect consumer interests. At the same time, 52 percent said that they agreed with the statement that another bureaucracy would just lead to more red tape and higher taxes, and probably wouldn't help protect the consumer at all.

It seems in a case like this that public opinion is itself contradictory. The respondents are in favor of this new government agency, but they are also against government regulation and bureaucracy and, therefore, by inference, against the creation of a new government agency that regulates business. It seems like the respondents want to "have their cake and eat it too." They don't want to be regulated by yet another government agency, and yet they want the benefits that may be gained from having such an agency. Is this really a contradiction or not? In a way, the apparent contradiction is understandable, because other things being equal, people would like the benefits of a consumer protection agency. But if the costs of setting up and paying for such an agency, plus all the restrictions on business it would introduce, and its costs, are pointed out, then many people are going to be much less enthusiastic. But by just asking the simple yes-no question, "Are you for or against it?" the more complex aspects of the question are pushed into the background. The poll result gives a simplistic and misleading picture of what people are really thinking about the issue.

As it has become more and more obvious to the public that advocacy groups get alarming statistics by asking loaded questions and twisting definitions, people have lost confidence in the polls. They have doubts about the ethics of polling and no longer have the confidence in the scientific accuracy of the polls they once had. Loss of confidence in polling has often been observed by the pollsters themselves. Evans Witt, president of Princeton Survey Research Associates, reported that the public is increasingly skeptical of both the ethics and the output of the polling industry.

The public is not sure about the scientific basis for polls. What value Americans see in polling is dribbling away through misuse. They say pollsters aren't asking the right questions to get what they really think. And they think that polls can be twisted and tortured to produce whatever results deep-pocketed sponsors desire. (Witt 2001, p. 2)

The pollsters themselves have become concerned about this loss of public confidence because they are finding it harder to get respondents to reply to telephone polls. More and more polls are being done on the Internet, partly for this reason. Witt even reported that according to a poll conducted by the Pew Research Center in 2000, pollsters were rated lower by the public for their performance in the presidental election of 2000 than talk show hosts and campaign consultants. Part of the reason for this loss of confidence is that so many polls announced in the media and in ads are carried out by media who want a good "story" or by advocates of one kind or another who are using the poll to support their own cause or product.

The problem posed by misuse of polls has two dimensions. One is the production of the poll itself. The other is the reporting of the poll in the media, or by advocates. When a poll is carried out by a reputable company, the statistical procedures used are very carefully designed to prevent skewed results due to samples that are too small or not representative of the population. These statistical methods have been well tried and tested, and they are very accurate in certain respects. The accuracy figures reported along with the poll results by reputable firms show that the proper statistical procedures for gathering data have been followed. But what is misleading is that these figures don't tell the reader anything about other factors, like the use of loaded questions or emotive terminology, or how the terms used in the poll have been defined. These omissions allow such a latitude for variation in the poll outcome that the appearance of scientific accuracy can be quite misleading. But that is just the first dimension of the problem. The second dimension is the use of the poll results by a party other than the company who carried out the poll. The poll results are typically reported in newspapers or other media. These reports may not include the accuracy figures originally given by the pollster. They may even reword the finding of the poll in a way that puffs the outcome up, making it appear more dramatic. Finally, the media may even have conducted the polls themselves, on their Web pages, for example. The polls may even have been conducted by someone who has no training in polling. For example, phone polls conducted by politicians or promoters of a product can use questions that are highly biased and contain argumentation and emotive terminology. They want to put a positive or negative spin on certain persons or products, and use the poll as device for this very purpose. Once this practice becomes evident to the public, it is small wonder they become skeptical about polls.

6. The Advent of Deliberative Polling

According to Yankelovich (1992, p. 22) public opinion polls can be very misleading, because people may not be aware of the consequences of a policy. Yankelovich noted (1991, pp. 38–44) that polls showed a more than 70 percent majority believing that the United States should have protectionist legislation. But when subsequent polls indicated that people might then have less choice of products, have to pay more for certain products, or have less quality, support for protectionism went down 26 to 28 percent.

The general problem, according to Yankelovich, is that when polls are used to estimate public opinion on issues of public policy, they too often oversimplify how the public is thinking. As shown in chapter 6, section 7, Yankelovich viewed public deliberation as a dynamic process that evolves as the public becomes aware of a problem and thinks out possible solutions. His criticism of the polls we are so familiar with in the mass media is that they oversimplify this process by taking only a snapshot of one stage in a dynamic process of deliberation. Yankelovich (1992, p. 24) divided the process of public deliberation into seven stages:

1. People become aware of the existence of a problem.
2. A sense of urgency develops about doing something to solve the problem.
3. Policy makers begin to offer proposals for change.
4. Resistance to change arises as people become aware of difficult trade-offs.
5. People wrestle with the trade-offs, trying to reconcile conflicting values.
6. People reach an intellectual resolution on what to do.
7. People personally, emotionally, and morally accept the resolution of the issue.

The problem with public opinion polls, according to Yankelovich (p. 25), is that because the media see their job as making people aware of new issues, they tend to emphasize stages one and two, because they see the public as a passive receptacle of information. But the most important thing about a public opinion poll as a basis for forming a public policy is the stage where people's opinions are being measured, in the sequence of deliberations that leads to a public judgment.

The process of thinking described by Yankelovich is a distinctive type of reasoning that is normatively classified in the typology of dialogues in chapter 1 as goal-directed practical reasoning used in deliberation. What people are doing in thinking about a political issue or policy that affects them personally is to judge its worth as a goal. But at the same time the actions needed to bring about this goal, and the consequences of bringing it about, need to be weighed in a balance. So trying to determine how people are really thinking about a political issue of this sort by taking a poll, based on asking a one-shot multiple choice question, "Are you in favor of or against this policy?" is inherently misleading. The poll cannot represent their real thinking on the issue, because that thinking will be a balancing of goals, actions, and consequences. In certain respects, they may be for the policy, while in other respects, they are against it. From the point of view of the inductive sampling inference based on the polling questions, there is a contradiction. But from the point of view of the practical reasoning that represents the real thinking of the respondents, the contradiction can be resolved.

Because of the deficiencies of standard polling techniques when it comes to getting a less flawed and distorted picture of what the public is thinking on important matters, Fishkin (1991) has proposed moving to a different model of polling called deliberative polling. The basic problem revealed by the various examples outlined above is that a poll provides only a simplistic snapshot of public opinion that can be highly misleading. Citizens may lack knowledge on a question in a poll, but do not want to reveal their ignorance or want to try to help the pollster. Hence, as noted above, they will venture an opinion, even if they really do not know anything at all about the issue. Even though they may realize that they have not thought about an issue enough to have a firm opinion, most respondents feel obliged to venture an opinion in answer to a pollster's question, just to help the pollster out. As Fishkin (1991, p. 83) summed up the problem, "most opinions are invented on the spot," and thus the polls are often distorted to make things appear a lot more definite than they really are. Fishkin's proposal that deliberative polls be used to solicit public opinion could overcome these deficiencies. The respondent could engage in a dialogue with the pollster, instead of just answering "yes" or "no" to a loaded question based on questionable definitions or emotively suggestive language. The respondent could admit his ignorance in a dialogue format that would permit finer shades of opinion to come out.

The purpose of an ordinary public opinion poll is to answer the question of what the opinion of the public is on some issue, at a particular time. On many issues, many of those polled will lack information about the issue. But that will not prevent them from venturing an opinion. And indeed, as noted above, the question of the poll is designed typically to force them to declare an opinion, one way or the other, on the issue. The purpose of a deliberative poll is to answer the question of what the opinion of the public would be if it had a better opportunity to consider the question at issue (Fishkin 1995, p. 162). The method of conducting a deliberative public opinion poll has been concisely described by Fishkin.

Take a national random sample of the electorate and transport those people from all over the country to a single place. Immerse the sample in the issues, with carefully balanced briefing materials, with intensive discussions in small groups, and with the chance to question competing experts and politicians. At the end of several days of working through the issues face to face, poll the participants in detail. The resulting survey offers a representation of the considered judgments of the public – the views the entire country would come to if it had the same experience of behaving more like ideal citizens immersed in the issues for an extended period. (1995, p. 162)

There are several respects in which the deliberative poll can be contrasted to the usual type of public opinion poll we are so familiar with. Instead of being a snapshot of public opinion at one point in time, the deliberative poll is the outcome of a dialogue that develops over time, passing through various stages. The deliberation goes through an opening stage, and then an argumentation stage in which there is interaction among the participants. As the deliberation dialogue proceeds, there is an interjection of information from experts and politicians. The deliberations can thus become better informed and more intelligent. There is what is called an embedding of the information-seeking dialogue in a deliberation dialogue. In the usual poll, the respondent tends to be forced to give an answer even if she is ignorant about the issue. In the deliberative poll, this ignorance of the respondent is gradually overcome as the deliberation proceeds. This difference means that many of the fallacies that inevitably occur in the ordinary polls, because of the way the poll is designed and has to be carried out, are much less likely to occur in the deliberative poll. A further major difference is stated by Fishkin above. The purpose of the deliberative poll is different from that of the usual poll. The usual poll has the aim of simply collecting information about what view the public is holding. The deliberative poll has the aim of judging what view the public would hold if it was thoughtfully informed about the issue and the arguments on both sides.

Traditional polling is a method of estimating public opinion on political issues that takes no account of the reasons a respondent has for holding an opinion. To get a better grasp of public opinion, critical questions about the questions used in the poll need to be asked. In particular, the extent of the known consequences of a policy at issue needs to be considered, in judging the worth of a conclusion derived by inference from a public opinion poll. To get a deeper analysis of how the respondents are reacting to the question posed in the poll, it is necessary to adopt a broader viewpoint. In this viewpoint the question and reply are seen as part of an ongoing deliberation on some issue the public is thinking about. By adopting a dialectical model of deliberation, a critical thinker can resolve the apparent contradictions in the public responses to the question put in the poll. Fortunately, the ordinary poll is not the only method of judging public opinion on an issue. Focus groups, discussion groups, and deliberative polls are alternative methods that offer deeper insight into how the public is thinking about that issue. Deliberation is one of the dialectical models of argument analyzed in Walton and Krabbe (1995).

Recent research in AI and argumentation has begun to study formal models of deliberation, as noted in chapter 2, section 5. In this research, deliberation is seen as a kind of conversation or dialogue in which two parties communicate with each other collaboratively. The conversation is modeled as a formal dialogue in which there are rules binding on the moves made by the participants. The rules govern the kinds of moves that can be made at each stage of the dialogue. As shown in chapter 2, section 5, Hitchcock et al. (2001) have set out a formal model of deliberation with the intent of making the model precise enough to be implemented by computer software. The obvious setting for such a dialogue model is that of multi-agent systems in computing. In multi-agent systems, software entities need to communicate in order to carry out various tasks collaboratively. In a deliberation dialogue of the kind modeled by Hitchcock et al., the two participants take turns making proposals and counter-proposals. But they also need to make other kinds of moves (speech acts), like asking and replying to questions. As shown in chapter 2, Hitchcock et al. structure deliberation as a type of dialogue that goes through eight stages as it moves toward its goal. The goal of a deliberation dialogue is to solve a problem by taking action on a question that poses a choice among possible courses of action. As deliberation proceeds, the two parties put forward various proposals for dealing with the problem, and examine arguments for and against them. The following itemization of the eight different types of moves in a deliberation dialogue is quoted from Hitchcock et al. (2001, p. 7).

Open: Opening of the deliberation dialogue, and the raising of a governing question about what is to be done.

Inform: Discussion of: (a) the governing question; (b) desirable goals; (c) any constraints on the possible actions which may be considered; (d) perspectives by which proposals may be evaluated; and (e) any premises (facts) relevant to this evaluation.

Propose: Suggesting of possible action-options appropriate to the governing question.

Consider: Commenting on proposals from various perspectives.

Revise: Revising of: (a) the governing question, (b) goals, (c) constraints, (d) perspectives, and/or (e) action-options in the light of the comments presented; and the undertaking of any information-gathering or fact-checking required for resolution. (Note that other types of dialogues, such as information seeking or persuasion, may be embedded in the deliberation dialogue at this stage.)

Recommend: Recommending an option for action, and acceptance or non-acceptance of this recommendation by each participant.

Confirm: Confirming acceptance of a recommended option by each participant. We have assumed that all participants must confirm their acceptance of a recommended option for normal termination.

Close: Closing of the deliberation dialogue.

Hitchcock et al. provided a set of rules that determine what each participant can say at each move in the dialogue. When all the relevant proposals have been examined by both sides, and the arguments for and against each proposal have been considered, the participants need to reach agreement on which course of action to go ahead with. This formal model of deliberation conforms to the standard model in recent argumentation theory in that it is commitment-based. Commitments are defined by the speech acts of the participants and by the commitment rules. In a commitment-based system, the premises of one participant's arguments are furnished by the commitments of the other. The commitment-based model is contrasted with the belief-desire-intention (BDI) model. In the latter model, belief is used instead of commitment as providing the basic structure underlying the rules of the system.

Polls are currently being abused by cause advocacy groups, public relations firms, corporate advertisers, and government agencies, in ways that are clearly fallacious and deceptive. They are among the most persuasive argumentation tools for deceptive advocacy, propaganda, and manipulation of public opinion. These claims have surely been proved quite convincingly by the examples cited above, which resonate with familiarity. But what can we do about it? It would be unrealistic to think that we could stop such manipulative argumentation tactics or that we can ignore polls. We do need public opinion polls as social indicators that are vital to the intelligent formation of public policies in a democracy. Polls should not be seen as inherently fallacious or as something we can do without. The best solution is to teach better awareness of the fallacies and tricky techniques of argumentation that polling is susceptible to. The best solution is to educate the public in critical thinking about polls and to promote wider public awareness about the importance of these fallacies, especially in policy formation and political deliberation in a democracy. The movement toward deliberative polling, in place of an uncritical reliance on the traditional methods, should be regarded as a step in the right direction.

7. Argumentation Schemes and Critical Questions

Part of the solution to the problem is to recognize that citing a statistic based on a poll to support a claim is allied with several distinctive forms of argument. In many cases, the form of argument used fits the pattern of one of the following argumentation schemes. The argumentation scheme most applicable to the cases studied above is the following one, the basic type of argument used to report the result of a poll.

The Report of a Public Opinion Poll Argument
> *X* percent of respondents answered question *Q* giving answer *A*.
> Answer *A* implies that statement *B* is true (or false).
> Therefore, *X* percent of respondents are of the opinion that *B* is true (or false).

The critical questions for the Report of a Public Opinion Poll argument focus on the question asked in the poll. As shown above, the readers of the poll are often not even told what this question is. Thus the key critical question is to ask what the question was. The other two critical questions also concern the question wording.

Critical Questions for the Report of a Public Opinion Poll Argument
1. What is the specific wording of question *Q*?
2. Can key terms in *Q* be defined precisely, in line with standards of precision appropriate for the poll?
3. Is there a bias in question *Q*, due to emotive terms or the structure of the question?

These three questions are not the only ones that can or should be asked in response to a Report of a Public Opinion Poll argument. But as shown by the case studies, they are the basic ones needed to spot weak points or reveal fallacies in such an argument. The Report of a Public Opinion Poll argument is always based on a question worded in a particular way. The wording is always based on a definition of at least one key term. The statistic depends on how the key term was defined. Various aspects of the definition will affect the outcome of the poll by inflating or deflating the numbers of the outcome. As we have seen, for example, the wider the definition is, the larger will be the number cited as the finding of the poll. What is important to recognize is that in response to any argument of this type, or any argument based on a poll or statistical finding, a very important focus of critical questioning should be on how the key term should be defined.

The key role of definitions and the need to question them has already been revealed by the previous case studies. But to underline the point, it may be helpful to quote another common type of example studied by Best (2001, p. 42).

Case 7.11

> When someone announces that millions of Americans are illiterate, it is important to ask how that announcement defines illiteracy. Some might assume that illiteracy means that a person cannot read or write at all, but a speaker may be referring to "functional illiteracy" (that is, the inability to read a newspaper or a map or to fill out a job application or an income tax form). Does illiterate mean not reading at all? Not reading at the third grade level? Defining illiteracy narrowly (as being unable to read at all) will include far fewer people and therefore produce far lower statistical estimates than a broad definition (being unable to read at the sixth grade level).

A similar case, also cited by Best (p. 43), is that of the various statistics on homelessness that have so often been stressed by social activists. Competing definitions of homelessness have often been given. Should we count only persons whose poverty made them homeless, for example? Or should we include disaster victims? Advocates for the homeless have argued for much broader definitions. Under such a broader definition, for example, people living with a relative might have to be counted as homeless. In such cases, then, the first critical question should always be how the key term is defined. There is usually considerable scope on how widely or narrowly to define a term. Thus, asking probing critical questions may be necessary in order to grasp how inclusive the definition is, and to think of alternative definitions that may be wider or narrower. Once a respondent carries out this form of critical examination of the argument, it will become clear how the statistic is dependent on the definition. By this means, the power of the statistic to persuade is eroded. The argument based on the numerical finding at first appears objective and even unchallengeable. But once the critical question of definition is raised, the power of the argument may simply evaporate.

In connection with the study of fallacies of polling, it is very useful to be aware of two other forms of argument that commonly play a role in arguments based on public opinion polls. The first one has to do with the use of public opinion polls by advocacy groups of various kinds to try to get public action on an issue.

The Call for Action Argument

> Because of statistical finding *S*, it is shown that *P* is a big problem.
> Therefore we should take action *A* in order to solve *P*.

Critical Questions for the Call for Action Argument
1. How are key terms defined in the question used to get S from a poll?
2. Do the definitions or terms used in the poll have a bias?
3. Are there actions other than A that might solve the alleged problem?

Note that the conclusion of this form of argument is not a claim that a statement is true or false. Instead, the conclusion is a call for action. It is a recommendation that a particular course of action would be a good idea. Thus this is a practical form of argument. Its logic is that of goal-directed practical reasoning. The context in which it should be evaluated is that of a deliberation.

Another form of argument associated with polling, and often based on a public opinion poll, is the appeal to popular opinion. This form of argument has long been recognized as potentially fallacious in logic. The *argumentum ad populum* is the traditional logical fallacy studied in chapter 6. As shown in chapter 6, there can be various forms of appeal to popular opinion, and not all of them are fallacious. The form presented below is a special subtype based on polling.

Appeal to Popular Opinion
Poll results S show that many people (or a majority) accept statement A.
Therefore, statement A is (probably, plausibly) true.

Critical Questions for the Appeal to Popular Opinion Argument
1. What reason is there to think that majority acceptance of A is relevant to accepting A as true?
2. Could the poll be biased in some way to inflate statistic S?

This form of argument is normally quite weak in itself, and an audience may easily detect the weakness of it. But it is often bolstered by other forms of argument. For example, suppose the majority includes the experts. Then this would make the argument stronger and harder to attack. The problem in such cases is one of disentangling the appeal to popular opinion type of argument from other types of argument, such as the appeal to expert opinion.

The call for action argument and the appeal to popular opinion argument are common forms of argument used by advocacy groups, public relations firms, and others in the business of manipulating public opinion. Neither is inherently fallacious. There is nothing wrong with advocacy or with using such arguments to advocate a cause or a political viewpoint or to sell a product. Persuasion by using arguments is a legitimate type of dialogue. But such arguments often conceal a shift. They are supposed to be part of intelligent public deliberations on how to solve social problems, like the plight of the homeless. But then they slide into advocacy argumentation that can properly be used in persuasion dialogue, but may be misleading when it is presented as supposedly part of deliberation dialogue. The fallacy aspect enters in through the deceptive shift from the one type of dialogue to the other. Such an argument may be all right as part of a persuasion dialogue, but it may fall short of the rules and standards appropriate for deliberation. Here the dialectical model of deliberation as a model of rational argumentation is extremely important for evaluating these forms of argument.

One key problem posed by our case studies is how to determine, in a particular case, whether a given argument is strong or weak. An associated problem of evaluation is to judge whether it is merely weak or fallacious. A fallacious argument is worse than one that is merely weak, or open to critical questioning. It is one that can't be critically questioned or has features making it difficult to critically question. A fallacy is a bad argument that disrupts a dialogue by either blocking it or making it problematic or difficult for the dialogue to continue properly. Fallacies often involve deception and deliberate tactics of confusion or unfairly trying to get the best of a speech partner. To prove that an argument based on a poll is fallacious, you have to show not only that critical questions have not been answered but that there is some factor at work in the context of dialogue that blocks off or interferes with the asking of critical questions, due to the way the argument has been put forward in a given case. The context of dialogue is all-important here. That is why the dialectical models of persuasion dialogue and deliberation dialogue are needed to prove that an argument based on a poll is fallacious.

8. Using Formal Dialectical Models of Argumentation

It is shown in this section that it is necessary and especially important to use the dialogue methodology in current argumentation theory to frame the asking of the question in a poll in a context of dialogue. This chapter has already set out a number of paradigm examples (or so-called cases) of fallacious reasoning employed in or based on polls. It concludes by offering a dialectical (dialogue-based) technique that can be used to probe into a question-reply dialogue in a given case and to ask the right critical questions about the actual wording of questions in a poll. It is argued that the best way to offset the potential for deception and bias in polling is to anticipate and deal with specific fallacies by developing a dialectical model of question asking and answering. But it will also be shown how the dialectical methods need to be combined with empirical methods that measure statistical effects of the question wordings in polls called "response effects" (Schuman and Presser 1981). Empirical methods combined with dialectical methods provide a precise way of measuring wording bias of a question and identifying fallacies due to this bias.

Since Hamblin (1970) constructed several simple formal models of dialogue to study fallacies, the use of normative models of dialogue to evaluate argumentation use in particular cases has developed in various directions. Formal models of persuasion dialogue along the lines set out by Hamblin have been constructed in Walton and Krabbe (1995). As noted in chapter 1, Hitchcock et al. have constructed a formal model of deliberation dialogue that can be applied to polling, especially to deliberative polling. Van Eemeren et al. (1996) have brought together a useful survey of the latest developments in argumentation theory based on this dialogue approach to the study of argumentation. The problem arising from the cases of fallacies of polling studied so far is that the use of syntactic and semantic methods to analyze the various kinds of problematic questions used in polls is not sufficient. What is also needed is to examine how the questions have been used in a context of dialogue. Let us then ask how some of the problems raised could be addressed in a dialectical framework.

The first problem that needs to be addressed is how we can use the method to distinguish between inappropriately loaded questions – or statements or terms – and genuine argumentative moves (that also go some distance toward proving the respondent's thesis false). This question is an excellent one, and fully deserves to be answered, but it is useful to observe that it is a loaded question itself, especially in regard to one particular presumption. The question presumes that there is a dichotomy between inappropriately loaded questions that should be critically questioned or may even be fallacious and genuine argumentative moves. That is, it presumes that loaded questions are inherently non-genuine or even illegitimate, spurious, or fallacious. But thinking that such a judgment can be made without taking the context of dialogue into account is a simplistic misconception (Walton 1995). While the spouse abuse question (to cite the modern classic case based on the ancient one) is fallacious as used in some cases, there are cases where asking the question, "Have you stopped abusing your spouse?" could be perfectly reasonable. In other words, loaded questions are not always fallacious, or non-genuine argumentative moves. Whether such a question has been used reasonably or not in a given case is determined by constructing a normative model of dialogue for the case. Then what needs to be done is to evaluate the prior sequence of questioning in light of the known details of the case and the appropriate normative model of dialogue for the case (Hamblin 1970; Walton and Krabbe 1995).

The second problem can be expressed in the following questions and assertions. What is the connection between the dialectical analysis – using the models of dialogue and the projected chains of argumentation used to determine the distance between the given proposition and the respondent's thesis – and the empirical test of response effects proposed by Schuman and Presser? Why even assume that there is any connection here? To assume such a connection is to assume that people's patterns of responses to questions are, at least to some degree, connected to judgments about the ways in which ideal chains of argumentation might proceed. But in fact, responses to poll questions might be much less rational than that. To respond to the worries expressed by this set of questions and assertions, it is best to begin by once again pointing out certain potentially misleading implications in them.

One factor in the method for judging how loaded a question is in a given case is connected to judgments about the ways in which ideal chains of argumentation might proceed. Citing this factor by itself, in relation to people's patterns of responses to poll questions, makes the method sound hopelessly idealistic. It makes it seem to assume, unjustifiably, that poll respondents really think out or are aware of chains of logical reasoning in some ideal model of argumentation. Can we assume that poll respondents are all that rational? It would seem to be unjustified (and worrisome) to make any such assumption.

To respond to these worries, some comments need to be made about the use of dialectical models as a method for evaluating argumentation. Yes, the method does assume that a respondent in a given case is rational in a certain sense, because it applies a normative model of dialogue, and the projecting forward of a chain of reasoning in that model of dialogue, toward the respondent's thesis. Because it is an ideal model, like all models, it does not apply or fit perfectly to the details of any particular case. Thus the evaluation of a loaded question in any particular case will inevitably be based on certain assumptions that may not fit the case exactly. Indeed, the evaluation of any particular case will have to be, in certain respects, and to some extent, conditional in nature. Is that a problem? It is not. What the evaluation of a case does is to place the asking of the question in the given case in relation to a context of dialogue that can be extrapolated (by presumption) from the information given in the text of discourse of the case. So the question is evaluated as loaded from the point of view that one can reasonably attribute to the respondent (in the absence of indications to the contrary). This evaluation of a case on a basis of attributing commitments to a participant in a dialogue is typical of normative methods. What has to be recognized is that commitment is not the same as actual belief (Hamblin 1970), but it can serve as a kind of dialectically constructed profile of belief.

Another point to be made about this particular method of judging loaded questions is that it is tailored to the data given in the particulars of the individual case it is being applied to. What is especially important to note is that the evaluation of how heavily a question is loaded in a given case depends on the commitments of the respondent, insofar as these are known. And how heavily a question is loaded depends on that respondent, or on a group of respondents, in the case of a statistical poll. So it is important to realize that, according to the method proposed above, a question can be heavily loaded for one respondent and less heavily loaded (or not loaded at all) for another respondent. So the determination of how heavily a question is loaded in a given case is not as strongly idealized as the worries expressed above suggest.

Another factor to be clear about is that the test for response effects used by statisticians is far from a perfect instrument. It arises from the worry that a question used in a poll might be loaded or biased in a way that the pollster did not anticipate. The worry is that such a bias would make the announcement of the finding of the poll (expressed as a scientific finding, with numerical measures of chance of error announced) misleading to users of the poll. Testing for a response effect is one way of getting confirming evidence that a problem of this kind exists in a given case. And the validity of the test, in a given case, depends on various statistical assumptions about sampling – in particular, on the assumption that the respondents used in the second test are the same kind of respondents as those used in the first test. These are the usual statistical assumptions about selecting a sample of respondents using methods that do not contain biases of various kinds well known to statisticians. So there are plenty of worries about any running of a statistical test for a response effect. It is not a perfect instrument, any more than any statistical test used in any poll is.

The general dialectical method proposed for evaluating whether and how heavily a statement, term, or question is loaded in a given case can be summed up as follows. A statement is loaded in a particular case (in a context of dialogue) if it goes some distance toward proving the respondent's thesis false. A term is loaded if it occurs in a loaded statement. A question is loaded if it contains or presupposes terms or propositions that are loaded. So defined, then, whether and how heavily a proposition (term, question) is loaded, in a given case, is determined by four factors: (1) the commitments of the respondent in a dialogue, (2) more generally, the context of dialogue for the given case (insofar as that is known), (3) the type of dialogue the participants are supposed to be engaged in (insofar as that is known, or has been determined), and (4) the projected distance between the proposition (or term or question), as used in the dialogue exchange, and the respondent's thesis. This method involves applying a normative (ideal) model of dialogue to the argumentation used in a particular case, embedded in the text of discourse given in an actual case. How heavily the proposition (or term or question) is loaded is determined by applying the normative model of dialogue to the given details of the particular case. In carrying out such an application, it is necessary to also use the tool of the profile of dialogue, as explained in section 1 above. In addition to this normative method, an empirical test is proposed. A question is loaded, or contains loaded terms, if individuals respond to it differently in statistical polls when it is reformulated in an equivalent way using other words. It is not necessary, or practically useful, to use this empirical test to evaluate how heavily a question is loaded in all cases (of the kind illustrated above as typically of concern in logic and critical thinking textbooks). Still, in principle, it is salutary to see that there is an empirical test that can be used for this purpose, particularly in evaluating questions used in statistical polls.

9. Combining Dialectical and Empirical Methods

What an empirical test for a response effect tells you is that there is something in the wording of the question that is loading the question or biasing it in a certain direction. The problem could be either in the connotations of the words used or in the logical structure of the question. The bias is in relation to the conventional word usage and commonly accepted opinions of a particular class of respondents, chosen according to criteria of the kinds commonly recommended by statisticians for polling. The test is a clue to or indicator of a trick or twist in the wording of the question that a pollster may not have been aware of until it was thus revealed and confirmed. This empirical test does not measure, in general, how heavily a question is loaded. It is only designed to measure unanticipated response effects due to question wording. It measures how one term in a question is loaded, in relation to how an apparently equivalent term is loaded in the same question, for a selected group of respondents. Thus it tells us something about loaded terms but does not measure, nor has anyone claimed that it measures, how heavily a question is loaded with respect to a particular respondent or group of respondents.

So why should we assume that there is any connection between this kind of empirical test for response effects of the wording of a question and the dialectical method of evaluating how heavily a question is loaded in a given case that was proposed above? The reason is that the dialectical method proposed above judges how heavily a question is loaded, in a given case, in relation to the commitments of the respondent in that actual case. Such a judgment presumes that these factors are known or can be judged by applying the profile of dialogue to the particulars of the case. When the statistical test for response effects of the wording of a question is run, it is on a particular group of respondents, where the characteristics of this group have been chosen by the statistical survey methodology. What is being estimated is how heavily the question is loaded, in virtue of its wording for that group of respondents. So when it is judged that the question is loaded or "biased" to a certain degree, for that particular group of respondents (as extrapolated to a wider population by the usual methods of statistical surveying), the result of the test applies to that group of respondents. In using such a test, it is both natural and necessary to make assumptions and to use these assumptions about the known views or positions of this group of respondents. These factors, which correspond to the known characteristics of the group selected, represent (in the dialectical model) the thesis (and the known commitments generally) of the respondent.

Collection of data in research and in statistical polls and public opinion surveys is always based on the asking of questions. But if natural language wording is used in the question, the question is bound to be more or less loaded in a particular direction, and therefore bound to have significant persuasive implications. Yet because of the way the results of scientific investigations and surveys are typically announced, it appears that the finding has been obtained by an objective and unbiased collection of data. The epistemological significance of this dissonance between appearance and reality should be regarded as extremely important from a viewpoint of critical thinking. We need to realize that before we act on these omnipresent polls, or take them seriously as results that have been scientifically validated and proved, and as constituting good evidence for a conclusion, some way of measuring the bias of the question has to be taken into account. But how do you measure the connotations of words and the innuendo or implicatures in a question? This is the problem, and statisticians are not used to dealing with problems of this kind. Indeed, they are not well equipped to deal with it, because the problem is a dialectical one, best solved by pragmatic methods on a case-by-case basis.

Work needs to be done by social scientists to investigate the relationship between normative models of dialogue and empirical methods of judging the attitudes and commitments of respondent groups in statistical polls and surveys. Normative structures of dialogue that have been developed (as cited above) are especially interesting precisely because they do seem to model everyday argumentation much more naturally than the deductive and inductive logical calculi that have dominated the field of logic for so long. But exactly how the formal dialectical modeling of loaded questions (and the tricky problems associated with them) correlates with statistical techniques for empirically estimating attitudes and commitments of respondents is really a field of inquiry in its own right, and one that, so far, has been explored very little. As more and more people become aware of the abuses of statistics in push polling and similarly dubious practices now so widely operative in the collection of data, the need for taking critical thinking seriously in this area has become more and more evident.

As noted above, Graesser et al. (1996) developed the computer program called QUEST to study strategies used by respondents when answering questions in polls. The QUEST model views questioning and answering within a process of communication in which both the questioner and the respondent have goals. Thus the QUEST model can be seen as dialectical. It has four components (p. 149). In the question interpretation component, the question is parsed into a logical form and its presuppositions identified. In the information sources component, scripts, concept, and frames are used to identify the knowledge structures. In the pragmatic component, three factors are identified: the goals of the questioner and the respondent, the common ground between the questioner and the respondent, and the informativeness of the answer. In the convergence to relevant answers component, matters of relevance are considered. The purpose of QUEST is to identify problems that respondents typically have with attempting to answer specific types of questions. An example cited above (p. 154) is the kind of case in which there are problems with presuppositions of questions. The ultimate aim of developing a program such as QUEST is to improve survey questions by identifying poor questions and diagnosing particular problems with them (p. 166). A cognitive computational model such as QUEST is both normative and dialectical in the way it classifies and processes the asking and answering of questions in polls and surveys.

Any method that is useful for analyzing fallacies of question bias in polling needs to be dialectical as well as empirical. For judging how heavily a question, term, or statement is loaded has been shown to require a method that is both dialectical and empirical. The judgment needs to be made by applying a normative model of dialogue to a particular case in which a question was asked. The normative model is prompted by the conversational context of the case, insofar as it can be determined from the question itself and the text of discourse surrounding it (as known in the case). The method is both normative and dialectical in that it works by applying an abstract model of dialogue to the known particulars of question use in a given case. However, as has been shown, empirical tests (of the kinds used in statistical surveys) can be brought to bear, to some extent, as well. The answer to whether a question can rightly be judged to be loaded, as used in a given case, turns out to depend on the context of dialogue in which the question was asked. The same method applies to loaded terms. How can we judge whether a term used in, say, a question or an argument is loaded? How can we judge how heavily the question is loaded? These are questions that need to be answered by looking at the details of the sequence of dialogue in which that term appeared, in a given question or statement. One part of the method is the use of empirical techniques to test for response effects. Another part of the method is to apply a cognitive model such as QUEST to the questions used in the poll, and diagnose specific problems and instances where bias is likely to occur. Underlying both methods should be a dialectical model of question-reply dialogue.

10. Conclusion and Summary of Fallacies

It needs to be emphasized that for the most part, this chapter has been about fallacies not in polls themselves but in media arguments derived from polls. Statistical methods used to design and validate polls are very precise and have been very well tested, so that the most elementary fallacies, such as drawing a conclusion based on too small a sample or on an unrepresentative sample, are dealt with very well by the professional pollsters. The main problems we have studied in this chapter concern the unwarranted and misleading inferences drawn from polls by their readers and users, often an audience that may not be well aware of the limitations of statistical methodology. However, some of these problems are created by the designers of the polls and by the media who report poll findings. Many statistical polls are run not by professional statisticians but by those in the media who are under the pressure of deadlines, and also under the pressure to puff up a poll by making a finding that appears exciting to the readers. Also, it might be noted that some of the fallacies and other problems studied in this chapter result inherently from the use of ordinary language and are not limited to polls.

What should we conclude about the use of undefined terms, loaded terms, persuasive definitions, and so forth, in arguments generally, and especially in public opinion polls? The first thing that we found was that there is nothing inherently wrong or fallacious about using a question that has emotive terms in it or has a bias or response effect due to question wording. In a parallel fashion, there is nothing wrong with using loaded terms in an argument. Nor should using persuasive definitions be seen as fallacious per se, whether in polling or in other arguments. For persuasion is a legitimate function of argumentation. There is nothing intrinsically wrong with the general practice of using loaded terms in a question or statement. But being aware of how polls can be biased is vitally important when the poll is used to argue for a policy or support an argument. Critical questions should be asked before accepting the poll outcome or drawing inferences from it. But polls based on a friendly (persuasive) definition should not automatically be judged fallacious. The use of persuasive definitions in mass media argumentation is a subject for further study in the next two chapters.

Where then is the fallacy in the use of such questions and arguments? The initial problem is really one of identifying bias that tends to be hidden because wording bias is not usually measured or even mentioned when a poll is published. Concealment is often the basis of deception. By showing how response effects due to question wording can be measured in a cognitive model, it can be shown how the problem with such questions is one of concealment. The question, on the surface, appears to have a purely information-seeking function in the collection of data. But underlying the appearance, the question has a function of persuasion. The question is really an argument, or is being used as an argument for the purpose of persuasion. And the argument becomes fallacious when-ever the biased poll is used as a systematic tactic of argumentation to mislead an audience. A fallacy, in this sense, is a deceptive tactic of argu-mentation used to get the best of a speech partner in a dialogue unfairly. As shown above, biased polls are routinely used by advocates as argumen-tation tactics to mobilize support for causes. This technique is known in politics as "spin control." Polling fallacies work by concealing a bias in question wording, and then using the biased poll to advocate a cause by statistically inflating the outcome. It is proper to speak of a fallacy being committed in such cases because the argument can be a serious obsta-cle to the dialogue of which the question or statement are supposed to be a part. Biased questions can, of course, be properly used in a persua-sion dialogue. But the standards for argumentation in an information-seeking dialogue are different from those of a persuasion dialogue. Delib-eration dialogue is often based on information-seeking dialogue. Thus it is often in the transition from one type of dialogue to another that an argument becomes fallacious. For example, if the context is one of public deliberation on how to spend money, the proper standards for a deliberation type of dialogue should be followed (Hitchcock et al. 2001). But how is intelligent deliberation possible if it is based on biased infor-mation coming from a supposedly scientific poll? If the poll is supposed to be an objective collecting of information, it should not be judged by the normative standards of a persuasion type of dialogue. The problem is even worse if the poll outcome cannot be questioned because no infor-mation is forthcoming on how key terms were defined. Thus what makes the use of loaded terms fallacious in both questions and statements is that the question or statement at issue is used inappropriately as part of a normative framework of dialogue that surrounds its contextual use. If it misuses loaded terms in various ways, asking a question in what appears to be a scientific public opinion poll can be seriously deceptive. By exploit-ing and actively promoting the assumption that such polls are objective, the poll that uses a loaded question can give a highly misleading account of the way the public is really thinking on some issue of current public deliberation.

The following fallacies were identified and analyzed above. The fallacy of the inappropriate persuasive definition is committed where a persua-sive (emotive, friendly, biased) definition is explicitly used in a poll as part of a tactic to deceptively manipulate the poll users. The fallacy of the concealed persuasive definition is committed when the persuasive spin introduced into the poll by an implicit persuasive definition has not been revealed by the poll outcome presentation. Two other fallacies are converses of each other. One is the use of a broad definition to inflate a statistical result; the other is the use of a definition that is too narrow to deflate a statistical result. The fallacy of meaningless statistics is committed through the use of a vague term that has not been defined, coupled with the announcement of a precise statistical result of a poll. The fallacy of using an atypical example in place of a definition in a poll is committed when there has been a failure to give a needed definition, and this failure is masked by the use of an example designed to have emotional impact on the users of the poll. The fallacy of question structure bias in polling is committed where the structure of the question introduces a bias into the poll that is deceptive, concealing a "yea-say effect." This tactic is often employed in push polling in political polls. The question is really being used as an attempt to persuade or to influence voters, but on the surface it is paraded as merely a collecting of information by taking a poll. The double negative fallacy of question wording is a tactic to confuse both poll respondents and users by violating standards of asking a clear question. This too is a fallacy related to the structure of a question used in a poll. The fallacy of false dichotomy is a general fallacy in logic that can occur in many different contexts of dialogue, including so-called objective or multiple-choice testing. However, this fallacy is especially prominent and important in polling. As shown above, there is a general tendency on the part of pollsters to try to force an answer in order to get a more dramatic and newsworthy poll outcome.

In many cases, polls are useful and accurate. In a presidential election, for example, a simple dichotomous question like, "Which candidate are you voting for?" can be appropriate, and the poll results coming from it could be highly accurate. The move to deliberative polling is also something to be applauded. A deliberative poll can take finer shadings of opinion into account, especially on matters of public policy in a deliberation that goes through several stages as information comes in on an issue. Too often in the past, on more subtle and complex matters of public opinion and attitude, the use of a simple dichotomous question, especially one containing emotive wording, has been fallacious. It has become increasingly evident in recent years that in many cases, especially in matters of public policy, polls have been abused. The cases analyzed above show this pattern of deceptive manipulation of polls to influence public opinion only too well. Common experience confirms it. The polls themselves are not only biased, but they are used to draw unjustified inferences and even to commit fallacies by means of tactics designed to mislead, inflate, and advocate. Misusing polls has turned out to be profitable and highly successful for those in the business of manipulating public opinion. Leading pollsters themselves are conscious of the erosion of public faith in polling caused by these abuses, and have made efforts to set standards. However, it is doubtful that we will ever be able to rely on those who run polls and use them for various purposes. We will never be able to be sure that they are fallacy-free. It is up to us as critical thinkers to become aware of the biases and fallacies and to take a "buyer beware" attitude to accepting media arguments based on polls and to forming public policies based on them.

8

Persuasive Definitions and Public Policy Arguments

Stevenson's theory of the persuasive definition has been applied only to abstract ethical theory and to philosophical discussions. It has perhaps been seen as not too widely significant when confined to that framework. But its implications are of sweeping significance once it is applied to media argumentation. It is shown in this chapter how many media arguments are based on emotively loaded words or phrases that raise questions about the values, verbal classifications, and definitions of these terms. The persuasive definition, or as it is sometimes called in statistics, the friendly definition, is the definition that is stacked in such a way as to put a positive spin on the argument of the definer. This chapter shows how persuasive definitions are extremely powerful media tools, and how they are often used to influence public policy arguments. Five cases based on the use of persuasive definitions in public policy arguments are presented, analyzed, and evaluated below. In all of these cases, the use of the persuasive definition as an argumentative technique had consequences that changed social policies in a way that led to significant gains in the interests of some advocacy groups and losses in the interests of others.

Using these rhetorical case studies, some basic dialectical problems are posed about the legitimacy of persuasive definitions, about how to reconstruct the chains of argumentation they are based on, and about how to evaluate them. The traditional approach, with its dichotomy between nominal and real definition, is shown to be inadequate; it is confining and misleading in many ways. It is shown that we need to begin with a case-based approach that illustrates how persuasive definitions are actually deployed as media argumentation devices in different contexts. Then it is shown how a method can be developed that classifies, analyzes, and evaluates definitions, and arguments based on them, with reference to the way each definition was used for some conversational purpose in a given case.

It is shown that persuasive definitions are inherently legitimate when used in a dialectically appropriate way in a context of dialogue. Now that the speech act of persuasion has been defined in chapter 2, it becomes possible to investigate, at a much deeper level than was possible before, the conditions under which persuasive definitions should be regarded as legitimate and appropriate as devices of persuasion. But to get deeper, we also have to identify the argumentation schemes in which arguments based on verbal classifications, values, and definitions are put forward. This chapter shows that persuasive definitions can be appropriate in a persuasion dialogue, provided the right conditions are met concerning the chain of argumentation in which the definition is put forward by the proponent and reacted to by the respondent. But if persuasive definitions can be legitimate under the right conditions in some cases, how is it that they can be tricky, deceptive, and even fallacious in other cases, where they are powerful instruments of deception? This difficult question is the final one taken up in this chapter. Rhetoric by itself, before the advent of argumentation schemes, and methods from AI, such as tools for argumentation diagramming that can incorporate schemes, could never solve the problem posed by this question. This chapter shows that with the advent of the new dialectical tools, we are now getting close to solving it.

1. Stevenson's Theory of Persuasive Definitions

The concept of the persuasive definition, as used in a certain way in argumentation, is a theory introduced by philosopher Charles L. Stevenson in his article published in the journal *Mind* (1938). It was then elaborated and presented in the form most of us are familiar with it today in his book, *Ethics and Language* (1944). A basic assumption behind Stevenson's concept of the persuasive definition is that words used in argumentation, for example, in ethical discussions, have both an emotive and a descriptive meaning. This distinction between the two types of meaning appears to have been drawn from earlier theoreticians of language use. According to the account given by Aomi (1985, p. 187), the phrase "emotive meaning" was coined by Ogden and Richards in their book, *The Meaning of Meaning* (1923). Ogden and Richards postulated that the descriptive meaning is the core factual or descriptive content of a word, while the emotive meaning represents the feelings or attitudes (positive or negative) that the use of the word suggests to respondents. Stevenson's theory of how persuasive definitions work in argumentation is built on this distinction. How a persuasive definition works, according to Stevenson's theory, is by redefining the descriptive meaning of the word, while covertly retaining its old familiar emotive meaning. The potential deception in this technique is that while the word ostensibly appears to have been given an entirely new meaning, it continues to retain its past emotional meaning. The emotional connotation expressed by the old meaning could be positive or negative. For example, the word "liberation" has positive connotations, while the word "oppression" has negative connotations. Because of the lingering of this emotive meaning, the respondent is covertly persuaded to accept (or reject) the new definition, based on persuasive positive or negative connotations in the existing usage of the word.

To show how Stevenson's concept of the persuasive definition works in practice, it is best to give an example. Stevenson himself (1944, p. 211) offered the following illustration, in the form of a dialogue between two parties called **A** and **B**.

Case 8.1

A: He has had but little formal education, as is plainly evident from his conversation. His sentences are often roughly cast, his historical and literary references rather obvious, and his thinking is wanting, in that subtlety and sophistication which mark a trained intellect. He is definitely lacking in culture.

B: Much of what you say is true, but I should call him a man of culture notwithstanding.

A: Aren't the characteristics I mention the antithesis of culture, contrary to the very meaning, of the term?

B: By no means. You are stressing the outward forms, simply the empty shell of culture. In the true and full sense of the term, "culture" means imaginative sensitivity and originality. These qualities he has; and so I say, and indeed with no little humility, that he is a man of far deeper culture than many of us who have had superior advantages in education.

B is arguing that the conventionally accepted definition of "culture" is superficial, and he proposes a new definition that redefines the term "culture" in terms of sensitivity and originality, and not just outward appearances.

What might be the effects of such a redefinition if applied to a case of ethical judgment? We can pose this question by extending Stevenson's example to a new one, which we now invent and call case 8.1a.

Case 8.1a

> Suppose Rodney uses bad grammar, has bad table manners, and displays an ignorance of history, literature, and classical music, but is emotionally sensitive, and highly original, even eccentric in his behavior. By the standard meaning of "culture," Rodney would definitely not be said to be a cultured person. But suppose that Rodney's boorish behavior is excused by claiming that according to the new definition, he is a cultured person.

In case 8.1a, Rodney's (apparently) bad behavior is being justified or excused by arguing that in the way that really counts, or really should count, he is a cultured person. What's really happening is that a kind of positive spin is being put on the case by using language that makes Rodney's behavior seem okay. How does the technique work? It works because the term "culture" retains its positive emotive meaning, thus seeming to support the view that Rodney is really behaving in an acceptable way. Stevenson's theory (1938, p. 333) can be used to explain how the argumentation works to create a deception in such a case. The redefined word retains the old positive emotive connotations that it always had, as noted above. But people tend not to realize that they are still being influenced by them, even though they have agreed to change to the new descriptive meaning, which perhaps should not still continue to have positive connotations, at least of the same kind. The technique works because the shift of descriptive meaning is typically not accompanied by a shift of emotive meaning. The result is a deceptive kind of blurring or ambiguity of meaning in the sequence of argumentation. This deceptive aspect has often evoked quite a critical attitude toward persuasive definitions in logic textbooks, where they are treated as, if not fallacious, at least something to be wary about. However, persuasive definitions sometimes appear to be acceptable.

A leading characteristic that helps us to recognize persuasive definitions, according to Stevenson (1944, p. 214), is that they are often preceded by the words "true" or "real." In case 8.1, for example, **B** says that she is talking about the "true" meaning of culture. Another illustration presented by Stevenson (1938, p. 334) defines "courage" as "strength against adverse public opinion." Persuasive definitions are commonly found in intellectual writings, such as on philosophy, literary criticism, and the social sciences. Philosophical arguments and ethical treatises in particular are full of persuasive definitions. Hallden (1960) has described many cases of such writings that give persuasive definitions of concepts like love, humor, poetry, culture, life, and democracy. It would be a sweeping condemnation to reject all these arguments as being somehow logically deficient, or even fallacious, just because persuasive definitions are used in them. So the diagnosis of exactly what is wrong with using persuasive definitions appears to be an unsolved problem. Whatever the solution to the problem is, Stevenson was certainly right to warn that persuasive definitions can be quite tricky and powerful tools of persuasion.

Aomi (1985, p. 187) explained the basic components of Stevenson's theory very well by stating the following four requirements of the effectiveness of a persuasive definition.

1. The word being defined has strong emotive connotations.
2. The descriptive meaning of the word is vague and ambiguous enough to be semantically manipulated.
3. The change of meaning by redefinition is not noticed by naïve listeners.
4. The emotive meaning of the word remains unaltered.

This four-tiered account of how persuasive definitions work shows how an emotive inertia factor is a key aspect of the process showing how the use of such definitions can be both persuasive and deceptive. The third and fourth requirements show how the function of a persuasive definition in persuading an audience depends on two factors: (1) how the people in the audience react emotionally to the word being redefined and (2) whether they notice the meaning shift implied by the redefinition.

Stevenson's theory seems mainly applicable to ordinary conversational argumentation and philosophical discussions, as indicated by the examples. But when one tries to apply it to mass media argumentation, other factors come into play. Persuasive definitions used in political arguments are most often designed to influence public opinion but are sometimes used to change public policies, regulations, or even laws or legal definitions. But once a definition is set in place in a bureaucracy, there is an inertia effect. It can't be changed easily by a single individual retracting it. In such cases, we are dealing not just with a proponent and respondent who are single agents. We are dealing with a community of arguers.

It is common that issues concerning the definition of terms used in mass media argumentation have a legal aspect. In such cases, there is a shift from the framework of a political or philosophical discussion to a legal one. But the rules and standards by which definitions and arguments are judged is quite different in the legal framework. To put the point in a more graphic way, two distinct communities of arguers are involved. A community is generally thought of as a group of actual persons. But McKerrow (1990) has suggested that the term has a different meaning as applied to the normative evaluation of argumentation. In this sense, a community of arguers can be seen as a set of agents or participants in dialogue who share a set of rules and common goals guided by their wish to collaborate verbally in order to discuss an unsettled issue. A community in this sense is defined by the collaborative willingness of a set of participants to abide by a set of social practices. There can be different communities guided by different sets of rules. One type of community cited by McKerrow (1990, p. 30) is the personal, but other types include the social, the technical, and the philosophical. McKerrow also noted (p. 29) that communities can be composed of individuals who follow the rules of a community out of free choice or "as a result of an edict from others in positions of authority." One can see that the freedom to put forward and to accept or reject definitions can be expected to vary considerably from one community of arguers to another.

For example, in a personal or philosophical discussion, a proponent is free to put forward a definition at any time, and the respondent in the discussion is free to accept it, reject it, or raise critical questions about it. If it is a persuasive definition, just because it is a speech act of persuasion, of the kind that might be found in an argument, the conclusion that it is wrong does not necessarily follow. Of course, words already have established meanings in ordinary usage. But it is quite possible to redefine a term as part of an argument. The respondent to whom the definition was directed should, however, have the right to question it or even to put forward an opposed persuasive definition. In a philosophical discussion, perhaps the respondent could even be said to be obliged to question the definition, and probe into it philosophically instead of accepting it uncritically. However, the situation will be quite different in argumentation in a legal community. For example, in a trial or in another legal proceeding, many terms have a meaning that has long been established by legal usage, statute, or a court ruling. The legal community is bound by these definitions and accepted usages of terms, once established. Of course, legal definitions and usages of terms can change, and often do as new cases or rulings modify, extend, or even replace old meanings with new definitions. But in this community, one is not free to simply advocate a persuasive definition of a term that already has an accepted legal meaning. Of course, one can do that, but that does not mean that the respondent will accept it or should even be bound to give it weight as a presumption overturning the existing presumption in law.

2. Cases of Public Redefinitions

The case studies in this investigation show how persuasive redefinitions of terms already defined in science, law, or everyday usage are very often, in a clever and subtle way, deployed to serve the interest of the definer. Persuasive definitions are commonly treated in logic textbooks. There have been studies of how they work as rhetorical tools used in argumentation, most notably by Stevenson (1944). However, in the literature, they tend to be treated as potentially confusing but fairly harmless logic-chopping devices used to boost up the plausibility of arguments in intellectual philosophical discussions. The case studies analyzed below show that persuasive definitions are far from the harmless verbal tricks they may appear to be. They are extremely powerful and significant argumentation tactics in legal and political argumentation with serious financial implications at all levels of government and at all levels of the justice system. Politics, in the view of Sederberg (1984) can even be seen as the attempt to control shared meaning. It can be seen as an arena in which "the contenders struggle to impose their respective meanings upon one another" or as a stable situation in which the powerful try to impose on others shared meanings underlying existing social arrangements (Sederberg 1984, p. 56). Definitions, on this view, are among the most powerful instruments of politics. Arguments about definitions are often taken to be trivial, but a brief investigation of some cases of political mass media argumentation will show that this impression is far from accurate.

In the following two cases, a U.S. president used a key term in the media, but then later, under the pressure of events, redefined it in a way suggesting a persuasive definition. Both cases are very interesting, in relation to the subject of investigating definitions, because they reveal the scope and importance of the subject. Far from being trivial, definitions, especially in legal and political cases, can involve vast sums of money, can affect the interests of powerful groups, and can be important in shaping public policies at the national level. Both cases are summarized from the much more detailed accounts given in the sources cited. Neither case should be taken as unusual. The interesting phenomena they illustrate would appear to be extremely common in political argumentation. A number of other cases in which definitions have had considerable impact in the domain of public argument can be found in a recent special issue of *Argumentation and Advocacy* on this subject (vol. 35, no. 4, 1999). For example, Titsworth (1999) has shown how the definition of "learning disability" has had an ideological basis in public discourse.

In the following case, President Ronald Reagan had proposed tax cuts to the federal domestic budget, but did not want to appear to be cutting programs in a way that would make his policies unpopular or offend particular groups. He proceeded with the strategy described below, summarized from the account in Zarefsky, Miller-Tutzauer, and Tutzauer (1984).

Case 8.2

> In a speech given in 1981, Reagan pledged to trim spending in federal domestic assistance programs while maintaining benefits for the "truly needy." Under pressure to clarify this key phrase, five days later the administration presented a specific list of programs that constituted the country's "social safety net" and would be exempt from cuts. The implication was that those who were "truly needy" would not have their "safety net" program cut (p. 115). Later in the year, however, Reagan cut social security and disability programs, but continued the pledge that the government would respond to the "truly needy," thus narrowing the list of "safety net" programs. By redefining "truly needy" and "safety net," he could propose making these reductions without breaking his earlier promise. These redefinitions proceeded gradually, and were not widely recognized by the public (p. 117). But they reassured those dependent on social services, because they could feel that as long as they were "truly needy," their programs would not be cut.

In this case, the use of the word "truly" in the phrase "truly needy" indicates the use of a persuasive definition. Even though it is admitted that the word "needy" is being redefined or altered, the word "truly" suggests that those who are really in need will not have programs cut. And anyone who depends on such a program will feel that they are definitely in the class of the truly needy. The use of the persuasive definition is reassuring to voters, while at the same time it leaves open a lot of latitude for making cuts without the danger of breaking a promise.

A definition can be used by someone as powerful as an American president to set the terms of a discussion taking place at the national and international levels of politics. Zarefsky (1986) used the case of President Johnson's "War on Poverty" to illustrate this point. According to Zarefsky

(p. 11), "The function of presidential definition is primarily to shape the context in which events or proposals are viewed by the public." Context can determine response, in Zarefsky's view, by containing presumptions. Once a presumption is set in place by a presidential definition, a burden of proof is put on any respondent who would argue in a way that appears to go against the presumption. Thus once President Johnson had defined his initiative to get the Economic Opportunity Act passed as part of what he called a War on Poverty, opponents found it difficult to make objections against a proposal described by such an appealing phrase. You have to remember that this phrase was appealing during the time before the Vietnam War became such a focus of dissent. Johnson's opponents tried to criticize the "anti-poverty" label as a rhetorical trick, but were unsuccessful. President Johnson even referred to some of these objections by remarking, "Why anyone should hate an antipoverty program, I don't know" (Zarefsky 1986, p. 35). This kind of example shows how a president can mobilize resources behind an initiative by defining the issue in a way that invokes a presumption in favor of one side. The presumption is set in place by the language that is used. It may not be explicit definitions of terms that sets the presumption in place so much as the way certain things are categorized using terms that have a positive or negative emotive spin. At that time, the expression "War on Poverty" had such a positive spin that it was almost irresistible. To question or criticize it, an opponent would immediately risk looking bad, and would be heavily on the defensive.

Both the safety net case and the War on Poverty case involve argumentation in which definition is covertly used. In the safety net case, a term was originally defined in a certain way, but then later, the criteria were changed so that the definition itself was covertly altered. In the War on Poverty case, Johnson used emotionally loaded language to invoke a presumption in favor of his own initiative that labeled opposition to his viewpoint as against "anti-poverty." He did not explicitly use a specific definition of the term "poverty" as the lynchpin of his rhetorical strategy, as far as I can tell. But he covertly used a tactic of persuasion relating to definition by conjoining the two terms "war" and "poverty" in a way that made it seem difficult to oppose his legislation. His proposal came under this positive-sounding category, and anyone who opposed it would appear to be arguing against the "anti-poverty" side of the issue. This tactic of using emotive terms to give a positive spin to an argument had been noticed early on by Jeremy Bentham. Bentham was familiar with parliamentary and legal debates, and identified what he called "laudatory" (emotively positive) and "vituperative" (emotively negative) terms used as rhetorical strategies in these disputes. He proposed a three-way classification of such terms used in argumentation (1969, p. 337). They are eulogistic (laudatory) if they evoke general approbation, dyslogistic (vituperative) if they evoke disapprobation, or neutral, if they fall into neither category. In the War on Poverty case, Johnson invented a eulogistic expression to define the viewpoint he wished to advocate. Because "poverty" is something negative, a "War on Poverty," he thought, would be something positive. The phrase seems to identify a cause that everyone would want to join. The use of this laudatory expression, similar to the terms "pro-choice" and "pro-life" in the abortion debate, set the discussion for the subsequent political and mass media argumentation on a tilted playing field. What it is vitally important to recognize in such cases is the persuasive role in mass media argumentation played by terminology. The argumentation can be explicitly founded on a persuasive definition. Or it can be based on emotive use of language grounded on a categorization covertly based on an unstated definition that invokes a continuing presumption in favor of one side in a dispute. Once the terms of the dispute are set in place, it becomes very hard for the opposing side to have a real voice. Until that side can raise critical questions and pry out the overt definition-based move, it remains in a very difficult position. That side always seems to be on the defensive. How can anyone deal with this tactic? What is needed is to expose the structure underlying the forms of argument used in such strategies, and also the dialogue structure that determines how such arguments should be critically questioned.

The next case is more complicated, because it involves the definition of a term that played an important role in political debate, but is basically a scientific term. The account below is summarized from the detailed description and analysis given by Schiappa (1996, pp. 213–220).

Case 8.3

> The term "wetlands" came to prominence in the environmental debates of the late 1960s and early 1970s. It refers to an area saturated by water to the extent that only specially adapted plants can grow in it. Wetlands are very valuable to the ecology, according to scientists. Environmentalists, concerned about the disappearance of wetlands, especially due to building, have lobbied to protect these areas from development. Large amounts of money are at stake, and developers have engaged in many widely publicized legal actions and debates on the issue with environmentalists. Starting in the

1970s efforts were made to introduce a standardized ecological definition of the term "wetlands." A 1979 definition cited features such as the kind of soil, the kind of vegetation, and the way water is present. In 1989 a definition of this kind was codified in a federal government manual for identifying wetlands.

In the presidential election campaign of 1988, George Bush committed his administration to a policy of "no net loss" of wetlands. By 1990, it became clear that if Bush kept to this commitment, he was in danger of alienating many of his pro-business, pro-development constituents. Accordingly, in August 1991, a document produced by a vice presidential task force proposed a redefinition of the term "wetlands" making the criteria stricter than those given in the 1989 manual. According to studies by scientists and environmentalists, under the new definition, 50 million acres previously designated "wetlands" would now be excluded. This so-called codification of the definition in the 1989 manual was implemented in federal agencies without approval by the White House or Congress and without inviting public comment, even though it met with intense opposition from environmentalists.

Schiappa commented that it is important to recognize that this dispute over defining "wetlands" needs to be seen as a matter of competing interests. The problem is that "wetlands" is a scientific term that should be defined by the scientific experts, using a so-called real definition. But when politics is involved, and hence also competing interests, it is easy to slip over into a persuasive definition that suits political needs, driven by powerful interest groups. The problem is that such redefinitions tend to merge scientific and political discourse in a way that misleads the public and allows a "technocratic elite" to be granted "definitional hegemony" to promote their own interests and causes under the guise of scientific neutrality. When you look at the details of the rhetoric in this case, as described by Schiappa, it is clear that the debate is not really about science, but is driven more by the competing interests of groups. Those involved in land development, building, real estate, logging, and so forth, are all on one side, and the environmentalists are all on the other side. The politicians are trying to steer their way rhetorically between these competing interests while retaining a majority of supporters, and redefinition of contested terms is an extremely useful tool for this purpose. In his book on definitions, Schiappa (2003) has given an even fuller account of how the term "wetlands" evolved in mass media argumentation.

The third case is one of a legal redefinition of a term that has not only legal implications, but all kinds of consequences for public policies and programs supported by government. Picking out any one case of this sort is arbitrary, because so many legal decisions, especially in the interpretation of statutes, are so heavily dependent on how key terms are defined or redefined. But this particular area has even attracted quite a bit of philosophical discussion in recent years.

Case 8.4

> Burgess-Jackson (1995) has argued for the claim that radical feminists' redefinition of the word "rape" is a persuasive definition. Burgess-Jackson cited several definitions of "rape" put forward by radical feminists (p. 428), including the one by law professor Catharine MacKinnon, which says that rape is "sex by compulsion, of which physical force is one form." A notable implication of this definition is that an act of sex in which no physical force is involved could come under the category of rape. Another definition cited by Burgess-Jackson, one put forward by the American College Health Association, includes "verbal coercion" as part of the definition of "rape." These definitions appear to depart from the lexical meaning of the word "rape." The Merriam-Webster's Collegiate Dictionary (1993, p. 968) defines "rape" as "sexual intercourse with a woman by a man without her consent, and chiefly by force or deception." The feminist redefinitions, by adding "verbal coercion," take the opening made by the qualifier "chiefly" in the lexical definition further, and extend it to cases that would not have been considered rape in the past. A case of this sort would be one in which, during amatory activities, the woman says "no," but the man persists, and although no physical coercion (or deception) was involved, the two end up having sex. Under the feminist redefinition, many cases of this sort that were formerly not considered to be rape would now be judged to be rape.

Burgess-Jackson argued that the feminist redefinition of "rape" cited above should be classified as an instance of persuasive definition. Does it meet the four requirements? It seems that it could. The word "rape" has strong emotive connotations. The descriptive meaning of the word is vague enough to be semantically manipulated. What about the change of meaning not being noticed by naïve listeners? It is possible that this requirement could be met. Although ignorance of the law is no excuse, in

fact many of us do not keep up with changes in the way words are interpreted in new legal rulings. And then there is the fourth requirement
that the emotive meaning remains unaltered. This requirement would
seem plausibly enough to be met in the case of the word "rape." In short,
there does seem to be the basis of a case for arguing that the feminist
redefinition of rape fits the category of a persuasive definition, according
to Stevenson's theory.

The legal history of the changing definitions of the term "rape" has
been chronicled by Schiappa (2003, ch. 4). The traditional legal definition of "rape" excluded the possibility that a man could rape his wife,
because it was based on the old notion of the woman as the property of
the man. According to this notion, when the man and woman entered
into the contract of marriage, the woman agreed to give the man the
exclusive rights to sexual intercourse with her. Given this agreement,
she couldn't then argue later that her husband had raped her. Feminists
were opposed to this notion of the woman as property because it failed
to see women as equal to men. Thus the current argument was that the
traditional definition of "rape" should be expanded. In the new definition it should be possible for a husband to rape his wife. It should also
be expanded to include the possibility of one man raping another man.
Thus the new definition of "rape" would also come to cover homosexual
activities. Advocates of the new definition argued that the notion of consent should be central to rape. So, for example, if a married woman does
not agree to have sex with her husband, and he forces her to have sexual
intercourse, then she should be allowed to charge him with rape. As Schiappa shows, the acceptance of the new definition in law has been slow
and dogged by controversy. At the time of writing, according to Schiappa
(2003, p. 68) seventeen states have abolished the marital rape exemption
by deleting words such as "not his wife." The exemption survives in some
form or other in the majority of states.

What can be observed in this case is that the redefinition of "rape" advocated by the feminists is more than just a matter of academic theorizing
or of abstract philosophical discussion. It has had legal implications that
affect everyone. The persuasive discussions of rape prompted by feminists
have gradually been followed by changes in the legal definitions of the
term. Of course, it is one thing to have critical discussion or to engage in
abstract philosophical theorizing. It is quite another to have a definition
accepted in law. The change in legal definitions comes about very slowly
within a massive institutional framework. Normally, in a critical discussion
or persuasion type of dialogue, as we have emphasized, the proponent

should be free to bring forward a definition and the respondent should be free to accept or reject it. Of course, putting forward a definition acts as a presumption. If the respondent doesn't accept the definition, then he should give some sort of reason or offer an alternative. But at any rate, the respondent should be free to ask appropriate critical questions. Once a definition becomes established in law, however, through statutes and legal rulings, it can be very hard to overturn it. Once it's there, it's there, and it may take a massive mobilization of effort, and a long time, to change it. The important thing to note here is the shift of context. It may be one thing to define a term like "rape" in a philosophical discussion. It is quite another thing to get it redefined once the definition has entered the legal area. The legal system takes over and an individual is no longer free to accept or reject a definition.

3. Wider Implications of These Cases

The study of persuasive definitions is not new to logic. Since Stevenson's analysis, it has now become common to have a section on definitions in logic textbooks that warns of the deceptiveness of persuasive definitions. But the wider implications of the use of persuasive definitions in political and legal settings have not been fully taken into account in these treatments of the subject. Definition is widely taken to be a relatively trivial business of "logic-chopping" that, while it can be tricky, can easily be sorted out by being careful with words. But quite to the contrary, the case studies above show that matters of verbal redefinition are far from trivial, and can be extremely difficult and costly to deal with. What they show is that not only can definitions and redefinitions be deceptive, but they can support particular interests. Once they are lodged into place in statutes, government manuals, and institutional regulations, they can be coercive in empowering some groups and disempowering other groups. The battle about words is part of, and is a tool used in, a larger battle about values, politics, and often money.

It should not be news to us that words as well as pictures are instruments of public relations techniques used in politics, war, propaganda, and advertising. But a realization of the extent to which persuasive definitions are woven into our legal system and our democratic system of government may come as something of a surprise. The reason for its unexpectedness is that popular opinion tends to take certain assumptions about definitions for granted, without reflecting on them too deeply. It is taken for granted that words, especially scientific terms and terms used in legal statutes and government regulations, have an objective meaning. On the other hand, it is often assumed that when there are verbal disputes about the definitions of words, such disputes are relatively trivial, and can easily be resolved by simply clarifying the meanings of the words. The case studies above clearly show that these assumptions are simply not true in some cases, and that the cases in which they are not true can be quite important. The case studies also suggest that deeply problematic cases may be a lot more common than we think.

One especially disturbing aspect of these cases is that they involve not only political and legal definitions, but also scientific definitions. Supposedly, it is up to the biologists to define "wetlands" and up to the economists to define "needy." Part of the problem is that such terms have been transferred from a scientific context to a legal or political context. The nature of the shift was most marked in the case of "wetlands." At first, this term was given a definition by scientists. But then, because of the cases brought to trial, the term took on a legal meaning. What happened was that scientists were brought into courts by both sides to testify as expert witnesses. As such trials became commonplace, a legal meaning of the term "wetlands" came to be defined. Then, as Schiappa's case illustrated so well, the term "wetlands" was redefined politically, and the new definition, now codified in an important government manual, had important consequences for the way land was officially designated by the government and for whether it could be developed for commercial purposes or not. This kind of shift is very significant, for there may be important differences between how a term should be defined scientifically and how it should be defined legally or politically. Scientific definitions are supposed to be objective and precise. They are not supposed to be subject to manipulation by competing interests, in the way that political definitions are. Legal definitions are often supposed to depend on scientific definitions. But still, in law the aim is not only discovery of the truth of a matter, but also fairness to the persons involved. For this reason, politics, and also law to some extent, are widely taken to be subjective in a way that science is supposed not to be.

But these matters are now widely subject to dispute. In recent years the claim has been made that objective scientific rationality is a sham and that scientific definitions are also influenced by the interests of scientists as a group. Thomas Kuhn is often cited as an exponent of this kind of view of scientific argumentation. Scientific hypotheses and definitions, according to this view, should always be seen as subject to change in the future. Kuhn (1970, p. 50) has shown that the term "molecule" is defined differently in physics than in chemistry; what counts as a molecule differs according to the current needs of the two fields of physics and chemistry. According to this postmodernist view, not only can a non-scientific definition of a term be different from a scientific definition, but the scientific definition serves the interests of scientists in just the same way that a non-scientific definition commonly serves the special interests of groups who advocate its usage.

While there is something in this postmodernist view, I believe it goes a bit too far. Surely, a scientific definition should be seen as different from a legal definition, and both should be seen as different from a political definition. A scientific definition, for example, is different from a legal definition because it has a different purpose, and because the standards for evaluating it are, and should be, quite different. A scientific definition should be judged by scientific standards appropriate for the scientific discipline it is part of. A legal definition should be accepted, rejected, or criticized on legal grounds. When a scientific definition is introduced as evidence in court, by an expert witness, for example, it is either accepted in that science or it is not. The participants in the trial, for example, the judge or the lawyers, can't redefine the term as it is used in that science. They can argue about what the legal implications of it should be, or they can bring opposing scientific experts to testify that previous testimony about the accepted scientific definition was not accurate.

Schiappa (1993, pp. 408–412) has shown how the definition of "death" raises an interesting kind of controversy. The term "death," as applied to a person, is a medical and scientific term that has legal implications. In recent times, new medical life-support technology has made possible a kind of situation in which a person whose brain function has been irreversibly destroyed can still be maintained so that his or her breathing and blood circulation functions are maintained. Is such a person alive, or can he or she be declared dead, for organ removal purposes? This question is one of considerable public significance. So it has led to active ethical discussions about how the word "death" should be defined. As Schiappa showed, many of the arguments put forward by philosophers, physicians, and other commentators supported what the participants in the debate apparently took to be real definitions with some sort of scientific or at least objective validity. Ethical disputes have been very common and, as Schiappa shows, have shared a certain characteristic pattern of argumentation. An onlooker to the debate, or someone who reads about it later, may see the participants as offering competing persuasive definitions. But the participants themselves put forward their definitions as though their claims were objective assertions of what is true, and represent accounts of the facts that can be verified. As Schiappa shows, the philosophical argumentation supports a particular definition by proceeding through two stages. First, fixed criteria that are portrayed as "essential" or objectively true are set up. Then it is argued that the recommended definition meets these criteria, while opposing definitions fail to meet them. Study of this sort of case seems to suggest that such controversies, not only about legal and philosophical definitions, but even about medical and scientific ones, are best viewed as comprised of argumentation putting forward persuasive definitions. It seems to be a distortion or misconception to view the definitions as true and verifiable propositions about factual or objective properties.

One of the most fascinating aspects of Schiappa's case study of ethical discussions on the definition of "death" stems from a leading characteristic that helps us to recognize a persuasive definition cited above. In persuasive definitions the term being defined is often prefixed by use of the words "true" or "real." So although it seems almost paradoxical to say this, the philosophical notion of "real definition" may in fact itself be seen as a kind of persuasive definition. Schiappa observed that when participants put forward their own definitions of "death" in the ethical debate on the redefinition of death, they tended to portray their own proposed redefinition as being the "real" definition. Is this move in argument itself a kind of attempt to use the technique of persuasive definition? The idea is an odd one, and has a postmodernist ring to it.

The postmodernist views are that definitions can change, that they are more persuasive than tradition indicates, and that they are bound to disciplines and other groups that have interests at stake. All these views seem to be justified, up to a point, by case studies of how the argumentation actually works when terms of public significance are redefined. But what seems to follow, that the term in question can freely be redefined by a different interest group simply to meet the rhetorical needs of the moment, seems wrong. The view that definitions can rightly be used for different purposes in different contexts seems right. But the implication that a scientific definition is therefore not only subject to redefinition in the same way as a political definition is, by pressure of competing interest groups and majorities, does not seem to be right. What is needed is a new approach to definitions, along the dialectical lines proposed by Perelman and Olbrechts-Tyteca (1969), an approach that accepts the contextual variability of definitions without being stuck with some of the more paradoxical and anti-dialectical consequences of radical postmodernistic views.

4. Definitions in the New Dialectic

There are two old ideas about definitions that can get us into a lot of trouble when relying on definitions in argumentation. One is the idea that words have a precisely determined objective meaning. This view, called essentialism, holds that each word has a fixed meaning or "essence," and the object of any verbal discussion is to find the essence of the term in question. The other idea is that the meanings of words are relatively trivial and unimportant. A corollary of this second view is the assumption that definitions can be stipulated arbitrarily by one party in a discussion. The second view stems from the empiricism that is dominant in Western culture. This common version of empiricism accepts the inference that because collection of data (the facts) is all that really matters, therefore questions of definition are really trivial. These two ideas are not necessarily consistent with each other, but they are preconceptions that are commonly held in an unreflective way, as popular beliefs. As Perelman and Olbrechts-Tyteca (1969, p. 211) showed, philosophical analyses of definitions have tended to be fairly consistent with these commonly held beliefs. Philosophical analyses have tended to operate within a dichotomy between so-called real definitions and nominal definitions. A real definition is supposed to be an objective account of the way things are. A real definition (supposedly) describes the true essence of the thing being defined. A nominal definition is supposed to be merely conventional or arbitrary. According to Perelman's analysis, definitions are human agreements about how words should be used. Thus according to Perelman's analysis, the dichotomy between real and nominal definitions is a false and misleading abstraction. For Perelman, a definition should always be regarded and evaluated as an argument. Definition should not be categorized as either purely arbitrary or as purely descriptive accounts of fixed meanings.

The approach to definitions taken in the new dialectic is directly at odds with these popular views. In the new dialectic, argumentation is always evaluated as used for some purpose in a conversation. Definitions are viewed in the same contextual way. To understand a definition, you have to understand the purpose that it was put forward by one party to fulfill, in relation to some other party in a conversational exchange. This dialectical view of definitions is opposed to essentialism. According to essentialism, the definition is based on a fixed meaning that does not vary with the context of conversation in which a word is used. According to the new dialectical view, a definition should be evaluated in light of the purpose it was put forward to fulfill, and this purpose changes, depending on what type of conversation the definition was supposed to be part of. Also, in the new dialectic, definitions are not trivial, because putting forward a definition of a key term or phrase can relate directly to the purpose of a conversation. For example, in a persuasion dialogue, the purpose of the one party is to persuade the other party to come to accept some proposition that he did not accept before. In such a context of use, a persuasive definition could be quite appropriate. But in much of traditional logic, persuasive definitions are regarded as highly suspect, if not altogether illegitimate.

The difference between essentialism and the new dialectic can be seen with reference to lexical definitions, the kind found in dictionaries. According to essentialism, a word has an objective meaning, or "essence," and the dictionary tries to provide that meaning by giving the genus and differentia. According to the new dialectical view, the purpose of a lexical definition is to explain the meaning (or usage) of the term to someone who already knows the meanings of other terms closely related to it. These other terms are likely to be more familiar and common. So I may not know the meaning of "hauberk," for example, an uncommon term. But I am likely to know the meaning of terms like "coat" and "chain mail" that are used to explain what a hauberk is. In the new dialectical view, the purpose of putting forward a lexical definition of a term, as in a dictionary entry, for example, is to explain the meaning (or usage) of the term to someone who does not understand it. The purpose of a lexical definition is to explain the meaning of a term that is unfamiliar by expressing it in terms that readers are likely to be familiar with.

The distinction between argument and explanation is very important in the new dialectic. An argument is made up of propositions called premises and conclusions, where the conclusion is unsettled or subject to doubt. The purpose of putting forward the argument is to fulfill the so-called probative function, meaning that the premises can be used to remove the doubt attached to the conclusion and thereby settle the argument. On this view, it is always characteristic of an argument that the conclusion is being doubted or is unsettled with respect to being true or false. In contrast, in the case of an explanation, the presumption is that the proposition to be explained (the so-called *explanandum*) is true and is not unsettled or doubted. For example, if you ask me to explain why the radiators are normally under the outside windows in a room, there is a presumption that we both accept that radiators are normally under the outside windows in a room. In contrast, suppose we are having an argument about whether Columbus discovered America. It is implied that one of us doubts, or has expressed doubts, that Columbus discovered America. The purpose of having an argument is to try to resolve these doubts, one way or the other. On the new dialectical view, the distinction between an argument and an explanation derives from the purpose of the conversation. Because we sometimes confuse this distinction, the understanding of how to distinguish between an explanation and an argument is very important in the new dialectic.

One of the main confusions about definitions is that we tend to presume that there must be just one reason for putting forward a definition, and that therefore all definitions need to be evaluated in the same way. But in many cases, the purpose of putting forward a definition is not to offer an explanation but to offer or support an argument. For example, if you and I are arguing about the abortion issue, and you define abortion as "the murder of unborn babies," it should be clear that you are putting forward an argument. The proposition that an aborted fetus is a person or "baby" would almost certainly be strenuously denied by the other (the pro-choice) party to the dispute. And because "murder" is one of the worst of crimes, by defining abortion as murder, the proponent of the definition has already put in place premises that can be easily used to prove that abortion is wrong. In this case, the offering of the definition can be analyzed as an argument, and should be seen as an argument. Putting forward a definition that really has the function of an argument is extremely common in everyday discourse, because words often have an argumentative spin or can be defined in such a way that such a spin is placed on them. Once we have been made aware of these phenomena, we begin to see how common they are.

In some cases, the definition of a term, once it has been repeated enough to have an impact on the way controversy is expressed, can have a powerful rhetorical effect on public policies and views. Zarefsky (1998) has presented several case studies of current ethical and political controversies in which the power of an advocate group to persuade the public to come to accept its view of the matter, and to act on it, has clearly depended on definition. One case, summarized below, concerns the abortion debate.

Case 8.5

> At one point, both the courts and public opinion reached "some-
> thing resembling a conclusion." The case of *Roe v. Wade* had legal-
> ized abortion in a way that established a kind of balance in favor
> of the pro-choice side. But then some years later, the pro-life side
> took the controversy in a different direction by redefining what
> was formerly called "intact dilation and extraction" as "partial-birth
> abortion." The effect of this redefinition was to direct the focus of
> public attention to a "gruesome procedure" that invoked a power-
> ful image to the public of the "baby" being torn to pieces. (Zarefsky
> 1998, pp. 3–4)

The rhetorical effect of this redefinition redirected the dialogue from an
abstract level to an emphasis on concrete details of a kind that proved to
be powerfully persuasive to the public audience. Careful analysis of case
studies of public controversies of the kind found in Zarefsky (1998) can
awaken one from a dogmatic slumber about the power of definition.

It has been quite clear in the abortion debate that the issue turns
very much, from a point of view of argumentation, on how the fetus is
classified and defined. Legally, the fetus in the womb is not a person. It
does not have the rights of a person until it is born. Pro-choice advocates
avoid the use of "person" terminology when describing the fetus. Pro-life
advocates insist on framing the debate in such a way that the unborn
fetus is classified as a "person." They often describe it as a "baby." And as
indicated above, they use argumentation that tries to get public opinion
to assume that the fetus should be viewed in person-like terms as a baby,
with human qualities and a human appearance. Thus the debate, as indicated above, often turns on the implicit but key prior issue of how the
fetus is to be defined or classified. The debate about terminology is, of
course, not purely ethical or even purely political. It has all kinds of legal
implications and dimensions. At bottom, the debate, in practical terms,
often seems to turn on whether abortions will be paid for by government
agencies.

On February 1, 2002, CBS News announced that the Bush administration "will make embryos and developing fetuses eligible for health
care under the State Children's Health Insurance Program, saying they
qualify from the moment of conception" ("White House: It's Not about
Abortion" 2002). This move is based on the implicit assumption that the
unborn fetus can be or should be classified as a child. Thus as a definition

or classificatory move it has highly significant implications for argumentation in the abortion debate. It would also have legal implications, for by beginning to treat the fetus under the classification of "child," it could be used later to bring public pressure influencing subsequent legal rulings. However, Bush administration officials denied these implications, as quoted in the CBS News report (p. 1).

But the White House maintained that the decision had nothing to do with abortion or establishing the rights of a fetus. The administration heralded the plan as a way to provide prenatal coverage to the 10.9 million women of child-bearing age who don't have insurance. . . . "All we're doing is providing care for poor mothers so their children are going to be born healthy," Health and Human Services Secretary Tommy Thompson said. "How anybody can now turn this into a pro-choice or pro-life argument, I can't understand it."

This denial is part of a clever strategy of not only making an argumentative move, but at the same time of putting a positive terminological spin on it. The wording "providing care for poor mothers" makes the decision sound good. How could anyone be against providing aid for poor mothers? But that is putting a spin on a spin. It is not too hard with even a little reflective critical analysis of the argumentation to see what the implications are of this move of definition and classification with respect to the abortion debate. Participants on both sides were quick to see it. Advocates on both sides quickly labeled the decision a "victory for the anti-abortion movement." Thus it is not hard to see how, at every turn in the abortion debate, argumentation turns pivotally on how the fetus is to be defined and classified.

A typical reaction to realization of the rhetorical power of definitions has been to swing to the opposite extreme of essentialism, called postmodernism. According to postmodernism the meanings of all existing words and phrases have emotive connotations built into them that are up for grabs by those in a position to manipulate them for political purposes. Thus the way commonly used terms are defined serves special interests of certain groups through both persuasion and coercion. For example, meanings of some commonly used words and phrases may serve the interests of traditional groups that have been in power in the past. Arguing from these premises, the postmodernist concludes that redefining terms to wrest political power from older groups by persuasion or even coercion is justifiable. The postmodernist does not see persuasive definitions as logically unacceptable or fallacious. She sees them as inevitable, and so they might as well be turned to your own advantage.

The new dialectic takes a view of definitions that is somewhere in between the more extreme essentialist and the postmodernist views of them. The new dialectical view recognizes the emotive and political spin that already exists in many commonly used terms, and appreciates how this spin can be redirected by the use of persuasive redefinitions. The new dialectical view recognizes the argumentative function of many definitions, unlike the essentialist view, which sees meaning as fixed and objective. But the new dialectical view does not draw the postmodernist conclusion that all definitions, even highly loaded, persuasive, or coercive ones used to promote special interests, are equally justifiable. According to the new dialectical view, a definition can be evaluated, and some properly judged to be better than others, depending on the purpose the definition is supposed to fulfill. When definitions are argumentative, as they often are, then according to the new dialectic they should be judged as arguments, in the way that other arguments are evaluated dialectically.

A problem for the new dialectic is how to define persuasive definitions (the self-reference in the problem notwithstanding). Are all definitions persuasive? Or are lexical definitions different from persuasive definitions? According to the postmodernist view, all lexical definitions have an argumentative spin or bias to favor special interests or viewpoints. A central problem then is how to define the expression "persuasive definition" itself so that some new dialectical classification system of the various kinds of definition can be given. So far, this problem is unsolved.

5. Proof of Legitimacy of Persuasive Definitions

Logic textbooks have often warned about the potential for deception in persuasive definitions, but they tend to stop somewhere short of condemning them as fallacious or illegitimate. Copi and Cohen (1998, p. 133) write that because "emotional coloration may be slyly injected into the language of a definition that purports to be accurate and appears to be objective," we must "be on our guard against persuasive definitions." This advice steers a middle way between outright condemnation and acceptance of persuasive definition. It is implied that persuasive definitions could be reasonable in some cases, but we are warned that they can also be dangerously deceptive. The basic problem is to find some basis for sorting out these two categories of cases. The prior theoretical problem behind the basic problem is to find some systematic theory for grasping what persuasive definitions are all about. What is their supposed purpose as a type of definition? And what are the conditions under which this purpose can be fulfilled in a given case, so that it can be judged that the use of the persuasive definition in that case was reasonable? These questions are, so far, unanswered. But it is only once the first question has been answered that we can even begin to investigate the second. Only when the first question is answered can it be understood why persuasive definitions are wrong or logically defective or deceptive. The analysis of the speech act of persuasion presented above in chapter 2 offers an answer to the first question. Let us reflect on this answer, letting its implications sink in. Then in the next section the investigation required to begin to answer the second question can be launched.

The speech act of persuasion shows what the goal is in a persuasion dialogue, and shows what should be the proper means for achieving that goal. Before the advent of the speech act of persuasion, the notion of a persuasive definition seemed hard to grasp as a coherent or legitimate notion in argumentation. Persuasion tended to be linked to the "mob orator," and even now it is often thought to belong to the realm of "spin doctors" and public relations experts. Persuasion, after all, had historically been associated with rhetoric and the Sophists. From a logical point of view, it seemed like a suspicious notion that could be at odds with truth or even dangerous. But once the speech act of persuasion has been defined, and its place in persuasion dialogue clarified, it begins to seem like persuasive definitions could be legitimate, under the right conditions. Of course, they can also be deceptive and tricky, as Stevenson rightly pointed out. But once the speech act of persuasion has been defined, we are now in a better position to understand the sorts of conditions under which persuasive definitions are misleading, and how they can be used as argumentation strategies to exploit the conventional meaning of a word. Thus the theory of definitions as a branch of argumentation stands to benefit greatly from a classification of the speech act of persuasion that shows it as a clear notion that has a central place in argumentation theory.

What the speech act of persuasion shows is that persuasive definitions can be legitimate where the context of a discussion is properly that of persuasion. For example, in a philosophical discussion, such as a Socratic dialogue, a persuasive definition of a key term like "virtue" might be put forward. The other party in the discussion might question the definition, and perhaps even attack it by making objections against it. This use of a persuasive definition could be perfectly legitimate, as long as the respondent in the discussion has the right to raise questions, and the proponent is open to revising or even giving up the proposed definition, in response to these critical questions. In such a case, the persuasive definition can be part of a sequence (chaining) of argumentation on one side. The proponent uses the definition as part of his attempt to prove his thesis in the dialogue. As part of such a chain of argumentation, the persuasive definition could be considered legitimate, on the grounds that it meets the proper requirement for the speech act of persuasion as set out in the last chapter.

But the problem is that there are different kinds of definitions, with different purposes. The purpose of a persuasive definition is to persuade rationally, in the sense laid out in the conditions for the speech act of persuasion. But the purpose of a lexical definition is to explain the meaning of a word that already has a conventional meaning accepted by native speakers of a language. Of course, the persuasive definition, too, although it may purport to be stipulative, may be of a term that already has an established usage. Thus a potential for confusion exists. If the respondent to the persuasive definition continues on with the same conventional meaning of the word, with its positive or negative connotations, there may arise an ambivalence or confusion of the kind explained by Stevenson's theory of emotive language. For example, the positive connotations that the word already has in the language may be carried over, casting a misleading aura of approval over the newly defined concept. And yet the newly defined concept may be taken by the proponent's argumentation to be something quite different from the traditional lexical meaning of the term in common speech.

The problem can be compounded by several other factors. Suppose the proponent is a member of an interest group, and the group has something to gain through getting wider acceptance for their view. Suppose also that this interest group is advocating a cause, and they place a higher value on advocacy for the cause than they do on really throwing light on the issue being discussed. In other words, suppose the advocacy group, although they make a show of engaging in a critical discussion of the issue, is never really willing to concede in the discussion. In other words, the group is not really open to critical questioning of its viewpoint, even though their advocates may insist that they are. Let's suppose that the past history of the dialogue shows that they continue to advocate their chosen viewpoint in a single-minded way, even when presented with good evidence that raises critical questions about their arguments defending that viewpoint. It is at this point, in a given case, that there is evidence of a dialectical shift. The evidence of the dialogue could indicate that the advocacy group is really engaging in interest-based negotiation, as contrasted with persuasion dialogue. In this type of case, there would be evidence that the advocacy group was biased. Bias, or advocacy, is not in itself a bad thing. But it can be deceptive. The purpose of a persuasive definition should be to persuade rationally. If its purpose is to promote the interest of a group by advocating a cause, as opposed to merely discussing the issue in a free and open way characteristic of persuasion dialogue, then the definition should be questioned. The problem with this kind of definition is that it makes what is supposedly a persuasive definition too much like a stipulative definition. The thing about a stipulative definition is that it is not open to objections or to critical questioning at all. Once it is stipulated, it is laid down axiomatically, so to speak, and no evidence counts against it. Mathematical definitions in axiom systems can be of this type. The definition is laid down stipulatively as a beginning point. You can question whether a theorem follows from the axiom. But it not appropriate to question the axiom itself.

Theoretically, then, persuasive definitions can be reasonable when put forward under the right conditions. If the context of a case is supposed to be that of a persuasion dialogue or critical discussion, a proponent is supposed to be an advocate for his viewpoint, putting forward arguments that meet the requirements for the speech act of persuasion. He is allowed to put definitions forward as well. Indeed, we can say that a proponent is obliged to put forward arguments meant to be rationally persuasive to the respondent, in order to fulfill requirements of burden of proof in a persuasion dialogue. At some points in such a dialogue, he will also be obliged to define his terms. The putting forward of persuasive definitions is thus reasonable in a persuasion dialogue. And we can go even further than merely saying that persuasive definitions are allowed or that they are legitimate. Under the right conditions, they can be moves that are required in order to contribute to the proper progress of the dialogue.

6. Argumentation Schemes Relating to Definitions

Having established that it is legitimate in principle to put forward a persuasive definition in a persuasion dialogue, it is now necessary to approach the formal problem of how such a definition should be put forward. What form should it take as a legitimate move in a dialogue? The literature on this subject is scarce. It is a question that appears to have been rarely asked.

To get at least the beginnings of an answer, it is necessary to go back to the Ph.D. thesis of Arthur Hastings at Northwestern University (1963). Hastings set out forms for a number of common types of arguments. He explained the form of each argument using a Toulmin model, which identified its premises and the conclusion. One premise, called a "warrant," is expressed in the form of a defeasible generalization that is subject to exceptions. Typically, the warrant combines with a more factual or specific type of premise to generate the conclusion. Although such forms of argument can be deductively valid in some instances, generally they are not. They are defeasible forms of argument that are best evaluated by asking critical questions. Matching each argumentation scheme, Hastings set out a list of appropriate critical questions. Thus the argument, when put forward in an actual case, has a certain standing. Or, as we might say, it temporarily occupies a ground. But then, if an appropriate critical question is asked, the standing of the argument is temporarily held in abeyance until the critical question has been satisfactorily answered.

Of all the various argumentation schemes, the one most applicable to arguments that are based on a proposed definition is called "argument from definition." Argument from definition is used when it is maintained that some object *a* has property *F* because *a* falls under category *C*, and every object falling under category C, by definition, has property *F*. For example, consider the following argument.

The Kangaroo Argument

> Bob (this animal I am pointing to) is a marsupial. How do I know that? Because Bob is a kangaroo, and all kangaroos are marsupials. How do I know that? Because a kangaroo is defined as a herbivorous, leaping marsupial mammal.

There are two aspects of this type of argument requiring comment right away. First, it seems like a deductively valid argument, because one premise is the universal claim that all kangaroos are marsupials. Also, it is an argument that might be further supported by appealing to a source, like a dictionary. If asked to support or justify the definition of "kangaroo," the arguer might cite a dictionary entry, for example. This example is a very simple one, perhaps making the form of argument seem almost trivial. Other examples will reveal that the argument can be far from trivial in some instances.

The following example is from a speech of Abraham Lincoln, quoted by Hastings (1963, p. 48).

The Contract Argument

> If the United States not be a government proper, but an association
> of States in the nature of a contract merely, can it, as a contract be
> peaceably unmade, by less than all the parties who made it? One
> party to a contract may violate it – break it, so to speak, but does it
> not require all to lawfully rescind it?

This argument is quite a powerful one. It gives a reason why it should not
be lawful for the southern states unilaterally to secede from the union.
The backing for the argument comes from a definition. It is argued that
by the definition of the term "contract," a contract can be peacefully
rescinded only by all the parties who made it. Therefore, if one party
to the contract tries to undo it without the agreement of the others,
that party "violates" the contract. He "breaks" it, as opposed to lawfully
rescinding it. One can easily see from this example how common this
form of argument from definition must be, in both legal and political
argumentation. Weaver (1953) has cited many instances where Lincoln
used this form of argumentation in his speeches.

In addition to argument from definition, there is another argumentation scheme that is important to know about when examining arguments
based on definitions. The importance of this type of argument is more
subtle, because it is a type of argumentation that is based on a definition
that has not been stated or made explicit as part of the argument it occurs
in. This type of argumentation can easily be illustrated using the case of
the abortion dispute as represented in case 8.5 above. Suppose that one
side in such a dispute argues, "Abortion is wrong because it is murder of
the fetus." In this case, it is unclear whether the arguer has defined or
is defining "abortion" as "murder of the fetus." That is possible. But it is
also possible that he is merely classifying the act of abortion under the
category of murder of the fetus. The pro-choice respondent, of course,
when confronted with this sort of argument, would react to it vigorously.
She might reply, for example, that to classify abortion as "murder" of
the fetus implies that the fetus is a person. She might argue that this
assumption is unwarranted. She might even argue that it begs the question. She would certainly (and should) react to it strongly, for in this case,
the issue is extremely controversial. However, in many cases, argument
from classification is not this visible. It often passes unnoticed in an argument, perhaps because it tends to be assumed that definitions and verbal classifications are trivial and unimportant. But argument from verbal

classification is extremely important, most clearly in legal argumentation, but also in mass media argumentation.

Argument from verbal classification is so common in everyday argumentation that the typical arguer is not aware that his argument is relying on it. It is typically implicit in a line of argument. It is for this reason that the burden of proof attached to argument from verbal classification tends to be invisible. It can slip into the argument without an audience being aware of it. And yet it can have a powerful persuasive impact, even determining the direction a chaining of argumentation in a discussion will take. Hastings gave the first structured analysis of this form of argument as an argumentation scheme with a matching set of critical questions. He called the form of argument "argument from criteria to a verbal classification" (p. 36). To explain this form of argument, it is best to begin with an example. A good example would be the following simple argument: "Ten percent is an excellent rate of return on a fixed-term investment, so this bond is a good investment" (this example is based on Hastings 1963, pp. 36–37). The form of argument can be made more explicit by identifying its premises and conclusion as follows.

> **Classificatory Premise**: Ten percent may be classified as an excellent rate of return on a fixed-term investment.
> **Major Premise**: Any fixed-term investment that has an excellent rate of return is a good investment.
> **Minor Premise**: This bond (a fixed-term investment) has a 10 percent rate of return.
> **Conclusion**: This bond is a good investment.

The reason that argument from a verbal classification can so often be deceptive, as noted above, is that the classificatory premise is unstated, and hence no visible burden of proof is attached to it by the respondent. Thus arguments based on verbal classification, although highly significant in many cases, tend to merge unobtrusively into a line of argumentation, without being challenged or even noticed.

As noted above, Hastings analyzed argument from a verbal classification using the device of a Toulmin warrant diagram. A more abstract formalization of the argumentation scheme has been presented in Walton (1996, p. 54). The argumentation scheme presented below is a modified version of this earlier abstract formalization. Below, the argumentation scheme for argument from verbal classification (Walton 2006, p. 129) is presented, showing the premises and conclusion of this type of argument, and labeling each premise by giving a name indicating its function in the argument. In this argumentation scheme, individuals and properties are represented as constants, while the variable x ranges over individuals $a, b, c, \ldots, n$. A set of critical questions matching the argumentation scheme is presented below it. The critical questions represent appropriate questions that can be used in a dialog to probe into weak points of any argument that fits the argument scheme for argument from verbal classification that can be questioned or criticized. Thus the set of critical questions matching a scheme provides a device that can assist in the evaluation of an argument fitting the scheme by suggesting to a critic some of the most important kinds of questions that should be asked when responding to this type of argument in a dialogue. The two devices of the argumentation scheme and the matching set of critical questions work together to provide a dialog structure that can be used both to analyze and to evaluate argumentation used in a text of discourse in a given case, provided the argument fits a scheme.

Argument from Verbal Classification

INDIVIDUAL PREMISE: a has property F.
CLASSIFICATION PREMISE: For all x, if x has property F, then x can be classified as having property G.
CONCLUSION: a has property G.

Critical questions

CQ$_1$: What evidence is there that a definitely has property F, as opposed to evidence indicating room for doubt on whether it should be so classified?

CQ$_2$: Is the verbal classification in the classification premise based merely on an assumption about word usage that is subject to doubt?

The persuasive definition in Stevenson's culture example is used as an argument to refute a prior implicit argument that works by classifying some particular thing into a verbal category. The counter-argument based on the persuasive definition is put forward as a refutation of a prior argument based on the existing conventional meaning of a word in natural language discourse. The counter-argument postulates a new invented meaning that goes against the existing conventional meaning. We can now see that both arguments have a particular structure, based on the argumentation scheme for argument from verbal classification. This analysis is quite revealing, as far as it goes, but Stevenson's example is highly complex, because of the implicit argumentation existing under the surface of the explicit text of discourse. Much more remains to be discussed in attempting to analyze it. The first point remaining to be discussed is that each of the counter-poised arguments from verbal classification is based on a definition. This type of argumentation is quite common, especially in legal reasoning where an argument is defended by supporting it by means of classifying a particular term, like "contract" or "wetlands," and then backing up the classification by definition that is accepted in law, generally in a statute or in a previous court ruling. If the verbal classification is in question, it can be supported by invoking a definition that has, on some grounds or other, been previously accepted. As shown in Stevenson's culture example, one common ground for acceptance is that of conventional meaning. Another common ground could be a redefinition of the term, perhaps for example based on a scientific meaning that has been accepted in a domain of knowledge or a legal meaning that has been accepted by a court that has jurisdiction over the case being tried. Thus we can see from considering such examples how argument from verbal classification can be backed up by citing a definition that has some grounds for acceptance supporting it. Such considerations lead us to consider a new argumentation scheme called argument from definition to verbal classification.

Argument from Definition to Verbal Classification

DEFINITION PREMISE:	*a* fits definition *D*.
CLASSIFICATION PREMISE:	For all *x*, if *a* fits definition *D*, then *x* can be classified as having property *G*.
CONCLUSION:	*a* has property *G*.

Critical questions

CQ$_1$: What evidence is there that *D* is an adequate definition, in light of other possible alternative definitions that might exclude *a*'s having *G*?

CQ$_2$: Is the verbal classification in the classification premise based merely on a stipulative or biased definition that is subject to doubt?

According to this argumentation scheme, the reason offered for classifying a particular entity as having a particular property is that the entity fits a definition. Thus the classification premise is a kind of conditional or generalization that links a classification to a definition. The definition premise makes the claim that some particular thing fits under the definition that is cited in the classification premise. In a given case the structure represents a linked type of argument in which the definition premise and the classification premise function together to support the conclusion that the particular entity cited has the property in question. So far so good, but if we are to better understand how the argumentation works in a typical case, like Stephenson's culture example, we have to probe more deeply into how the argument from persuasive definition is related to emotive language as well as to definitions. Let's tackle this problem next.

The problem now confronted is to try to figure out how argument from definition to verbal classification supports the argumentation in a kind of case, like the one cited in Stevenson's culture example, by linking a persuasive definition to values. In Stevenson's example we have two counter-poised definitions, each of which supports an argument from verbal classification. One is grounded on a conventional definition in existing usage, while the other, the counter-argument meant to refute the first one, is grounded on a new definition. The new definition is supported by reasons that appeal to positive or negative values. The argumentation scheme representing the structure of this part of the argument is that for argument from values. In the standard example (Bench-Capon 2003a, 2003b) diabetic Hal needs insulin to survive, but cannot get any in time to save his life except by taking some from Carla's house without her permission. The argument from positive value for preserving life is weighed against the argument from negative value of taking someone's property without his or her permission. Now the problem is to see how all three schemes – argument from definition, argument from values, and argument from verbal classification – are related in cases where a persuasive definition has been used.

Let's go back to considering the scheme for argument from verbal classification. In Hastings's analysis of this type of argument, he made it clear that normally the argument is based on some sort of definition that may or may not be stated. But typically, the definition is not stated. Hastings (pp. 42–45) cited seven critical questions that should be considered when evaluating any instance of argument from a verbal classification.

1. What is the implicit definition being used?
2. Is the definition acceptable, or are the criteria acceptable?

3. Are there exceptions or qualifications to the definition and criteria?
4. Are other criteria necessary for an adequate definition?
5. Do the characteristics described meet the criteria?
6. Are there enough characteristics described to justify inclusion in this category?
7. Could the object fit better into another category?

The device of listing critical questions is also used in Walton (1996, p. 54), but only two critical questions are given.

1. Does *a* definitely have *F*, or is there room for doubt?
2. Can the verbal classification be said to hold strongly, or is it one of those weak classifications that is subject to doubt?

It would seem that Hastings's list is a bit too long, while my list is a bit too short. As a compromise, I would suggest the following list attaching to the argumentation scheme for argument from a verbal classification above.

1. What definition backs up the classification of *a* under category *C*?
2. Is the definition acceptable?
3. Should alternative definitions be considered?

This list of critical questions emphasizes the importance of some sort of definition, whether implicit or explicit, as backing the argument from a verbal classification. You could say that one main function of the set of critical questions is to bring the need for a definition to the surface, in order to back up the argument.

Both argument from verbal classification and argument from definition are, in principle, reasonable forms of argumentation in all the types of dialogue. It follows that they are reasonable forms of argumentation in persuasion dialogue. On the other hand, they can be illegitimate or go wrong in various ways if they are used inappropriately or in such a fashion as to impede a persuasion dialogue, perhaps by deceiving the respondent. This much can be established, as a matter of theory. But what happens when we apply this theory to actual tricky and controversial cases, of the kind introduced above? A number of more specific questions are raised. These are specific questions about how these two types of argumentation are used in different types of dialogue. As shown below, problems, deceptions, and fallacies tend to arise when there has been a problematic or tricky dialectical shift from one type of dialogue to another.

7. The Speech Act of Defining

Argument from a definition involves appealing to a definition as one premise of an argument. Argument from verbal classification is a more subtle and more common strategy in argumentation. The use of laudatory or vituperative terms in argumentation sets the language of a dispute by using emotive spin to favor one's own side. Of course, this strategy depends on a verbal classification that, once the argument has been analyzed, can be shown to rest on a prior covert definition. When argument from a verbal classification is properly challenged by a respondent by raising critical questions, the dialogue should then shift to a verbal dispute about competing definitions. In such a dispute, opposed definitions may even be put forward by the opposed sides, and then the argumentation will ascend to a different level, that of a so-called verbal dispute. But in many cases, that doesn't happen. As illustrated by Zarefsky's example of the War on Poverty, the opponents may not recognize how the dispute has been covertly framed to tilt the playing field against them even before the game begins. Thus they go on and on fighting an uphill battle. At least in the short term, the definer tends to win. This tactic must surely be well known to public relations experts in mass media today, and routinely exploited as a fundamental part of any attempt to influence public opinion. But how does it really work? What are the mechanics of argumentation underlying its structure? These questions have not been systematically investigated in argumentation theory, apart from the growing body of case studies that bring out their importance.

Observing how common this sort of phenomenon is in mass media argumentation, the basic questions remain. What is the structural platform of this argument strategy? When laudatory or vituperative categorization is deployed as a tactic of mass media argumentation, how is it based on a form of argument? When a definition is put forward, to defend an argument from verbal classification or for any other reason, what form docs it have as an argument? How are these argument forms used as platforms to drive a chain of argumentation forward, enabling an opponent to be hemmed in or even silenced? The answers to these questions can be given only by recognizing the underlying forms of argument represented by the argumentation schemes for argument from definition and argument from verbal classification. But there is an underlying question as well. It is even harder to answer, and the best we can do here is to advocate a new direction for research. To take this direction, the act of putting forward a definition in a dialogue needs to be seen as having a rhetorical function, but having an underlying dialectical function as well. Putting forward a definition is not an argument, in itself, although it certainly can be part of a chain of argumentation. Putting forward a definition needs to be seen as a special kind of speech act in its own right.

When I say, "I define term T as meaning X," where X is a so-called *definiens*, or string of words offered as a definition, what sort of action am I undertaking? The answer is that I am making a proposal to the respondent. I am proposing that both of us, in future moves in the dialogue, should always plug in X as the meaning of T whenever T occurs in any argumentation in the dialogue. The speech act here is less like an argument than a recommendation. It is a recommendation that the respondent should be free to accept or reject. The speech act of putting forward a definition can be compared with the speech act of persuasion. It is similar because it also has implications for the rest of the dialogue. In other words, there is a kind of chaining forward involved. Once the proponent has put forward a definition, and the respondent has accepted it, then both parties are bound to accept that definition for the rest of the dialogue. This clause of the speech act of definition has implications with respect to the cases studied above. For suppose the proponent puts forward a certain definition for a key term but then later uses the term in a different way. This chain of argumentation displays a kind of inconsistency. The respondent should have a right to challenge or criticize the inconsistency. The problem, as noted in the cases above, is that the change may slip by unnoticed. It may even be covered up by the proponent. Here then is a key problem with persuasive definitions, and with all kinds of definitions used in argumentation. The problem is the shifting to a different meaning from one proposed in an earlier definition.

Another basis for comparison is also interesting to pursue. In the speech act of persuasion, the respondent must be free to challenge the persuasion attempt by asking critical questions or by bringing forward counter-arguments. But what about the kind of case where a definition is offered? Should the respondent be free to reject the proposed definition or even to offer a contrary one in its place? Normally, the answer in a persuasion dialogue should be affirmative. This capability is one of the freedoms both parties should have in a persuasion dialogue. It should even be possible for the proponent to offer a persuasive definition that supports her viewpoint while the respondent offers a contrary persuasive definition (of the same term) that supports his viewpoint. This situation in a persuasion dialogue should not be seen as inconsistent or contradictory in a way that makes it wrong or requiring resolution by getting rid of the inconsistency right away, even banning it altogether. Such conflict is all part of the normal conflict of opinions in a persuasion dialogue. But in actual cases of argumentation, reality may not be so simple or so free. What may happen is that the proponent may insist on both parties accepting the definition.

Cases in point routinely occur in legal and scientific argumentation. Once a term has an accepted legal meaning, you can propose a new definition that goes against the old one. But the reply may be that well, that's just the way the term is legally defined in law. You're not a judge, and you don't have the power to change the law. So although you may advocate a new definition of some term with a legally accepted meaning, you can't change the accepted meaning of the term. Similarly, in the case of a term having an accepted scientific meaning in a certain discipline, you may try to argue against this definition or propose a different one. But if you are not an expert in this field, what you say will have little effect. Even if you are an expert, if the majority in the field accept the given scientific definition, your proposing a new definition will not be an acceptable move in argumentation. It's more or less the same with public opinion. If a certain term is conventionally defined in a certain way, and this way of defining it is widely accepted and approved in the public opinion, your public audience is not going to be persuaded by your moving to a different definition of the term. The reality is that in many mixed cases, there isn't the same freedom that is there with respect to definitions that are characteristic of a pure persuasion dialogue. Mass media argumentation being what it is, the freedom to put forward a persuasive definition is not always there. And perhaps even more significantly, the freedom to question or reject an existing definition is not always there. The problem is that in many cases of mass media argumentation, the dialogue is not simply that of a persuasion dialogue. Persuasion is centrally involved, but there are often other types of dialogue mixed in, making the analysis of the definition in the case more complex.

8. Evaluating Persuasive Definitions

According to the analysis of the speech act presented in chapter 2, persuasion dialogue is a legitimate type of framework of argumentation, and there is nothing inherently fallacious or deceptive about persuasion in itself. The speech act of persuasion that sets the goal for argumentation in a persuasion dialogue aims at a kind of rational persuasion, provided the appropriate rules for persuasion dialogue are followed. But the cases noted above pose more specific questions. Is legal argumentation a kind of persuasion dialogue? Is political argumentation, for example, in an election campaign in a democratic system, a kind of persuasion dialogue? Is scientific argumentation best seen, as Kuhn seems to suggest, as a kind of persuasion dialogue, or perhaps even as a kind of interest-based negotiation dialogue? Some of these questions are addressed in Walton (1998b), but some are still under investigation. Until they are answered, the study of persuasive definitions will remain an open subject. But some provisional remarks can be made on evaluating the use of persuasive definitions in the cases cited above. The new dialectical approach suggests a new perspective on how to judge the use of persuasive definitions in these four cases and in other comparable cases.

Let's go back to Stevenson's original case of the dialogue on culture (case 8.1 above), and try to reconstruct the chain of argumentation in it. We begin by identifying all the propositions in the argument in the following key list of them.

Key List for the Culture Example

He has had but little formal education.

His sentences are often roughly cast, his historical and literary references rather obvious.

His thinking is wanting in that subtlety and sophistication which mark a trained intellect. He is definitely lacking in culture.

The characteristics I mention are the antithesis of culture, contrary to the very meaning of the term.

He is not a man of culture.

I should call him a man of culture notwithstanding.

In the true and full sense of the term, "culture" means imaginative sensitivity and originality.

These qualities he has.

He is a man of far deeper culture than many of us who have had superior advantages in education.

Using this key list, we can now construct an Araucaria argument diagram representing the chain of argumentation in Stevenson's culture example. There has been an implicit conclusion, "He is not a man of culture," inserted into the argument. Even though this implicit assumption was not present explicitly in the argumentation in Stevenson's dialogue, it appears on the diagram in Plate 3 in the darkened box with the dashed borderline. The arguments supporting this proposition are shown on the right side of the diagram under the proposition, "He is not a man of culture." Shown to the left of this text box is another one, also in a darkened box, "I should call him a man of culture notwithstanding." This proposition is opposed to the proposition "He is not a man of culture" and is diagrammed as a refutation, indicated by the double arrow joining it to the proposition it is put forward to refute. Underneath the refutation, on the left, is the sequence of argumentation supporting it. Thus the diagram falls into two parts. On the right is shown a linked argument pattern supporting the proposition that he is definitely lacking in culture, which in turn supports the ultimate conclusion that he is not a man of culture. On the left the refutation of this argumentation is leading to the conclusion that he is a man of far deeper culture than many of us who have had superior advantages in education. This conclusion is then used as a premise to support the conclusion, "I should call him a man of culture notwithstanding." To some extent, then, the argument does display both the original argument and the counter-argument in Stephenson's dialogue and culture, bringing out the opposition between the pro and contra argumentation, and showing its dialogue structure.

Notice that in the argument diagram in the figure, both the argument on the right hand and the counter-argument on the left have a shaded area surrounding them, indicating which propositions are joined together in the argument structure, and marked on the shaded area is an expression indicating the type of argument. Both arguments are labeled by the expression "argument from verbal classification." This label represents the argumentation scheme for the argument from verbal classification. This form of argument concludes that some particular object has a property in virtue of its falling under a verbal classification of some particular type. Thus the argument diagram in Plate 3 is instructive in that it shows, for the first time, how Stephenson's key example used to illustrate how persuasive definitions work can be modeled as a sequence of argumentation with specific premises and conclusions joined together in an argument structure.

The argument diagram in Plate 3 only begins to probe into the structure of the culture dialogue, however. We still have to see how argument from definition to a verbal classification, as well as argument from values, are involved. The first point to be made is that we can easily see how argument from definition to a verbal classification is involved. It is used to support the premise shown in the lowest left text box of Plate 3. It is used to redefine the term "culture" originally used in the part of the argument shown on the right side of the figure. The problem is that this argument is based on argument from values in a curious way. To see better how it works, we turn back to case 8.1a.

In case 8.1, **B** is trying to persuade **A** to have a better opinion of Rodney. She is trying to persuade **A** to give up the "superficial" view that Rodney is uncultured and move to the more favorable view that, in the "true" sense of the word, he can be seen as a cultured person. In this case, the persuasive definition seems pretty harmless. It is fairly obvious what **B** is up to. And **A** can always disagree, if he wishes, by arguing that he takes a different view of culture, and would define the term in a different way than **A** has. The remaining three cases are different. In the Reagan case, the redefinition of the term "safety net" took place gradually in a way that made it appear that Reagan was keeping his pledge to retain benefits for the "truly needy." Zarefsky et al. (1984, p. 114) describe this rhetorical tactic as a species of what is called "dissociation" in Perelman and Olbrechts-Tyteca (1969). In dissociation, a seemingly unitary term is split in two by pairing it with opposed terms, one favorable and one unfavorable. Then the speaker's position is linked to the favorable term and opposed to the unfavorable term. But is dissociation a rhetorical tactic that is fallacious, or somehow represents an unfair or deceptive kind of argumentation that ought to be condemned as illegitimate? Zarefsky et al. seem to stop short of this claim. They see the use of this tactic by the Reagan administration as involving ambiguity and subtle shifts in definition (p. 119). But surely in the persuasion dialogues characteristic of political rhetoric, a good deal of ambiguity and subtle shifts in definitions should be expected and accepted as reasonably normal for this kind of argumentation. The opposition can offer critiques of what they perceive as deceptions or logical shortcomings in such tactical redefinitions, but redefining the terms of a debate is not a logical defect or error in every case.

What needs to be seen in this kind of case is that both sides have a right to put forward an argument from verbal classification that puts its own viewpoint in a favorable light. Why? The answer, as shown above, is that argument from verbal classification is an inherently reasonable form of argumentation. You have every right to put it forward. And, as also shown above, the speech act of persuasion represents a legitimate move to make in a persuasion dialogue. Hence in a persuasion dialogue, you even have a right to put forward a persuasive definition, using the form of argument called argument from definition. It should be accepted that there is nothing wrong, in principle, with making this sort of move in a dialogue. But the problem is, typically, that the buck does not stop there. Both forms of argumentation should be seen, following Hastings's schemata representing their structures, as open to critical questioning. As noted in the cases above, too often the proponent of the argument adopts specious tactics designed to prevent the asking of critical questions by the respondent in a dialogue. For example, in the abortion dispute, the side who has defined abortion as the murder of the fetus might simply deflect critical questioning by arguing that scientifically and medically, the fetus has to be classified as a human being or patient. She might argue that these classifications cannot be questioned by a layperson who is not a scientist or physician. For the argument would then be merely "anecdotal" and worthless as scientific evidence. The problem here partly arises from a dialectical shift. The original dispute was supposed to be a persuasion dialogue, but somehow the imputation crept in that only arguments appropriate for a scientific or medical investigation or clinical study have any further worth in the discussion. The tactic is meant to shut the respondent up and prevent him from taking any further meaningful part in the dialogue.

In the wetlands case, there are more problems, because the initial perception, which seems to be right, is that "wetlands" is a scientific term that ought to be defined by the scientific experts. But then, in case 8.3, there was a dialectical shift, when the term was redefined (evidently) for political purposes. Schiappa (1996, p. 227) sees the problem as a "dream of escaping politics altogether" by letting the scientific experts define terms for us. He sees this "dream" as one that "potentially ends in disaster"(p. 227). But from a new dialectical perspective, the shift from a scientific context to that of a political debate on policies is not necessarily a bad thing. For in many cases (Walton 1998b), such a shift can be constructive. For example, a shift from an information-seeking dialogue to a persuasion dialogue could improve the quality of the persuasion dialogue by making it better informed on the issue. On the other hand, the redefinition in case 8.3 can be criticized as deceptive, on the grounds that the tightening up of the criteria for "wetlands" was introduced in such a way that what was really going on was not widely realized by the public.

Case 8.4, about the term "rape," seems different from the previous three cases. It was a legal redefinition proposed by an advocacy group, and the issue was given much publicity at the time. It is harder to see in this case how deception was involved, if it was. But case 8.4 is similar to cases 8.2 and 8.3, because, unlike case 8.1, the redefinition was a matter of public policy that served identifiable interests. If it is hard to argue that the redefinition was logically illicit in cases 8.2 and 8.3, however, it is even harder in case 8.4. According to Burgess-Jackson, the redefinition in case 8.4 is not an "objectionable" form of persuasive definition, because the word "rape" is vague and ambiguous to begin with, and because it represents a feminist point of view that is legitimate as a "theory" of rape (p. 433). Based on his analysis of this case, Burgess-Jackson has argued for the general thesis that putting forward a persuasive definition should not be regarded as an inherently objectionable or disreputable move in argumentation. What needs to be noted in this case is that the intellectual discussions about the term "rape" by feminists and others could be seen as persuasion dialogue. If so, the redefinition of the term "rape" advocated by some at that stage could be seen as a persuasive definition. By the same token, the old definition opposed by the feminists could also be seen as a persuasive definition. Once the speech act of persuasion has been clearly defined, and we can see how persuasion can be rational in argumentation, there is surely no real objection to seeing argumentation about the redefinition of even something as controversial as rape in this light.

Surely, the postmodernists are right to make the following argument. Because virtually all terms used in everyday discourse already contain emotive connotations that reflect existing values and traditions, arguing for a new ethical view that redefines such a term should be seen as, in principle, a reasonable kind of move to make in ethical argumentation. Because this argument does seem to be reasonable, it signals caution in condemning all use of persuasive definitions.

The objection to persuasive redefinitions, when they should properly be regarded as objectionable, seems to center more on the potential for confusion and deception. And as Stevenson's analysis brought out, that potential is certainly there. But an even more worrisome aspect of persuasive definitions was brought out quite clearly by cases 8.2, 8.3, and 8.4. Once they are lodged into place, in law, government regulations, or public policies, the capability for critically questioning them undergoes a shift. Now the legal experts take over. As a layperson, you as an individual can't realistically decide any more whether you will accept this definition or not. Legally, you are bound to accept it. Of course, you can still argue against it or question it as a private citizen, as long as we have freedom to engage in philosophical discussions on public issues. Of course, the legal definition is supposed to somehow be based on some underlying community acceptance and on moral thinking that reflects what is acceptable or not in light of the changing times. But it is important to note that once we enter the legal area, there is a sharp shift in the rules for putting forward definitions and for dealing with argumentation based on definitions and accepted meaning of terms.

9. What Should the Rules for Persuasive Definitions Be?

Persuasive definitions have not been studied very much. We have not really advanced far beyond the point reached by Stevenson's investigation of them, and there are many unanswered questions. Presumably, persuasive definitions are closely related to stipulative definitions, and possibly they should be treated as a species of them, as Robinson (1950) proposed. Rules for stipulative definitions, as opposed to other kinds of definitions, tend to be more permissive. In a dialogue, a participant should generally be free to offer a stipulative definition at any point, and there are few restrictions on stipulative definition that apply to other definitions. For example, a stipulative definition can ignore previous lexical usage. This same freedom seems to attach to persuasive definitions. But the degree of freedom certainly should vary contextually. For example, if one party offers a persuasive definition in a persuasion dialogue, then it is up to that party to defend it and to stick to it, while it is up to the other party to accept it or not. The other party should be free to propose an opposed persuasive definition and to argue against the persuasive definition put forward by the first party. The rules might be quite different in a scientific or legal context, however. In law, statutes and rulings of various kinds lay down definitions of significant legal terms. While such definitions can sometimes be disputed, they have a certain standing. Thus an attorney arguing a case in court is far from free to start basing her arguments on stipulated or persuasive definitions that she herself has invented. Similarly, in a scientific discipline, certain definitions, like those of "mass" and "force" in physics, are accepted generally in the field. They have a firm standing. Such definitions can be challenged, but not by just pulling a new persuasive definition out of a hat. The rules for putting forward, challenging, and accepting definitions clearly vary with the type of conversational exchange an argument is supposed to be part of. So there are no easy or pat solutions to the problems of when definitions should be judged proper and when not.

In an interesting study of collegiate debating, Shepard (1973) showed that stipulative definitions are freely allowed in these debates and that this possibility offers debaters a creative freedom to exploit persuasive definitions and other stipulated definitions that are fanciful in departing from lexical usage. The problem is that the audience will simply not accept a proposed definition that is too fanciful, and because the debater's argument is based on the definition, the audience will simply not find the argument persuasive. The problem is that proposing a stipulative definition may be proper or acceptable as a move in a debate, but it may be self-defeating as a strategic move. What is suggested is that the following two questions should be distinguished. When is using a stipulative definition proper or acceptable as a move in a dialogue? When is using a stipulative definition a good strategy to help you achieve your goal in a dialogue?

In all four cases above, the move to redefine a key term by introducing a persuasive definition would seem to be a proper or acceptable move in the argumentation in the case. Arguments supporting this way of evaluating the cases were presented above. But the question of whether these redefinition attempts were good strategy is another matter, not yet discussed. In case 8.1, the redefinition of "culture" might have been a good argument strategy for **B**. For all we are told about the details of the case, it seemed that **B**'s argument was a good strategy in helping her to persuade **A** that Rodney was a good guy. In cases 8.2 and 8.3, the strategy seemed like a good one, because by the time the public became aware of what was going on, the budget had been cut and the wetlands had been developed. The deception was successful. But what happened when the public realized that they had been duped by a persuasive redefinition? It is much harder to say about long-term effects. Possibly, it could be just this kind of deception that makes the public cynical about politics. On the other hand, because a considerable segment of the public presumably supported the side of the developers, the effect was more diluted. In case 8.4, one long-term possible effect may be the trivialization of the crime of rape. The public thinks of rape as a horrible and intolerable assault that demands a very strong penalty. The emotive connotation of the word "rape" in previous usage is that of a horrific, repellant kind of crime. But suppose that lesser offenses describable as "verbal coercion" are widely publicized as rape convictions. The strong emotive connotations in public opinion attached to the word "rape" may become diluted. As long as the public is unaware of the redefinition and its implications, the strategy of women's rights advocates could be successful, if the law is changed to a wider definition of "rape." But once the public gains a wider awareness of what is going on, the redefinition could have other effects that go against that strategy.

In all these cases, the problem with the persuasive redefinition resides in the awareness of the audience, the other party in the dialogue, or the general public, in making the adjustment between the new meaning and the emotive connotations of the old meaning. The problem is the potential for confusion, dissociation, and ambiguity created by the failure of matching between these two things. The persuasive redefiner can get a temporary advantage from this ambiguity, making it a powerful rhetorical device of persuasion. The long-term effects may not be so good, however. Thus the strategic trade-off may be between a temporary gain and potential long-term problems. Zarefsky (1986) in his study of President Johnson's War on Poverty observed that Johnson's persuasive definition strategy was extremely successful in the short term. It enabled him to get his Economic Opportunity Act passed. But in the long term, it made failure inevitable by setting up the goal of winning a war that could never be won. As Zarefsky analyzed the case, the reason for the defeat was not economic but rhetorical. The temporary gain that can be achieved makes the use of persuasive definitions very attractive as a rhetorical tactic, especially where the redefinition can be lodged long enough into legal, governmental, or some form of public acceptance long enough to have the effects its advocates want. On balance, what is called for is recognition of the use of persuasive definition as an argumentation tactic that is, in principle, legitimate. In the right context of dialogue, at the right point in the development of a line of argumentation, the putting forward of a persuasive definition can be a reasonable move. But the potential for deception is there, as soon as the redefinition of the old term departs from the existing usage of the audience or respondent of the argument. So from a logical point of view, we should be wary of persuasive definitions, and treat them with caution. Definitions, especially those affecting public policies, are often a lot more complex from a viewpoint of argumentation than they seem. They need to be thoroughly discussed by both sides. Freedom of speech is vitally important, for if the respondent is prohibited from asking critical questions, long-term consequences can be problematic; once a definition hardens into legal rulings, it cannot be easily changed.

From a logical point of view, the most important thing about handling cases like those considered above is that a persuasive definition should be treated as an argument. It should be regarded as open to critical questioning and to the posing of counter-definitions. It should be regarded as having a burden of proof attached. It should be recognized that the audience or respondent of the redefinition should have the right to argue for retaining the existing usage, if it seems to them to better represent their views on the matter. When a proponent puts forward a persuasive definition, she should be held to it, unless she changes to a redefinition, and she should also have that option. But at the same time she should be open to criticism if she argues in such a way that presumes or exploits the previously existing usage in a way that could be deceptive, inconsistent, and confusing. The dialectical problem posed by such cases is one of retraction of commitment to definitions to which one was previously committed in argumentation, either by posing explicit definitions or by presuming the existing usage of a term. It is not possible to make up any one set of rules to govern all such cases, because, according to the new dialectic, the rules will vary depending on the type of dialogue in which the parties are supposedly engaged.

10. Conclusions

Very little if any advance has been made on studying persuasive definitions since Stevenson first began the systematic study of them as tools of persuasion. Precise determination of when their use is legitimate or illegitimate in the kinds of significant cases studied below is too much to hope for at this point in the development of the subject. In this concluding section, it is good to begin by recapitulating what we don't know about definitions in mass media argumentation, at this point in the study of the subject. First, it needs to be emphasized, in agreement with Schiappa (2003), that essentialism has historically been a bad influence on the study of definitions and that this ancient doctrine does not stand up to critical scrutiny. Schiappa's extensive case studies in his new book show that definitions are always political. By analyzing the structure of argumentation schemes and types of dialogue, this chapter has shown that definitions are always inherently persuasive in nature, in ways that have not been fully recognized. On the other hand, I continue to think that there is some place for something like the notion of an essential attribute in a definition. When defining a term by genus and difference (a good method in at least some instances), one needs to differentiate between the more important or central attributes and those that are less important or central to the meaning of the term. Some notion of essentiality is useful, I think. But maybe instead of talking about "essential" attributes, we should talk about "important" attributes. Even if essentialism is a bad old doctrine that is no longer useful or plausible, there may still be a role for some doctrine that is like essentialism but much less absolutistic and Platonic. What this role is remains to be determined. The study of definitions in argumentation has scarcely begun.

There are also a lot of unanswered questions about the changing role of philosophy as a discipline. In the older Platonic view, the philosopher investigated the truth, and thus he opposed the Sophists who merely engaged in persuasion. But is this a realistic view of critical discussion in philosophy, or is it only a stance that philosophers like to adopt as a presumption that they somehow have a privileged access to the truth? What Perelman and Olbrechts-Tyteca (1969) would add is that a philosopher who claims to know the truth and who claims that only sophists engage in persuasion is using the tactic called dissociation. This tactic divides any question into a yes-no choice, implying that the opposed viewpoint is the negative side. One can see that dissociation represents part of the strategy of persuasive definition on Stevenson's analysis. But one can also see that dissociation is a natural part of advocacy in discourse, resembling philosophical argumentation. When a philosopher argues for a certain view, naturally he is expected to accept that view as the "right" one, and the opposed view as the "wrong" one. Of course, he is also supposed to be open-minded and to look at the evidence on both sides. And he is also expected to speak or write with some conviction. In line with these reasonable expectations, you would expect him to use dissociation. Of course, it is a bad thing if a philosopher goes too far, and sees only his own view or definition as "real," refusing to consider the opposed views at all because they are "illusory" or whatever. But you expect the philosopher to take the position that his own view is right or represents reality better than any opposed view. Otherwise, the rational thing for him to do is to change his mind, and embrace one of the opposed views, once it has been supported by enough evidence to warrant acceptance.

Posing your own definition of a key term in a philosophical discussion as "real" or "essential" might be quite normal, expected, and even reasonable (to a degree). This practice might not be quite so bad as it may initially appear. Much of the issue turns on what one takes a philosophical discussion to be. Is it an objective investigation into the truth (what is called an inquiry in chapter 1)? Or is it a discussion with two opposed theses where each side tries to persuade the other using reasoned argumentation? The first view is positivistic, and might have been quite acceptable to Stevenson and the philosophers of his era. But it does not seem very plausible in this era, when many are now using the term "postphilosophy." If the second view is the right one, then you would expect the participants to use persuasive definitions. You would even expect them to contend that the persuasive definitions they advocated to be "right" represent the real essence of the thing being defined. The question that is raised turns on one's view of what philosophical discussion is or should be. This is the area often called metaphilosophy. I like to think of philosophy as a kind of persuasion dialogue, and according to this view, you expect the proponent of a view to argue strongly for his view and adopt the stance that it is the "right" view of the matter being discussed. Of course, you should also expect the philosophical discussant to be open to conceding that his view was not the right one, if rational arguments presented evidence to justify that conclusion. The worst problem with essentialism is that it appears closed to possible refutation, dismissing all opposed views as "unreal." None of these questions can be answered at the present time, but this chapter offers a new basis for discussing them.

What can be said about positive conclusions that can be drawn from the new approach to persuasive definitions? The case studies above cast light on how persuasive definitions work rhetorically and how they ought to be evaluated from a logical point of view. The new dialectical approach required to cope with these rhetorical phenomena needs to overcome the old, but still widely accepted viewpoint of essentialism, and the newer and recently more influential viewpoint of postmodernism. According to the new dialectical view, a definition should always be evaluated in light of the purpose it was supposedly put forward to fulfill in a context of conversation. It has also been shown why definitions should often be presumed to be argumentative in nature, even though in some cases the purpose of putting forward a definition is supposedly that of explanation rather than argumentation. The hypothesis suggested by our analysis of these cases is that putting forward a persuasive definition should be treated as a speech act, but also as a particular kind of persuasion attempt.

What has been revealed more than anything is the incredible rhetorical power of the persuasive definition in media argumentation. The study of definitions has languished in logic, because it has not really advanced beyond its ancient Aristotelian framework. In particular, logic has not known how to handle persuasive definitions. On the other hand, recent studies of persuasion have shown that the power to define is the power to frame a whole debate and to dictate the direction the argumentation in it will take. But without a dialectical structure of types of dialogue and argumentation schemes, rhetoric by itself is powerless to study systematically how arguments based on definitions are persuasive. It takes a dialectical analysis to really see what is going on, by identifying the types of argument used, the argumentation strategies, and how these arguments and strategies are used to influence mass media persuasion. Zarefsky (1986) linked the three subjects of rhetoric, persuasion, and definitions together in a way that brings out how all three are vital to mass media argumentation. He defined rhetoric as "the study of the process of public persuasion" (p. 5). He added that rhetoric "encompasses a concern for the terms in which issues are defined, since a definition will highlight some aspects of an issue while diminishing others, and the choice of what is highlighted will make the issue more or less persuasive." Thus the new approach to the study of definitions in argumentation needs to get beyond the essentialism of logic and to stop thinking of a definition as a merely lexical entry in a dictionary. Argumentation is heavily based on definition and verbal classification, and that includes persuasive definitions most emphatically. Persuasive definitions must come to be seen as inherently legitimate, and even normal, in a context of persuasion dialogue. On the other hand, the use of persuasive definitions is such a powerful technique partly because we understand so little about how it works, and partly because persuasion dialogue is so mixed in with other types of dialogue. We still understand very little about special contexts of argumentation, like scientific and legal argumentation, where different communities of arguers are involved. This chapter has shown that how the important notion of persuasive definition works in media argumentation needs to be much more firmly based on dialectical tools, especially the argumentation schemes and argument diagramming methods that show how the schemes apply over extended chains of argumentation. But at the same time they also need to be grounded in the application of these tools to real cases of media argumentation.

9

The Structure of Media Argumentation

The cases studied in the previous chapters have suggested how dialectical and rhetorical methods need to be combined to reveal tactical argument moves and strategies underlying media argumentation. But the respondent-to-dialogue problem posed in chapter 4 remains unsolved. In this chapter, a solution to the problem is presented, using some technology from AI. We begin by reviewing the RTD problem and other unsolved problems brought out in the preceding chapters. These problems continue to be exacerbated by the troubled relationship between rhetoric and dialectic, and one problem is how to integrate the methods of each approach with the other. There is an inevitable tension between them, but paradoxically, one is not much good without the other when it comes to grasping how mass media argumentation works and getting better insights into both the strengths and weaknesses of this important type of argumentation. Solutions to these problems are proposed by putting forward several hypotheses that form a theory of how a proponent attempts to persuade an audience using argumentation across media.

The main elements of the theory are the following propositions. Both the audience and the arguer need to be seen as agents that share common knowledge that enables them to communicate. But some cases are more dialectically complex. In these cases, three agents are involved. Two basic types of media argumentation are distinguished. In direct media argumentation, only the proponent and the audience have the roles of agents. In indirect media argumentation, there is a proponent who argues with a respondent in order to influence a third-party audience.

Five stages in the rhetorical/dialectical structure of media argumentation are distinguished. The invention stage is especially important, both for bringing out the role of strategy and for clarifying the difference between rhetoric and dialectic. I show how strategy, in the invention stage especially, needs to be based on a capability for what was called simulative reasoning in chapter 4, section 5. Simulative reasoning allows one agent to grasp how another thinks. The capability for combining practical reasoning and simulative reasoning is shown to rest on a multi-agent structure of communication based on a technology called plan recognition. By using these hypotheses as parts of a new theory, this chapter offers a new way of articulating and clarifying the mutually supportive roles of rhetorical and dialectical methods of argumentation. A new way of integrating rhetoric and dialectic is proposed. At the end there is a summary of the methods developed through the whole book, presenting a list of the fifteen basic components of media argumentation.

1. Rhetoric and Dialectic Reconfigured

A central problem brought out in the previous chapters is the fundamental difficulty of somehow reconciling the tension between rhetoric and dialectic in a coherent and theoretically well-organized model of argumentation. Dialectic is an objective structure, based on argumentation schemes and types of dialogue, for critically identifying, analyzing, and evaluating argumentation and fallacies. Its critics would say, among other things, that it is a purely abstract subject, a branch of logic that cannot tell an arguer how to persuade any actual audience or how to use arguments that are effective for persuasion. Persuasion has often been portrayed in the past as either a literary style of presentation or a psychological subject that requires empirical methods to measure the impact of a message on an audience, for example, by using polls or other scientific techniques. This dichotomy leaves no room for seeing rhetorical argumentation as based on dialectical strategies of argumentation used in persuasion, deliberation, and other frameworks of communication. Why does it seem so hard to get to get over this dilemma? It is hard to say. It may be because popular opinion, and also the widely accepted opinion of the scientific experts, just accepts a positivistic view of academic research in which all that matters is "the facts" – for example, a collection of empirical data by scientific methods, such as polling. The whole thrust of this book has been to try to crack that monolithic and pervasive *endoxon* by moving forward in a direction that goes between the horns of the dilemma posed by public perceptions.

What has emerged from the cases of rhetorical argumentation studied in the previous chapters is a new approach. This approach freely concedes the importance of empirical research and the collection of data. But it counsels against a blind acceptance of these methods as applied to mass media argumentation and points up the need for using dialectical methods to identify the biases and fallacies inherent in these methods. Especially, it identifies and analyzes the abuses of these methods as rhetorical strategies that commit fallacies and use dubious arguments for mass persuasion to make corporate profits, to manipulate public opinion for purposes of cause advocacy, and even to use argumentation as propaganda. Many in the fields of rhetoric and mass media influence will think that this dialectical approach is too negative because it stresses fallacies and criticisms. It even seems to make rhetoric and mass influence in communication look deceptive and guilty of a Sophistic kind of fraud, which this field has for so long been accused of perpetrating. Is there some way the new dialectic can be fitted in with the positive aims of rhetoric in a middle way that overcomes the existing dilemma and the negative aspects associated for so long with the Sophists as tricksters and con artists? The answer is yes, that there is a very good way.

The approach taken in the previous chapters has shown time and time again how dialectic and rhetoric can work together and, when so integrated, can benefit greatly from each other. Rhetoric can take actual cases of mass media argumentation, like those studied by David Zarefsky and Edward Schiappa, and show how they are based on persuasive definitions and other forms of argumentation. Dialectic can study these cases as well, identifying the argumentation schemes and common structures, like appeals to fear and pity, used in them. These cases show that audiences are successfully persuaded by arguments they think are reasonable. For example, fear appeal arguments, even though they are emotive in nature, were shown in chapter 4 to have a structure that takes the form of practical reasoning. In other words, the audience is persuaded by the argument because it is essentially reasonable, based on premises that accurately represent their commitments and goals, their hopes and fears, and their normal means-end ways of thinking about practical affairs of life. The audience is persuaded because it thinks the argument is a good one. It appeals to them because it has premises that represent their commitments, and it gets them to draw inferences to the recommended conclusion by forms of argument or argumentation schemes that properly represent rational thinking. In other words, there is a cognitive element involved. The audience is not misleadingly regarded as just a raw mass of positive or negative emotions like fear and greed that can be manipulated like Skinner's rats. Persuasion does in part work in that way. But the more significant part is how the proponent's strategy of persuasion, appealing to both positive and negative emotions, can be channeled into specific responses, persuading an audience to come to a conclusion about how to act or what to accept as an opinion. This process of channeling, and how argumentation strategies can be based on it in successful mass media persuasion, is the cognitive part revealed by the new dialectic. It is the structure underlying the argumentation schemes and types of dialogue used.

But in the previous chapters there has been a central problem that leaves a gap between dialectical theory and the reality of mass media argumentation. The RTD problem was posed by the apparent mismatch between dialectical models of argumentation and what happens in most cases of mass media influence attempts. In dialectic, the proponent and the respondent take turns making moves (speech acts) that form a dialogue by connecting up into an orderly sequence of argumentation. This continuity is lacking in typical cases of mass media argumentation. The proponent sends out a message directed to a mass audience. But he doesn't normally then engage in dialogue with the mass audience. The communication seems to be a one-shot event. As shown in chapter 1, Leff (2000, p. 247) also noted this very difference, but considered it a characteristic of difference between rhetoric and dialectic. Dialectic proceeds by question and answer, whereas rhetoric proceeds through a longer sequence of continuous discourse. Participants in dialectic take turns, whereas in rhetoric discourse is continuous. In dialectic, the proponent makes a move, and then the respondent replies with a following move. But in traditional rhetoric, the speaker makes a presentation to an audience, and the audience passively takes it in. In mass media presentations and in written rhetoric, the audience doesn't reply as part of the interaction. When a politician makes a televised speech in an election campaign, there may be various reactions. The crowd may shout "Hurrah!" Commentators may be interviewed after the speech. Reports and editorials on the speech may appear the next day in the media. But these reactions are not normally part of the rhetorical presentation of the speaker's argumentation. The speaker has delivered his persuasive appeal with a mass audience in mind, using what he takes to be their beliefs or opinions into account. But they do not actually intervene or raise questions during the phase when the speech is being written or prepared.

2. The Respondent-to-Dialogue Problem Revisited

Many instances of rhetorical argumentation, as shown by the RTD problem first formulated in chapter 4, section 4, do not appear to fit the dialogue model. The reason is that in the paradigm case of a dialogue, there is an exchange of questions and replies (so-called speech acts) between two participants. In some cases of mass media arguments, for example, in televised political debates, this turn-taking exchange of verbal moves between the two parties actually exists. But there are many cases of mass media arguments where the role of the respondent is diffuse or even appears to be absent. Consider a speech given at a national convention or by a president. There may be no reply by a commentator. Because the speech was televised, presumably it had an impact on an audience. But who was that audience, and how did they react? What questions or criticisms did they have? We may not know. Or consider the case of an advertisement for a product in a magazine or TV commercial. There may have been arguments in it, but who were the respondents, and how did they react? Did the arguments influence them? Of course, there are many ways of testing hypotheses on the answers to these questions. If sales shot up after the ad aired, that may be a pretty good sign that the argument in the ad reached the target audience and successfully persuaded them to buy the product. But the answers in such a case are provided only by the testing of the hypothesis. The case is different from one in which there is a dialogue in the sense of a verbal exchange between speech partners. The proponent can perhaps be identified as the one who put forward the argument in the ad, and the discourse in which the argument was expressed may be available in the form of a tape or transcript. This part of the dialogue is reproducible. But there may be nothing corresponding to the response move as a speech act in the dialogue.

The solution to the RTD problem of mass media argumentation has several components. One is the breaking down of the typical dialectical model of a sequence of turn-taking, question-reply moves into a different sequence. This sequence is the modified dialectical sequence for rhetorical argumentation. Let us call it the rhetorical argumentation sequence (RAS). The following five stages are characteristic of an RAS. First, the proponent goes through an argument invention stage in which he devises an argumentation strategy to persuade the audience or respondent. Second, there is a construction stage, where he builds the message. For example, the message could be a TV commercial. The construction stage would consist of the work of preparing the commercial. Third, there is a sending stage in which the message is printed or broadcast to a mass audience. Fourth, there is a message processing stage where the audience takes in the argument. Each member of the audience does this individually and, depending on format, in different ways. The message may be printed or stored on a tape, and each person who reads or sees it individually processes the message. Fifth, there is a feedback stage, where some results of having sent the message are fed back to the proponent. These results represent the supposed impact of the message on the audience. The five stages constitute a normative model of mass media argumentation. They do not necessarily represent the actual temporal sequence of how things proceed in a real case. For example, an early version of the commercial could be televised, and viewers might make it clear by phone calls that they do not like the commercial for some reason. Let's say, for example, that viewers find that the commercial is distasteful or think that it portrays them in a bad light. In response to this feedback, a new version of the commercial may then be constructed and broadcast. Notice also that each stage is not necessarily a discrete or continuous single event in time. For example, a commercial may be run for a few days, and then run again a month later for a few days.

The profile of dialogue is a technique used to represent a connected sequence of speech acts that are moves in a local segment that is part of a longer sequence of argumentation in a dialogue. The profile is a short selected sequence of moves that represents only a fragment of a longer sequence of moves comprising a lengthy exchange between two participants who have taken turns arguing in a dialogue. More correctly (Krabbe 1999), a profile of dialogue is not always just a single sequence. It may also exhibit several sequences organized as branches in a tree structure. Thus Krabbe (1999, p. 25) described a profile as a tool that "is supposed to give us some general features of such sequences at some intermediate level of abstraction" between an actual case and a formal model of dialogue. Despite its incompleteness, a profile can be useful for analyzing or evaluating an argument or argument strategy that was played out mainly in certain moves in a dialogue. The profile technique is useful in cases where bringing in additional lengthy parts of a dialogue in full is not necessary or can be condensed. The term "profile of dialogue" was first introduced in Walton (1989b, pp. 65–71) to analyze and evaluate examples of question-asking strategies, and especially the fallacy of many questions. A well-known example of the kind of question that is associated with this traditional fallacy is, "Have you stopped abusing your spouse?" The fallacy arises from the fact that no matter which way the respondent answers, he automatically commits himself to the proposition that he has abused his spouse at some time or other. Thus the question can be used as a tactic to force even the non-spouse-abuser to concede that he has abused his spouse. One might parenthetically note that such a question would be not be fallacious if used to interview a defendant in court who had just admitted that he had abused his spouse. The question could be fallacious, though, where it represents an attempt by the questioner to force the respondent to admit guilt without leaving him any room to air his real opinions. Thus this tactic falls under the heading of the kind of questioning tactic of forcing an answer studied in relation to polling in chapter 7, section 4.

One diagnosis of the problem with some of the questions used in polls, and with the fallacy of many questions, is that such questions do not allow the respondent to give a proper answer because the question is too complex. To deal with this problem, the questioner should break the question down into several simpler questions that the respondent can answer separately without being forced into concessions he does not want to make. These simpler questions, once answered, can then lead to more complex questions that can now be answered without committing any fallacies or being forced to admit something that the respondent does not want to admit. A profile of dialogue can be used to show what the right sequence of questioning should ideally look like.

Profile 9.1

    Q1: Do you have a spouse? (If answer is "no," end of sequence.)

    Q2: Have you ever abused your spouse? (If answer is "no," end of sequence.)

    Q3: Have you stopped abusing your spouse?

Suppose the respondent has already answered "yes" to both Q1 and Q2. At the next move in the dialogue, it would not be inappropriate for the proponent to pose the question Q3. In such a case, there is no forcing of an answer that unfairly limits the respondent's options. Although the famous complex question would be asked at move Q3, it would not be fallacious. To evaluate problematic cases, like the kinds of questions used in polling studied in chapter 7, the profile of dialogue technique is the best method. This technique is normative. It is used to indicate how the right sequence of dialogue should ideally go. Then this sequence or profile can be compared with the real dialogue sequence of argumentation in the given case being analyzed. The comparison of the two sequences can reveal the evidence needed to judge whether the questioning in the actual case should be seen as fallacious or not.

Now we come to the basic problem for using dialectical models to apply to real cases of rhetorical argumentation. The problem is that when you look at a real case of mass media argument, such as a commercial, there appears to be no basis for building up a profile of dialogue that could be applied to the case. For, as observed above, the RAS seems to be a one-shot affair. There is not the same kind of more protracted sequence of questions and replies between the proponent and the respondent so typical of dialectical argumentation. Thus it is questionable whether dialectical models apply usefully to mass media argumentation. To deal with this problem we need to take a closer look at how mass media argumentation works, as shown by the case studies discussed in the previous chapters.

3. Direct and Indirect Media Argumentation

Two classes of media argumentation need to be distinguished. The first is that of arguments based on the commitments of the audience. Typical of this class are the appeals to fear and pity studied in chapters 2 and 4. For example, in the appeal to pity, the proponent bases the argument on the recognition that the audience will feel pity when a situation that seems unfortunate to them is presented. He then uses this evocation of pity as a premise in practical reasoning designed to get the audience to take a recommended course of action. For example, he may recommend that the audience send a check or credit card number. In this kind of case, the proponent must devise his strategy of argumentation based on what he takes to be the commitments and the presumed thinking of the target audience. Chapters 2 and 4 showed some of the argumentation schemes used in appeals to fear and pity, and showed how such arguments are based on the presumed commitments of the target audience. The typical *ad hominem* argument studied in chapter 5 has a different and more complex dialectical structure. In the circumstantial *ad hominem* argument, like the Gore example, the proponent bases his argument on the commitments of the respondent. He finds a pair of propositions that are commitments of that specific respondent and that are (arguably) inconsistent with each other. Then he uses this whole apparatus to try to get

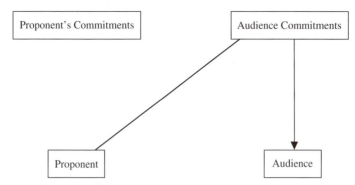

FIGURE 9.1 Direct media argumentation.

the audience to draw a conclusion by inference from what has been put before them. The audience is supposed to see that the respondent is inconsistent in that he does not practice what he preaches. The audience is expected to draw the conclusion that the respondent is a hypocrite. By this means the proponent hopes to discredit the respondent before the mass audience, and thereby get the mass audience to reject his argument. This class of arguments has a more complex dialectical structure than the previous one. It is first directed to the commitments of the single respondent, but then it uses this first segment of the argument to try to influence a wider, often mass audience.

The strategies for these two classes of arguments are essentially different. In the first, the respondent is the mass audience. This class of arguments could be called direct media arguments. The dialectical structure of direct media argumentation is displayed in Figure 9.1.

The direct class of media arguments is dialectically simpler. The proponent directly aims his strategy at the audience. His task is to try to figure out what their commitments are likely to be, what their goals and interests are likely to be, and how they are likely to feel about situations that are familiar and evocative to them.

The second class of media arguments is rhetorically more complex. The proponent has more work to do here. He must first figure out a plausible account of what the respondent's commitments are likely to be, or at any rate how they can be plausibly portrayed. Then he must work with these data using an argumentation scheme to try to influence the audience. From the argument based on the respondent's presumed commitments, he must try to get the audience to draw a conclusion. To do this, he needs to know something about the commitments and the thinking

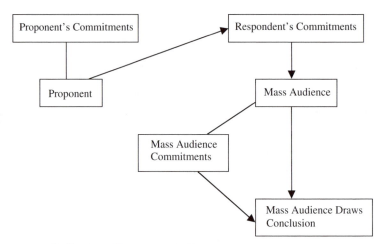

FIGURE 9.2 Indirect media argumentation.

of the audience. So in the indirect type of media argumentation, the proponent must base his argument first on premises that are (arguably) commitments of the respondent. Second, he must direct this first stage of the argument to the commitments of the audience. The dialectical structure of indirect media argumentation is displayed in Figure 9.2.

This distinction between the two types of mass arguments is important for the speech act of persuasion. The direct type of media argument can be viewed dialectically as being based on the speech act of persuasion. The indirect type does not fit the model of the speech act of persuasion outlined in chapter 2, at least not without modifications. The speech act of persuasion in the indirect mass media argument is one directed to the audience as respondent. The aim is to persuade the audience to accept a conclusion by using argumentation based on their commitments, or what are taken to represent their commitments, as premises. But this aim is pursued indirectly by means of argumentation in a prior context of persuasion dialogue between the proponent and the respondent who is attacked or otherwise confronted in argumentation. Thus what is involved in the indirect type of argument is a double persuasion dialogue. There is a shift from one persuasion dialogue to another. In this type of argument, we can say that the speech act of persuasion is involved at two levels. The distinction between direct and indirect media arguments is essential to solving the RTD problem by matching the commitment-based structure of media argumentation to the dialectical model.

In both direct and indirect argumentation, the audience plays a complex role as both spectator and judge. The audience may seem to be a silent spectator. But in many cases it is evident that the audience is meant to be a participant. Tindale (1999, p. 66) noted that the dialectical approach may insist that a dialogue is involved whether you look at the role of the audience the one way or the other. To appreciate this point, it is useful to look at political arguments, such as *ad hominem* arguments used in campaign ads. The audience appears to be a spectator, but the ad works because the audience is invited to draw conclusions on a basis of innuendo. It is in such cases that the Gricean notions of implicature and rules for collaborative conversation come into play. The problem then posed (Tindale 1999, p. 67) is to integrate the dialectical notion of rules for a collaborative conversation with a rhetorically based account of the role of the audience.

Another component necessary for the solution of the RTD problem is a dialectical reconstruction of the invention stage. How is it that the invention stage can be dialectical if the typical sequence of question-reply moves in a dialogue is not there? The configuration of argument strategies, set out as the explanation of appeals to fear and pity as fallacious arguments in chapter 4, still seems very mysterious in certain respects. How does the one agent "enter into" the mind of the other to anticipate the objections or future argumentation moves of the other? It sounds like what is involved is the rhetorical ability of persuasion called empathy. How could empathy work in argumentation? How is it a part of the rhetorical argumentation commonly used in mass media persuasion attempts? When the proponent constructs the persuasive message, in order for the argument to be successful, it must be based on premises that are commitments of the target mass audience. But the problem is how the proponent can find the right premises. How can he effectively know or try to guess the commitments of the target audience? Answers to these questions need to be based on the assumption that the proponent can simulate the thinking of the audience on the issue that is the topic of the persuasion dialogue. To do this, he must use what is called simulative reasoning.

When the proponent goes through the invention stage, the first stage in persuading a mass audience, he develops and acts on an argumentation strategy. To devise the strategy, the proponent must try to judge what the commitments of the audience are with respect to the matter at issue. How does he do this? The key is simulative reasoning. The proponent has to use empathy to try to put himself in the mind of the audience, so to speak. Then he can proceed to the construction stage, where he builds the argumentation that will lead the audience from their commitment-based premises to the conclusion the proponent wants them to accept. It is this process of simulative reasoning, trying to anticipate the response of the audience through *prolepsis*, that constitutes the main dialectical element of rhetorical argumentation. The dialogue between proponent and respondent is "mental," so to speak. There is a profile of dialogue there implicitly, but it may not be articulated verbally by the proponent. Indeed, it is generally better for the proponent if his audience is unaware of the rhetorical/dialectical mechanics of his argument strategy. And yet to make the strategy work, the proponent needs to "think ahead" in a dialogue to try to anticipate how the audience will react to each move in his sequence of argumentation.

4. Star Trek: The Rhetorical Dimension

In presenting an argument, an arguer who is engaged in a public attempt at rational persuasion typically has a social audience in mind. However, as Vorobej (2006, p. 5) has shown, a speaker's social audience is a socially constructed entity. It represents not the actual audience a speaker is addressing, but a kind of construct simulating the collective viewpoint the speaker is aiming at as his persuasion target. To be successful in carrying out the speech act of persuasion in a dialogue, the speaker must use arguments based on premises that are propositions the audience either accepts or can be persuaded to accept (its commitments). Moreover, as we now hope to show, to be successful in this enterprise the speaker must base his arguments on the values of the audience or on the values of particular groups of individuals comprising the audience.

In chapter 1, section 9, the automated method of argument diagramming called Araucaria was used to identify the premises and conclusions in the argumentation in Captain Picard's speech, showing how the chain of argumentation fits together to support an ultimate conclusion. Importantly, we saw how each of these arguments is based on certain argumentation schemes. One is the scheme for argument from values. Another is the scheme for practical reasoning. A third is the argument from value-based practical reasoning that combines the former two schemes, leading to the ultimate conclusion that the three groups should go ahead with a mission. The argument diagram in Plate 2 showed clearly how each of the three arguments supporting this conclusion is based on an argument from value that has an implicit premise based on what Picard takes to be the value of each group. The argument diagram also represented the refutation, or counter-argument, that went against the conclusion. This part of the dialectical reconstruction of the argument could have been developed further, but we did not attempt to do so in order to keep the illustration reasonably simple. Once we constructed the argument diagram, displaying the arguments for and against the conclusion, we are then in a position to evaluate these arguments as weak or strong, based on the argumentation schemes and the data we have concerning whether the premises are true or false. The next step is to look at the same speech with its three constituent arguments from a different viewpoint, that of rhetoric. Our way of doing so will use the same tools identified during the dialectical reconstruction of the argument, namely, argumentation schemes, and the identification of the premises and conclusions in the argument as propositions in argumentation chains leading to an ultimate conclusion. We now return to the example of Captain Picard's speech in order to show how his rhetorical presentation of the argumentation to the three groups can be shown to be an instance of value-based practical reasoning. To do this we have to take a different temporal viewpoint on the argumentation. Instead of seeing it as a completed process in which the arguments have already been set out, and where our aim is to identify their premises and conclusions, including the implicit ones, and see how they are parts of arguments leading to an ultimate conclusion, we have to look at it in a future-oriented way. We have to look at it from the point of view of Picard's assignment set by Starfleet Command. That assignment is to persuade the target audience to go ahead with the mission that has been set. The rhetorical problem is that there are three different groups, and three different kinds of arguments will be needed to persuade them that they should go ahead. From the rhetorical point of view, the three kinds of arguments needed for the purpose of persuasion are separated not by their logical structure but by the different values their premises need to be based on. As in the dialectical reconstruction of the argument, the value-based nature of the argumentation, requiring the argumentation schemes for value-based reasoning, and more specifically for value-based practical reasoning, is vitally important. But the way these schemes are used is quite different. For this purpose, an argument diagram is not very suitable, because it is based on the assumption that the argument already exists, at least partially, so that it can be completed by filling in unstated premises and conclusions. But from a rhetorical point of view, at the beginning point where the speech first needs to be made, the arguments do not yet exist, except in the mind of the speaker as *topoi*, or patterns of argument that could be used to invent sequences of argumentation tailored to the needs of a specific audience. How could such a structure be diagrammed? Here we propose that something similar to an argument diagram, but in certain ways quite different from it, can be used to represent the rhetorical structure of an argument. It will use the same tools as the dialectical reconstruction of an argument, as shown in Plate 2. But the tools will be used in a different way. They will be used for the purpose of constructing an argument, a method traditionally called argument invention. This structure is displayed in Plate 4.

In Plate 4, the ultimate conclusion of the argumentation in the speech is shown at the top, in a way comparable to the argument diagram in Plate 2. Below the top text boxes, the three arguments supporting the ultimate conclusion are displayed. At the next level, just below the level where the three arguments are displayed, one can see how each argument is based on a specific goal attributed to an audience group. At the level below that, it is shown how each, goal, in turn, is based on a value thought to be specific to that group. The bottom level shows which group is thought to hold that particular value.

Plate 4 is an example of a rhetorical structure that represents a sequence of direct media argumentation based on premises supported by values of specific target audience groups to be persuaded, leading to an ultimate conclusion to undertake an action that requires collaboration by all the groups involved. The format of the argumentation structure is thus based on two types of dialogue. One is a persuasion type of dialogue, while the other is a group deliberation to undertake an action requiring collaborative action by all the groups involved. From this rhetorical point of view we are looking at the argumentation structure from a viewpoint of needing to persuade a group with diverse values to undertake a specific course of action. This perspective is a distinctively rhetorical one, as contrasted with the dialectical one previously analyzed. Deliberation uses the type of argumentation called practical reasoning, and this kind of reasoning is central to planning. Picard has already adopted a plan, in this case, and is trying to persuade those who will be involved in carrying it out to accept it. To do this, he makes a proposal to the audience, supported by his arguments in favor of it.

Recent research has shown that the speech act of making a proposal has three essential components (Kauffeld 1998, p. 248). In this analysis, what is proposed is a proposition that is addressed by the speaker to the audience or hearer in a way in that meets three following conditions.

1. The speaker must present a statement of resolve, such as "We should carry out his action," and act as if this statement expresses a conclusion that the speaker has reached.[1]
2. The speaker must give it to be believed that he is speaking with the goal of answering doubts and objections regarding the statement put forward.
3. The speaker must have a commitment to provide the audience with reasons to raise questions, doubts, and objections with regard to the proposition.

Kauffeld sees these three kinds of conditions as essential to some speaker's utterance as properly being classified as an instance of the speech act of making of a proposal.

In Searle's (1969) classification of speech acts, proposing lies between a directive, a speech act in which the speaker tries to get the hearer to carry out a course of action, and a commissive, a speech act that commits the speaker to a course of action. In the analysis of the speech act of making a proposal put forward by Aakhus (2006), there is a future act that requires collaboration (joint action) between the speaker and audience, and the speaker tries to get the audience to take part in it. It is assumed that the two parties are acting together to solve a problem and take turns in attempts to collaborate in doing so (p. 7). Kauffeld (1995) proposes that the speaker's purpose in such a context is to get the audience to consider some proposition as worthy that the audience has doubts about or would otherwise tend to dismiss or overlook. The speaker and the audience are able to contribute to the accomplishment of carrying out this action together, and it is not obvious that each can do it of their own accord in the normal course of events. The speech made by the speaker is an attempt to enlist the audience in this action, taken to be mutually beneficial. In the Star Trek example, Captain Picard puts forward the proposal to go to Dozaria, and he offers arguments for this course of action. It is a course of action he is already committed to, and he makes the speech to try to persuade his audience that they can act together to solve the problem by participating in the proposed venture.

The analysis of Searle, Kauffeld, and Aakhus shows how the speech act of making a proposal contains potential for the speaker's defense of the

---

[1] The exception would be during the early stage of a deliberation, say, a brainstorming session, where the point is to collect alternatives to discuss, without committing the participants to the suggested ideas.

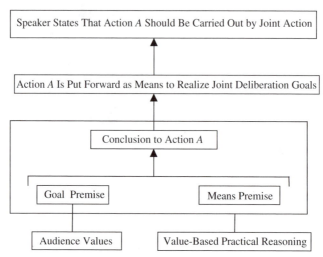

FIGURE 9.3 Argumentation structure of the speech act of making a proposal.

proposal and potential for the audience to have doubts or reservations about it. But what structure of argumentation underlies the making of the proposal, framing the arguments that might be offered to support it, as well as the rebuttals that might be used to attack it? This question can be answered by using the scheme for value-based practical reasoning, as shown in Figure 9.3.

The argumentation structure shown in Figure 9.3 shows how value-based practical reasoning underlies the speech act of making a proposal in a deliberation dialogue. The part of the diagram below the first box displays the argumentation needed to support the proposal. The argumentation needed to defend the proposal, if it is questioned or attacked, is the scheme for value-based practical reasoning presented in chapter 1, section 8. We can see, for example, how the structure of value-based practical reasoning is embedded into the deliberation dialogue in the Star Trek example.

5. Argumentation Strategies

In deliberation dialogue, each agent has a plan of action based on practical reasoning. A plan is based on a goal and a set of actions that are connected to the goal (Russell and Norvig 1995, p. 339). Characteristic of planning is a chaining forward of actions from a "start state" to a "goal state" (p. 365). A plan is also based on plausible hypotheses about what is likely to happen in the future. There is a useful literature on the theory of action that can be applied to planning. Segerberg (1984) developed a formal theory of action in which actions are composed of subactions chained together in a way very similar to the way states form a plan in planning theory in AI. The chaining takes the form of action sequences of the kinds described by Goldman (1970). An example would be me moving my arm to make a signal. The action of me moving my arm is related to my action of making a signal in a sequence of actions. Such a sequence of actions could be part of a plan. Segerberg (1985, pp. 185–187) gave the example of using a recipe to make a meal. During the sequence of actions required to make the meal, there are many so-called routines or habitual actions that are "run." For example, I might have to whip the potatoes. The recipe could be thought of as representing a plan. The connected sequences of actions in cooking the meal represent routines that are connected together in a more complex sequence of actions performed to carry out the plan.

Planning is closely related to the notion of a strategy in deliberation. You could say that a plan is an action strategy, or represents a strategy of deliberation. Hamblin (1987) constructed a formal theory of action strategies based around the notion of a "deed." In his logic of imperatives, he defined a deed as an elementary independent action attributable to a particular agent (p. 140). A partial allocation of deeds to an agent is called a partial strategy (p. 157). Walton and Krabbe (1995, pp. 189–195) presented a formal precis of Hamblin's action-state semantics in which a partial strategy specifies a sequence of actions with gaps in it. The gaps can later on be filled in as events actually unfold in the given situation in which the action is being carried out. It has also been shown in Walton and Krabbe (pp. 15–21) how the notion of a partial strategy is fundamental to understanding the notion of commitment. A person is said to be "living up to a commitment" as long as his actions are based on a partial strategy, his actions forming a sequence leading toward the fulfillment of that commitment as a goal state. All these notions from planning theory and action theory are extremely useful in helping us to understand argumentation in the context of a deliberation. Each agent has goals that represent commitments, and has plans or action strategies that are hypothesized as means to lead to these goals.

In going through the five stages of presenting an argument to be sent across media, whether the format is one of direct or indirect communication, the proponent has to use practical reasoning to devise a persuasive message. The respondent has to use practical reasoning to comprehend the message and then act on it. But the proponent must use simulative reasoning to anticipate the plausible response and thinking of the respondent. What is at work is a simulative use of practical reasoning by the proponent, especially at the invention stage. Simulation must be used to try to devise an argumentation strategy that will achieve an action goal, to persuade the respondent, or to achieve the goal of the dialogue, whatever type of dialogue is involved.

When we examine the other types of dialogue set out in chapter 2, we find the concept of strategy is different for each type of dialogue. In a persuasion dialogue, each participant has a strategy for persuading the other participant to accept the first party's thesis. Van Eemeren and Houtlosser (1999a, p. 164) have described argumentation strategies as arising from the balance between rhetoric and dialectic in argumentation. The balancing of a resolution-minded dialectical objective with the rhetorical objective of having one's own position accepted tends to give rise to strategic maneuvering. The capability to devise such useful strategies demands the ability to think ahead in a dialogue and to judge proactively how one's respondent will react to future moves. In a persuasion dialogue, a participant's strategy can be modeled as a chaining forward of inferences of the kind described in chapter 2, section 3. This chaining forward must meet all four requirements (R1–R4) for argumentation in a persuasion dialogue set out in chapter 2, section 2. The respondent must accept the premises. Each inference in the chain must be structurally correct. The chain of argumentation must have the proponent's thesis as its end point (goal-state). And these three requirements are the only means allowed as fulfilling the proponent's goal. This notion of a persuasion strategy requires several abilities. One is the simulative ability to judge what the respondent's commitments are. Another is the ability to think up chains of argumentation using these commitments as premises. Still another is the ability to anticipate the future moves and sequences of moves that will be used by the respondent in the dialogue. An agent in a dialogue tries to extrapolate a line of argumentation forward aiming at a particular end point that is his thesis to be proved in the dialogue. This notion of the extrapolation forward of a chain of argumentation is the basis of dialectical relevance. An argument should be judged to be relevant in a persuasion dialogue if it can be extrapolated forward so that it reaches, or at least aims at reaching, the conclusion the proponent is supposed to prove. This normative and dialectical concept of relevance is vitally important for modeling argumentation in persuasion dialogue and especially for analyzing alleged fallacies of relevance.

Strategy in a persuasion dialogue is structurally similar to the notion of action in a deliberation type of dialogue. Both are based on chaining forward a sequence of argumentation aimed at an end point. But the two kinds of strategy are qualitatively different. Strategy in deliberation is based on goals, sequences of actions, and planning. It is aimed at a goal state and is concerned with hypothetical sequences of actions that represent alternative means for bringing about the action that is the goal. Persuasion strategy is based on the four components (R_1–R_4) that are characteristic of argumentation in persuasion dialogue. In some cases, a strategy has actually been played out, and we may try to figure out what the arguer's strategy was, based on the given text of discourse representing his argumentation. But strategy is normally a future-directed notion that is vital to the invention stage of a mass media argument. It is a sequence of argumentation that exists in the agent in a simulative and partial representation. It is a device that an arguer needs to deploy in a hypothetical dialogue that he anticipates might be played out in the future. To devise a strategy at the invention stage, what an arguer must do is to take the commitments of the other party and to try to use them in a sequence of argumentation leading the respondent to a designated conclusion. The proponent must use structurally correct inferences in the chain. Mostly, he must use plausible reasoning and implicature to try to get the other party to incur new commitments that can also be used as premises. The whole sequence should eventuate in the proving of the designated conclusion. Strategy in rhetorical argumentation characteristically requires the ability to use simulative reasoning to judge what the commitments of the audience are, and how they will draw conclusions based on those commitments.

A system of argument invention of the following kind can be built on the structure of persuasion strategy outlined above. The first component of the system is a set of statements that are premises acceptable to an audience that can be used in arguments designed to persuade them to accept the target conclusion. The second component is a set of argumentation schemes that can be used inferentially to draw conclusions from these premises. The third is a device like an Araucaria diagram that can be used for constructing chains of argumentation recursively from the first two components. How such a chaining device works can be illustrated as follows. To use the chaining device, the argument inventor takes the set of premises and applies each scheme to them generating a conclusion. This conclusion is then added to the set of premises. The argument inventor repeats the process, each time using the new conclusion as one of the premises in the new inference. Following this recursive procedure, the statement formerly drawn as a conclusion becomes, during the next round of argument invention, a premise in a new argument used to move closer toward the conclusion to be proved.

To see more precisely how simulative "thinking ahead" needs to be done as part of the process of rhetorical argument invention, there are several technologies recently developed in AI that can be extremely helpful. One is the technology called plan recognition.

6. **Plan Recognition**

Plan recognition technology is an active area of research in artificial intelligence, and many software packages have been developed. In plan recognition, one agent attributes goals and planned actions to another agent on the basis of observing that other agent carrying out actions. What sorts of dialogue are involved in cases of argumentation based on plan recognition? Obviously, deliberation is involved. The agent whose actions were observed must be presumed to be engaged in deliberation. The other agent must have the capability to understand how deliberation works. But Carberry argued that there is also an information-seeking type of dialogue involved. As she put it (1990, p. 3) the one agent is "seeking information" and the other is "attempting to provide that information." She cited the example of apprentice-expert dialogues. The apprentice begins by attempting to perform a given task. But then, if confronted with a problem, he may discuss the problem with the expert teacher. Generally, then, we can say that two types of dialogue are involved. One is a deliberation, in which a primary agent uses practical reasoning to solve a problem or carry out a plan. The other is an information-seeking dialogue in which the secondary agent seeks information relevant to the deliberation. But there are other types of dialogue that can be involved as well in some cases. Chu-Carroll and Carberry have shown how negotiation and persuasion dialogue often need to be involved as well. The following case has been summarized from their more lengthy account (Chu-Carroll and Carberry 1995, p. 111).

Case 9.1

> The air-traffic control systems in a country have gone down. Two neighbouring countries, X and Y, negotiate with each other on how to track and deal with all affected flights. In this scenario, the agents deliberating on how to solve the problem are the air-traffic control

systems representing countries X and Y. But in order to success-fully deliberate, they have to exchange relevant information. For example, they will have to give each other information about their individual equipment to determine which terminal is more capable of guiding which flights. But there is also another type of dialogue required. The air-traffic controllers in countries X and Y will also have to negotiate with each other on how to best divide the work load. If one has a work load that is too heavy at some times, it will have to try to trade off with other flights it could take on during less busy times.

Based on cases like this one, Chu-Carroll and Carberry proposed a model of plan recognition that includes negotiation as well as deliberation and information-seeking dialogue. But their model needs to be extended even further. In some cases persuasion dialogue needs to be involved as well. Chu-Carrol and Carberry acknowledged this necessity (p. 121) in their statement that there are intervals in communication where one agent needs to justify beliefs to another agent. If the two agents have a difference of opinion about some issue, they will have to engage in persuasion dialogue to resolve that issue.

Multi-agent systems and other new advances in AI like computational dialectics and plan recognition technologies can be applied to rhetorical argumentation.[2] What they do is to give new structure to argumentation that can be used to solve many problems that have been around for a long time. Most importantly, they can be used to model the notion of an arguer having a strategy of argumentation when communicating in a dialogue with another arguer. Traditional dialectical models in argu-mentation theory have seen the participant in the dialogue as a kind of primitive, unanalyzed entity. If we can model a participant as an agent, we can see the agent as having a strategy, organized in advance in order to interact in a dialogue with another agent. Thus, for example, if the pur-pose of a dialogue is for one agent to persuade another agent, then we can see the first agent as building up a strategy, in the form of rhetorical argu-mentation that can be used for this purpose. Exactly how such a strategy can best be modeled is currently controversial. Some say that the agent has to be seen as having beliefs, desires, and intentions. Others think that the agent should be seen as having what are called commitments. These

---

[2] In fact, of course, the original motivation of the dialogue systems of Hamblin (1970) was to study argumentation, and especially fallacies of the kind that commonly occur in argumentation.

are entities that can be reconstructed from a dialogue without necessarily representing the beliefs, desires, or intentions of the agent.

Plan recognition is most directly applicable to argumentation in the deliberation type of dialogue based on practical reasoning. As advocated in the previous chapters, the structure needed to accommodate such a communication is one of multi-agent dialogue. Both the proponent and the respondent are agents, capable of action, of taking in information, and of seeing the consequences of his or her own actions. Both are capable of planning. Now we return to the question posed in chapter 4, section 5, of how one agent can simulatively see into the "mind" or plans of the other, based on external evidence. An agent is presumed to be capable of receiving and processing information about its immediate environment. The one agent can also presumably see the actions of other agents. An agent can also receive messages from another agent in a dialogue. Using practical reasoning, an agent can draw inferences from this information.

For practical reasoning to be used in mass media argumentation, the message presenter has to be able to understand the thinking of the audience, especially the means-end reasoning the audience would presumably use in trying to solve a problem. The proponent of an argument has to figure out what the commitments of the audience are, as indicated above. He also has to figure out which arguments can be used to influence the audience, based on their commitments. But there is also another component of strategy in mass media argumentation. The proponent must try to figure out what line of argumentation is likely to be used by the respondent. The situation here is similar to the kinds of simulative reasoning used in chess as described by Gordon (1986) in chapter 4, section 5. In the case of mass media argumentation, the proponent must try to put himself into the position of the audience as if he were one of them. He must, in effect, try to figure out what the strategy of the audience would be. How would they respond? How would they think? Would they have some further agenda that might lead them to oppose the argumentation they are about to be faced with? In the case of a deliberation dialogue, a proponent needs to figure out what the goals of the audience are and what sort of strategy they currently have for realizing these goals. An argument will be ineffective if it fails to deal with this existing strategy.

The message presenter, in the language of recent developments in computer science, must have a capability for plan recognition. Carberry (1990, p. 17) has defined plan recognition as the method whereby "an agent attempts to reconstruct from the available evidence a plan that was previously constructed by another agent." The air controllers example (case 9.1) can be used to illustrate plan recognition. But to see how plan recognition can be applied to argumentation strategy, it is best to use another simple example. Carberry (1990, p. 17) used the following example from ordinary life to illustrate plan recognition, summarized below as case 9.2.

Case 9.2: The Motorist Example

    A motorist driving along the freeway sees an empty car parked along the edge of the road. She sees that the car has a missing tire. As she drives a little further, she sees a man rolling a tire along the edge of the freeway. He is carrying a baby in one arm as he rolls the tire. Three small children are walking behind him. By observing these facts, the driver draws several conclusions. She concludes that this man she saw rolling the tire was the driver of the empty car with the missing tire. She concludes that the man was rolling the tire along in order to get it repaired. She concludes that he did not want to leave the three small children alone in the car along the highway. The motorist did not see these conclusions as facts. They were all conclusions drawn by inference from what she saw. She drew them by attributing a plan of action to the man she saw rolling the tire. This capability is plan recognition.

How does plan recognition work? One agent observes the actions of another agent. So it is partly based on observations. But the observer can't see directly what is going on the other agent's mind. How the process works is that the observer attributes practical reasoning to the agent whose actions she has observed. She then draws conclusions in the form of hypotheses that seem to explain what she has observed. She attributes goals to this agent, and hypothesizes that he sees actions and pursues goals in much the same way she does. But of course, the conclusions drawn by the motorist could be wrong. They are just plausible attributions or hypotheses. What sort of further evidence could be used to test these hypotheses? Carberry (1990) built a system of plan recognition called TRACK that uses a dialogue method to test inferences drawn by plan recognition. Basically, the method is for the one agent to ask the other questions about his observed actions. Carberry (p. 75) explained how TRACK works as a dialogue system: "TRACK assimilates utterances from an ongoing dialogue and incrementally updates and expands the system's beliefs about the underlying task-related plan motivating the information-seeker's queries." In other words, the agent who carries out plan recognition engages in a dialogue with the agent whose actions were observed. As the dialogue continues, new information comes in about this agent's plan. The other agent can then use this new information as evidence to update his earlier hypothesis about the plan of this agent.

One agent has to grasp the practical reasoning of another agent in plan recognition. But there is also a lot of domain-dependent knowledge required. For example, in case 9.2, the observer agent needs to understand that a tire is part of the wheel on the car, that a tire can go flat if punctured, that a tire can be removed from the car, and so forth. She also needs to understand that it would be dangerous to leave children alone in a car at the side of the highway. Of course, we all know such things, and we taken for granted that others know them. This so-called common knowledge is the basis of all human communication. When you present an argument in mass media communication, for example, you presume that the audience already has much knowledge about the way things commonly work in daily life. However, when devising computer software, you can't take it for granted that a computer has such knowledge. To make a computer reason like a human, it has to be programmed with many factual assumptions representing common knowledge. The fact that a computer lacks such knowledge presents a main problem for AI. One way to deal with it is to restrict common knowledge to a particular domain in a given case. For example, in order to make the computer capable of plan recognition in case 9.2, many facts representing common knowledge about cars, tires, leaving children in the car, and so forth could be programmed into the computer's data base. All these facts represent the domain-dependent knowledge in that case.

Plan recognition is very important for understanding the structure of simulative reasoning in mass media argumentation. When an agent constructs an argument through the five stages of mass media argumentation, whether of the direct or indirect type, he needs to have an argumentation strategy. To have a strategy, he needs to grasp the commitments of the audience. He needs to use these commitments as premises of his argument. He also has to try to anticipate how the audience will use practical reasoning to draw inferences from these premises. These tasks require simulative reasoning. The arguer has to try to think like the audience thinks and to try to see how they will be persuaded to arrive at the conclusion he wants to convince them to accept. Plan recognition can be a useful tool for this purpose. If the arguer can get some grasp of the plan of action that can be attributed to the audience, this hypothesis could be extremely useful for devising a strategy to persuade the audience or influence them toward a particular course of action.

Plan recognition is especially important to understanding at the invention stage. Understanding how the invention stage works and relates to the other four stages is vital to coming to a new and useful understanding of how dialectic and rhetoric should be integrated. Dialectic is seen primarily as a critical art of identifying, analyzing, and evaluating argumentation already given in a text of discourse. Rhetoric is seen primarily as a tool for the construction of argumentation to persuade an audience.

7. The Solution to the RTD Problem

A problem that loomed large throughout this book was the RTD problem of how media argumentation can be based on the speech act of persuasion if, as it appears to be in many cases, it is a one-shot argument as opposed to a sequence of connected dialogue moves between proponent and respondent. Now in this chapter, computational dialectic has offered a solution to the problem. Media argumentation can be amenable to the speech act of persuasion because the arguer has to interact dialectically with the audience by using simulative reasoning, most visibly at the invention stage of the argument. The rhetorical arguer must judge the commitments and values of the audience, as shown in the Star Trek example. He must figure out how to use forms of argumentation to persuade the audience based on their commitments. He must use value-based practical reasoning and plan recognition to judge and anticipate how the audience is thinking in the domain and on the issue of the case. In a nutshell, the arguer must try to devise a rhetorical argumentation trajectory that probes into the thinking of the audience. This strategic task of argumentation (1) is commitment-based, (2) has its goal as the speech act of persuasion, (3) uses value-based practical reasoning, as well as other argumentation schemes, and (4) can shift from deliberation to persuasion. The latter point brings out the importance of the traditional distinction between deliberative argumentation and argumentation used for persuasion, emphasizing that argumentation can be understood at a deeper level only if different types of dialogue are recognized. Computational dialectic in AI is now widely based on this recognition.

Carberry, as shown above, used a dialogue technique in plan recognition. She studied many cases of plan recognition in dialogues between two parties where one party was trying to understand the plan of another party whose actions had been observed. Central to her analysis of plan recognition was the idea that the plan recognition process could be conceived as a dialogue. The dialogue is initiated when one agent sees the actions of another and forms a hypothesis to try to explain these actions. But the dialogue process can, in many cases, be continued as an actual dialogue between the two parties. The plan recognizer can ask the other agent, for example, "What were you trying to do?" Similarly applying the dialogue model can also work with cases of rhetorical argumentation. The arguer is devising an argumentation strategy at the invention stage, and is thus implicitly engaging in a dialogue interaction with the audience. But in some instances, the argumentation actually carries over into a real dialogue. For example, the designer of a pilot for a television ad may engage in discussion with a focus group to try to foresee likely reactions to the ad. Or he may take a poll to see how viewers felt about it. Or he may get e-mail from the viewers once the ad has been run. Or he may collect data on whether sales of the product have increased after the ad was run. All these interactions with the audience, or selected groups in the mass audience, can be seen as instances of dialogue. Then, using feedback, the ad designer can modify the ad or adopt a different strategy, if he feels that the ad as presently constructed is not achieving the desired effect. There are many possibilities of feedback of various kinds. But they can all be seen as a kind of continuation of dialogue between the proponent and the mass audience that the argument is designed to persuade.

But the RTD problem, as posed above, is that profiles of dialogue do not seem to apply to mass media argumentation, because there is no sequence of questions and replies between the proponent and the respondent, as required by the dialectical model. It can now be replied that there is such a sequence, because the mass media argument presenter is interacting with the audience dialectically when he uses simulative reasoning to try to anticipate the audience's response to the argument. And in fact, for planning strategy in mass media argumentation, the profiles technique can be extremely helpful. The other useful dialectical tool is the chaining forward of an argument. Both techniques are useful because they enable the arguer to anticipate the responses of the audience proactively. What is essential for the mass media arguer to do, according to the commitment model, is to use the commitments of the audience as premises. Using the Star Trek example as a simple model, the arguer selects an argumentation scheme, or a chain of argumentation having different kinds of arguments as links in the chain, and uses it to get by a rhetorical trajectory from the premises to the conclusion at issue. The commitments of the audience are the data, subject to change by updating as new information comes in through dialogue. Profiles of dialogue are then used to infer new audience commitments. The inference engine applied to these data is the set of argumentation schemes. They need to be applied to the data one at a time and then sequentially. The result of multiple applications is an argumentation chain. The argumentation represents the arguer's best strategy for persuading the audience to come to accept the conclusion. Thus we can see that the procedure could be automated and that it is inherently dialectical in nature.

Too late to be included for extensive commentary, a paper has just appeared (Bench-Capon, Doutre, and Dunne (2007) that presents a formal argumentation framework for modeling practical reasoning in which values can be represented in such a way as to allow divergent opinions for different audiences. In this framework, every argument is explicitly associated with a value promoted by its acceptance. Consequently, the formal model built to represent use of value-based practical reasoning to persuade an audience is called a value-based argumentation framework (VAF). In the model, whether an argument is acceptable or not depends on how well it stands up to critical questions and counter-arguments put forward in a dialogue with the audience to whom the argument is directed. Another feature of the model is that rankings of values emerge during the course of the dialogue as argumentation on both sides is put forward (p. 43). The model is thus sensitive to preferences between arguments with respect to particular audiences, and can account for disagreements of values among different audiences (p. 66)

Of course, applying dialectical methods to rhetorical argumentation is a new and undeveloped branch of argumentation theory. It has not been automated yet, and in some respects it is still a crude technology at the earliest stage of its potential development. For one thing, the current analysis of argumentation schemes is still at a rough and preliminary stage. As noted in chapter 1, the list of presumptive argumentation schemes in Walton (1996) is not complete, although it has identified many of the most common forms of presumptive argument that would apply in cases of mass media argumentation. Perelman and Olbrechts-Tyteca (1969) have identified many of these forms of argument, and many of them were also evident in Aristotle's writings on rhetoric and so-called topics. Arthur Hastings's Ph.D. thesis (1963) made an even more systematic taxonomy and analysis of the most important schemes along with useful examples of them. Recently, Kienpointner (1992) has produced an even more comprehensive account of many argumentation schemes, stressing deductive and inductive forms as well as presumptive forms. Among the presumptive argumentation schemes in Walton (1996) are such familiar types of argumentation as argument from sign, argument from example, argument from commitment, argument from position to know, argument from expert opinion, argument from analogy, argument from precedent, argument from gradualism, and the slippery slope argument. Van Eemeren and Grootendorst (1992) have also analyzed important argumentation schemes. The existing formulations of the argumentation schemes are not at a stage of precise formal development yet. They have arisen mainly out of practical concerns arising from studying real cases. However, there is currently a joint research project under way that has the aim of formalizing argumentation schemes. And the importance of argumentation schemes has been more widely recognized in the field of computing. These new developments show the power of computational dialectics as applied to media argumentation.

8. Fifteen Basic Components of Media Argumentation

The analysis of cases in the previous chapters has revealed the following fifteen basic components of media argumentation. Each component represents an important normative characteristic of media argumentation that helps us to properly analyze and evaluate it in particular cases. Thus these fifteen components provide a summary of what has been achieved so far in revealing the deep structure of media argumentation.

1. Media argumentation is basically made up of arguments that are meant to be plausible. Although they can be deductive or inductive in some cases, for the most part they are presumptive arguments of the kind identified by Cialdini (1993) as cognitive short cuts, as listed in chapter 1, section 5. They are arguments such as appeal to popular opinion, appeal to pity, and the other forms of argument mentioned in the previous chapters and in the literature on argumentation and fallacies.

2. To analyze and evaluate given cases of media argumentation, identification of the premises and the conclusion is an important step. Another separate step is the identification of the link of inference between the premises and the conclusion.

3. These arguments have a structure represented by argumentation schemes. In the presumptive argumentation schemes so typically

used in arguments in media argumentation, the major premise is a warrant that is not absolutely true but is defeasible and holds presumptively, subject to exceptions.

4. Practical reasoning is a very important type of argumentation scheme for media argumentation. It is ubiquitous in commercial ads, for example. The structure of the ad is often in the form, "Here is a problem. Buying this product (e.g., taking this medication) is the solution." Practical reasoning is also the basic structure of media argumentation in political deliberation in a democracy.

5. Argumentation schemes need to be evaluated in a context of dialogue by asking appropriate critical questions. Burden of proof and turn taking in dialogue are very important in evaluating the plausibility or doubtfulness of an argument.

6. The premises of such arguments are based on what the proponent takes to be the commitments of the audience to whom the message was directed. Very often the premises are *endoxa*, or propositions generally accepted by the public and the experts.

7. One common way of trying to judge popular opinion on an issue is the public opinion poll. These polls are ubiquitous. They can be very valuable in some instances. They can also be very misleading. They are often abused, or executed in an uncritical manner, and subject to fallacies that can be highly deceptive. Having dialogue with members of a target audience, for example, in focus groups, can be a much more accurate and less misleading way of judging popular opinion in some cases.

8. The formation of public opinion should be seen as a deliberation process that goes through several stages. A problem is formulated, ways and means of solving it are discussed, and solutions are arrived at and evaluated. Along the way, further information is injected into the deliberation at various points.

9. Media argumentation needs to be analyzed and evaluated in different contexts of dialogue, of the kind outlined in chapter 2, section 4. Dialectical shifts need to be taken into account. For example, as indicated in the point just above, an information-seeking dialogue can be embedded in a deliberation dialogue.

10. Persuasion is central to media argumentation. Typically, the goal of media argumentation is to persuade a mass audience to take action or to accept a viewpoint. Persuasion can now be defined as an objective of media argumentation much more precisely than

in the past through the analysis of the speech act of persuasion presented in chapter 2.

11. Media argumentation takes the form of five stages in a feedback cycle. The proponent devises and tries out an argument designed to reach an interlocutor or mass audience. He gets feedback in the form of polling, observing how sales go up or not, and by various other indirect means of communicating with the audience. While this process is under way, information often comes in, suggesting a change or redirection of the argumentation. Thus the premises in the original argument can be modified and corrected so the argument is made more plausible.

12. Based on argumentation schemes, argumentation strategies are very important to understanding the structure of media argumentation. For example, the strategy called dissociation by Pereleman and Olbrects-Tyteca and the strategy of contrast cited by Cialdini are not themselves argumentation schemes or forms of argument. Instead, they represent rhetorical trajectories used by a proponent of an argument to put that argument within a longer sequence of argumentation leading to a conclusion.

13. To model the notion of an argumentation strategy, both the proponent and the respondent in a dialogue need to be seen as agents, in the sense of the term now widely used in multi-agent systems. In media argumentation, the proponent and the respondent share information and knowledge about commonly accepted ways of doing things. The proponent as agent can then devise a strategy using simulative reasoning based on his anticipation of how the respondent is likely to react to certain assertions or arguments.

14. When devising an argument strategy to persuade an audience, Gricean implicature is vitally important. Plan recognition enables each agent to anticipate the implicatures that the other agent can reasonably be expected to draw. It is by these means that the proponent structures the strategy of his selected line of argumentation with missing assumptions so that the audience can draw its own conclusions or fill in unstated premises. As shown in chapter 5, section 8, suggestion and innuendo are vitally important tools of mass media argumentation.

15. Bias is a central category for evaluating media argumentation. Rhetorical argumentation is very often biased, because it is advocacy, but that in itself is not necessarily a critical defect or dialectical fault. An argument is biased in a sense implying a critical defect if

it purports to be a two-sided dialogue, whereas in reality it is one-sided. Propaganda is hard to define, but following the analysis of chapter 3, argumentation in propaganda should not necessarily be judged to be critically defective or fallacious. However, there is a strong tendency for propaganda to be deceptive.

These fifteen components represent the basic characteristics of media argumentation. All that remains is to show how they are tied together in a system that displays their interlocking dialectical and rhetorical structure.

9. The Persuasion System

In this section we organize the components of media argumentation into a structure called the Persuasion System that shows where the premises come from, what type of reasoning is used to draw inferences from them, and what the ultimate conclusion of the chain of reasoning is supposed to be. The Persuasion System of media argumentation is a five-tuple {C, T, A, D, K}. C is the set of commitments of the audience; T is a designated proposition representing the conclusion (thesis) that the proponent is trying to get the audience to accept as a new commitment; A is a set of argumentation schemes (forms of argument), used to infer propositions from other propositions; and D is a set of dialogues, of various kinds, but deliberation dialogue, persuasion dialogue, and negotiation dialogue are three of the most important types. Each dialogue contains a pair of agents called the proponent and the respondent. The proponent is an agent represented by an individual constant p. The audience is an agent represented by a constant r, meaning that the audience has the dialectical role of respondent. K is a set of propositions representing the common knowledge shared by the proponent and the audience. K breaks down into two subsets. One is the domain-dependent set of facts of the case. The other subset represents the common ways of doing things and common knowledge broadly familiar to any audience and proponent who would be involved in media argumentation.

What makes media argumentation possible is the simulative reasoning used by the participants. The proponent uses simulative reasoning to judge how the audience is thinking, what their commitments are, what inferences they are likely to draw, and generally, how they are likely to respond. The proponent can anticipate the critical questions the respondent will ask, and can judge in advance whether any answers to these questions he may venture in his argumentation will be seen as plausible or implausible. Because both participants are agents, they will tend to formulate and solve practical problems by the same process of thinking. In particular, the proponent can use plan recognition to devise an argumentation strategy that will fit the commitments and the thinking of the audience. Plan recognition is coupled with the use of argumentation schemes in the chaining structure of reasoning described in chapter 2, section 3. The proponent constructs an argument strategy by chaining forward from the audience's commitments, C, to his own conclusion T. Because of common knowledge K shared with the audience, and argumentation schemes representing ways of reasoning shared with the audience, the proponent can use simulative reasoning to persuade the audience.

One of the most fundamental of these argumentation schemes is the one called practical reasoning. The critical questions matching the argumentation scheme for basic practical reasoning are reprinted below from chapter 1, section 7.

(Q1) Are there alternative courses of action apart from B?
(Q2) Is B the best (or most acceptable) among the alternatives?
(Q3) Should goals other than A be considered?
(Q4) Is it really possible to bring about B, in the situation?
(Q5) What bad consequences of bringing about B should be taken into account?

If the two premises of the practical inference above are commitments of the respondent, and the conclusion follows, then it should also become a commitment of the respondent. But if the respondent poses any of the appropriate critical questions cited above, then his commitment to the conclusion of the practical inference can be retracted. Using this argumentation scheme, the proponent has the ability to foresee the inferences the respondent is likely to draw when presented with the argumentation. Thus argumentation schemes, in this case the one for basic practical reasoning, are an important element in simulative reasoning and strategy in mass media argumentation. This simulative process of arguing by grasping the position of the other side mentally, and using this knowledge to anticipate his reactions and counter-moves, may seem like the most mysterious aspect of mass media argumentation. But once the Persuasion System exhibits the dialectical structure of mass media argumentation, the mystery disappears. It becomes clear how the proponent can extrapolate the respondent's line of argumentation forward, using chaining and profiles of dialogue, basing the extrapolation on the respondent's commitments.

Simulative reasoning of the kind used in mass media argumentation in the past appeared to be subjective. But now it can be seen to be based on evidence that can be extracted from a given case and then used in a chain of logical reasoning. Plan recognition shows how such judgments are based on a body of evidence that is verifiable or falsifiable. The data are drawn from the proponent's observing the actions of the respondent, and also from his engaging in dialogue with the respondent. The proponent can construct a hypothesis about the respondent's commitments and goals based on this evidence. It can be strengthened or defeated by new evidence that comes in as the dialogue proceeds. It can also be challenged by questioning the inferences drawn in the logical reasoning used to hypothesize from the data in a case. This way of inventing a strategy has traditionally been thought of as subjective. And, in a way, it can rightly be called subjective, because the process of generating such a hypothesis is simulative. One agent constructs a hypothesis about what he thinks represents the thinking of another agent. Such an estimate can be wrong. The possibility of deception is very real in argumentation. As has been observed in philosophy under the heading of "the problem of other minds," you can't get direct access to what is going on in another person's mind. But the Persuasion System reveals how simulative strategy can be based on a testable assessment of objective and reproducible evidence. It can be based on a process of logical reasoning originating from premises that can be tested by the observed or documented evidence in a case. As emphasized, this process is fallible. It is based on plausible reasoning, because one agent can infer only indirectly what another agent is really thinking. The evidence rarely tends to be conclusive, and simulative reasoning is hypothetical and conjectural in nature. But it can be analyzed and evaluated by using objective criteria to apply to an actual case. Thus what the Persuasion System shows is that, in theory at any rate, media argumentation has an objective rhetorical/dialectical structure.

10. Computational Dialectics for Rhetorical Invention

We started out this book with describing the longstanding tension between rhetoric and dialectic, especially stemming from the philosophers' perception of rhetoric as a sham and deception. Rhetoric was portrayed as trading on the bias of an audience and as a device of manipulative persuasion that has no regard for the truth of the matter being discussed. This view sees dialectic and rhetoric as opposed subjects, locked into a conflict with each other. The Star Trek example, as treated first in chapter 1 from a dialectical viewpoint, and then as treated in this chapter from a rhetorical viewpoint, showed how both subjects simply represent different uses of the same argumentation technology. Dialectic is a technology using tools like argumentation schemes and argument diagramming for critical analysis and evaluation of a given argument that already exists. Rhetoric is a technology that uses the same tools, adapted to the Persuasion System, and thus used in a different way, primarily for the invention of new arguments that might be used to persuade a target audience, given what is known or can be reasonably assumed about the beliefs and values of that audience.

The Star Trek example reveals how each of these views is a false portrayal. Both subjects are based on use of rational argumentation for some purpose in a dialogue context, and on the same argumentation structures. The difference is that one uses argumentation in a reconstructive way by beginning with the text of discourse of a speech that already exists, while the other uses argumentation in a constructive way to aim it from premises representing the presumed values of the target group to the conclusion that they are to be persuaded to accept. The essential argumentation technology is the same. The difference lies in the purpose the technology is being used for and the way that argumentation tools are applied to the task of carrying out that purpose.

Analyzing the Star Trek example using tools from argumentation theory, such as argumentation schemes, and tools from artificial intelligence, such as Araucaria, has revealed connections between computing and argumentation. But recently there has been a convergence of research efforts between the argumentation (informal logic) community and the AI community in computing. Computing is coming to be based more and more on dialogue exchanges in the form of speech acts between artificially constructed software entities that transfer information, negotiate exchanges of information or commodities, and try to decide on a best course of action to carry out common goals. Communication between a user and a software entity is another form of dialogue that is vitally important in computing technology. Argumentation is being increasingly seen as extremely helpful in such interactive computer communications by those in the field of AI. Formal logic is too rigid and too limited to model such dialogue-based arguments in a flexible way – one that can model the defeasible type of argumentation that is so ubiquitous in computing. AI is moving to a social model of argumentation in which two parties called agents reason together to try to carry out a project or attain a goal by collaborating. The best explored of these new technologies is a branch of distributed computing called multi-agent systems.

Among the many recent research efforts in computing that could be cited here are the series of papers by Singh (1991, 1997, 1999), which develop a commitment-based approach to communication in multi-agent systems, and the recent books on rational agents by Wooldridge (2000, 2002). The concept of a rational agent is defined by Wooldridge (2000, p. 1) in terms of how the agent reasons. He offers the following simple example of agent reasoning: "if I have a goal of staying dry, and I believe it is raining, then it is rational of me to take an umbrella when I leave the house." This human goal-directed action is a case of an agent being rational. The agent engages in practical reasoning that leads from a goal to an action. On the other hand, agents are often irrational. They go against their own stated goals, and sometimes even contradict themselves. Sometimes they even commit fallacies and try to deceive themselves and other agents. Of course, the example of a rational agent represented by Wooldridge is a case of an agent acting alone. The larger problem now confronted in distributed computing concerns cases where two agents (in the simplest) case are attempting to communicate with each other in order to decide on a collaborative course of action. It has become evident that the idea of two rational agents trying to reason together needs to be based on the structure of rationality as a dialogue, developed by Hamblin (1970, 1971, 1987) in order to study fallacies in logic. The basic idea behind a Hamblin dialogue is that the two participants can reason and argue rationally together because each can identify and keep track of the commitments of the other. This commitment-based approach is an alternative to the belief-desire-intention approach advocated by Wooldridge (2000). Singh (1991, 1997) developed the commitment-based approach of Hamblin into a formal theory of communication and collective rational action for multi-agent systems. He bases his theory of multi-agent communication around agents seen as having a limited rationality. An agent is viewed as acting rationally under certain constraints that typically involve uncertain and incomplete information that can change rapidly. Thus a limited rational agent can make a mistake, but also has a (limited) capability to correct its mistakes.

Persuasion and other types of dialogue that are important for computing come under the field now called computational dialectics[3] in artificial

---

3 There is a computational dialectics research group in Germany (Forschergruppe Kommunikatives Verstehen), whose stated goal is to combine results from argumentation theory and AI to study the computational structure of argumentative dialogue. Tom

intelligence, or the new dialectic in argumentation theory.[4] "Dialectic" in this sense refers to the formal properties of speech acts as they occur in different types of dialogue. Formal dialectic studies structured sequences of speech acts in which two speech partners take turns contributing to a goal-directed and rule-governed conversation.[5] Formal models have now been developed for persuasion dialogue (Walton and Krabbe 1995), negotiation dialogue (Sierra, Jennings, Noriega, and Parsons 1998), and deliberation dialogue (Hitchcock et al. 2001). Another basic type of dialogue that has been studied in plan recognition research in AI is the information-seeking dialogue (Chu-Carroll and Carberry 1995). The inquiry and the eristic dialogue are two other types that are recognized in the literature on dialectical argumentation, as shown below. Obviously, in the study of the speech act of persuasion, persuasion dialogue will be prominent. But in realistic discourse containing argumentation, several different types of dialogue are often mixed in together. Thus an important task of argumentation analysis is to place a given argument in a dialectical frame (Reed 1998). There can also be shifts from one type of dialogue to another during an argument (Walton and Krabbe 1995).

When a practical logic of argumentation schemes is used for the invention of arguments in rhetoric, as well as for their analysis and evaluation in dialectic, the result is a powerful fusion of rhetoric and dialectic. Traditional logic, like syllogistic logic, emphasized analysis of argumentation based on context-free formal deductive systems of argument. Traditional analyses of economic and political argumentation featured cost-benefit analysis and decision theory based on Bayesian probability. The Persuasion System presents a new and quite different approach to mass media argumentation that is truly liberating to those used to the confines of the traditional approaches. Not only is it a more flexible and powerful approach, but it has a clear and precise structure and useful guidelines as applied to real cases of mass media argumentation in a democratic

Gordon, the leader of a project associated with this group (Project Zeno), is said to have been the originator of the expression "computational dialectics." I believe that the first time I heard it was during a talk given in Bonn by Henry Prakken in 1994.

[4] See Walton 1998b.

[5] Formal dialectic as a method of studying fallacies was founded by Hamblin (1970), but the Erlangen School of Lorenzen had earlier developed a system of formal dialectic as a method of modeling the structure of philosophical and mathematical argumentation. The history of how the subject came to life again in the twentieth century has been briefly chronicled in Walton and Krabbe (1995).

system with a free market economy. It is much more exciting and interesting than traditional methods of argument analysis because the user can so easily see how it represents the flow of real argumentation. It yields real insight into techniques of rhetorical argumentation instead of forcing them into narrowly defined, preconceived structures that abstract away from the most interesting aspects of the clever way arguments are used to persuade. It shows how to criticize an argument as well as how to invent one.

The Persuasion System is the best tool to answer the worry that rhetorical argumentation is a sham and a deception built on sophisms and faulty reasoning. Rhetorical argumentation seems to have nothing to do with truth or evidence, once it has been separated from the dialectical argumentation underlying it. It could be equally said that dialectic is an abstract and useless subject once it has been separated from its applications to rhetorical argumentation. The reintegration of rhetoric and dialectic can lead to a rehabilitation of rhetorical argumentation along Aristotelian lines. Of course, there is always a danger in using Aristotle to support one's own view of rhetoric. Leff (1993, p. 314) and Gross (2000, p. 26) have shown how those with strong views about rhetoric tended to cite Aristotle's *Rhetoric* as supporting their quite different visions of rhetoric as a subject. Aristotle is regarded as such a powerful theoretician that he has been constantly reinterpreted over the ages to fit many different conceptions of rhetoric as a discipline. But these past interpretations have been the source of much of the problem. They have exacerbated the tension between dialectic and rhetoric by distorting the aims and methods of both subjects.

Sophistry, or antilogic, as it was sometimes called by the ancients, does, after all, represent a very real danger of misuse in propaganda and other techniques of media persuasion that tend to trade on deception where it is effective. There should be a free marketplace of argumentation in a democratic system that allows for free speech. Thus, mob rhetoric, propaganda, and biased and fallacious argumentation will always be used deliberately to promote the causes of interest groups. Rhetorical and dialectical skills, however, can be used by both sides. If deliberative democracy is to work as a useful and reasoned method of arriving at prudent conclusions on how to act under conditions of uncertainty and disagreement, the mass media audience must also learn how to use argumentation skills to deal with the information and argumentation explosion due to both traditional mass media and the Internet, by learning to judge what kind of information is reliable and what kind of persuasion is fallacious.

The Persuasion System can be extremely helpful in devising formal models of media argumentation that not only are useful, but in fact are already being used in computer science.[6] When we eventually automate this type of argumentation more fully by implementing the formal models, they will be widely employed in developing new technologies for deliberation and persuasion in media argumentation. As this happens, they can be used to assist in the task of rhetorical invention of new arguments in advertising, debate, and political controversy on public policy issues. In having public input on policy issues, communication will be improved by an increased capacity to identify, analyze, and evaluate argumentation on an issue. Problems of public deliberation in law, ethics, and democracy were the original motivation for the founding of both rhetoric and dialectic as subjects by the Greeks, as noted in chapter 1. Dialectic is a new field (or a new revival of an old field) that is only now beginning to receive attention in the mainstream of academic research in the humanities and social sciences. By providing new foundations for the future development of software tools based on computational dialectics, computing technology research will show others what can be achieved by finding a better adjustment between rhetoric and dialectic.

---

[6] Gordon (1995) used dialogue models of argumentation to pioneer computational dialectic as applied to legal reasoning. An early project using these models was the application of computational dialectic by Gordon and Karacapilidis (1997) to provide communication technology for public deliberation in choices of routes for the fast trains in Europe. Reed (2006) has provided an overview of the many applications of dialogue-based argumentation developed in recent computing technology.

Bibliography

Aakhus, Mark. 2005. "The Act and Activity of Proposing in Deliberation." In *Engaging Argument: Selected Papers from the 2005 National Communication Association/American Forensic Association Summer Conference on Argumentation*, ed. P. Riley. Washington, D.C., National Communication Association, 2006, 402–408.

Adler, Jerry. 1994. "The Numbers Game." *Newsweek*, July 25, pp. 56–58.

Allossery, Patrick. 1999. "Anti-Tobacco Ads Go for the Throat." *Financial Post*, June 21, p. C4.

Aomi, Junichi. 1985. "Persuasive Definitions in Social Sciences and Social Thought." In *Man, Law and Modern Forms of Life*, ed. Eugenio Bulygin, Jean-Louis Gardies, and Ilkka Niiniluoto. Dordrecht: Reidel, 187–190.

Aristotle. 1939. *Topics*, trans. E. S. Forster. Loeb Classical Library. Cambridge, Mass.: Harvard University Press.

Aristotle. 1928. *On Sophistical Refutations*, trans. E. S. Forster. Loeb Classical Library. Cambridge, Mass.: Harvard University Press.

Aristotle. 1937. *The Art of Rhetoric*, trans. John Henry Freese. Loeb Classical Library. Cambridge, Mass.: Harvard University Press.

Atkinson, Katie, Trevor Bench-Capon, and Peter McBurney. 2004. "A Dialogue Game Protocol for Multi-Agent Argument over Proposals for Action." In *Argumentation in Multi-Agent Systems*, ed. I. Rahwan, P. Moraitis, and C. Reed. Berlin: Springer, 149–161.

Barnes, Jonathan. 1980. "Aristotle and the Methods of Ethics." *Revue Internationale de Philosophie* 34: 590–611.

Barth, Else M., and Jan L. Martens. 1977. "*Argumentum Ad Hominem*: From Chaos to Formal Dialectic." *Logique at Analyse* 77–78: 76–96.

Bench-Capon, Trevor. 2003a. "Agreeing to Differ: Modelling Persuasive Dialogue between Parties without a Consensus about Values." *Informal Logic* 22: 231–245.

Bench-Capon, Trevor. 2003b. "Persuasion in Practical Argument Using Value-Based Argumentation Frameworks." *Journal of Logic and Computation* 13: 429–448.

Bench-Capon, Trevor J. M., Sylvie Doutre, and Paul E. Dunne. 2007. "Audiences in Argumentation Frameworks." *Artificial Intelligence* 171: 42–71.

Bentham, Jeremy. 1969. *The Book of Fallacies.* In *A Bentham Reader*, ed. Mary Peter Mack. New York: Pegasus. First published in 1824.

Bernays, E. 1923. *Crystallizing Public Opinion.* New York: Boni and Liveright.

Best, Joel. 2001. *Damned Lies and Statistics.* Berkeley: University of California Press.

Blair, J. Anthony. 1977. "What Is Bias?" In *Selected Issues in Logic and Communication*, ed. Trudy Govier. Belmont: Wadsworth, 93–103.

Blair, J. Anthony. 1998. "The Limits of the Dialogue Model of Argument." In *Argumentation and Rhetoric*, ed. Hans V. Hansen, Christopher W. Tindale, and Athena V. Coleman. CD-Rom. St. Catherines, Ontario: Ontario Society for the Study of Argumentation.

Blair, J. Anthony, and Ralph H. Johnson. 1987. "Argumentation as Dialectical." *Argumentation* 1: 41–56.

Bloomer, W. Martin. 2001. "Topics." In *Encyclopedia of Rhetoric*, ed. Thomas O. Sloane. Oxford: Oxford University Press, 779–782.

Bratman, Michael E. 1987. *Intention, Plans and Practical Reason.* Cambridge, Mass.: Harvard University Press.

Brinton, Alan. 1985. "A Rhetorical View of the *Ad Hominem*." *Australasian Journal of Philosophy* 63: 50–63.

Brinton, Alan. 1995. "The *Ad Hominem*." In *Fallacies: Classical and Contemporary Readings*, ed. Hans V. Hansen and Robert C. Pinto. University Park: Pennsylvania State University Press, 213–222.

Burgess-Jackson, Keith. 1995. "Rape and Persuasive Definition." *Canadian Journal of Philosophy* 25: 415–454.

Burnyeat, Myles F. 1994. "Enthyeme: Aristotle on the Logic of Persuasion." In *Aristotle's Rhetoric: Philosophical Essays*, ed. David J. Furley and Alexander Nehemas. Princeton: Princeton University Press, 3–55.

Campbell, Stephen K. 1974. *Flaws and Fallacies in Statistical Thinking.* Englewood Cliffs, N.J.: Prentice-Hall.

Cantril, Albert H., James Fallows, Leonard Garment, Robert B. Hill, and Paul Warnke. 1990. "The User's Perspective: A Round Table on the Impact of Polls." In *The Classics of Polling*, ed. Michael L. Young. Metuchen, N.J.: Scarecrow Press, 374–388.

Carberry, Sandra. 1990. *Plan Recognition in Natural Language Dialogue.* Cambridge: MIT Press.

"Changed Law Fuels Statistics." 1992. *Winnipeg Free Press*, October 10, A3.

Childs, H. L. 1965. *Public Opinion: Nature, Formation and Role.* Princeton, N.J.: Van Nostrand.

Chu-Carroll, Jennifer, and Sandra Carberry. 1995. "Conflict Detection and Resolution in Collaborative Planning." In *Intelligent Agents II: Agent Theories, Architectures and Languages. IJCAI '95 Workshop.* Berlin: Springer-Verlag, 111–126.

Cialdini, Robert B. 1993. *Influence: Science and Practice*, 3rd ed. New York: Harper-Collins.

Clark, Herbert H., and Michael F. Schober. 1992. "Asking Questions and Influencing Answers." In *Questions about Questions: Inquiries into the Cognitive Biases of Surveys*, ed. Judith M. Tanur. New York: Russell Sage Foundation, 15–48.

Collingwood, Robin G. 1946. *The Idea of History*. Oxford: Clarendon Press.

Copi, Irving M. 1982. *Introduction to Logic*, 6th ed. New York: Macmillan.

Copi, Irving M., and Carl Cohen. 1998. *Introduction to Logic*, 10th ed. Upper Saddle River, N.J.: Prentice-Hall.

Cragan, John F., and Craig W. Cutbirth. 1984. "A Revisionist Perspective on Political *Ad Hominem* Argument: A Case Study." *Central States Speech Journal* 35: 228–237.

Crossen, Cynthia. 1994. *Tainted Truth: The Manipulation of Fact in America*. New York: Simon & Schuster.

Dascal, Marcelo, and Alan G. Gross. 1999. "The Marriage of Pragmatics and Rhetoric." *Philosophy and Rhetoric* 32: 107–130.

Devereux, Daniel. 1990. "Comments on Robert Bolton's The Epistemological Basis of Aristotelian Dialectic." In *Biologie, Logique et Metaphysique*, ed. Daniel Devereux and Pierre Pellegrin. Paris: Editions du Centre National de la Recherche Scientifique, 263–286.

Dillard, James Price. 1994. "Rethinking the Study of Fear Appeals: An Emotional Perspective." *Communication Theory* 4: 295–323.

Donohue, William A. 1981. "Development of a Model of Rule Use in Negotiation Interaction." *Communication Monographs* 48: 106–120.

Dray, William. 1964. *Philosophy of History*. Englewood Cliffs, N.J.: Prentice-Hall.

Dray, William. 1995. *History as Re-enactment: R. G. Collingwood's Idea of History*. Oxford: Oxford University Press.

Ellul, Jacques. 1967. *Histoire de la Propagande*. Paris: PUF.

Elster, Jon. 1989. *The Cement of Society*. Cambridge: Cambridge University Press.

Engel, S. Morris. 1976. *With Good Reason: An Introduction to Informal Fallacies*. New York: St. Martin's Press.

Evans, J. D. G. 1977. *Aristotle's Concept of Dialectic*. Cambridge: Cambridge University Press.

Feld, Karl G. 2001. "When Push Comes to Shove." In *The Public Perspective* 12, no. 5, p. 37. The Roper Center for Public Opinion Research.

Finocchiaro, Maurice. 1980. *Galileo and the Art of Reasoning*. Dordrecht: Reidel.

Finocchiaro, Maurice. 2005. *Arguments about Arguments*. New York: Cambridge University Press.

Fisher, Roger, and William Ury. 1991. *Getting to Yes*, 2nd ed. New York: Penguin.

Fishkin, James S. 1991. *Democracy and Deliberation*. New Haven: Yale University Press.

Fishkin, James S. 1995. *The Voice of the People: Public Opinion and Democracy*. New Haven: Yale University Press.

Freeman, James B. 1995. "The Appeal to Popularity and Presumption by Common Knowledge." In *Fallacies: Classical and Contemporary Readings*, ed. Hans V. Hansen and Robert C. Pinto. University Park: Pennsylvania State University Press, 263–273.

Freeman, James B. 2005. *Acceptable Premises: An Epistemic Approach to an Informal Logic Problem*. New York: Cambridge University Press.

Freeman, James B. 2006. *Acceptable Premises*. New York: Cambridge University Press.

Garner, Richard. 1993. "Are Convenient Fictions Harmful to Your Health?" *Philosophy East and West* 43: 87–106.

Garver, Eugene. 1994. *Aristotle's Rhetoric: An Art of Character.* Chicago: University of Chicago Press.

Goldman, Alvin. 1970. *A Theory of Human Action.* Englewood Cliffs: Prentice-Hall.

Goldman, Alvin I. 1995. "Empathy Mind and Morals." In *Mental Simulation: Evaluations and Applications,* ed. Martin Davies and Tony Stone. Oxford: Blackwell, 185–208.

Gordon, Robert M. 1986. "Folk Psychology as Simulation." *Mind and Language* 1: 158–171.

Gordon, Thomas F. 1995. *The Pleadings Game: An Artificial Intelligence Model of Procedural Justice.* Dordrecht: Kluwer.

Gordon, Thomas F., and Nikos Karacapilidis. 1997. "The Zeno Argumentation Framework." In *Proceedings of the Sixth International Conference on Artificial Intelligence and Law,* Melbourne, Australia, 10–18.

Govier, Trudy. 1987. *Problems in Argument Analysis and Evaluation.* Dordrecht: Foris.

Govier, Trudy. 1999. *The Philosophy of Argument.* Newport News, Va.: Vale Press.

Graesser, Arthur C., Sailaja Bommareddy, Shane Swamer, and Jonathan M. Golding. 1996. "Integrating Questionnaire Design with a Cognitive Computational Model of Human Question Answering." In *Answering Questions: Methodology for Determining Cognitive and Communicative Processes in Survey Research,* ed. Norbert Schwartz and Seymour Sudman. San Francisco: Jossey-Bass, 143–174.

Grennan, Wayne. 1997. *Informal Logic.* Montreal: McGill-Queen's University Press.

Grice, H. Paul. 1975. "Logic and Conversation." In *The Logic of Grammar,* ed. Donald Davidson and Gilbert Harman. Encino: Dickenson, 64–75.

Gross, Alan G. 2000. "What Aristotle Meant by Rhetoric." In *Rereading Aristotle's Rhetoric,* ed. Alan G. Gross and Arthur E. Walzer. Carbondale: Southern Illinois University Press, 24–37.

Hallden, Soren. 1960. *True Love, True Humour and True Religion: A Semantic Study.* Lund: Gleerlup.

Hamblin, Charles L. 1970. *Fallacies.* London: Methuen.

Hamblin, Charles L. 1971. "Mathematical Models of Dialogue." *Theoria* 37: 130–155.

Hamblin, Charles L. 1987. *Imperatives.* New York: Blackwell.

Harrah, David. 1984. "The Logic of Questions." In *Handbook of Philosophical Logic,* vol. 2, ed. Dov Gabbay and F. Guenther. Dordrecht: Reidel, 715–764.

Hart, Roderick P., and Courtney L. Dillard. 2001. "The Deliberative Genre." In *Encyclopedia of Rhetoric,* ed. Thomas O. Sloane. New York: Oxford University Press, 209–217.

Hastings, Arthur C. 1963. "A Reformulation of the Modes of Reasoning in Argumentation." Ph.D. dissertation, Northwestern University.

Herbst, Susan. 1993. *Numbered Voices: How Opinion Polling Has Shaped American Politics.* Chicago: University of Chicago Press.

Hitchcock, David. 1995. "Does the Traditional Treatment of Enthymemes Rest on a Mistake?" In *Analysis and Evaluation: Proceedings of the Third ISSA Conference on Argumentation,* vol. 2, ed. Frans H. van Eemeren, Rob Grootendorst, J. Anthony Blair, and Charles A. Willard. Amsterdam: SicSat, 113–129.

Hitchcock, David, Peter McBurney, and Simon Parsons. 2001. "A Framework for Deliberation Dialogues." In *Argument and Its Applications: Proceedings of the Fourth Biennial Conference of the Ontario Society for the Study of Argumentation (OSSA 2001)*, ed. H. V. Hansen, C. W. Tindale, J. A. Blair, and R. H. Johnson. Compact disk. Also available at http://www.csc.liv.ac.uk/~peter.

Hohmann, Hanns. 2000. "Rhetoric and Dialectic: Some Historical and Legal Perspectives." *Argumentation* 14: 223–234.

Horty, John, and Nuel D. Belnap. 1995. "The Deliberative Stit: A Study of Action, Omission, Ability, and Obligation." *Journal of Philosophical Logic* 24: 583–644.

Hurley, Patrick J. 1994. *A Concise Introduction to Logic*, 5th ed. Belmont, Calif.: Wadsworth.

Hurley, Patrick J. 2000. *A Concise Introduction to Logic*, 7th ed. Belmont, Calif.: Wadsworth.

Ivison, John. 2006. "Afghanistan: A Liberal Mission." *National Post* (Toronto), June 17, p. A1.

Jackson, Sally. 1996. "Fallacies and Heuristics." In *Logic and Argumentation*, ed. Johan van Benthem, Frans H. van Eemeren, Rob Grootendorst, and Frank Veltman. Amsterdam: North-Holland.

Jacobs, Scott. 2000. "Rhetoric and Dialectic from the Standpoint of Normative Pragmatics." *Argumentation* 14: 261–286.

Jacobs, Scott, and Sally Jackson. 1983. "Speech Act Structure in Conversation." In *Conversational Coherence: Form, Structure and Strategy*, ed. Robert T. Craig and Karen Tracy. Beverly Hills: Sage, 47–66.

Jacobs, Scott, and Sally Jackson. 1992. "Relevance and Digressions in Argumentative Discussion: A Pragmatic Approach." *Argumentation* 6: 161–176.

Johnson, Ralph H. 1987. "The Blaze of Her Splendors: Suggestions about Revitalizing Fallacy Theory." *Argumentation* 1: 239–254.

Johnson, Ralph H. 2000. *Manifest Rationality: A Pragmatic Theory of Argument*. Mahwah, N.J.: Lawrence Erlbaum Associates.

Johnstone, Henry W., Jr. 1952. "Philosophy and *Argumentum Ad Hominem.*" *Journal of Philosophy* 49: 489–498.

Johnstone, Henry W., Jr. 1959. *Philosophy and Argument*. University Park: Pennsylvania State University Press.

Johnstone, Henry W., Jr. 1981. "Toward an Ethics of Rhetoric." *Communication* 6: 305–314.

Kant, Immanuel. 1961. *Critique of Pure Reason*, trans. Norman Kemp Smith. London: Macmillan.

Kapp, Ernst. 1942. *Greek Foundations of Traditional Logic*. New York: Columbia University Press.

Kauffeld, Fred J. 1995. "The Persuasive Force of Arguments on Behalf of Proposals." In *Analysis and Evaluation: Proceedings of the Third ISSA Conference on Argumentation*, vol. 2. Amsterdam: SicSat.

Kauffeld, Fred J. 1998. "Presumptions and the Distribution of Argumentative Burdens in Acts of Proposing and Accusing." *Argumentation* 12: 245–266.

Kennedy, George A. 1963. *The Art of Persuasion in Greece*. London: Routledge and Kegan Paul.

Kennedy, George A., trans. 1991. *Aristotle on Rhetoric: A Theory of Civic Discourse.* New York: Oxford University Press.

Kennedy, George A. 1994. *A New History of Classical Rhetoric.* Princeton: Princeton University Press.

Kesterton, Michael. 1995. "Social Studies." *The Globe and Mail,* June 8, p. A24.

Kienpointner, Manfred. 1992. *Alltagslogik: Struktur und Funktion von Argumentationsmustern.* Stuttgart: Fromman-Holzboog.

Kienpointner, Manfred. 1997. "On the Art of Finding Arguments: What Ancient and Modern Masters of Invention Have to Tell Us about the *Ars Inveniendi.*" *Argumentation* 11: 225–236.

Kienpointner, Manfred, and Walther Kindt. 1997. "On the Problem of Bias in Political Argumentation." *Journal of Pragmatics* 27: 555–585.

Kneale, William, and Martha Kneale. 1962. *The Development of Logic.* Oxford: Clarendon Press.

Kock, Christian. 2003. "Multidimensionality and Non-deductiveness in Deliberative Argumentation." In *Anyone Who Has a View: Theoretical Contributions to the Study of Argumentation,* ed. Frans H. Eemeren, J. Anthony Blair, Charles A. Willard, and A. Francisca Snoeck Henkemans. Dordrecht: Kluwer, 157–171.

Kock, Christian. 2006. "The Domain of Rhetorical Argumentation." Paper to appear in the *Proceedings of the ISSA Conference,* Amsterdam.

Krabbe, Erik C. W. 1998. "Comments on Blair." In *Argumentation and Rhetoric,* ed. Hans V. Hansen, Christopher W. Tindale, and Athena V. Coleman. CD-Rom, St. Catherines, Ontario: Ontario Society for the Study of Argumentation.

Krabbe, Erik C. W. 1999. "Profiles of Dialogue." In *JFAK: Essays Dedicated to Johan van Benthem on the Occasion of His 50th Birthday,* ed. Jelle Gerbrandy, Maarten Marx, Maarten de Rijke, and Yde Venema. Amsterdam: Amsterdam University Press, 25–36.

Krabbe, Erik C. W. 2000. "Meeting in the House of Callias: Rhetoric and Dialectic." *Argumentation* 14: 205–217.

Krabbe, Erik C. W., and Douglas N. Walton. 1993. "It's All Very Well for You to Talk! Situationally Disqualifying *Ad Hominem* Attacks." *Informal Logic* 15: 79–91.

Kravetz, Stacy. 1999. "A Fad Flames Out, and Retailers Get Burned." *Wall Street Journal,* January 21, pp. B1 and B10.

Kuhn, Thomas S. 1970. *The Structure of Scientific Revolutions,* 2nd ed. Chicago: University of Chicago Press.

Lagerspetz, Eerik. 1995. "*Ad Hominem* Arguments in Practical Argumentation." *Argumentation* 9: 363–370.

LaTour, Michael S., and Shaker A. Zahra. 1989. "Fear Appeals as Advertising Strategy: Should They Be Used?" *Journal of Consumer Marketing* 6: 61–70.

Le Bon, Gustave. 1896. *The Crowd: A Study of the Popular Mind.* London: T. Fisher Unwin.

Leff, Michael. 1993. "The Uses of Aristotle's Rhetoric in Contemporary American Scholarship." *Argumentation* 7: 313–327.

Leff, Michael. 2000. "Rhetoric and Dialectic in the Twenty-first Century." *Argumentation* 14: 241–254.

Leventhal, H. 1970. "Findings and Theory in the Study of Fear Communications." In *Advances in Experimental Social Psychology*, ed. L. Berkowitz, vol. 5. New York: Academic Press, 119–186.

Leventhal, Howard. 1971. "Fear Appeals and Persuasion: The Differentiation of a Motivational Construct." *American Journal of Public Health* 61: 1205–1224.

Little, Bruce. 1996. "Gap in Jobless Rates a Puzzle." *The Globe and Mail*, February 12, p. B1.

Locke, John. 1961. *An Essay Concerning Human Understanding*, ed. John W. Yolton. London: Dent.

Maren, Michael. 1998. "The Faces of Famine." *Newsweek*, July 27, pp. 12–13.

Marlin, Randal. 1989. "Propaganda and the Ethics of Persuasion." *International Journal of Moral and Social Studies* 4: 37–72.

Marlin, Randal. 2002. *Propaganda and the Ethics of Persuasion*. Peterborough, Ontario: Broadview Press.

Martin, Rex. 1977. *Historical Explanation: Reenactment and Practical Inference*. Ithaca, N.Y.: Cornell University Press.

McClurg, Andrew J. 1992. "The Rhetoric of Gun Control." *American University Law Review* 42: 53–113.

McKerrow, Raymie E. 1990. "Argument Communities." In *Perspectives on Argumentation*, ed. Robert Trapp and Janice Schuetz. Prospect Heights, Ill.: Waveland Press.

"The Microscope." 2000. Canadian Broadcasting Corporation, *Marketplace*. February 29. Http://cbc.ca/consumers/market/news/00feb29.html.

Mitchell, Catherine. 1995. "Federal Violence Report Dishonest: Academics." *The Globe and Mail*, April 11, pp. A1 and B4.

Moore, David W. 1992. *The Super Pollsters: How They Measure and Manipulate Public Opinion in America*. New York: Four Walls Eight Windows.

Moore, Robert C. 1985. "Semantic Considerations on Nonmonotonic Logic." *Artificial Intelligence* 25: 75–94.

Morgan, C. 1987. "Explicit AIDS Campaign Offends TV Watchers in Australia." *Nature* 326: 732.

Nolt, John Eric. 1984. *Informal Logic: Possible Worlds and Imagination*. New York: McGraw-Hill.

Nuchelmans, Gabriel. 1993. "On the Fourfold Root of the *Argumentum Ad Hominem*." In *Empirical Logic and Public Debate*, ed. Erik C. W. Krabbe, Renee Jose Dalitz, and Pier A. Smit. Amsterdam: Rodopi, 37–47.

Ogden, Charles Kay, and Ivor Armstrong Richards. 1959. *The Meaning of Meaning*. New York: Harcourt Brace. First published in 1923.

O'Keefe, Daniel J. 1994. "Argumentation Studies and Dual-Process Models of Persuasion." In *Logic and Argumentation*, ed. Johan van Benthem, Frans H. van Eemeren, Rob Grootendorst, and Frank Veltman. Amsterdam: North-Holland.

O'Keefe, Daniel, J. 1996. *Persuasion: Theory and Research*. Thousand Oaks, Calif.

O'Keefe, Daniel J. 2001. "Persuasion." In *Encyclopedia of Rhetoric*, ed. Thomas O. Sloane. New York: Oxford University Press, 575–583.

Payne, Stanley L. 1951. *The Art of Asking Questions*. Princeton, N.J.: Princeton University Press.

Perelman, Chaim, and Lucie Olbrechts-Tyteca. 1969. *The New Rhetoric: A Treatise on Argumentation*, trans. J. Wilkinson and P. Weaver, 2nd ed. Notre Dame: University of Notre Dame Press. First published, as *La Nouvelle Rhetorique*, in 1958.

Pfau, Michael, and Michael Burgoon. 1989, "The Efficacy of Issue and Character Attack Message Strategies in Political Campaign Communication." *Communication Reports* 2: 53–61.

Pinto, Robert C., J. Anthony Blair, and Katherine E. Parr. 1993. *Reasoning: A Practical Guide for Canadian Students*. Scarborough: Prentice Hall.

Plato. 1961. *The Collected Dialogues of Plato*, ed. Edith Hamilton and Huntington Cairns. New York: Bollingen Foundation.

Premack, D., and G. Woodruff. 1978. "Does the Chimpanzee Have a Theory of Mind?" *Behavioral and Brain Sciences* 1: 515–526.

Rawls, John. 1993. *Political Liberalism*. New York: Columbia University Press.

Reed, Chris. 1998. "Dialogue Frames in Agent Communication." In *Proceedings of the Third International Conference on Multi-Agent Systems*, ed. Y. Demazeau. IEEE Press, 246–253.

Reed, Chris. 2006. "Representing Dialogic Argumentation." *Knowledge-Based Systems* 19: 22–31.

Reed, Chris, and Glenn Rowe. 2002. "Araucaria: Software for Puzzles in Argument Diagramming and XML." *Technical Report*, Department of Applied Computing, University of Dundee. Available at http://www.computing.dundee.ac.uk/staff/creed/araucaria.

Reed, Chris, and Douglas Walton. 2003. "Diagramming Argumentation Schemes and Critical Questions." In *Proceedings of the Fifth Conference of the International Society for the Study of Argumentation*, ed. Frans H. van Eemeren, J. Anthony Blair, Charles A. Willard, and Francisca Snoeck Henkemans. Amsterdam: SicSat, 881–885.

Regan, R. T. 1971. "Effects of a Favor and Liking on Compliance." *Journal of Experimental Social Psychology* 7: 627–639.

Reiter, Raymond. 1987. "Nonmonotonic Reasoning." *Annual Review of Computer Science* 2: 147–186.

Rescher, Nicholas. 1977. *Dialectics: A Controversy-Oriented Approach to the Theory of Knowledge*. Albany: State University of New York Press.

Robinson, Richard. 1950. *Definition*. Oxford: Clarendon Press.

Robinson, Richard. 1953. *Plato's Earlier Dialectic*. London: Oxford University Press.

Robinson, Richard. 1962. *Plato's Earlier Dialectic*, 2nd ed. Oxford: Clarendon Press.

Rogers, Richard W. 1983. "Cognitive and Physiological Processes in Fear Appeals and Attitude Change." In *Social Psychophysiology*, ed. John T. Cacioppo and Richard E. Petty. New York: Guilford, 153–176.

Roper, Burns W. 1990. "Are Polls Accurate?." In *The Classics of Polling*, ed. Michael L. Young. Metuchen, N.J.: Scarecrow Press, 218–232.

Russell, Stuart J., and Peter Norvig. 1995. *Artificial Intelligence: A Modern Approach*. Upper Saddle River, N.J.: Prentice Hall.

Schiappa, Edward. 1993. "Arguing about Definitions." *Argumentation* 7: 403–417.

Schiappa, Edward. 1995. "Introduction" to *Warranting Assent*, ed. Edward Schiappa. Albany: State University of New York Press, ix–xxix.

Schiappa, Edward. 1996. "Towards a Pragmatic Approach to Definition: 'Wetlands' and the Politics of Meaning." In *Environmental Pragmatism*, ed. Andrew Light and Eric Katz. London: Routledge, 209–230.

Schiappa, Edward. 2003. *Defining Reality: The Rhetoric of Definition and the Politics of Meaning*. Carbondale: Southern Illinois University Press.

Schuman, Howard, and Stanley Presser. 1981. *Questions and Answers in Attitude Surveys: Experiments on Question Form, Wording, and Context*. New York: Academic Press.

Searle, John. 1969. *Speech Acts*. Cambridge: Cambridge University Press.

Searle, John. 2001. *Rationality in Action*. Cambridge: MIT Press.

Sederberg, Peter C. 1984. *The Politics of Meaning: The Construction of Social Reality*. Tucson: University of Arizona Press.

Segerberg, Krister. 1984. "Towards an Exact Philosophy of Action." *Topoi* 3: 75–83.

Segerberg, Krister. 1985. "Routines." *Synthese* 65: 185–210.

Seligman, Daniel. 1961. "We're Drowning in Phony Statistics." *Fortune*, November, pp. 146–171.

"Senate Impeachment Trial of President Bill Clinton – Day 16." CNN transcript. *CNN AllPolitics.com Political Website for 1998*. Www.cnn.com/allpolitics/stories/1999/02/06/transcripts.

Shepard, David W. 1973. "Stipulative Definitions and Elementary Logic." *Central States Speech Journal* 24: 131–136.

Sierra, Carles, Nicholas R. Jennings, P. Noriega, and Simon Parsons. 1998. "A Framework for Argumentation-Based Negotiation." In *Intelligent Agents IV*, ed. M. P. Singh, A. Rao, and M. J. Wooldridge. Berlin: Springer Verlag.

Simons, Herbert W., Joanne Morreale, and Bruce Gronbeck. 2001. *Persuasion in Society*. Thousand Oaks, Calif.: Sage.

Singh, Munidar P. 1991. "Towards a Formal Theory of Communication for Multiagent Systems." In *Proceedings of the International Joint Conference on Artificial Intelligence (IJCAI)*. Available at http://www.csc.ncsu.edu/faculty/MSingh/papers/index.html.

Singh, Munindar P. 1997. "Commitment in the Architecture of a Limited, Rational Agent." In *Intelligent Agents Systems: Theoretical and Practical Issues*, ed. Lawrence Cavedon. Berlin: Springer Verlag, 72–87.

Singh, Munindar P. 1999. "A Semantics for Speech Acts." *Annals of Mathematics and Artificial Intelligence* 8: 47–71.

Stevenson, Charles L. 1938. "Persuasive Definitions." *Mind* 47: 331–350.

Stevenson, Charles L. 1944. *Ethics and Language*. New Haven: Yale University Press.

Sycara, K. P. 1990. "Persuasive Argument in Negotiation." *Theory and Decision* 28: 203–242.

Tanner, John F., Ellen Day, and Melvin R. Crask. 1989. "Protection Motivation Theory: An Extension of Fear Appeals in Communication Theory." *Journal of Business Research* 19: 267–276.

Thouless, Robert H. 1942. *Straight Thinking in War Time*. London: Hodder and Stoughton.

Tindale, Christopher W. 1999. *Acts of Arguing: A Rhetorical Model of Argument*. Albany: State University of New York Press.

Tindale, Christopher W. 2004. *Rhetorical Argumentation: Principles of Theory and Practice.* Thousand Oaks, Calif.: Sage.

Titsworth, B. Scott. 1999. "An Ideological Basis for Definition in Public Argument: A Case Study of the Individuals with Disabilities in Education Act." *Argumentation and Advocacy* 35: 171–184.

Tocqueville, Alexis de. 1966. *Democracy in America,* ed. J. P. Mayer and Max Lerner. New York: Harper and Row. Originally published in 1835.

Tripp, Garwood, and Alix Davenport. 1988. "Fear Advertising – It Doesn't Work." *Health Promotion* 27: 17–19.

van Eemeren, Frans H., and Rob Grootendorst. 1984. *Speech Acts in Argumentative Discussions.* Dordrecht: Foris.

van Eemeren, Frans H., and Rob Grootendorst. 1987. "Fallacies in Pragma-Dialectical Perspective." *Argumentation* 1: 283–301.

van Eemeren, Frans H., and Rob Grootendorst. 1992. *Argumentation, Communication and Fallacies.* Hillsdale, N.J.: Lawrence Erlbaum Associates.

van Eemeren, Frans H., and Rob Grootendorst. 1995. "*Argumentum Ad Hominem*: A Pragma-Dialectical Case." In *Fallacies: Classical and Contemporary Readings,* ed. Hans V. Hansen and Robert C. Pinto. University Park: Pennsylvania State University Press, 223–228.

van Eemeren, Frans H., Rob Grootendorst, Francisca Snoeck Henkemans, et al. 1996. *Fundamentals of Argumentation Theory.* Mahwah, N.J.: Erlbaum.

van Eemeren, Frans H., and Peter Houtlosser. 1999a. "Delivering the Goods in Critical Discussion." In *Proceedings of the Fourth International Conference of the International Society for the Study of Argumentation,* ed. Frans H. van Eemeren, Rob Grootendorst, J. Anthony Blair, and Charles A. Willard. Amsterdam: SicSat, 163–171.

van Eemeren, Frans H., and Peter Houtlosser. 1999b. "Strategic Manoeuvring in Argumentative Discourse." *Discourse Studies* 1: 479–497.

van Eemeren, Frans H., and Peter Houtlosser. 2000. "Rhetorical Analysis within a Pragma-Dialectical Framework: The Case of R. J. Reynolds." *Argumentation* 14: 293–305.

van Eemeren, Frans H., and Peter Houtlosser. 2001. "Managing Disagreement: Rhetorical Analysis within a Dialectical Framework." *Argumentation and Advocacy* 37: 150–157.

van Eemeren, Frans H., and Peter Houtlosser. 2002. "Strategic Manoeuvring: Maintaining a Delicate Balance." In *The Warp and Woof of Argumentation Analysis,* ed. Frans H. van Eemeren and Peter Houtlosser. Dordrecht: Kluwer, 131–160.

Vorobej, Mark. 2006. *A Theory of Argument.* New York: Cambridge University Press.

Walton, Douglas N. 1989a. *Informal Logic.* Cambridge: Cambridge University Press.

Walton, Douglas N. 1989b. *Question-Reply Argumentation.* New York: Greenwood Press.

Walton, Douglas. 1990. *Practical Reasoning.* Savage, Md.: Rowman and Littlefield.

Walton, Douglas. 1994. *The Place of Emotion in Argument.* University Park: Pennsylvania State University Press.

Walton, Douglas N. 1995. *A Pragmatic Theory of Fallacy.* Tuscaloosa: University of Alabama Press.

Walton, Douglas. 1996. *Argumentation Schemes for Presumptive Reasoning*. Mahwah, N.J.: Erlbaum.

Walton, Douglas. 1997a. *Appeal to Expert Opinion*. University Park: Pennsylvania State University Press.

Walton, Douglas. 1997b. *Appeal to Pity: Argumentum Ad Misericordiam*. Albany: State University of New York Press.

Walton, Douglas. 1998a. Ad Hominem *Arguments*. Tuscaloosa: University of Alabama Press.

Walton, Douglas. 1998b. *The New Dialectic: Conversational Contexts of Argument*. Toronto: University of Toronto Press.

Walton, Douglas. 1999a. *Appeal to Popular Opinion*. University Park: Pennsylvania State University Press.

Walton, Douglas. 1999b. *One-Sided Arguments: A Dialectical Analysis of Bias*. Albany: State University of New York Press.

Walton, Douglas. 2000. *Scare Tactics: Arguments That Appeal to Fear and Threats*. Dordrecht: Kluwer.

Walton, Douglas. 2006. *Fundamentals of Critical Argumentation*. New York: Cambridge University Press.

Walton, Douglas, and Chris Reed. 2005. "Argumentation Schemes and Enthymemes." *Synthese* 145: 339–370.

Walton, Douglas N., and Erik C. W. Krabbe. 1995. *Commitment in Dialogue: Basic Concepts of Interpersonal Reasoning*. Albany: State University of New York Press.

Warnick, Barbara. 2000. "Two Systems of Invention: The Topics in the Rhetoric and the New Rhetoric." In *Rereading Aristotle's Rhetoric*, ed. Alan G. Gross and Arthur E. Walzer. Carbondale: Southern Illinois University Press, 107–129.

Warnke, Paul. 1990. "The User's Perspective: A Round Table on the Impact of Polls." In *The Classics of Polling*, ed. Michael L. Young. Metuchen, N.J.: Scarecrow Press, 374–388.

Weaver, Richard M. 1953. *The Ethics of Rhetoric*. Chicago: Henry Regnery.

Wenzel, Joseph W. 1990. "Three Perspectives on Argument: Rhetoric, Dialectic, Logic." In *Perspectives on Argumentation*, ed. Robert Trapp and Janice Schuetz. Prospect Heights, Ill.: Waveland Press, 9–26.

Wheeler, Michael. 1990. "How to Read the Polls." In *The Classics of Polling*, ed. Michael L. Young. Metuchen, N.J.: Scarecrow Press.

"White House: It's Not about Abortion." 2002. CBS News, *Eye on Politics*. February 1. Www.cbsnews.com/now/story/0,1597,327803-412,00.shtml.

Wilensky, Robert. 1983. *Planning and Understanding: A Computational Approach to Human Reasoning*. Reading, Mass.: Addison-Wesley.

Witt, Evans. 2001. "People Who Count." *The Public Perspective* 12, July-August, pp. 1–5. The Roper Center for Public Opinion Research.

Wooldridge, Michael. 2000. *Reasoning about Rational Agents*. Cambridge: MIT Press.

Wooldridge, Mike. 2002. *Introduction to MultiAgent Systems*. Chichester: Wiley.

Wooldridge, Michael, and Nicholas R. Jennings. 1995. "Intelligent Agents: Theory and Practice." *The Knowledge Engineering Review* 10: 115–152.

Yankelovich, Daniel. 1991. *Coming to Public Judgment*. Syracuse, N.Y.: Syracuse University Press.

Yankelovich, Daniel. 1992. "A Widening Expert/Public Opinion Gap." *Challenge,* May–June: 20–27.

Young, Michael L. 1990. "Editor's Introduction to the Basics of Polling." In *The Classics of Polling,* ed. Michael L. Young. Metuchen, N.J.: Scarecrow Press, 47–50.

Zarefsky, David. 1986. *President Johnson's War on Poverty: Rhetoric and History.* University: University of Alabama Press.

Zarefsky, David. 1997. "Definitions." In *Argument in a Time of Change: Definitions, Frameworks, and Critiques,* ed. James F. Klumpp. Annandale, Va.: National Communication Association, 1–11.

Zarefsky, David. 1998. "Definitions." In *Argument in a Time of Change: Proceedings of the Tenth NCA/AFA Conference on Argumentation,* ed. James F. Klumpp. Annandale, Va.: National Communication Association, 1–11.

Zarefsky, David, Carol Miller-Tutzauer, and Frank E. Tutzauer. 1984. "Reagan's Safety Net for the Truly Needy: The Rhetorical Uses of Definition." *Central States Speech Journal* 35: 113–119.

Index